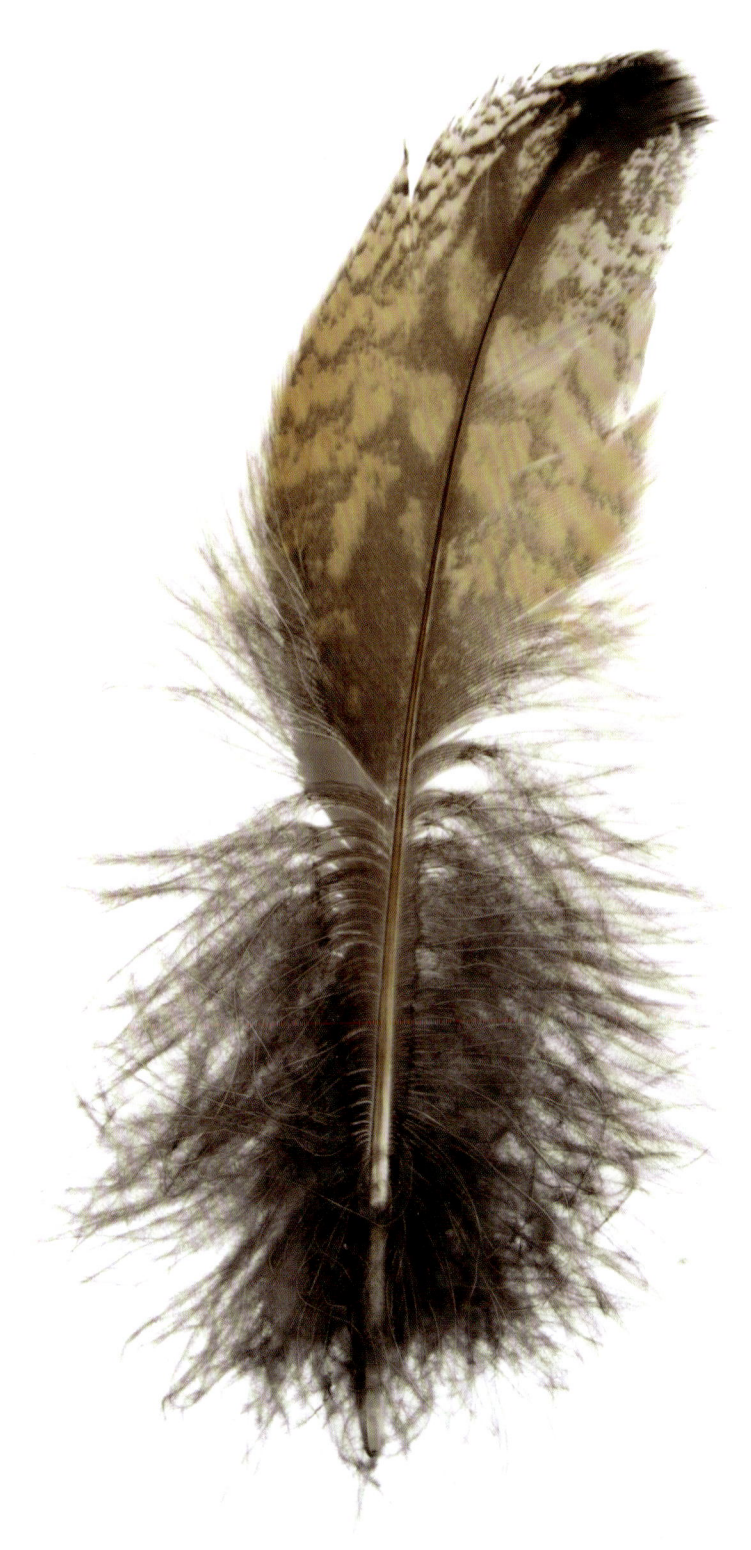

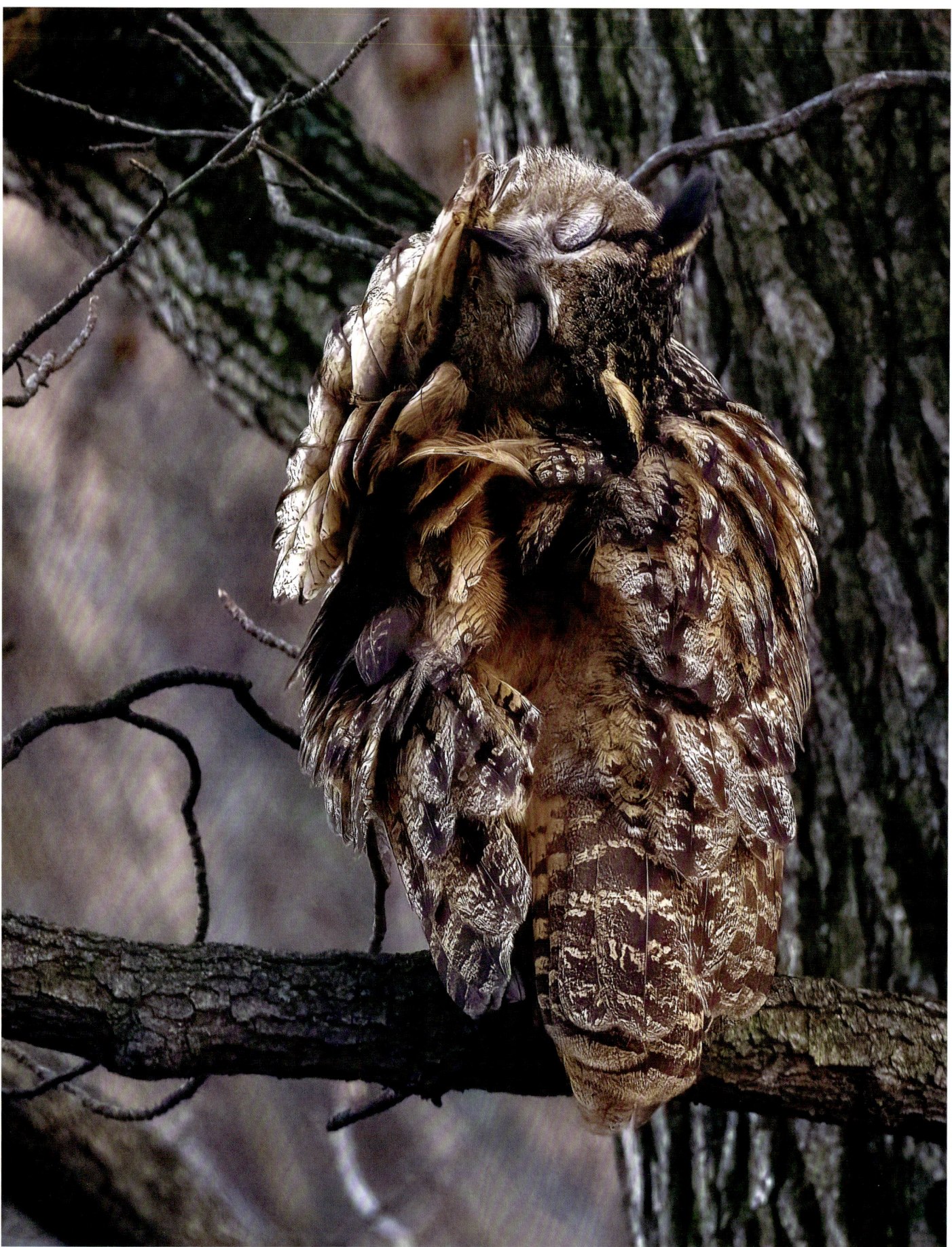

FLACO

The Owl Who Escaped Captivity
and Won the Hearts of the World

Edited by Jonathan Hollingsworth
Foreword by Carl Safina

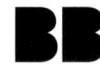

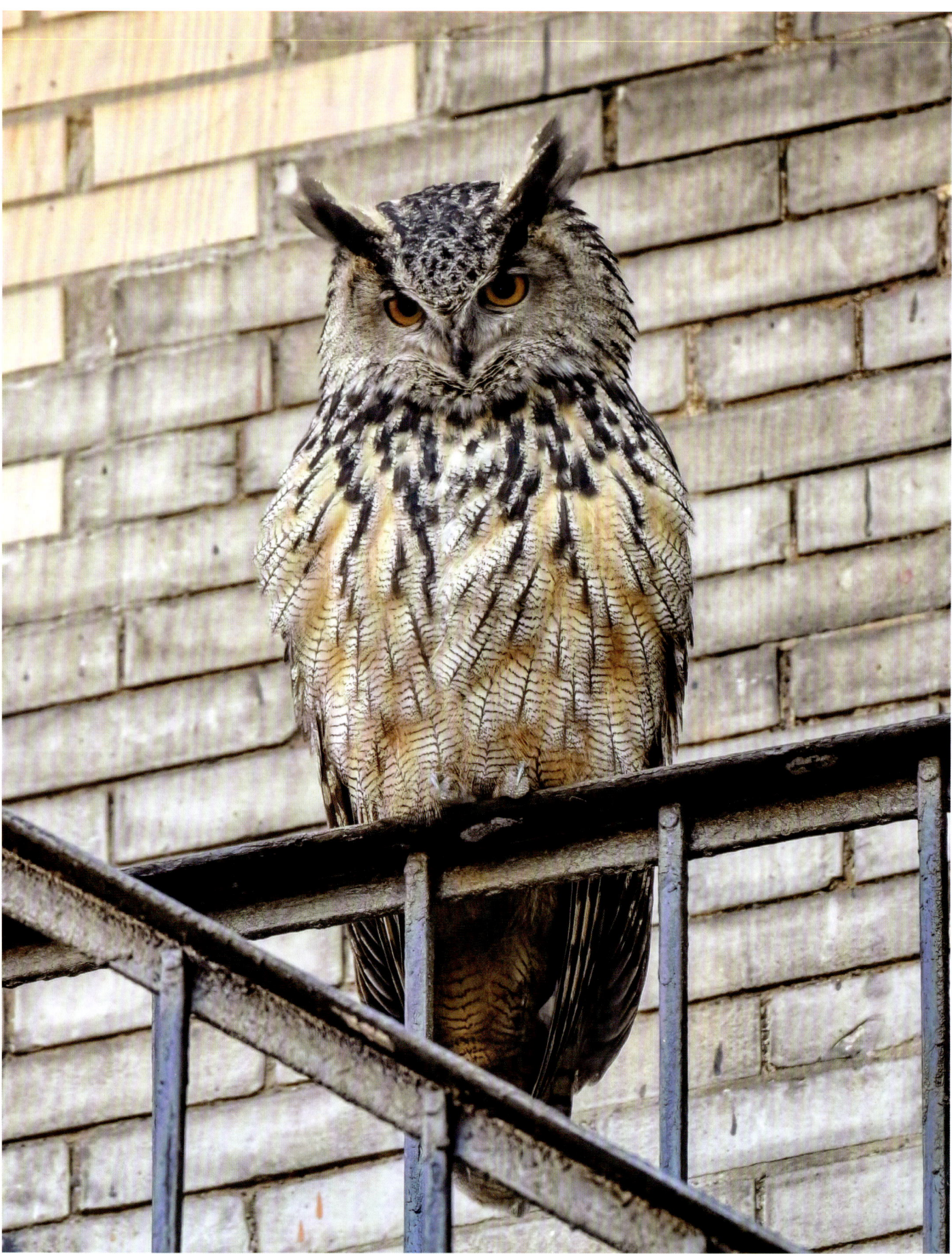

for Flaco —
and anyone with a cage to break out of . . .

This book is for you.

Title Page Paul Beiboer, *Flaco Preening,* The North Woods, Near the Huddlestone Arch, 2/26/23, 5:30 p.m.

It was always such a nice routine to visit Flaco just before flyout, as he was getting active. His pre-flyout routine would include slowly waking up, starting with some preening, and then stretching. On this particular day, after about ten minutes of preening, he flew out toward the Harlem Meer Construction Site around 5:40 p.m. to go hunting.

Opposite David Barrett, *Flaco Roosting on a Fire Escape,* 74th Street and Broadway, Upper West Side, 1/17/24, 4:19 p.m.

Flaco had visited this airy courtyard several times before, and a friendly resident invited us back again. By then we were getting multiple nightly reports of Flaco being seen on buildings and water tanks and being heard hooting at all hours of the night on the Upper West Side. A chance to see Flaco at relatively close range in daylight, though, was still a special experience, as Flaco had long ago ceased roosting in a public park. Minutes after this photo was taken, a disturbance from the floor directly above Flaco startled him and caused him to fly out early. Flaco never returned to roost in this courtyard.

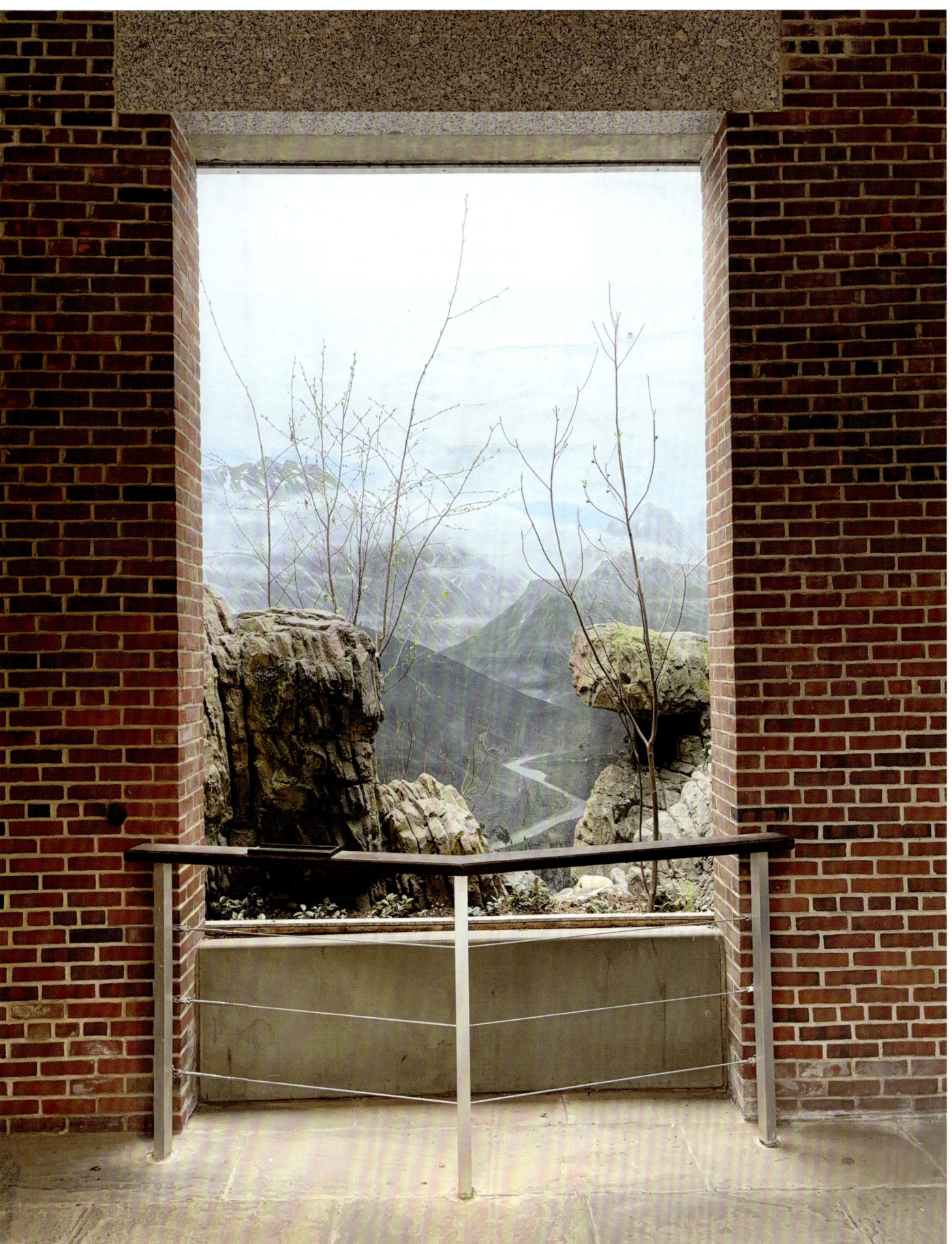

Introduction

The Escape

If you visited the Central Park Zoo between November 10th, 2010 and the day of Thursday, February 2nd, 2023, you could have seen Flaco the Eurasian eagle-owl in one of two small enclosures during his years of captivity.

The second enclosure, described as the size of a bus stop, or say, the luxury window display where he landed nearby on the night of his escape, was tucked between the zoo entrance, near the Delacorte Clock and the exit of the Polar Circle exhibit, which smells of penguins every time the door swings open.

Flaco's enclosure was outfitted with a series of stones to suggest rocky outcroppings and branches to perch, but for an owl with a six-foot wingspan, it was too small for flight and any desire for movement was reduced to a hop.

The Delacorte Clock, donated by philanthropist George Delacorte in 1965, was inspired by the animated clocks he observed in medieval town squares during his travels to Europe. The zoo clock, just above the entry arches and adjacent to Flaco's enclosure, springs to life every 30 minutes, between 8:00 a.m. and 6:00 p.m., with seasonal music "performed" by an orchestra of animal musicians — a penguin, kangaroo, bear, elephant, goat, and hippo — constructed for the delight of children. But for a nocturnal owl, it must have been infernal during critical hours of rest.

Cruellest of all, at least from a viewer's perspective, might have been the mural that covered the back wall of Flaco's enclosure: a mythical vista with a snaking river and mist-enveloped mountains, evoking the cover of a vintage fantasy novel, suggesting that there was *someplace else* to go.

Because the zoo has an open layout, where anyone can pass through the central thoroughfare without a ticket, it was possible to catch a glimpse of Flaco without paying, and thousands did, whether strolling to other parts of the park or making a daily commute. Unlike Flaco in the photographs of this book, the Flaco of the zoo was not a creature that inspired delight or wonder. Observers who passed his enclosure have described him as looking "bored," "grumpy," and "miserable." The Flaco that could hoot for hours from the city's rooftops and water towers with a decibel force as loud as a dog's bark rarely hooted in his enclosure.

Zoos can be safe havens for animals who are endangered or suffer dwindling habitats and a means for critical research on behaviors that cannot be observed easily in the wild. But to see Flaco in his enclosure in a boutique urban zoo, however, was to see an animal of keen intelligence whose life was not being lived for his own benefit but for the humans who happened to pass by his cage on their way in or out of the zoo.

Viewed as an art installation, it posed a question of ethics.

Left Flaco's former enclosure at the Central Park Zoo after the interior branches and steel mesh had been removed.

For one individual, described as a "vandal" and "radical activist," that question required an answer, which came on the night of February 2nd, 2023. The person (or persons) who cut a hole in Flaco's enclosure came prepared, using a professional-grade tool to cut the stainless steel mesh while standing out of the camera's view.

By 8:30 p.m., zoo staffers reported that Flaco was missing. NYPD's 19th Precinct reported that that night, Flaco explored the neighboring Upper East Side and spent time near the Sherry-Netherland Hotel on Fifth Avenue before notoriously landing on the sidewalk outside Bergdorf Goodman, where video footage shows him standing a few feet from an open pet carrier, in the flashing red lights of a squad car, as an officer paces in the background and onlookers stand at the ready, always with their phones, recording, recording.

It appeared that no one knew quite what to make of the scene, including Flaco, who flew off when the crowd grew too big. Within days, Flaco was reborn from a zoo B-lister to "The World's Most Famous Bird," a title more esteemed and burdensome than Flaco could have ever wanted.

A shaded branch, a rat's scurry, and the great wide world to explore might have been plenty.

An Uncertain Future: Captivity or Freedom

The Central Park Zoo staff and park rangers worked in tandem for 15 days, attempting to capture Flaco in a series of ill-fated, public-facing rescue efforts, while he remained in the south end of the park, in the Hallett Nature Sanctuary or Heckscher Ballfields and Playground. Their numbers grew in the successive days as they appeared in dark clothing that evoked a military operation, standing in wide-stance pairs looking into the trees with binoculars and keeping round-the-clock vigils in the unpleasant February weather. Despite the ominous presentation, their intentions were for the greater good.

The zoo's immediate messaging expressed concern that Flaco could not survive on his own. Having lived in captivity his entire life, the zoo's staff feared he was not equipped with the skills to hunt for his own prey, which, in his case, would be the city's abundant rat population.

The rats were the other risk: The New York Department of Health reported that in 2022, it had used 75,749 pounds of rat poison in the city, up from 62,511 pounds the year prior. Every meal presented a risk, which was not just a hypothetical because Flaco's Central Park celebrity bird predecessors had met early, tragic deaths with traces of rodenticide in their bodies.

In those volatile first days and weeks of Flaco's life on the lam, zoo keepers, conservation societies, ornithologists and birders weighed in with their expert *shoulds* pertaining to Flaco's

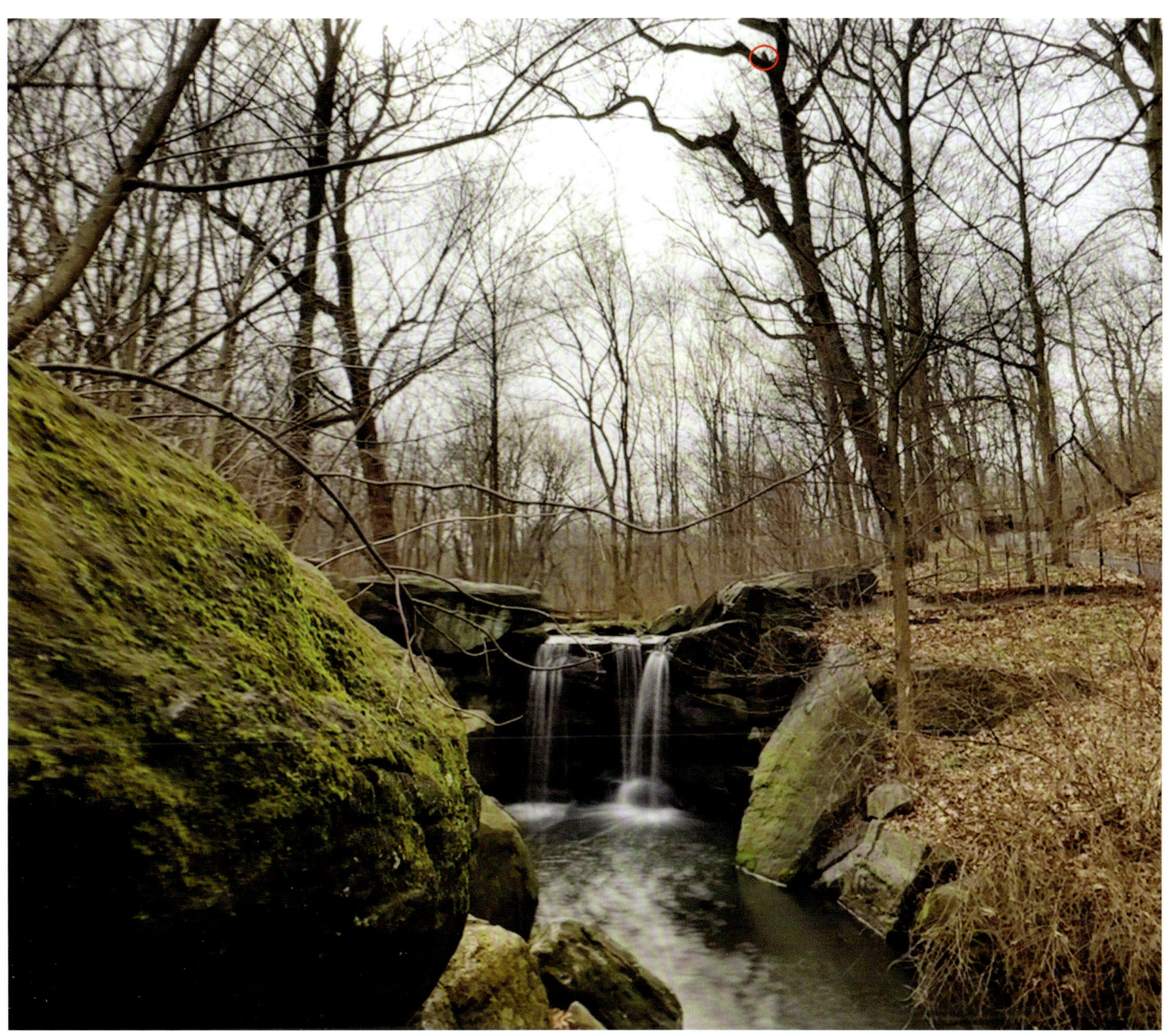

Above Howard Katz, *Flaco Perched in a Favorite Tree in the North Woods,* Loch Waterfall by Huddlestone Arch, 3/2/23, 2:09 p.m. (Flaco is circled in red at the top of the image.)

Following spread David Barrett, *Flaco by the Trap,* Central Park's Heckscher Ballfields, 2/9/23, 6:59 p.m.

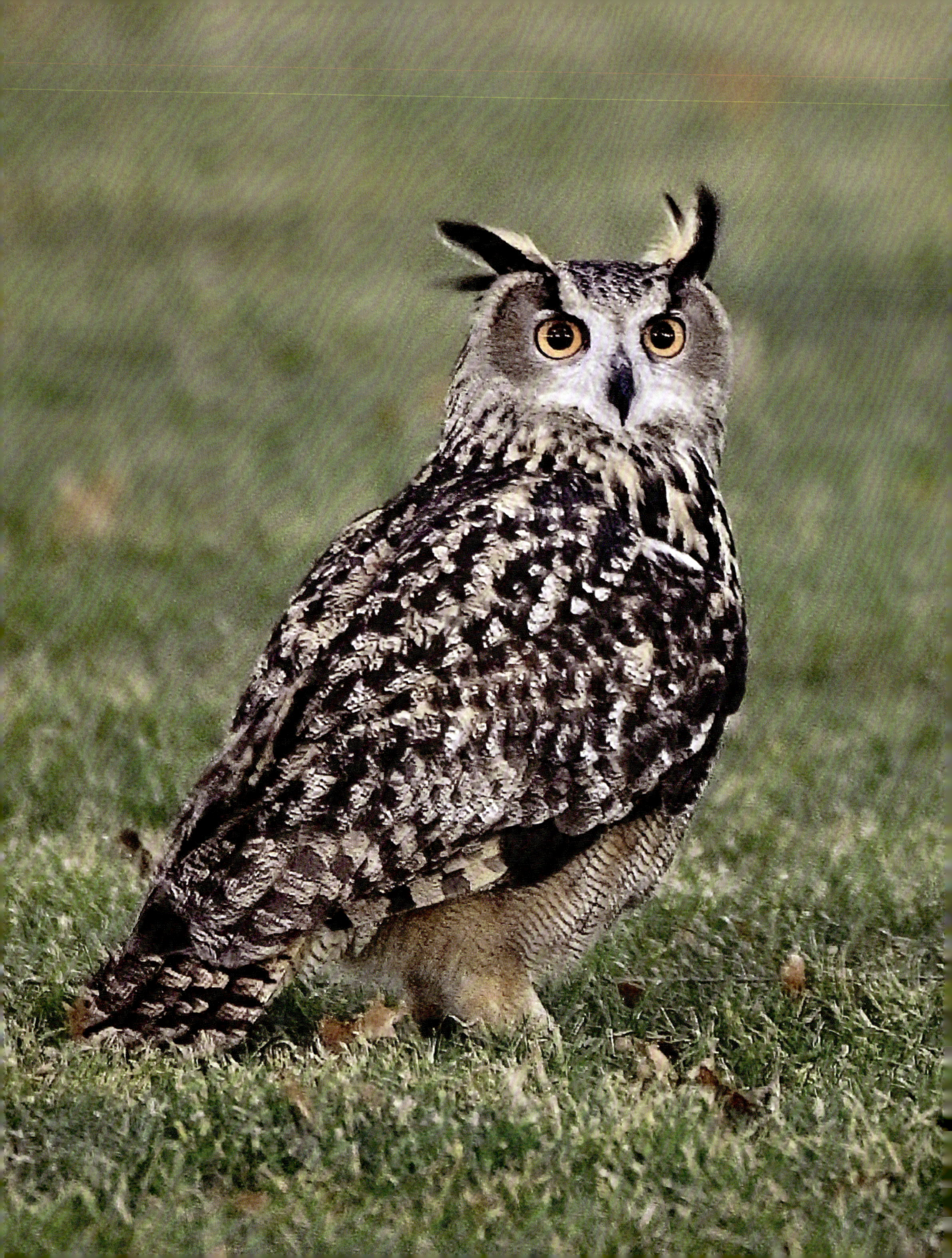

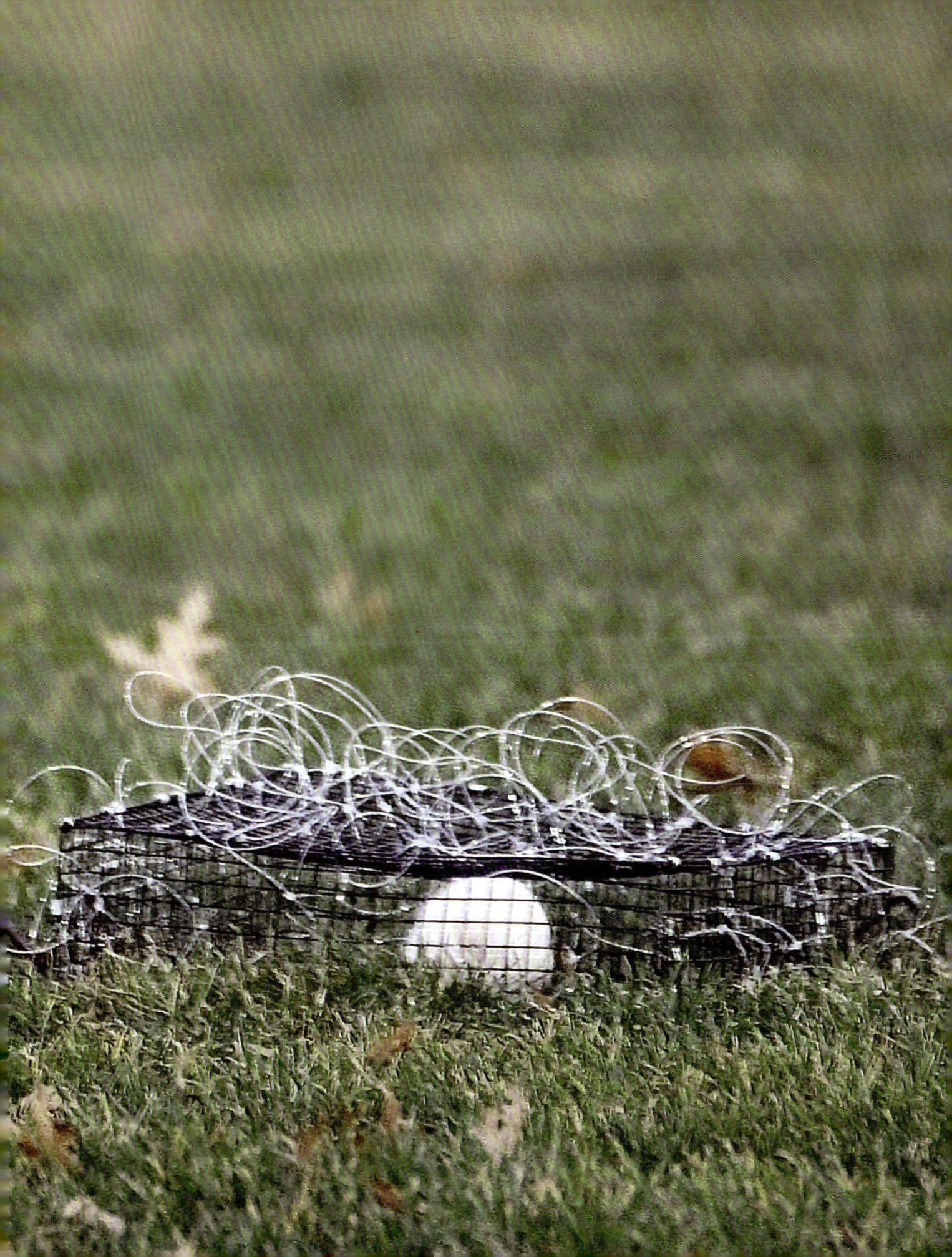

future: as an apex predator, he'd disrupt the park's ecosystem, competing for food and preying on native birds; he might cross-breed with a Great Horned Owl (and there was one in the park, Geraldine) producing compromised offspring; and lastly, Flaco would be in constant danger (rodenticide, window collisions, and vehicles) living in the city, a continent away from his native habitat.

Scott Weidensaul, author of *Peterson Reference Guide to Owls of North America and the Caribbean,* summed up the opinions of many: "The best thing for him, long-term, even though it might not be as full or enriching as life could be for him, is to be back in captivity," as published in *Audubon* magazine. The sentiment was prescient: in the wake of Flaco's death a year later, Weidensaul told *The New York Times,* "Sometimes it sucks to be right."

Meanwhile, public opinion took a turn as the prospect of returning Flaco to his minuscule enclosure struck a nerve with many New Yorkers. Nearly 1,700 people signed the petition "Free Flaco, the Central Park Zoo Owl," calling for the end of all recovery efforts.

The Central Park Zoo didn't help sway public opinion, issuing press releases through the Bronx-based nonprofit, The Wildlife Conservation Society, which manages the zoo, in lieu of deploying an official talking head to inform the public of its concerns and rescue efforts. Nor did its methods of trapping Flaco, which happened in full view and could amass large audiences.

When birder/photographer David Barrett posted Flaco's whereabouts in real-time on Manhattan Bird Alert (@BirdCentralPark), his X account devoted to the birds and wildlife of Manhattan, which is approaching 100K followers, a small group of observers could grow exponentially within minutes, though they were always instructed to follow the etiquette of unobtrusive bird watching.

On February 9th, a week after Flaco's escape, Barrett captured an iconic moment of the zoo's rescue efforts (featured in the previous spread) in which Flaco is standing on the lawn of the Heckscher Ballfield, next to a Bal-Chatri trap, a cage containing a live rat, outfitted with a series of filament nooses to snare Flaco's feet. This could pose its own danger, especially if Flaco were to take flight while his feet were ensnared. For a moment, that could have happened: Flaco landed on the cage briefly as zoo staff rushed forward with their nets, but Flaco miraculously unsnared himself and never approached a trap again.

Another release from the zoo, posted on February 12th, indicated that Flaco had been observed hunting, capturing and consuming prey, which allayed the most pressing concern that Flaco could starve. Within days, he made remarkable progress, not just hunting, but flying more than short, exhausting distances which had been punctuated by clumsy landings. Flaco was finally learning how to be an owl — and a highly capable one.

The final push — and failure — occurred on the evening of February 16th, when zoo staff and rangers played a recording of a female Eurasian eagle-owl from the park's Sheep Meadow, a bitter irony for an owl who had been branded "Do not breed" from the day he'd been hatched at Sylvan Heights Bird Park in Scotland Neck, North Carolina. When Barrett received a tip earlier that day from a Central Park birder who'd overheard the zoo's plans to bait Flaco with the female eagle-owl recordings, he posted the update on X, which ignited public outrage.

The next day, on February 17th, the zoo announced in a statement that it wasn't just suspending capture efforts (as it had on February 12th) but calling them off: "We are going to continue monitoring Flaco and his activities and to be prepared to resume recovery efforts if he shows any sign of difficulty or distress."

Flaco was a free bird.

Following spread   Anke Frohlich, *Surveying the Field for Rats*, North Meadow Baseball Fields, 8/26/23, 11:23 p.m.

Like the snowy owl I observed in Central Park in 2021, Flaco favored the North Meadow baseball field backstops. Finding him there involved walking around the entire area, checking every backstop and fence. He often flew from post to post several times before settling on a perch.

The backstops were the perfect height for him to hunt from. Flaco sat patiently, sometimes for hours. Then without warning, he would dive to the ground and grab a rat in his talons.

In this image, the Upper West Side provided a beautiful backdrop.

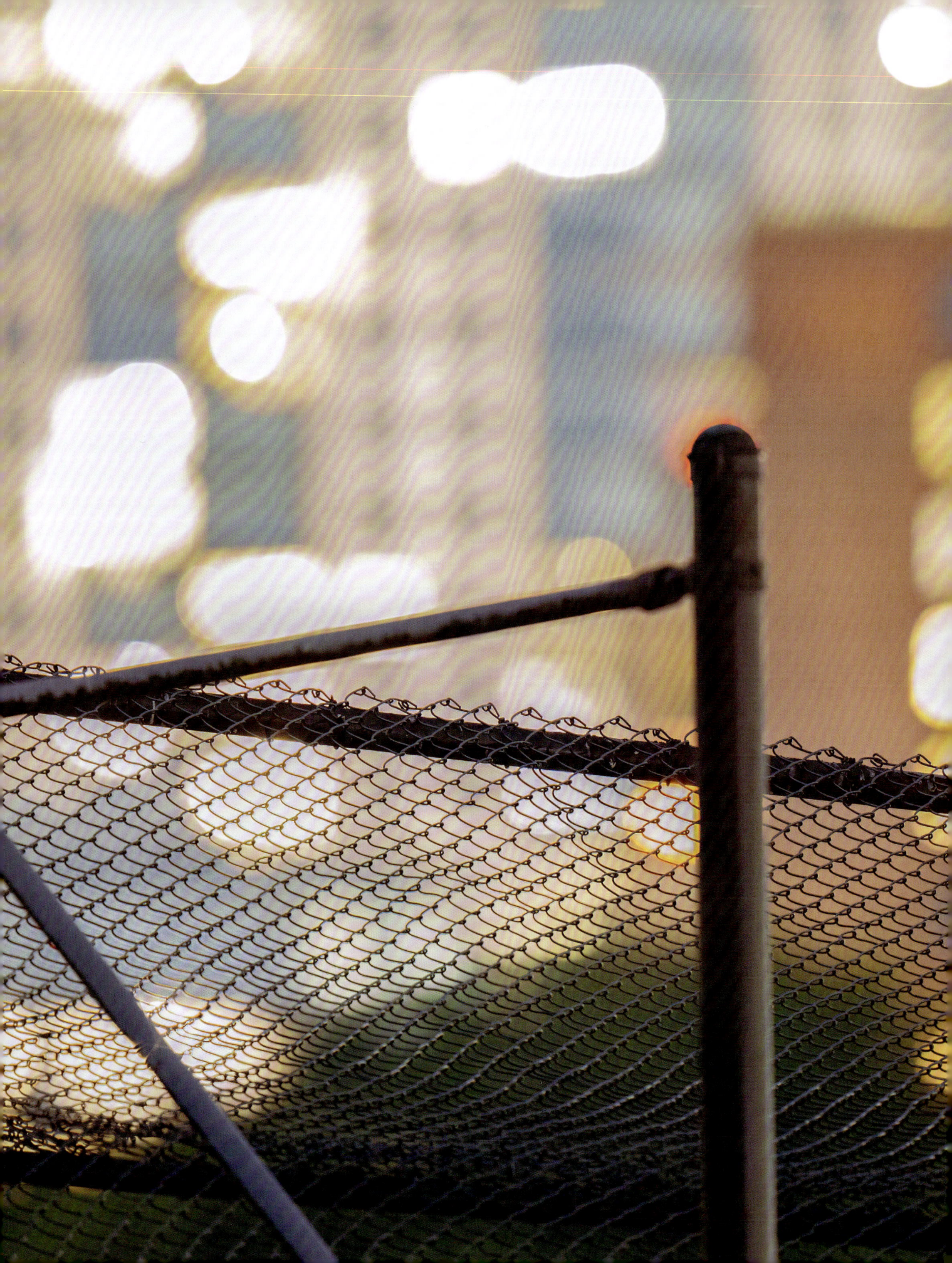

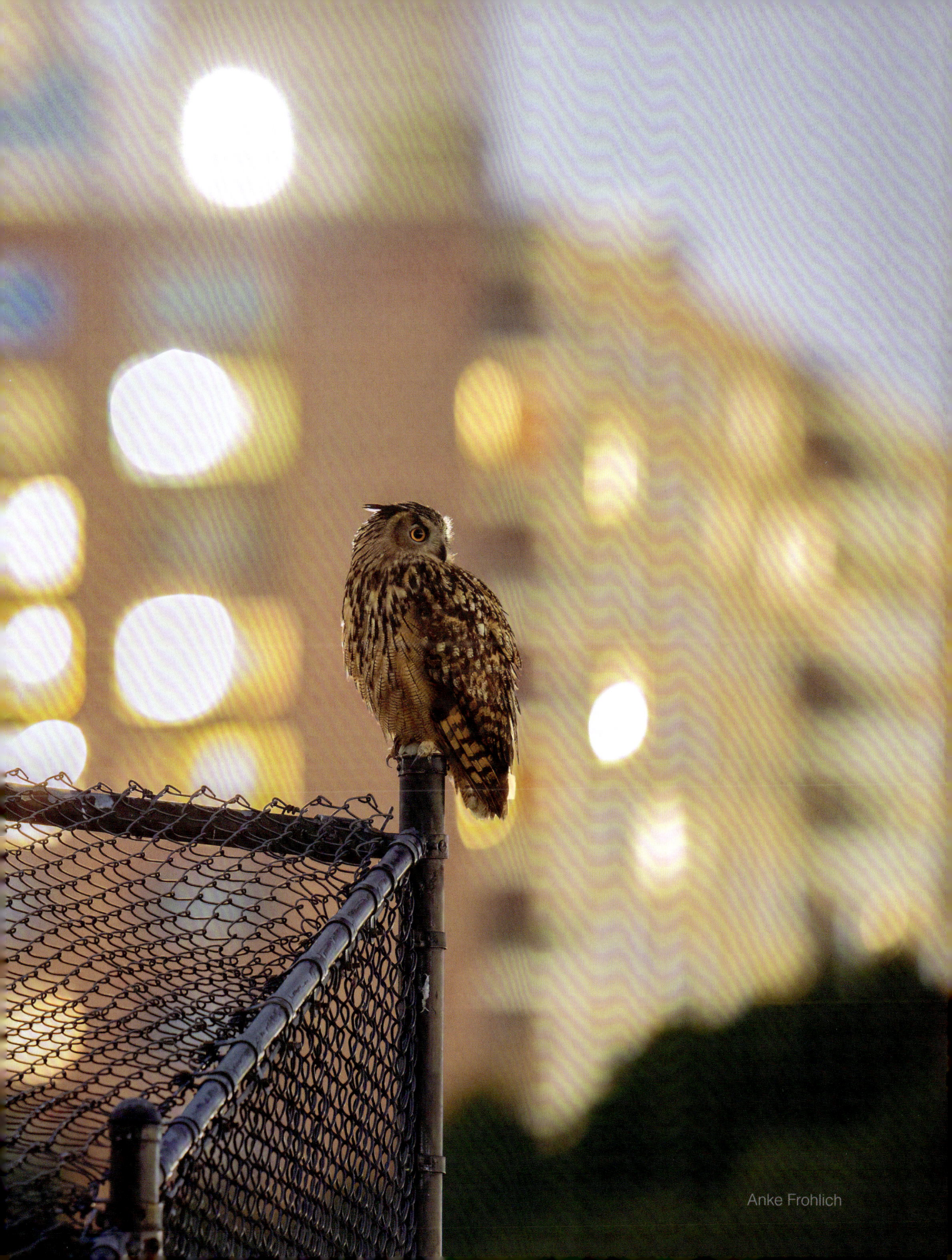
Anke Frohlich

A Year of Freedom

During his first weeks of freedom, Flaco lingered in the south end of the park — a runaway unwilling to go home but unsure where to fly to next. He was finally able to make sense of the sounds he'd been hearing in his enclosure for years: the Delacorte Clock as it sprung to life, the clop-clop of the horse-drawn carriages, the beeping of maintenance trucks, the tourists ringing the bells on their Citi Bikes and snapping pictures with commentary in every language.

By February 21st, Flaco retreated to the 40-acre North Woods at the top of Central Park, where one can wander the heavily wooded, shaded paths in peace and forget the surrounding metropolis, which is exactly what Frederick Law Olmstead and Calvert Vaux had in mind when they designed the park, beginning in 1858. Making use of the existing hills and rocky outcroppings, the famed landscape architectural duo planted trees, constructed new waterways and falls, and built rustic bridges and intimate paths. If the south end of the park sounds like a Little League game and carousel ride, the north end is the crunching of leaves and a babbling brook.

For an owl just getting his bearings in the new world of freedom, the North Woods was the perfect retreat. Ask most park-goers where "The Loch" is, and you'll probably receive blank stares. An intimate, cooling gem of the North Woods, the Loch begins as a shallow pool at its west end, which narrows to an east-bound stream that eventually cascades over falls and passes beneath the Huddlestone Arch (1866), an engineering marvel comprised of boulders held in place without mortar or any support system. Photographer Venus N. Sallay speculated that Flaco regularly roosted in a tree directly above the falls for the soothing sound of the breaking water below.

Though Flaco's appetite was limited to rats — and later, pigeons — Eurasian eagle-owls are known for hunting whatever they like, and the concerns for disruptions to the ecosystem were not unfounded, at least initially. Eagle-owls can prey on other raptors (Northern Goshawks, Peregrine Falcons, Long-eared Owls), the less glorious (coots, geese), the soft and fuzzy (rabbits), the clever (foxes), and the unlikely (European roe deer). No need to mention the ease of taking a cat or, perhaps, a small dog enjoying the freedom of Central Park's "off-leash" hours. Fortunately, no Chihuahuas, Frenchies, Dachshunds, Brussels Griffons, Papillons, Pomeranians, or Pugs were taken in Flaco's year of freedom.

In her essay "Owls," Mary Oliver considers terror's place in the natural world and how it runs parallel to even the most placid lives, including her own. Her exemplar, of course, is the owl who descends silently on its prey in the night, then cries out "with the sheer rollicking glory of the death-bringer." On the nights when Flaco did not consume his dinner in one go, head-first, it was possible to see him in a state of post-hunt-repose, with a headless rat in his clutches, as he dozed in the branches.

Eurasian eagle-owls, *Bubo bubo*, one of 260 species of owls, inhabit an impressive range of roughly 12 million square miles, from the rocky cliffs of the Asia—Pacific, to bell towers of Western Europe, "largely because," as ornithologist Jennifer Ackerman wrote in *What an Owl Knows*, "they can adapt to a wide variety of climatic conditions, habitats, and altitudes."

Adapt, indeed. One could imagine the ancestral flock looking west at Flaco hooting at the top of a Manhattan water tower, particularly as photographed here by Paul Beiboer, and giving him a collective thumbs-up with their primary feathers.

And of roughly 60 million years of owl evolution, the Eurasian eagle-owl is second in size only to Blackiston's fish owl of eastern Russia, a fellow ear-tufted owl that has a height of more than two feet and a wingspan of six feet, which Jonathan C. Slaght describes in *Owls of the Eastern Ice* as looking "almost too big and too comical to be a real bird, as if someone had hastily glued fistfuls of feathers to a yearling bear."

Flaco was no hasty assemblage: every part, from the pumpkin-colored, forward-facing eyes to the jaunty, expressive ear tufts and the luxurious shading of his plumage, seemed meticulously created. In North America, the go-to owls of our popular culture often have been Great Horned Owls, as featured in Disney's *Bambi* or *The Sword in the Stone,* or more recently, the Snowy Owl, Hedwig, in the *Harry Potter* franchise.

Flaco, in comparison, was bigger, more mysterious, and exotic. As an owl, he was a knockout.

The Eurasian eagle-owl (up to 30" height, 79" wingspan) is larger, whether in height or wingspan, than North America's largest counterparts: the Great Gray Owl (33.1"/60.2"), Snowy Owl (28"/57"), Great Horned Owl (24.8"/57.1"), and Barred Owl (19.7"/43.3"). The latter three owls lived in the park before or during Flaco's year of freedom.

The other key to Flaco's popularity was his accessibility: Flaco didn't hide in the deepest, highest branches to roost. He'd spent his entire life looking at—and being looked at—by people, and so it wasn't surprising that he chose spots that offered a view of the human traffic around him. The intimacies of preening or swallowing a rat didn't need to be done in private. Flaco, a name which amusingly translates to "skinny" in Spanish, was large, even plump, and the joy he delivered was democratic: with his six-foot wingspan, one didn't need binoculars or fancy equipment to look up and marvel.

A Turning Point

Once Flaco relocated to the North Woods, he did not return (as far as anyone observed) to the south end of the park. He cycled through a series of predictable, beloved locations at the north end. Favorite trees included the oak and black walnut flanking the East Drive, the elm by the North Meadow Recreation Center, or the trees in close proximity to the Gothic Bridge and Central Park Tennis Center.

In the evenings, after flyout, he often hunted in the North Meadow Ballfields, the Compost Heap (also called The Mount), or the Harlem Meer Construction Site, which offered key perches to observe the delicious, herky-jerky movements of his prey.

His hunter's instincts had been latent all along, waiting to be put to use, and every part of the eagle-owl's body conspired toward the singular purpose of survival. The facial feathers funnel sound to the advantageously asymmetrical ears, which are just openings on each side of the head covered with feathers designed to let sound pass through. (The eagle-owl's ear tufts, incidentally, are used for camouflage and have nothing to do with hearing.) The muscular, fine-feathered legs and sharp talons crush and kill on impact, sinking effortlessly into soft bodies. The digestive system allows an owl to consume its prey whole, sending the undigestible bits back up hours later, packaged as a tidy pellet, in a regurgitation process called "antiperistalsis." The pupils can dilate to almost the entire size of an owl's eye, and the disproportionate ratio of rods to cones is designed to help owls sense movement in low light. The Eurasian eagle-owl, with its shallow wingbeats and long, fast glides, has an aptitude for nearly soundless flight, producing up to ten decibels less sound than other species. These gifts of the kill were Flaco's all along, which is rich, considering the initial skepticism concerning his ability to hunt on his own.

Most of the contributors I spoke with hoped that Flaco would leave Manhattan, as other owls had done over the years — Great Horned Owls, Barred Owls, Northern Saw-whet Owls, and the Snowy Owl — whether relocating to New Jersey's Palisades Park across the Hudson River, or migrating upstate to the Catskills or Hudson Valley, following the well-worn path of fellow city-grizzled New Yorkers. The Central Park Conservancy confirmed that they had stopped using rodenticide during Flaco's time of freedom, but the rest of the city remained a hazard.

Flaco disappeared from Central Park in the first week of November and re-emerged in the late afternoon of Monday, November 6th, 2023, in the sculpture garden of Kenkeleba House on East Second Street in the East Village, five miles south of his Central Park haunts. With the new move, the dietary risks increased exponentially. By November 17th, Flaco was back in Central Park, spotted in his favorite oak, but from here on, he would no longer be a full-time resident of the park.

Some speculated that hectoring from other birds was among the causes of his departure.

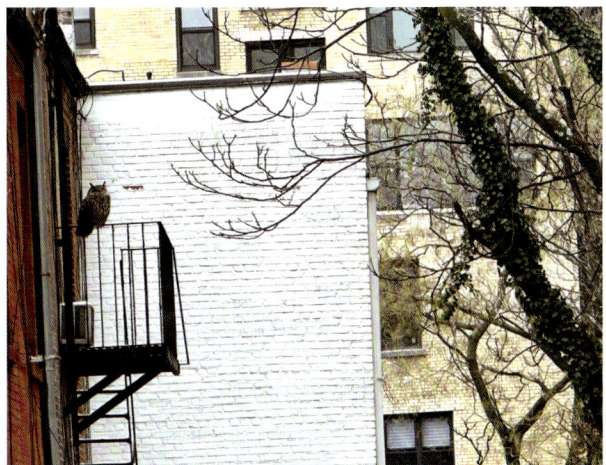

Howard Katz, *Flaco on a Fire Escape of a West 82nd Street Courtyard,* Upper West Side 1/18/24, 12:03 p.m.

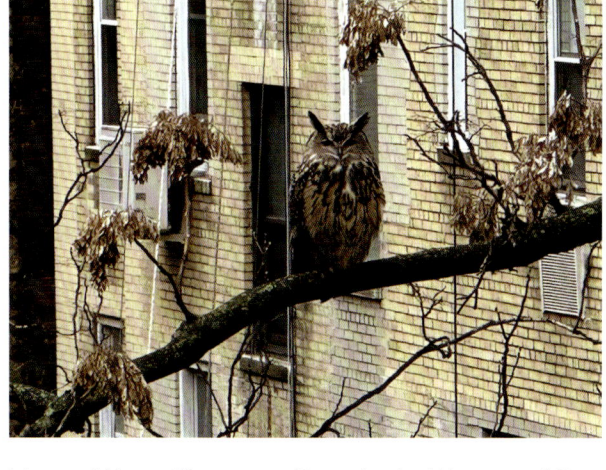

Howard Katz, *Flaco on a Branch of a West 82nd Street Courtyard,* Upper West Side 12/28/23, 2:02 p.m.

On day one, two Red-tailed Hawks had dive-bombed Flaco as he clung to a branch blowing in the February gusts. Photographer Mark Elliott observed groups of 20–30 crows, referred to as a "murder," when in a group, for good reason, sitting in the branches above Flaco, cawing relentlessly. Then there were the aggressions of smaller birds—occasionally the orioles and robins, but especially the strident blue jays as photographed here by @chrisangphoto.

The courtyards and fire escapes of the Upper East and Upper West Side would have offered sanctuary from aggressive birds and raptors and wintery gusts. They were the perfect location to roost peacefully by day, especially in a sunny spot, before the evening flyout or hours spent hooting from the city heights. Even in Flaco's last weeks, the photographers could not discern noticeable signs of illness or decline, but based on the Bronx Zoo's March 25th necropsy report, rodenticide was building up in his body, and the pigeon herpesvirus was attacking the tissue of vital organs—a virus that is fatal in Eurasian eagle-owls.

On Presidents Day, February 19th, a resident of West End Avenue on the Upper West Side snapped a picture of Flaco resting on a seat cushion on a fire escape before he was startled by workmen on the roof and flew off, leaving an uneaten rat. No one saw him again until he was discovered, downed, at 5:00 p.m. on Friday, February 23rd in the courtyard of a building on West 89th Street.

The dream of Flaco was over.

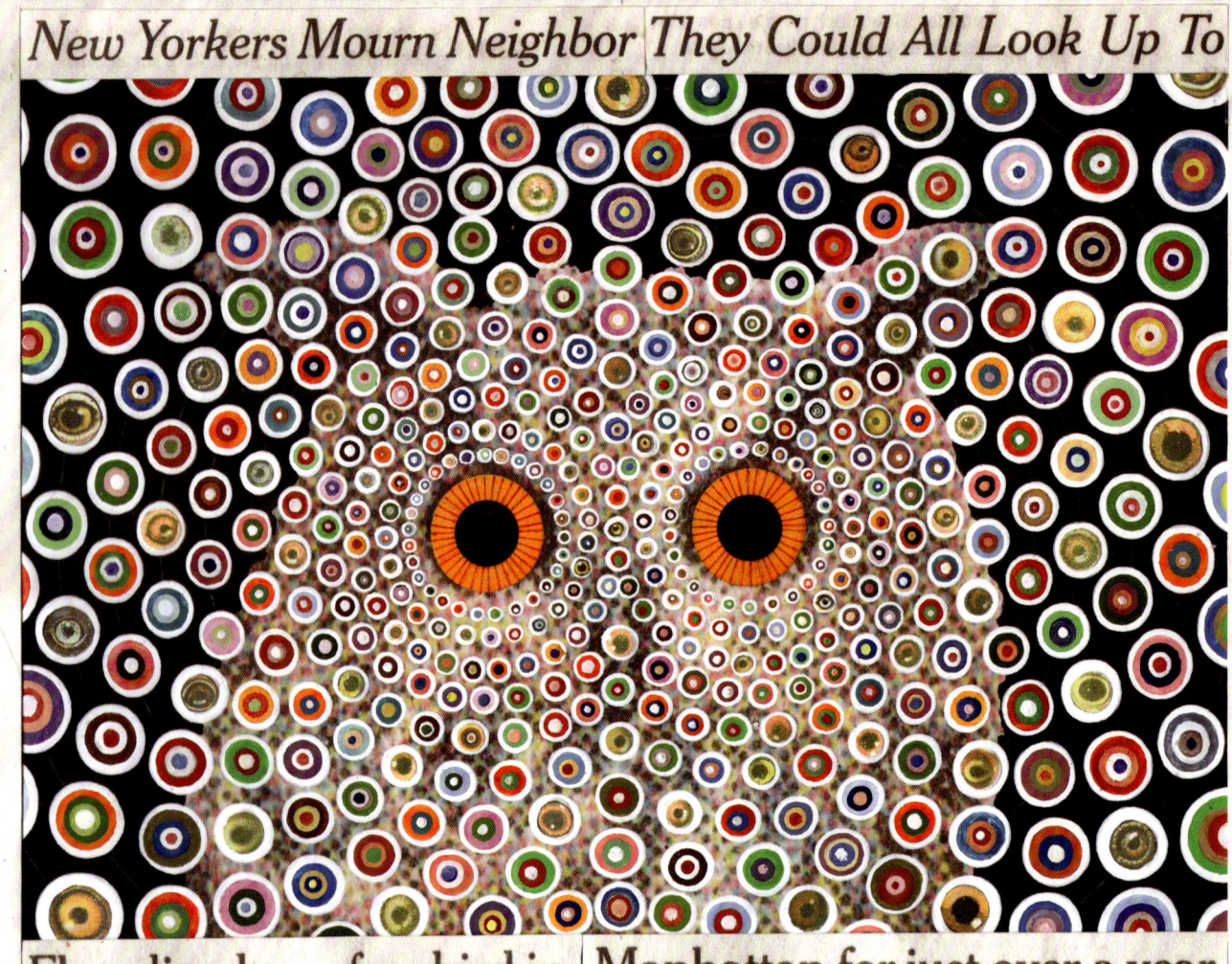

Fred Tomaselli, *February 25, 2024,* 2024, gouache and collage on archival inkjet print, 11 x 14 in.

The Legacy of Flaco: Finally His Own Owl

The individual who cut a hole in Flaco's Central Park enclosure released two Flacos into the world.

The first was the living, breathing Eurasian eagle-owl of Manhattan, un-taming himself before our eyes, who roosted in some of Central Park's oldest branches, removed the head first, plucked the mites from his feathers, assumed the "DeLorean" position before flyout, and hooted from the rooftops. The other Flaco is the owl of our imagination who occupies much larger real estate in the hearts, minds, and spirits of those around the world who were deeply moved by his story.

While we have tragically lost the real, singular Flaco, the Flaco of our dreams and imaginations is very much alive. This book aims to preserve and represent both.

We fell in love with Flaco not just because he was a majestic owl, easy to anthropomorphize and lay flat under the weight of symbolism and metaphor, but because we saw ourselves in him. We wanted for Flaco the same things we want for ourselves: to live in accordance with our own nature and abilities, exempt from judgment or interference.

Who among us wouldn't give up the equivalent cage—we've all got one—whether that's droning along year after year on the same hamster wheel of the 9-to-5 grind, working toward dreams that may or may not be realized, or navigating another round of anniversaries and holidays? There are deeper entrapments, too: our own bodies and minds, over whose shortcomings, histories, traumas, insecurities, and deterioration we preside.

Even the happiest, most enviable life has moments worthy of escape, so who among us wouldn't long to bend back the steel mesh of ourselves and our circumstances for greater freedoms and, in doing so, transform ordinary years into a diamond-pressed life that sparkles, shimmers, and shines?

Flaco's desire for coupling—and a mate—tapped into our individual longings, too.

"You can be lonely anywhere, but there is a particular flavour to the loneliness that comes from living in a city, surrounded by millions of people," Olivia Laing writes in *The Lonely City,* a sentiment that rings true when one considers Flaco in New York. Owls' vocalizations can tell us their species and gender. Among each other, they can warn of danger or establish territory with other owls . . . but they're also a call for a mate.

Observers have noted that Flaco seldom hooted within his Central Park enclosure, but while free, he flew to some of the highest points of the city and hooted for hours. Flaco wasn't the only Eurasian eagle-owl in North America, but as far as we know, he was the only one living in the wild, and there's something heartbreaking and quintessentially New York about the young hero calling night after night for a mate who would never come.

In addition to the extraordinary documentation

created by a cadre of photographers who set out with their equipment each evening, never knowing how long the dream of Flaco might last, artists used the language of their own creative practices across a broad range of media to preserve and memorialize Flaco.

Reporter/artist Bill Hutchinson carved a 13-foot Flaco totem pole in California to delight his elderly mother. Heide Hatry created altered books, incorporating Flaco imagery and delicate bones extracted from Flaco's pellets alongside the book's original text. Fred Tomaselli reimagined the cover of The New York Times with Ed Shanahan's article "New Yorkers Mourn Neighbor They Could All Look Up To" accompanying Tomaselli's gouache and collage portrait of Flaco in multi-colored circles . . . because "O" is for owl. Chicago-based artist (and former boxer) Tony Fitzpatrick folded Flaco into his aviary of bird-inspired collage work. Colombian muralist Calicho Arevalo painted 11 Flaco murals on the Lower East Side (most gone now); Martha Nishida created a stitchwork portrait of Flaco expressly for this book; and humorist Ian Frazier gave Flaco six lines in his annual holiday poem, entitled "Greetings, Friends!," published in The New Yorker on December 25th, 2023.

An outpouring of grief followed in the wake of Flaco's death: The New York Times sent a push notification at 10:56 p.m., February 23rd, announcing Flaco's death, in journalism's tolling of the bells typically reserved for heads of state and celebrities. On Sunday, March 3rd, 2024, hundreds of mourners gathered at the base of Flaco's oak for a remembrance ceremony where they had left flowers and 257 objects (most handmade), which are represented in the final section of the book.

* * *

Some have said, "If Flaco had not been released, he would still be alive today." That is true—possibly for another decade or two. Years upon years of being unable to fly, enduring stultifying boredom criminal for a bird of such keen intelligence, and fed a diet of frozen rats. What kind of life would that be? But then, some people love a cage.

Instead, Flaco got to experience all four seasons on his own terms: mastering the thrill of the hunt and the gift of flight which could take him from the emerald lawns of the North Meadow Ballfields to the water towers on the Upper West Side; feeling the sun warming feathers dampened by spring rain; napping through the heat of summer's hottest days under a leafy canopy; hearing the papery rustle of breezes moving through autumn leaves while hooting at the full moon; feeling the first snowfall landing on his head and ear tufts.

For one year, Flaco was his own owl, experiencing the life he had always deserved, finally making use of the exquisite mechanics and flight gear he'd been born with . . .

And what a spectacular year it was.

JONATHAN HOLLINGSWORTH
New York City, 2025

Right Juliet Schreckinger, Detail of *Flaco,* 2023, ink and graphite on Arches paper, 8 x 10 in.

Following spread Paul Beiboer, *Flaco on Water Tower,* Upper West Side, 86th Street & Columbus Avenue, 12/2/23, 11:00 p.m. (Exposure approximately one sec.)

After Flaco flew from the top of 5 West 86th Street earlier that night, he landed on top of what would become one of his favorite water towers on the Upper West Side. He stayed there for a few hours at least and hooted for more than an hour. He seemed interested in watching the airplanes coming into Newark, New Jersey.

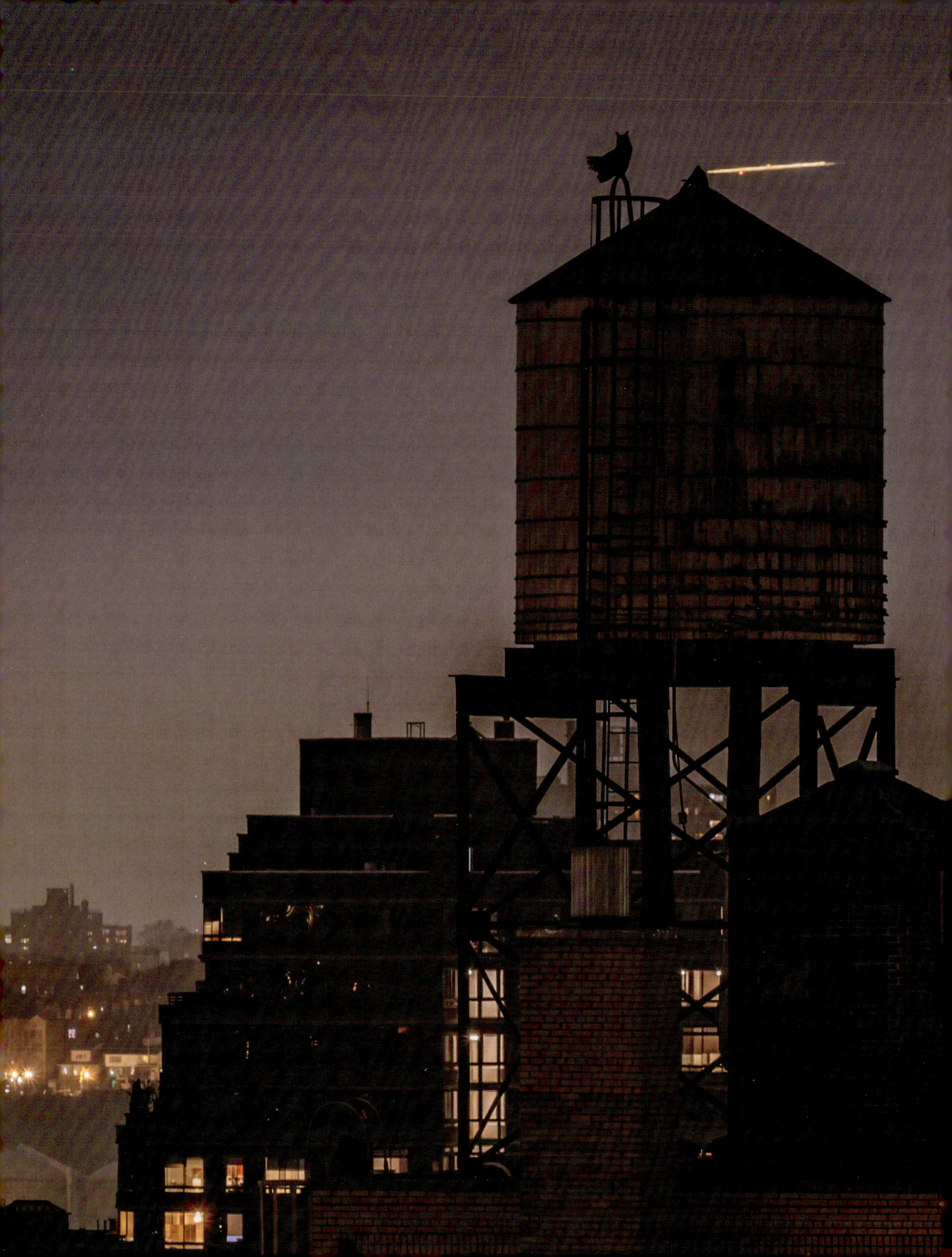

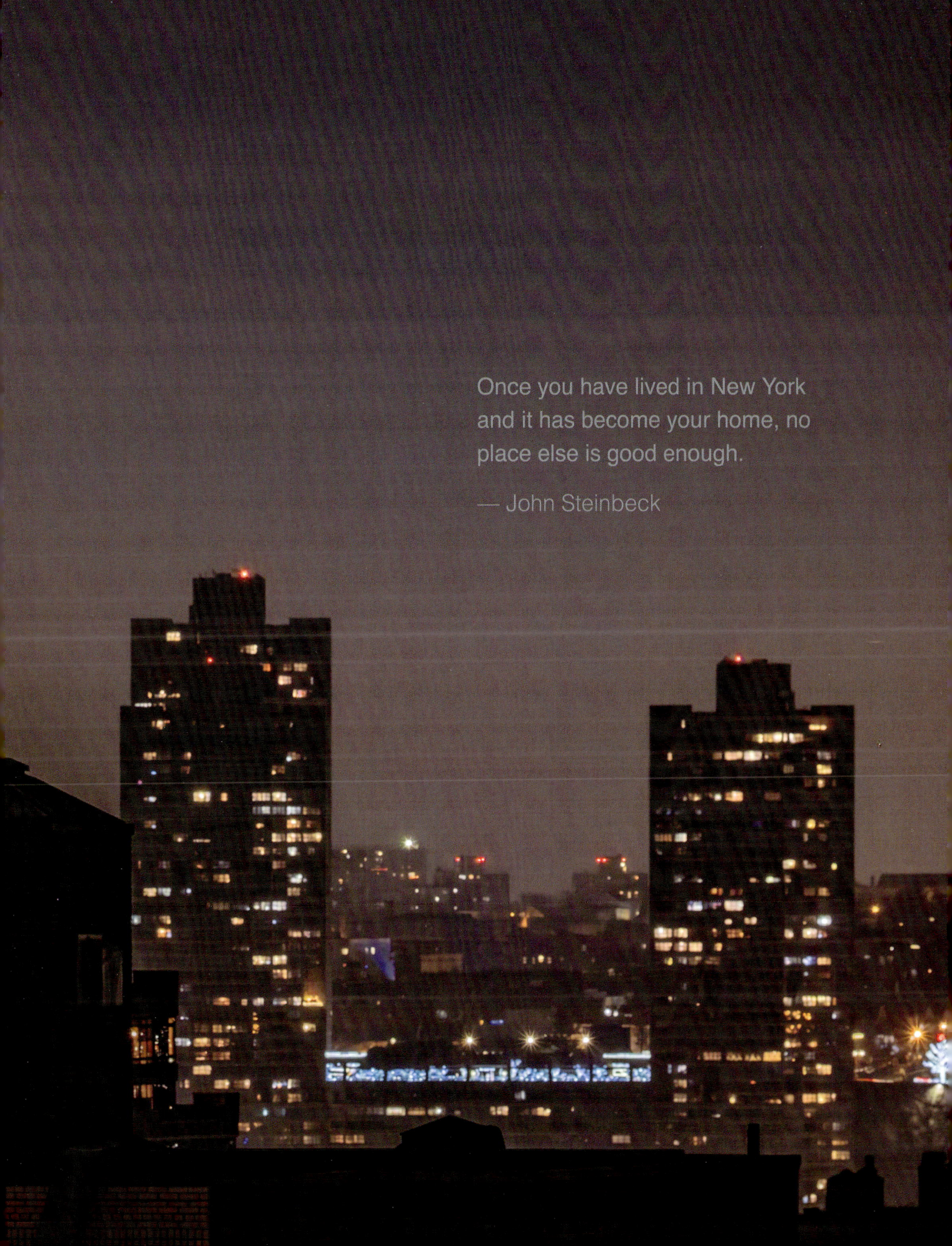

An owl that escaped from the Central Park Zoo is still loose – and hunting on his own – *NPR,* 2/16/23

Flaco, der ausgebüxte Uhu, begeistert die New Yorker – und nicht nur weil er so geheimnisvoll «Huuu» ruft
– *Neue Zürcher Zeitung,* 10/03/23

Flaco, Central Park Zoo Owl, Tastes

New Yorkers give a hoot about Flaco the Owl – *Le Monde,* 2/26/23

Il gufo Flaco rimarra libero: lo zoo di Central Park rinuncia alla cattura e lui diventa il beniamino di New York perche caccia i topi
– *la Repubblica,* 2/20/23

Flaco the owl doesn't give a hoot after escaping NYC zoo, and officials say he can fly free for now
– *CBC News,* 2/18/23

What Should Be Done About Flaco, the Eurasian Eagle-Owl Loose in New York? —*Audubon*, 3/7/23

Flaco the owl becomes New York's newest tourist attraction, as he settles into Central Park home
— *ABC News*, 2/20/23

Flaco the Escaped Central Park Zoo Owl Is My King — *Jezebel*, 2/21/23

Freedom and Isn't Rushing to Return
— *The New York Times*, 2/14/23

Freedom has been a hoot, but can Flaco the owl survive New York City?
—*The Guardian*, 11/24/23

New York City's Central Park Owl 'Flaco' is now TWICE as big as when vandals helped him escape zoo — after feeding off the Big Apple's huge rat population — *Daily Mail*, 10/2/23

An Owl Named "Flaco" Escaped A NYC Zoo 8 Months Ago And Has Been Living Freely In The City Ever Since — *Buzzfeed*, 11/10/23

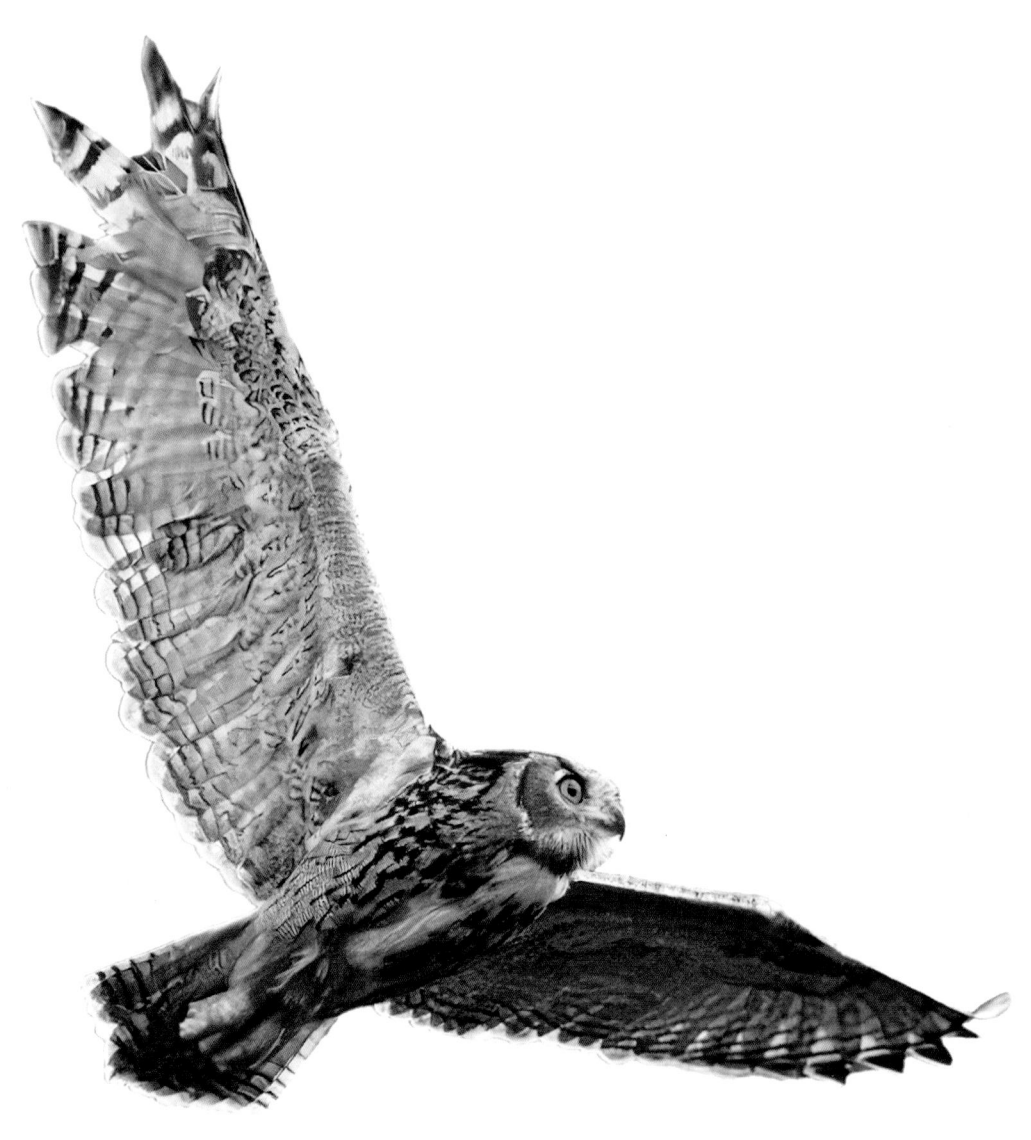

Anke Frohlich, Detail of *Flaco Soaring,* East Drive Opposite the Compost Heap, 10/5/23, Six Minutes After Sunset

The Short Happiness of Flaco

Flaco lived the classic question: At what price freedom? Was Flaco's liberation worth his relatively short, hazardous freedom, his death?

Almost from the moment he was reported loose, Flaco became a metaphor. The only member of his Eurasian species suddenly free in America, with no experience at making a living in New York, Flaco was the kind of immigrant that the city has long known and nurtured.

Stranger in a strange land, a legal alien in a city where millions had arrived alone and unconnected under the shadow of Lady Liberty, Flaco was an unlikely reflection of the American experience and a quintessential New Yorker. He was free, his choices were limited, he was self-reliant but still dependent on what the city—what we—had to offer. We could wish him well; we could not guarantee his safety.

We let his new life thrill us. But we all knew that the rats Flaco was catching bore traces of poison that would accumulate, and could kill him. Holding our breath, we wondered whether the city that cheered him on would ultimately undo him.

Flaco had succeeded. And when he fell, we had ourselves to blame.

So—Is a short span of being who you were born to be better than a long, safe, monotonous life? To varying degrees, it's the question we all answer for ourselves, with how we live our own lives.

CARL SAFINA

Flaco's Timeline

March 15, 2010

Flaco the Eurasian eagle-owl, identified as "#151," is born to Xena (#84) and Watson (#82) at Sylvan Heights Bird Park in Scotland Neck, North Carolina, an AZA-led (Association of Zoos & Aquariums) breeding program that provides Eurasian eagle-owls to zoos and institutions for conservation purposes.

November 10, 2010

The Wildlife Conservation Society, the Bronx-based parent non-profit of the Central Park Zoo, announces Flaco's arrival at the zoo, where he begins his life of captivity in the Temperate Territory section, among the snow leopards, snow monkeys, and red pandas, which will be the first of Flaco's two Central Park enclosures.

February 2, 2023

Between 4:30 p.m. (winter closing hours) and 8:30 p.m., approximately, an individual cuts a hole in the stainless steel mesh of Flaco's enclosure, while standing out of view of the cameras. The individual is never identified or apprehended.

At 8:30 p.m., zoo staff discover that Flaco is no longer in his enclosure. The 19th Police Precinct reports that Flaco explores the neighboring Upper East Side and lands on the sidewalk outside the Sherry-Netherland Hotel on Fifth Avenue, before landing outside the luxury department store, Bergdorf Goodman.

After emergency workers attempt to capture Flaco, unsuccessfully, with a pet carrier, the 19th Police Precinct posts on X: "Well. That was a hoot. We tried to save this little wise guy but he had had enough of his group of admirers and flew off."

The zoo's staff and Central Park rangers begin round-the-clock observation of Flaco, who spends the night in a tree near 59th Street.

February 3, 2023
By sunrise, Flaco returns to the south end of Central Park, where zoo workers maintain "visual contact." Flaco roosts in the upper branches of a tree in the Hallett Nature Sanctuary, approximately 60 feet above the ground, in frigid temperatures. The Hallett Nature Sanctuary is closed to pedestrian traffic.

February 9, 2023
In the early evening at Central Park's Heckscher Ballfields, zoo staff and park rangers bait Flaco with a Bal-Chatri trap—a metal cage containing a live rat with a series of filament nooses on top to ensnare Flaco's feet. Flaco briefly lands on the trap, but escapes as zoo staff rush forward with nets. He never approaches a trap again.

February 11, 2023
Flaco is observed expelling a pellet, evidence that he is successfully hunting on his own.

February 12, 2023
The Central Park Zoo announces that Flaco has been observed "successfully hunting, catching and consuming prey" in the previous days. "A major concern for everyone at the beginning was whether Flaco could be able to hunt and eat; that is no longer a concern." Zoo staff and rangers will continue to monitor Flaco, "though not as intensely."

February 16, 2023
On their final failed attempt to recover Flaco, zoo staff and rangers play a recording of a female Eurasian eagle-owl from Sheep Meadow. Flaco shows interest but declines to approach.

Nearly seventeen hundred individuals sign a petition, "Free Flaco, the Central Park Zoo Owl," on Change.org, calling for the end of all recovery efforts.

February 17, 2023
The Central Park Zoo announces that the results of the previous night's attempts were unsuccessful and they are effectively ending recovery efforts. "We are going to continue monitoring Flaco and his activities and to be prepared to resume recovery efforts if he shows any sign of difficulty or distress. We will issue additional updates if there is a change in the eagle owl's status or our plan changes."

February 18, 2023
Experiences first snowfall outside captivity.

February 21, 2023
Relocates from the south end of Central Park to the North Woods, where he roosts by day, until flyout, to hunt at the nearby Harlem Meer Construction Site, Compost Heap, or North Meadow Ballfields. The northern section of the park will remain Flaco's home through October 2023.

March 14, 2023
Seth Meyers devotes more than four minutes to the Flaco story on his show, *Late Night with Seth Meyers,* referencing Flaco's 'Shawshank' escape, which provides "the kind of story we need right now."

October 31, 2023
Departs Central Park.

November 6, 2023
Re-emerges at 5:00 p.m. in an enclosed sculpture garden beside Kenkeleba House, an artists' space on East Second Street, on the Lower East Side, between Avenues B and C. This marks Flaco's first significant foray outside the park.

November 14, 2023
Returns uptown, to the Upper East Side, alighting on the Fifth Avenue, 13th floor windowsill of playwright and poet, Nan Knighton, where he remains for three hours.

November 15, 2023
Makes a second apartment window visit, two blocks north, on Fifth Avenue and the East 90s.

November 17, 2023
Returns to the oak tree in Central Park, one of the primary trees where Flaco prefers to roost. While Flaco continues to spend time in Central Park, he is no longer a permanent resident.

November 27, 2023
Alights on the fire escape in a hidden courtyard on West 80th Street, between Columbus and Amsterdam Avenue. The enclosed courtyards of the Upper East Side and Upper West Side become prime roosting spots in fall, 2023 and winter, 2024.

January 12, 2024
Returns to Central Park to spend the day roosting low in a tree in the Loch, his last-known daytime visit to Central Park.

February 2, 2024
The one-year anniversary of Flaco's liberation is accompanied by extensive media coverage and fanfare celebrating his survival. A group of filmmakers, photographers, and devoted fans meet at the corner of West 90th Street and Broadway that evening, hoping to find Flaco, who makes a surprise appearance on the brownstone balconies along West 89th Street.

February 19, 2024
Flaco is believed to have stopped hooting, presumably compromised by illness. A resident on West End Avenue observes Flaco resting on a fire escape, abandoning an uneaten rat after being startled by workmen on the roof.

February 23, 2024
Flaco is found unresponsive at 5:00 p.m. in the courtyard of 267 West 89th Street on the Upper West Side. Volunteers from the Wild Bird Fund pronounce Flaco dead shortly thereafter.

February 24, 2024
David Barrett announces on Manhattan Bird Alert that the Central Park oak (104th Street and East Drive) will be the designated spot for Flaco's remembrances. Mourners begin placing flowers and tributes at the base of the tree.

Plans for a remembrance ceremony begin.

New York State Legislators rename The Bird Safe Buildings Act, S.7098/A.7808 the FLACO Act ("Feathered Lives Also Count" Act) to honor the impact Flaco had on New York City.

March 2024
Mike Hubbard, Jesse McGraw, and David X launch simultaneous petitions for the placement of a Flaco memorial in Central Park, which garner more than 5,000 signatures.

Sixty-three thousand individuals (as of September 2024) sign a petition on ThePetitionSite.com to "urge the NYPD and Central Park Zoo officials to relaunch the investigation into the vandalism of Flaco's habitat to prevent any further zoo inhabitant escapes."

March 3, 2024
Hundreds of mourners (and the media) gather at 4:00 p.m. at the base of Flaco's Central Park oak for a remembrance ceremony, where speakers pay tribute with stories, remembrances, poetry, and music.

March 15, 2024
Flaco would have turned 14 years old. He spent 7% of his life as a free bird.

March 25, 2024
The Wildlife Conservation Society announces the final findings of the Bronx Zoo's necropsy report: Flaco's body contained four kinds of rodenticide and the pigeon herpesvirus which affected the tissue of critical organs. Even without the acute traumatic injury brought on by the window collision or fall, these elements would have proved fatal.

April 11, 2024
East River Tattoo in Greenpoint, Brooklyn organizes "Flaco Day," where fans can get a Flaco tattoo designed and inked by visual artist Duke Riley. Multiple media outlets cover the event.

May 28, 2024
Flaco's wings and frozen tissue samples are transferred to the American Museum of Natural History. The remainder of Flaco's remains are archived at the Bronx Zoo's Wildlife Health Center.

January 31 — July 6, 2025
The New York Historical Society mounts the exhibition, "The Year of Flaco," which includes a selection of the memorial objects acquired for the museum's permanent collection.

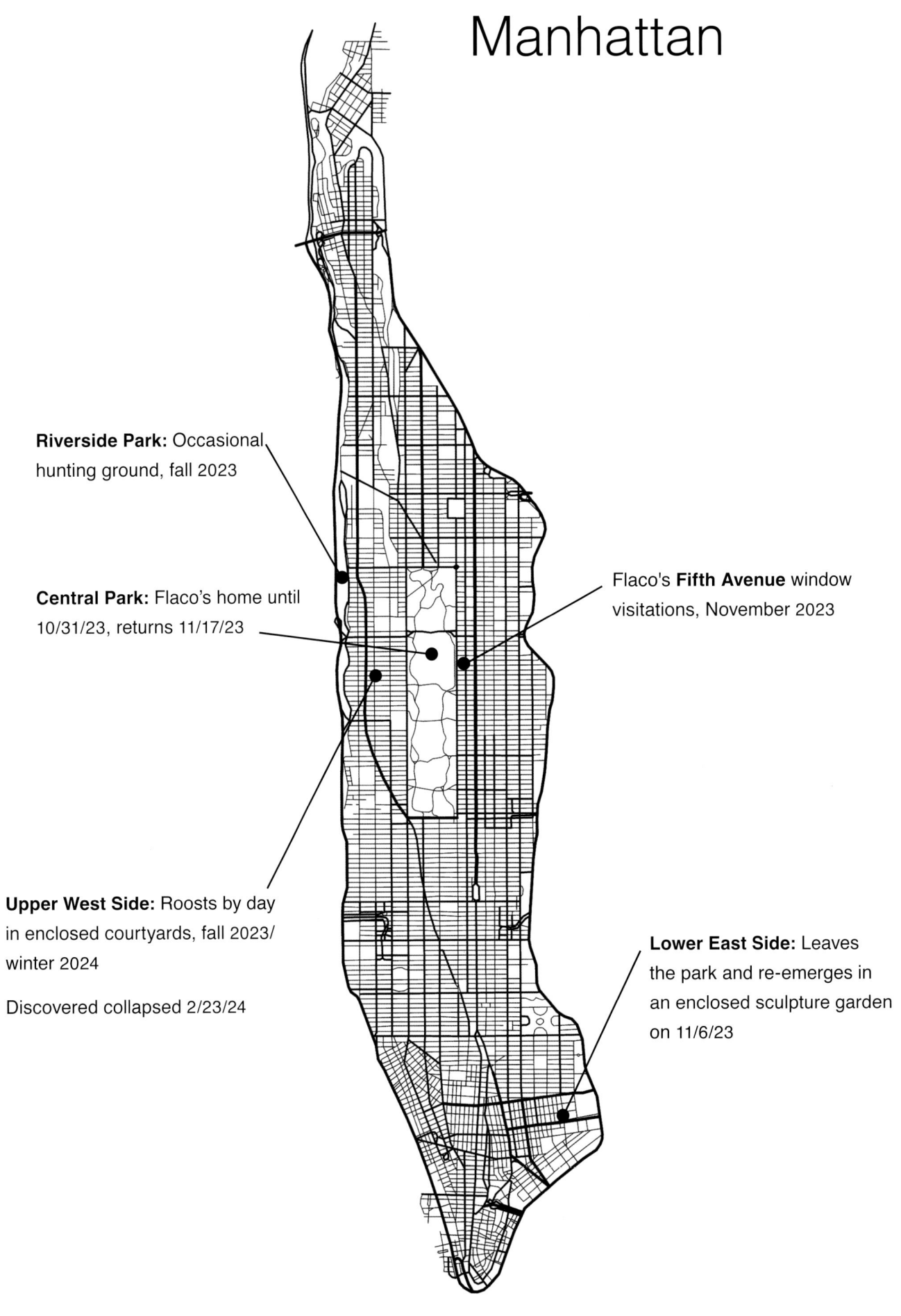

Central Park

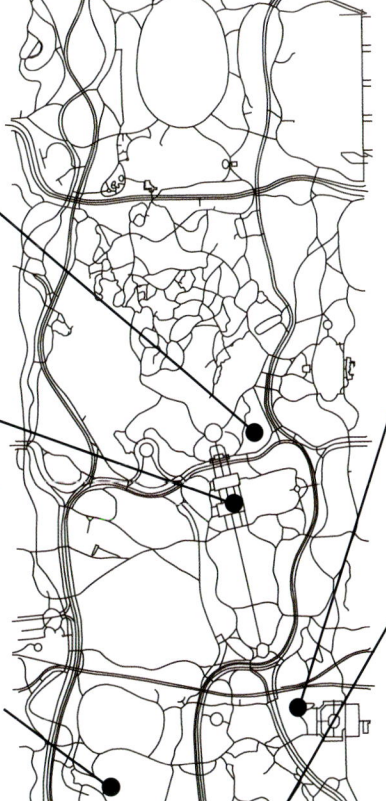

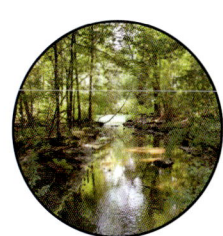

North Woods/ The Loch: First destination after leaving the southern end of the park

Harlem Meer Construction Site: Perches on beloved equipment, hunting for rats

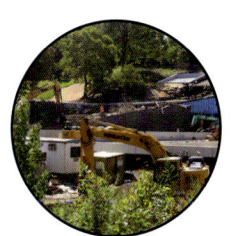

Flaco near

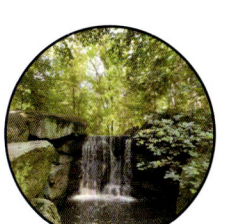

Huddlestone Arch: Flaco regularly roosts above the falls, winter 2023

Compost Area: Evening hunting ground

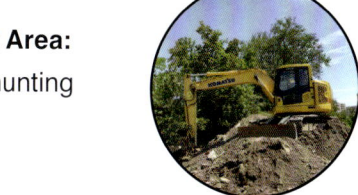

Flaco's Oak: A favorite roosting spot, admired by bikers/joggers on East Drive; site of memorial ceremony

Flaco's Black Walnut: Roosting spot

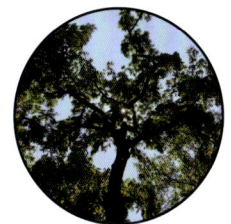

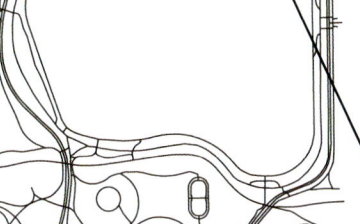

Literary Walk, The Mall: Roosting spot, February 2023

Flaco's Elm: Leafy canopy offering respite during the hottest days of summer

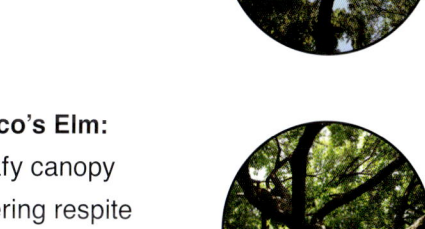

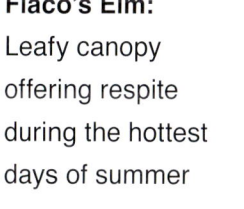

Naumburg Bandshell: Early February 2023, appears between the bandshell and south end of the Literary Walk

Central Park Zoo: Lives in captivity from 11/10/10 to 2/2/23

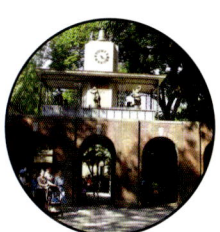

Hallett Nature Sanctuary: Takes refuge during his first weeks of liberation, early February 2023

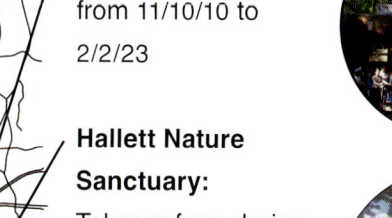

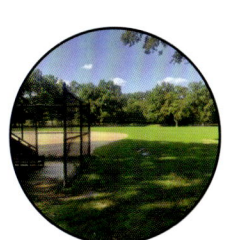

Heckscher Ballfield: Nearly captured by zoo staff, 2/9/23

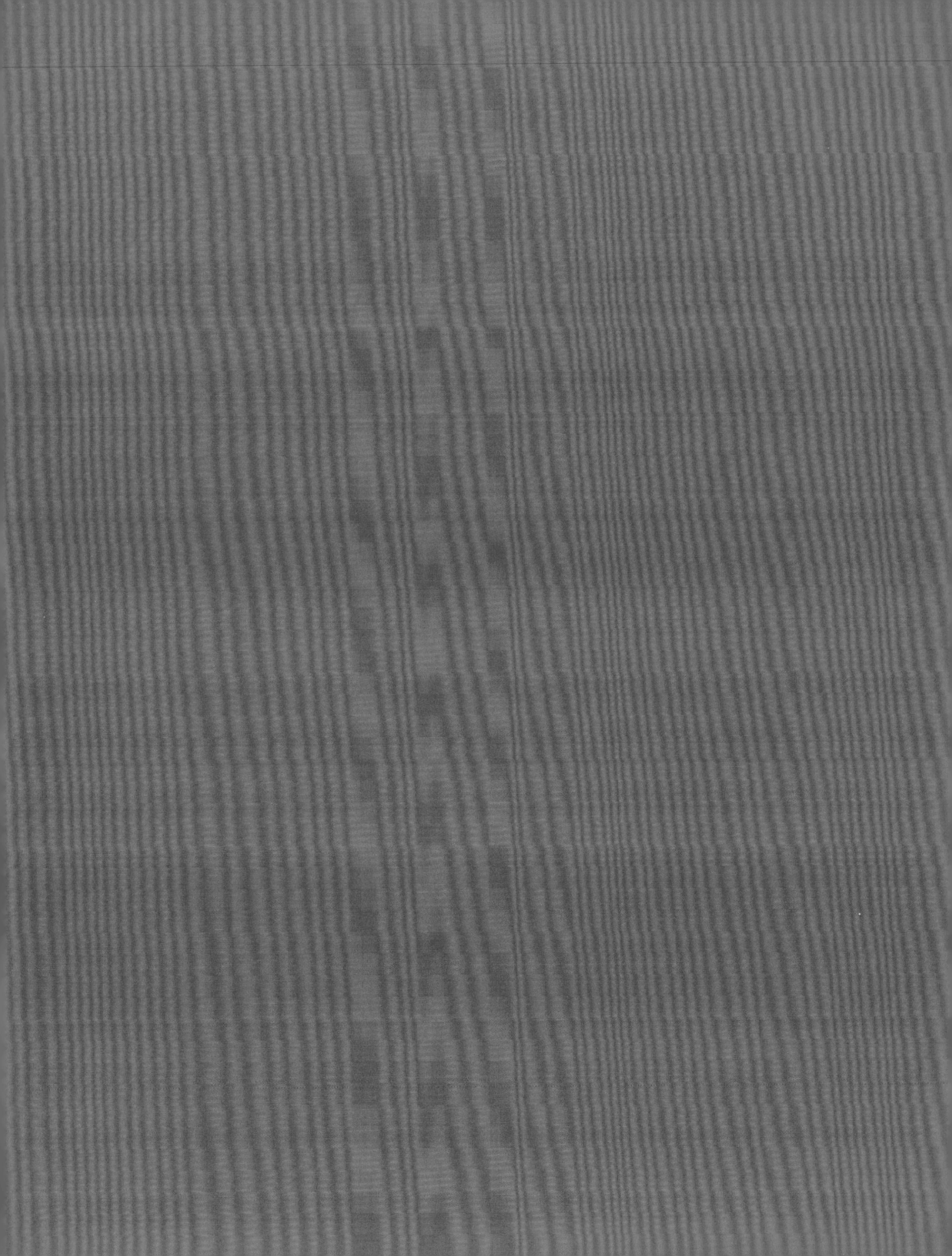

Notes from the Field
Insights from an Owl

> Keep only what is useful. Regurgitate the rest.

> Be patient. Eventually something will move.

> Learn through play.

> Only one out of four or five tries yields a mouse. Never give up.

> Accept help when it is offered.

> Adapt to stay resilient.

> Travel every four to six months.

> Take time to sit and observe.

> Death is a necessary ingredient to life. Accept the transformation.

> Never foul your own nest.

> Parenthood is temporary.

> The Great Grey Owl does not see what the Great Horned Owl sees. Perspective is everything.

> Withhold judgment. Nature does not take sides.

> Where you live is not nearly as important as where you are alive.

— Excerpt from *The Hidden Lives of Owls*
LEIGH CALVEZ

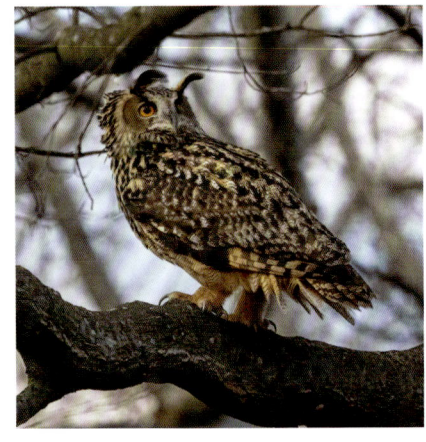

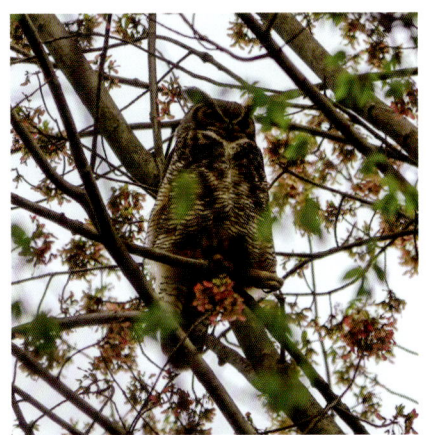

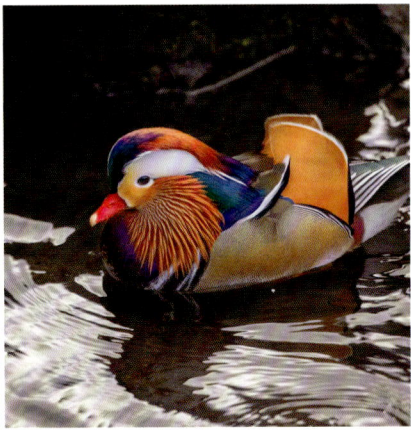

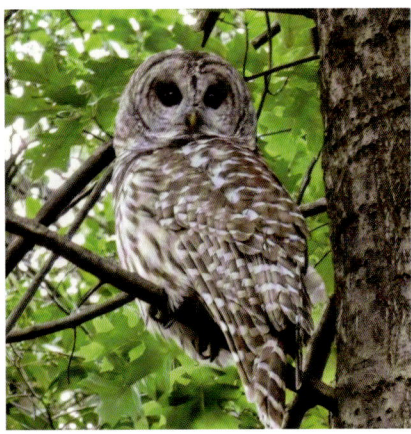

Photographers

Chris Ang
David Barrett
Paul Beiboer
Sheryl Checkman
Marianne DeMarco
Mark Elliott
Molly Eustis
Anke Frohlich
Venus N. Sallay

Top to bottom

Flaco, Eurasian eagle-owl
@chrisangphoto

Geraldine, Great Horned Owl
Molly Eustis

Mandarin Duck
Venus N. Sallay

Barry, Barred Owl
David Barrett

About the Photographs

From 2018 to 2024, Central Park enjoyed a rotation of celebrity birds who arrived, unbidden but beloved, right out of the avian ether, who either died tragically or at best, disappeared without ceremony, like the stars of a party who couldn't be bothered with goodbyes.

First, the Mandarin Duck, a species normally found in China and Japan, mysteriously arrived in the Pond in the southeast corner of the park on October 10th, 2018. His vibrant glam-rock plumage—the Ziggy Stardust of ducks—put the drab mallards to shame. Whether he'd been an abandoned pet or an escaped zoo inhabitant, no one knew, but the band around his leg suggested some tenuous tie with humanity. Having made national headlines and inspiring Bette Midler's children's book, *The Tale of the Mandarin Duck* (Penguin Random House, 2021), he had tired of fame by March of 2019 and travelled far enough that even the city's intrepid birders, who ventured to the region's lakes, ponds, and rivers, did not spot him again.

Then came the parliament of owls for whom Central Park was a chessboard. There was the Snowy Owl, the first of its species to return to Central Park since the winter of 1890, who perched on the same backstops, surveying the North Meadow Baseball Fields for rats, which Flaco would inherit and use for the same purpose. The attention from antagonistic birds and shutter-happy humans might have been too much because the Snowy Owl took flight after a mere month, in January 2021. However, it is still possible to see a Snowy Owl across from the park, mounted and stuffed at the American Museum of

Natural History—shot on Long Island in 1876 by teenaged Teddy Roosevelt.

Geraldine, a Great Horned Owl, arrived in January 2022, compromised from a left foot that was deformed or injured, and used the park to convalesce for 18 months before disappearing in summer 2023. Unlike Flaco, she was more elusive and harder to locate, camouflaging herself in the depths of a favorite pine in Cedar Hill or the Ramble.

One of Flaco's young mourners expressed regret that Flaco and Geraldine had never "married," but owls are not keen to share their turf, and an encounter between two apex predators would have been one of antipathy, not romance. Molly Eustis, a Flaco photographer and Geraldine devotee, often toggled between the two owls during her nights shooting in the park and worried about what would happen in an encounter during the six months the owls shared the park. There was at least one evening in which Eustis observed them in a similar section, but, fortunately, Geraldine fled before there could be an encounter.

Despite the proliferation of cutesy owl puns and professed love for its avian visitors whose presence could be fleeting, New York hasn't always been so hospitable to its owls. In 1900, William Braislin, M.D. recorded an event in his journal, in which he had witnessed a group of boys gathered in an empty lot, throwing stones (and epithets) at a Barred Owl roosting in the branches above them. Despite the indignity of the assault, the owl remained for several more days, until the neighboring households determined that the owl was a nuisance, as the crowd's onslaught of rogue stones was a danger to heads and windowpanes. The antagonists were not shot by the police, but the owl was.

More than a century later, a representative of the same species received a more favorable welcome. The young Barred Owl, cleverly named "Barry," before anyone realized there was a female under the feathers, was the precursor for Flaco. She arrived in the dark days of the pandemic, just when we needed her most: COVID-19 had already consumed three seasons, relegating us to long days indoors; there was still no vaccine available; a punctuation mark of the day was throwing open our windows at 7:00 p.m. to bang on pots and pans, thanking the essential workers and reminding our neighbors that there was still life happening behind the curtains. Who wouldn't perk up at the news that a Barred Owl, a plucky two-pound ingenue, had appeared in our year of grief and solitude?

A group of birders spotted her in the Loch, at the less-frequented north end of the park, on October 9th, 2020, almost two years to the day after the arrival of the Mandarin Duck. Some speculated that because she was young, approximately a year based on her coloration, she had not learned to be afraid of humans. Admirers might stand within 10 feet of her as she preened in the branches of a favorite hemlock. Unlike most owls, she was active during the daytime and could be seen splashing in shallow pools, turning her head at a 270-degree angle, or swooping down to snatch a frog.

Nearly 10 months later, at 2:30 a.m. on August 6th, Barry collided with a two-seater Central Park Conservancy maintenance vehicle on West Drive travelling at or below 15 miles per hour. The necropsy found traces of two kinds of anticoagulant rat poison, bromadiolone and difethialone, in her body, but the state Department of Environmental Conservation that performed the necropsy could not confirm whether her body had been under duress, with her senses impaired, before the collision.

An outpouring of grief followed. Barry had stayed in the park longer than any owl in recent history. She had been profiled in *The New York Times,* and Instagram and Twitter accounts had sprung up in her honor. Her fans and visitors knew that she might take flight without a farewell, but no one considered such a brutal, premature death or the more sinister effects that could have caused it. #RIPBarry trended on Twitter, while in the real world, Barry's admirers gathered for an informal evening vigil on Monday, August 9th, beneath her favorite hemlock tree near the Boathouse in the Central Park Ramble, where her fans left notes and marked what would have been her 10th month in the park.

Two days later, literary critic Michiko Kakutani wrote an essay in *The New York Times* titled "Barry the Owl Brought Us Together. What Will We Do Without Her?" It was a good question.

On the 27-degree morning of Friday, February 3rd, 2023, a group of photographers gathered to photograph a bewildered, freaked-out Flaco in the upper branches of the park's Hallett Nature Sanctuary in his first morning of freedom. They were not gathered as strangers, because most were well-acquainted through their days photographing Barry. The camaraderie, the lines of communication between them, and the social media accounts were all ready and waiting . . .

Cue the arrival of a resplendent, eminently photogenic, escaped owl . . .

During my interviews with the photographers, more than one said that they had been avid birders in their youth, a passion that had fallen to the wayside in adulthood, then re-awakened during the pandemic when old cameras came out or new ones were purchased. It makes sense. For those fortunate enough to live close to the park, afternoon walks offered a respite from the new universal practice of working from home. Rather than wandering masked and social distancing through Sheep Meadow, the Ramble, or along the Literary Walk, spotting an owl in a remote, out-of-the-way section of the park could add a sparkle to monotonous days in which any glimmer felt rare.

Flaco's liberation was a major life event for many of the photographers, which is not hyperbole: some were in the park every evening, documenting the variations of Flaco's nightly routines. Elements of the business of life that had once mattered fell away or were postponed. Collectively, they clocked thousands of hours, spending more time with Flaco than some might spend with their own families.

The photographers did not work in isolation. Every evening, there were the usual trees to canvas: the oak at 104th Street and East Drive, the black walnut by the Compost Heap, or the elm, whose branches are featured in the final pages of this book, close to the North Meadow Recreation Center. But if Flaco was not tucked among the usual branches, the thread of text messages picked up where it left off as the photographers worked together to find him, in a process that sometimes required night vision monoculars.

Imagine early August, that oppressively hot, swampy stretch when summer is its least charming, and everyone who can leave the city does. In these hottest months, Flaco roosts predictably in the elm, a tree with angling Gumby arms and a dense canopy that could have been around since Teddy Roosevelt's presidency. Each of Flaco's chosen trees has an inherent majesty, but to stand under the great elm, in particular, even after Flaco's passing, one can still sense the communion of spirits. If trees can feel wise, this one does: it is a holy place, even if pickleball is happening nearby.

In his sleep, Flaco lets his wings slacken with the heat, and by late afternoon, he begins to stir. His eyes open, followed by the meticulous and lengthy beauty treatment of preening, pulling out feathers, itching the mites. A small crowd of admirers has gathered in the quiet heat. There are unspoken rules to observing or photographing Flaco: no sudden movements, no loud sounds, no getting close, and no use of flash. (Even police cars patrolling the park at night were politely asked to turn off their flashing lights as they passed beneath the oak or black walnut tree flanking each side of East Drive.)

After preening, Flaco stretches his wings, extends his powerful legs, and opens and closes the four toes of his feet, a Zygodactyl arrangement in which one toe can rotate front or back, forming an X or V, depending on the needs of the hunt or the roost. He's moving through the series of motions that the photographers have come to recognize, photograph, and love before the take-your-breath-away moment when he crouches low, assuming the "DeLorean" pose from *Back to the Future* for "flyout," the magic hour for owlers when he leaves his sanctuary to hunt.

Sometimes, after flyout, Flaco could be followed to the predictable spots of the ballfields, the periphery of the Jackie Onassis Reservoir, the North Gate, the Compost Heap, or the Harlem Meer Construction Site. Other nights, he was gone.

In all of my interviews with the photographers, I waited until the end to ask the question, "What was it like after Flaco was gone?" The responses varied, but usually, there was a long pause as they considered it, while shoring up their composure. By then, a few months had passed since Flaco's death. In his interview with nature writer David Gessner, who published *Flaco: A Triptych* on Terrain.org in the months after Flaco's death, David Barrett confessed, "I don't know what to do with my nights anymore."

The underlying sentiment in the months after Flaco firmly established himself in the park had been one of tentative hope: "Okay, maybe he'll make it…" Others hoped he would eventually leave the risks of city living, but in every conversation, there was a deep appreciation for having had the experience and a lingering sorrow that the magic hours had ended.

For each image, I asked the photographers to include a basic caption, along with the time, because long exposures can make some images look like daylight hours when they were actually shot late at night. But more importantly, I wanted them to document their experiences, the moment, and the precarious, sometimes painful positions that went into making the images, whether shooting through the chain link surrounding the Harlem Meer Construction Site or holding an 8lb. camera still for 30 minutes, waiting for Flaco to cross their sightline, trying to predict whether their cameras were properly focused on his unpredictable flight path.

Wandering the park with tripods and backpacks with heavy cameras and lenses, climbing through heavily wooded, potentially dangerous sections of the park at night, and following Flaco's hoots to capture him against the full moon: these were just some of the feats that went into creating this collective body of work. Many of the photographers lived close to the park, but others might still be in the park after midnight, with a subway commute home, but still so keyed up that the night's work had to be reviewed before bed.

A tremendous amount of time, work, energy, money, risk, frustration, cunning, sweat, sore muscles, exhaustion, joy, failure, exhilaration, camaraderie — and most of all, love — went into making these images. Every portrait of Flaco is also a portrait of the individual on the other side of the lens, the woman or man who had the vision and captured a moment.

These pictures are all we have left.

Was it worth it in the end? I won't attempt to speak for the photographers, but I suspect the answer would be a resounding YES.

There was always something sacred about these experiences — a little brush with the divine — when the air was full of grace and possibility, like when Flaco swooped by a group of photographers, almost landing on Anke Frohlich's lens or sending an unforgettable *whoosh* of air past Sheryl Checkman.

Perhaps you might feel that same tingling *whoosh* as you turn these pages.

Day One

Molly Eustis, *Flaco's First Day,* Central Park, The Pond at 59th Street / The Hallett Nature Sanctuary, 2/3/23, 2:55 p.m.

This was Flaco's first full day outside of the zoo and my first time seeing him. It was bitterly cold and very windy, and at this point, I'd been out there for about 2 hours already. I had those disposable hand warmers and had to periodically take breaks to thaw my fingers. There was a sizable group of photographers, most of whom I knew, and several news outlets were on the scene.

Flaco was very high in a bare tree at the southeast edge of the Hallett Nature Sanctuary, and we were observing him from the path across the pond. It was a thrill to see him, and we were all a little giddy with excitement, but I think I can speak for everyone when I say we were also very nervous about his safety as a captive owl, now loose in the city. Two screaming red-tailed hawks circled overhead all afternoon, and Flaco stayed in that perch for a few hours, looking a bit shell-shocked, like he wasn't quite sure how he'd gotten himself into that situation or how to proceed.

When I was editing my photos later that night, it struck me that this was almost certainly the first time in his life he'd been up that high or experienced wind like that. I stayed and watched until just after sunset as he made a few short flights to trees lower and north in the sanctuary, and I left when I could no longer feel my (frozen) feet.

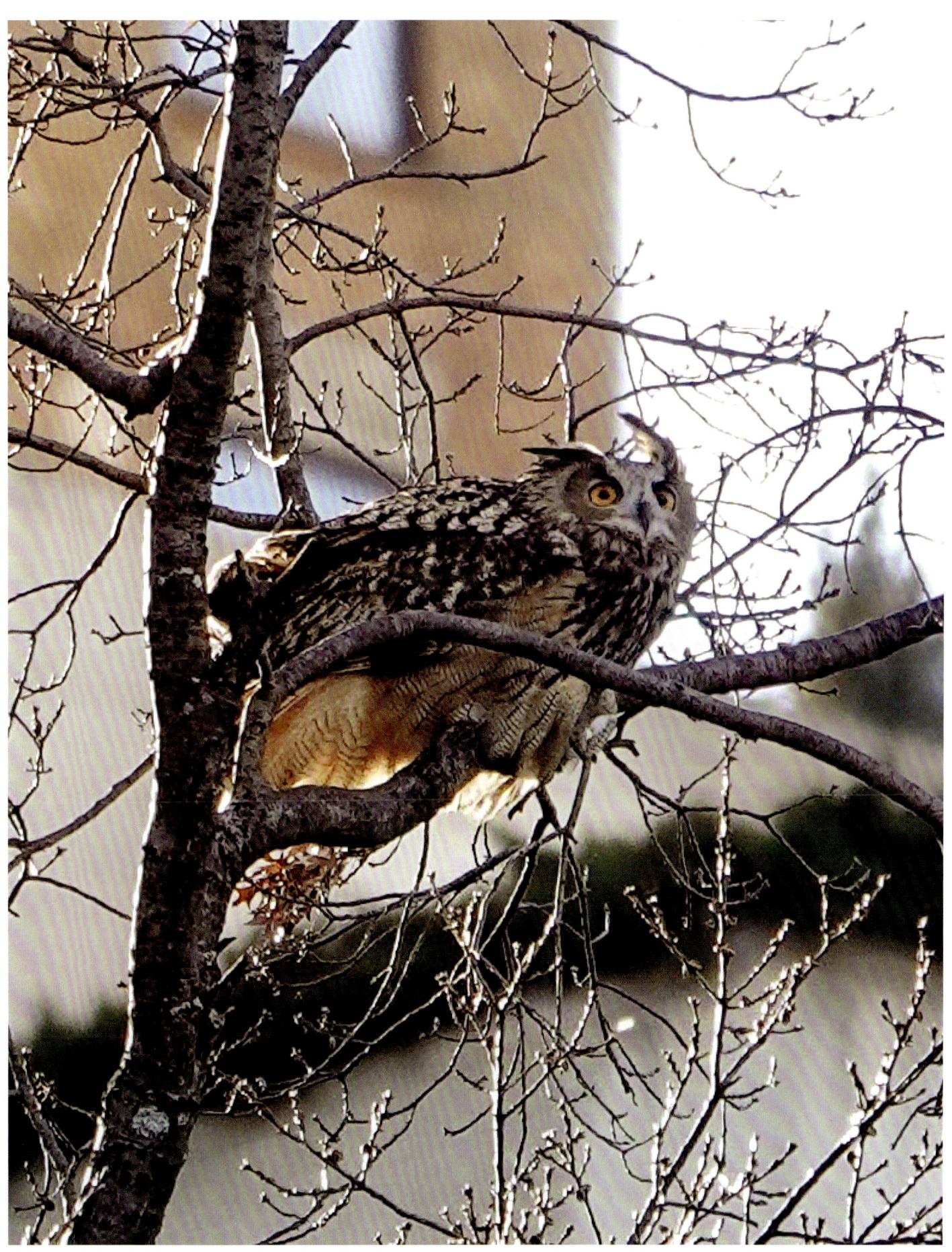

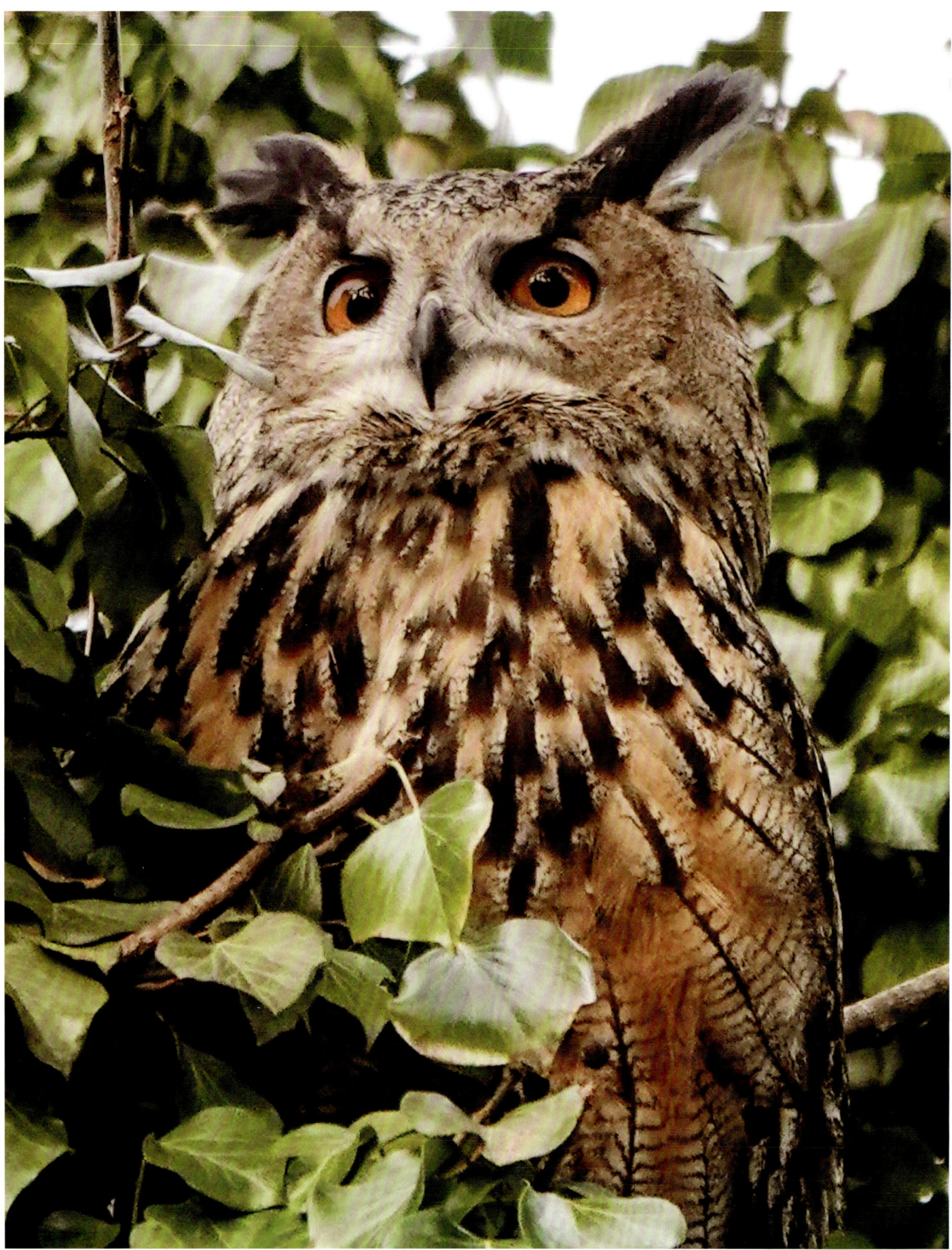

Molly Eustis, *Flaco in the Ivy,* East Drive Between 63rd–65th Street, Close to the Zoo, 2/7/23, 3:54 p.m.

There were many observers that afternoon on East Drive—birders and non-birders alike. We were more or less blocking an entire lane and would occasionally get yelled at by passing carriages, bikers, etc. Because this location is also a high foot-traffic area, there were a lot of passersby stopping to find out what all the hubbub was about, and many ended up staying for a while and watching with us.

This perch was particularly striking because of the abundant green ivy among otherwise mostly bare trees and the way the green of the ivy and orange of Flaco's irises complemented each other. I remember the sound of collective awe when he took flight from the ivy at sunset, though he did not go far, just to the next tree.

A small group of us stayed late that night, watching him make many short flights from tree to tree around that section of East Drive, even dipping down into the zoo at one point! He did not stay down there too long.

Zoo workers were around that night as well—some up on East Drive and some down on the zoo grounds. I was also keeping an eye out for our then-resident Great Horned Owl, Geraldine, who used to roost on Cedar Hill and in the Ramble but would cover large swaths of the park at night after flyout. I wondered and worried (for both of them) what would happen if they met.

Following spread (left and right) @chrisangphoto, *Flaco in a Favorite Tree,* Near the Tennis Courts and Gothic Bridge, 3/10/23, 10:50 a.m.

Double page spread @chrisangphoto, *Flaco Pre-Flight,* The Loch, 3/2/23, 3:30 p.m.

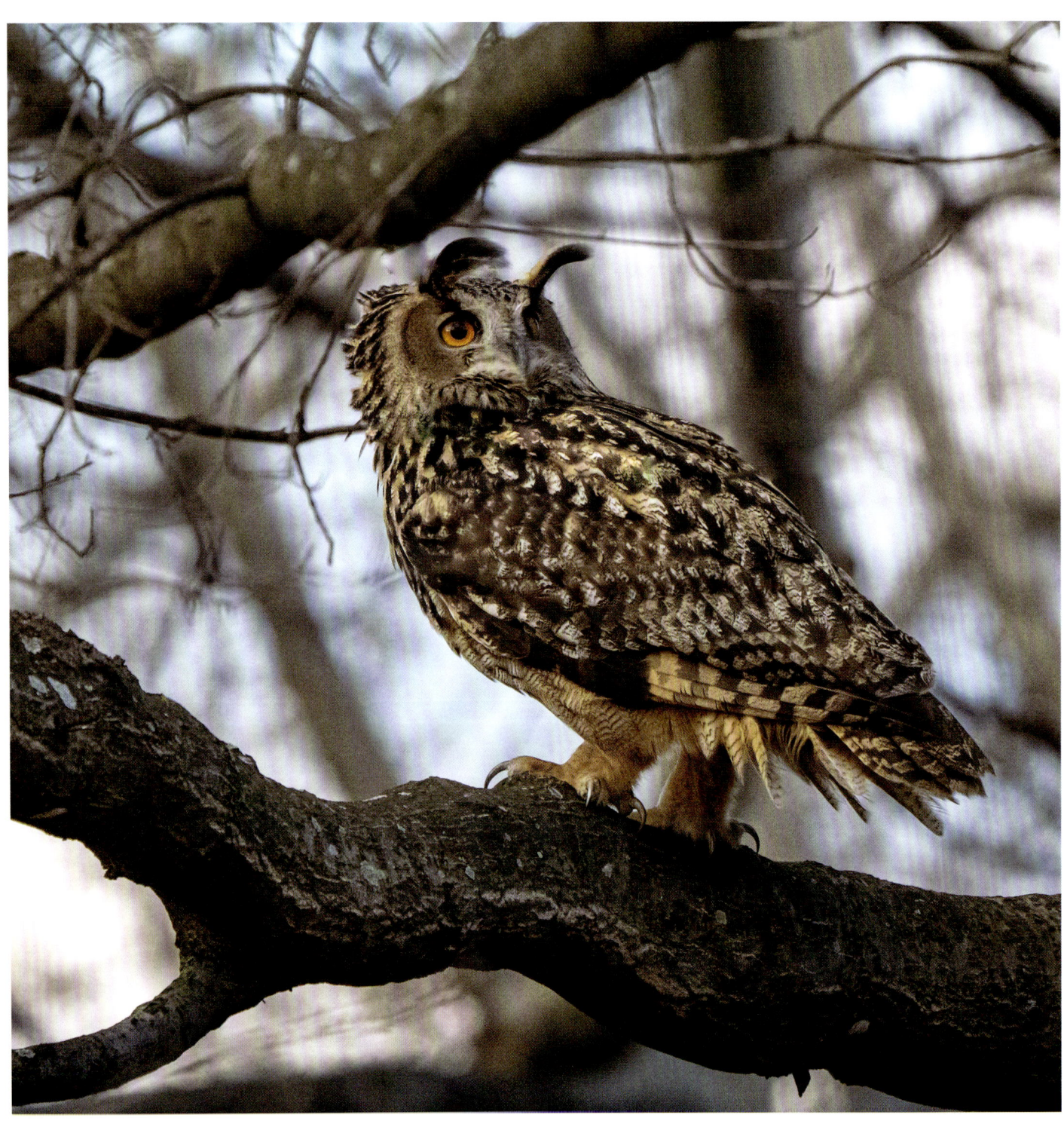

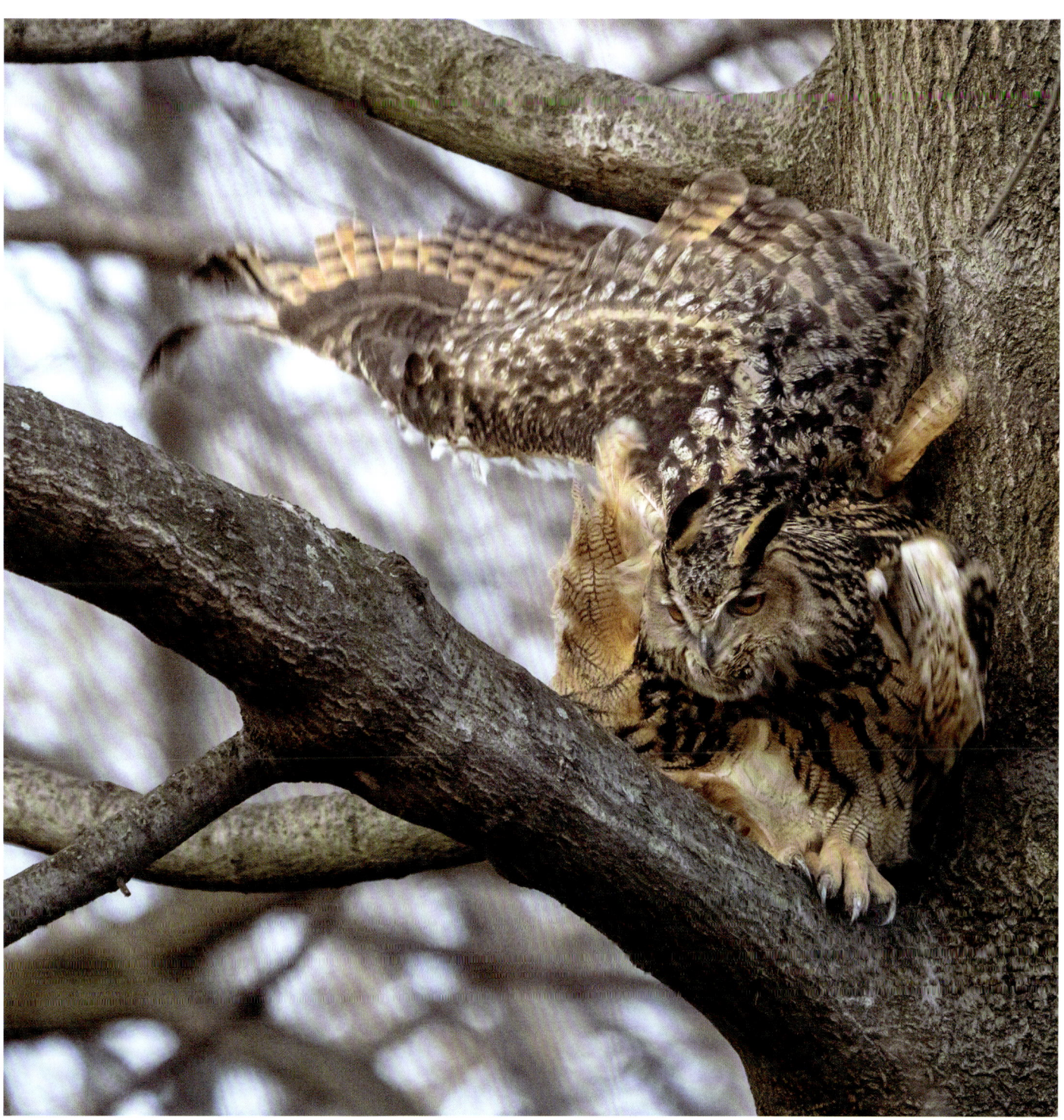

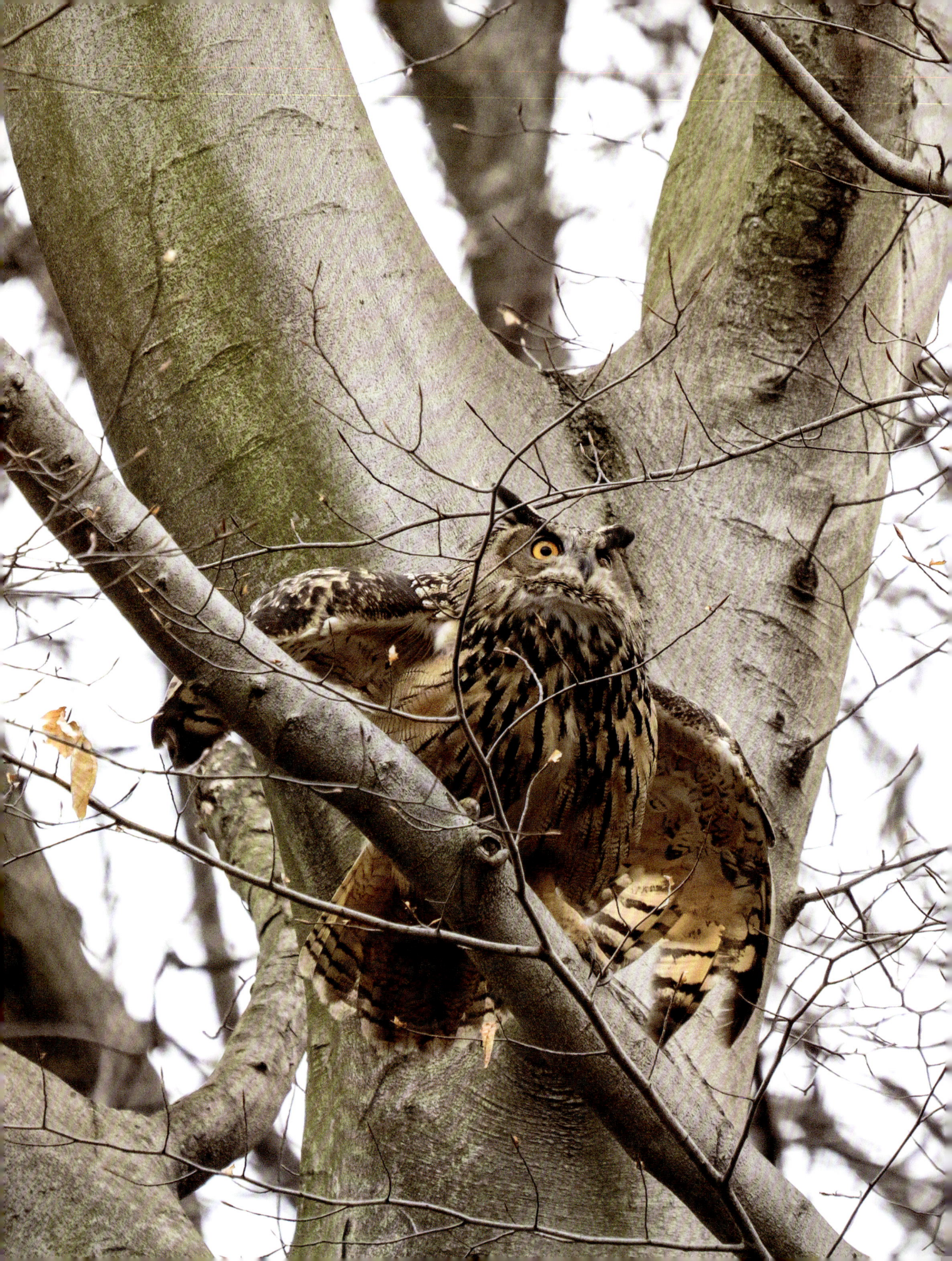

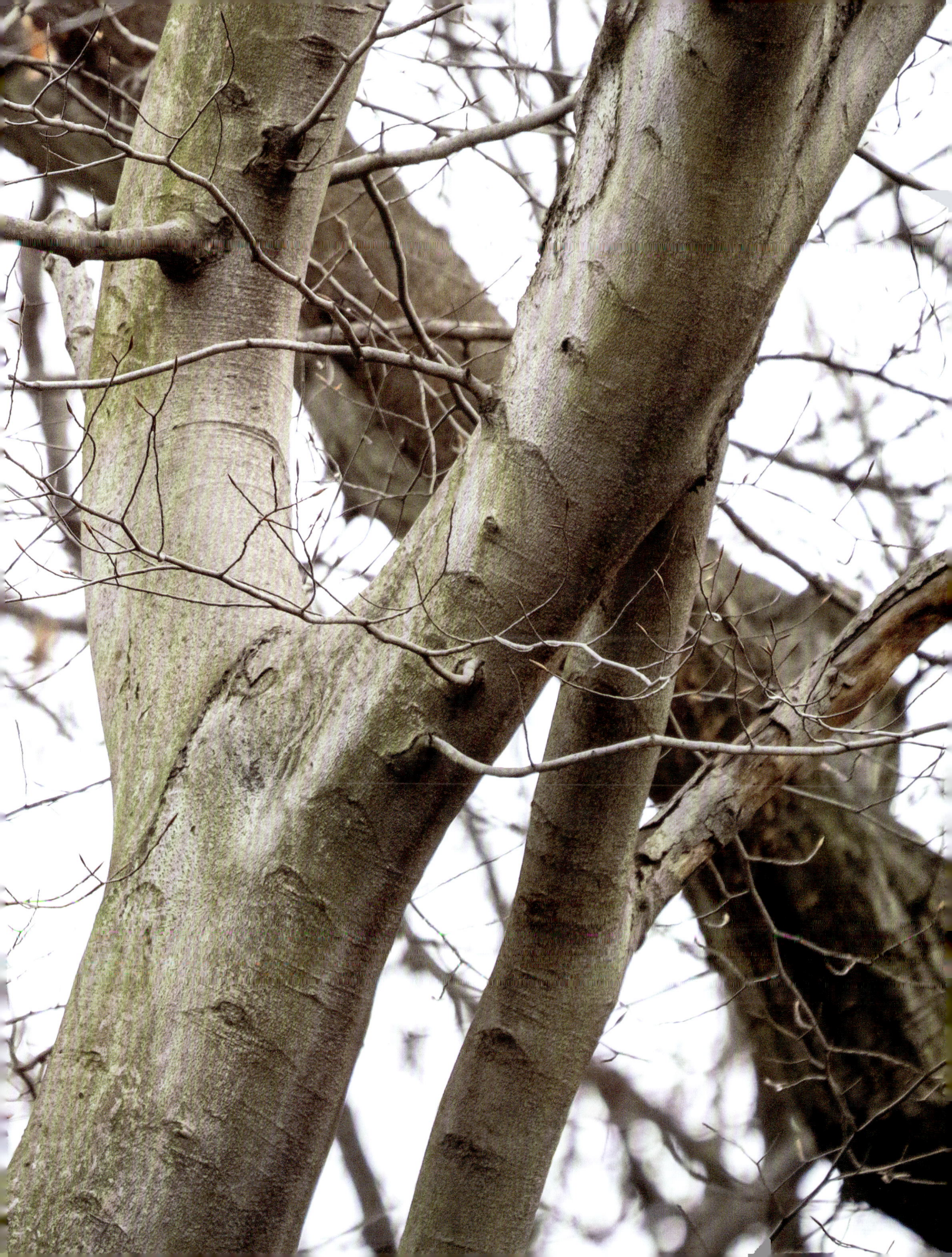

Venus N. Sallay, *Flaco with a Rat,* Heckscher Ballfields, 2/11/23, 8:45 p.m.

On this evening, I witnessed that Flaco was able to hunt on his own, as evidenced by the prey in his talons. Flaco stayed very high up in this tree, clutching his prized catch. From then on, I felt a sense of relief that there's no need to worry that Flaco would starve or not survive outside the Central Park Zoo after being captive for nearly 13 years. This night, Flaco hooted almost nonstop from the same tree.

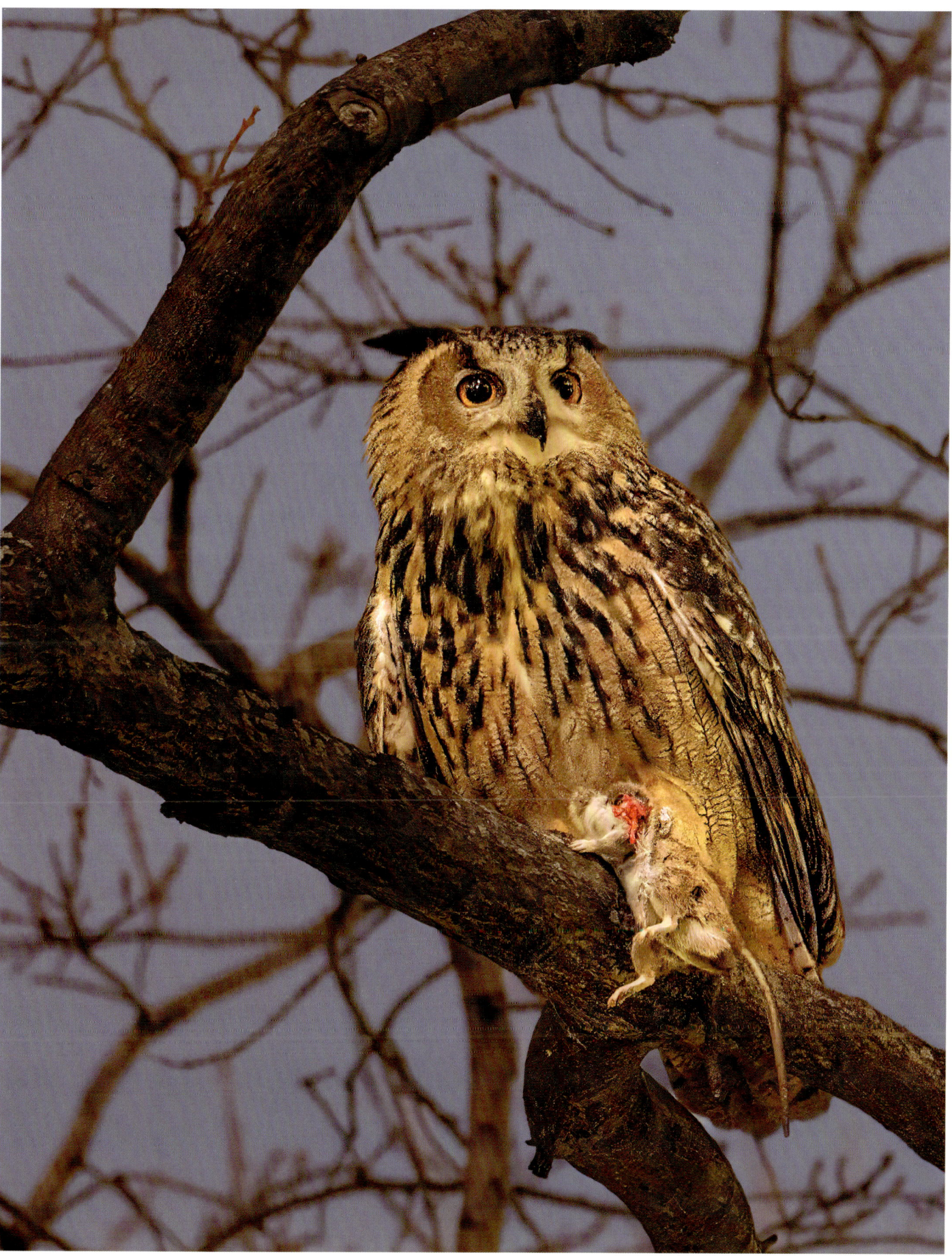

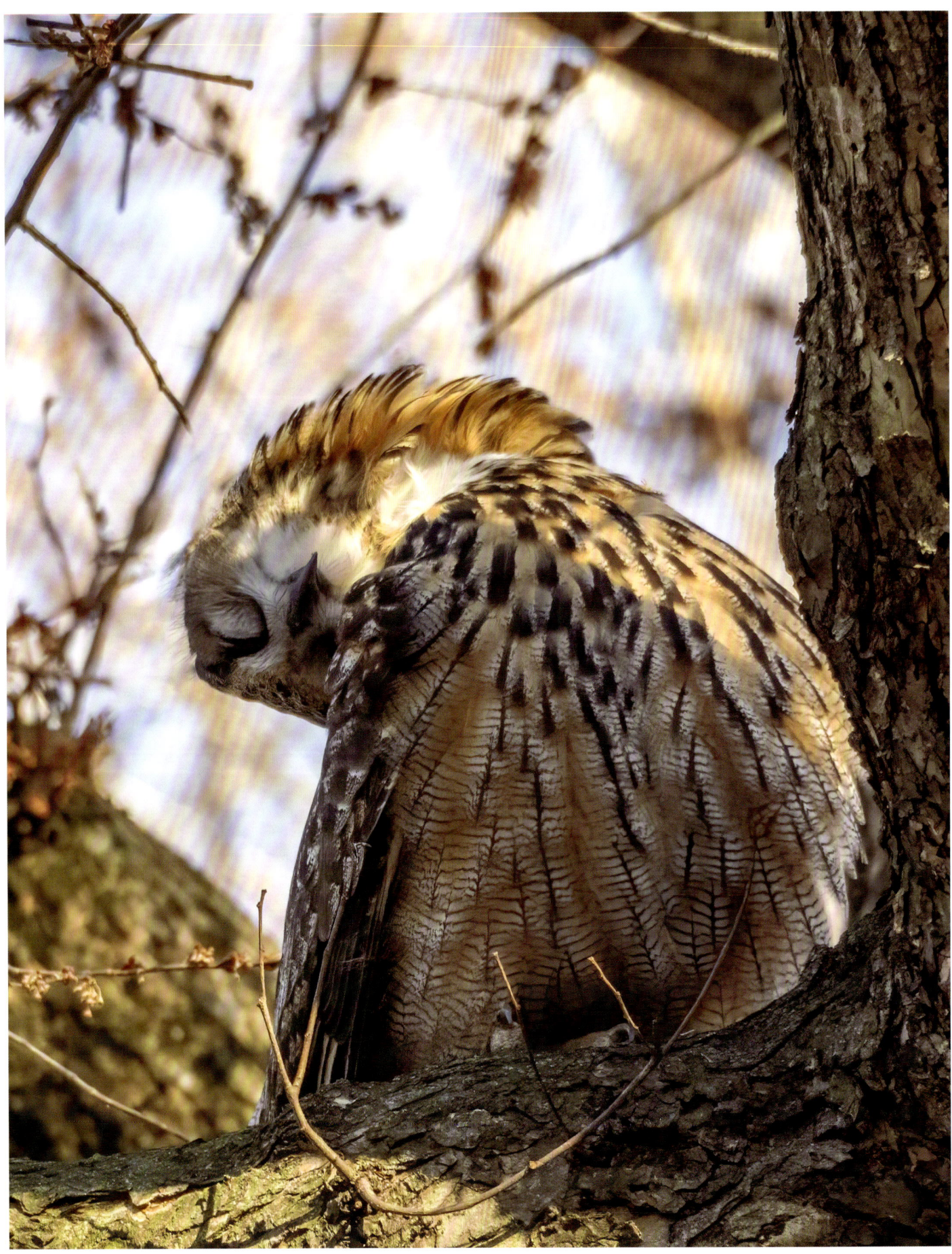

Sheryl Checkman, *Sweet Dreams Are Made of You,* The Mall, 2/18/23, 4:08 p.m.

On February 18, 2023, Flaco was holding court on the Mall. It was easy to find him that day since there was a large group of photographers standing about with tripods all pointed in his direction.

It was late afternoon when Flaco started to wake up. He stretched his neck sideways, eyes still closed as if to say, "I'm not quite ready to wake yet," and I was able to capture this image of him—perhaps holding on to that juicy rat in his dreams.

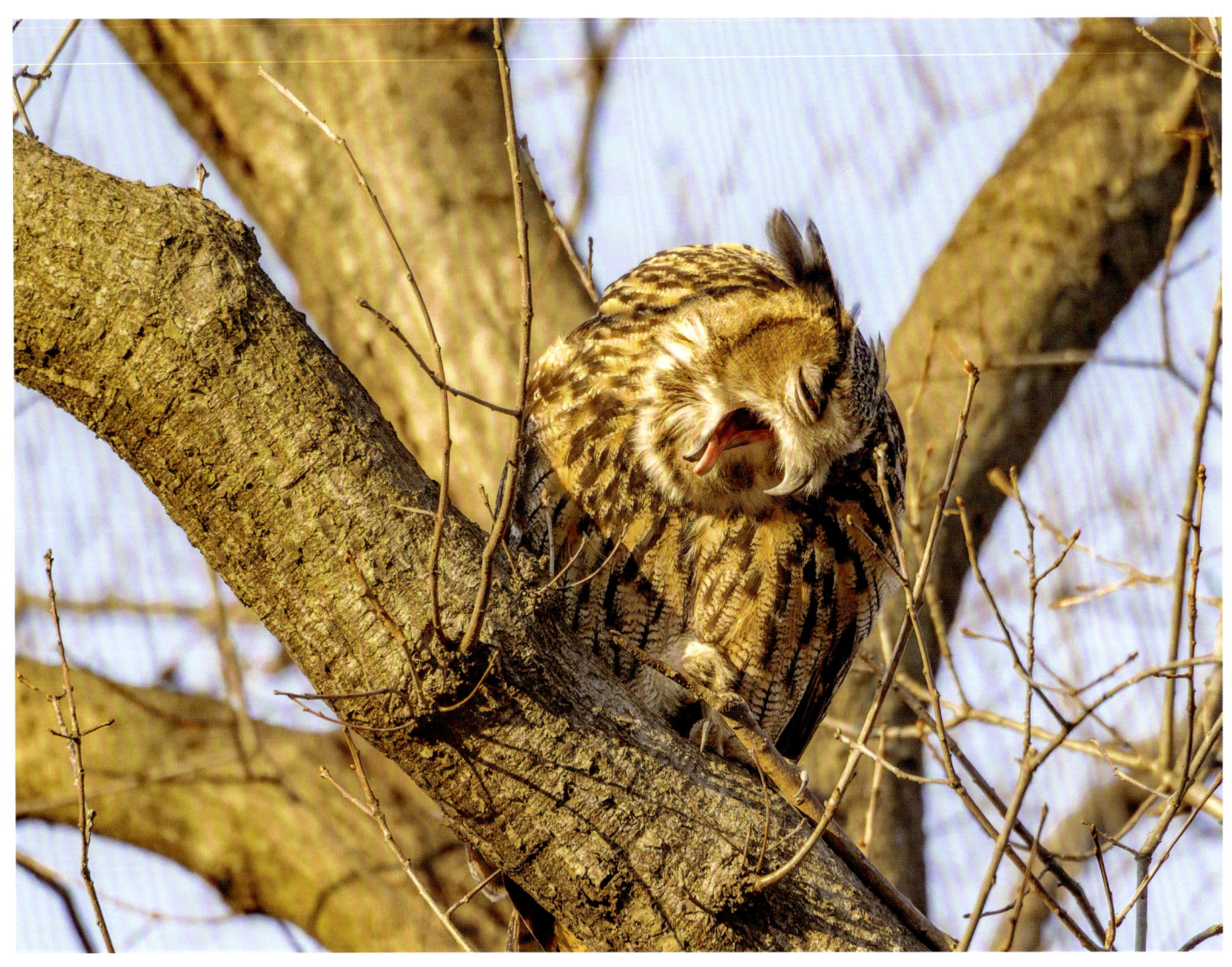

Sheryl Checkman, *Coughing up a Pellet,* North Woods, 2/20/23, 4:16 p.m.

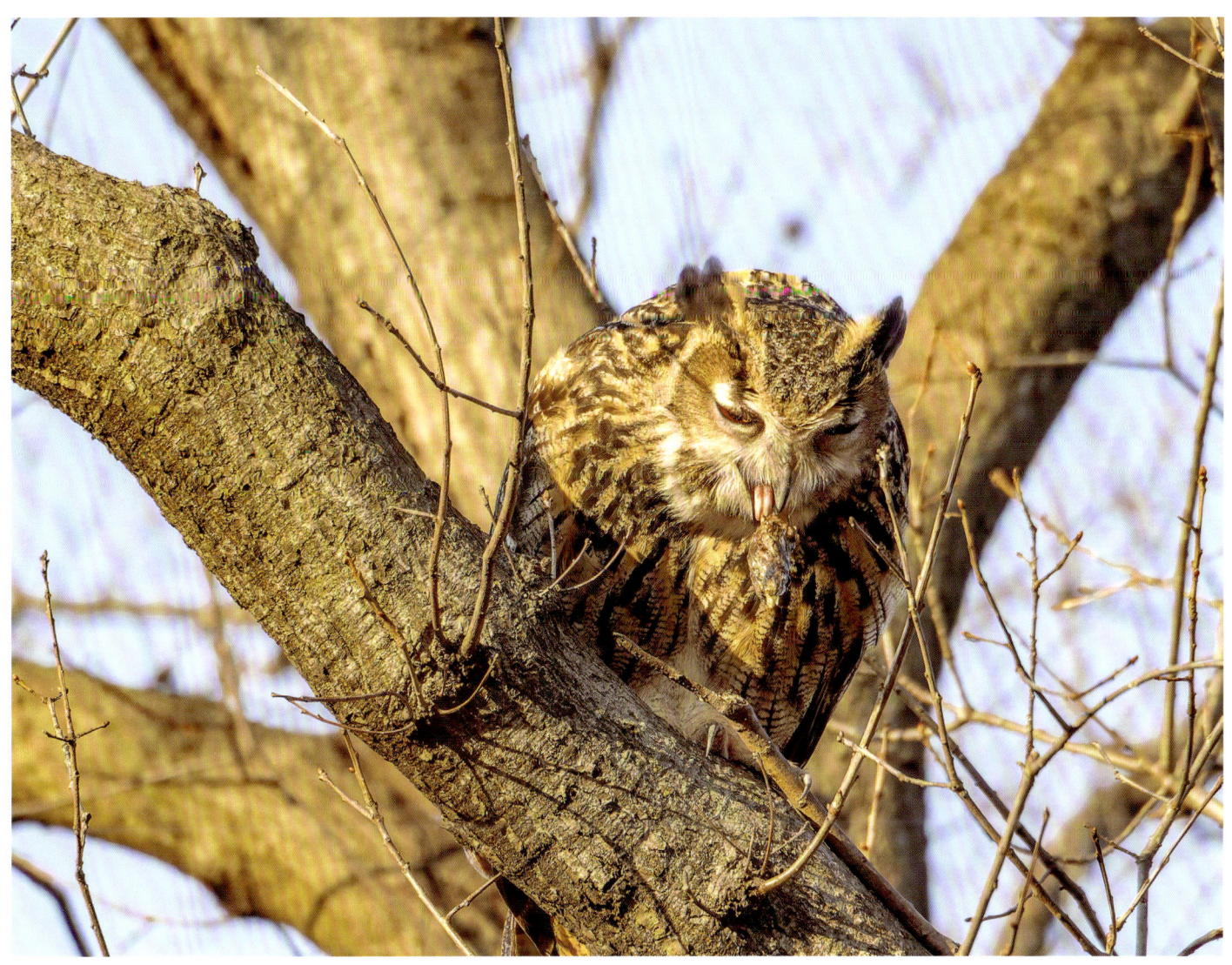

This photo was taken when Flaco first flew up to the North Woods and settled in a tree by West Drive at 107th Street. I remember joining a group of other photographers waiting at a respectful distance from the tree and setting my tripod up in a spot where I had a good, unobstructed view of Flaco.

It was late afternoon, the time when Flaco started to wake up, stretch, preen, and, in this shot, he was attempting to cough up a pellet—the undigestible bits from his last meal—in preparation for flyout. I took a few videos that day as well, and when I listen back to the audio, all that can be heard is the clicking of many camera shutters and the awed whispers of my fellow photographers.

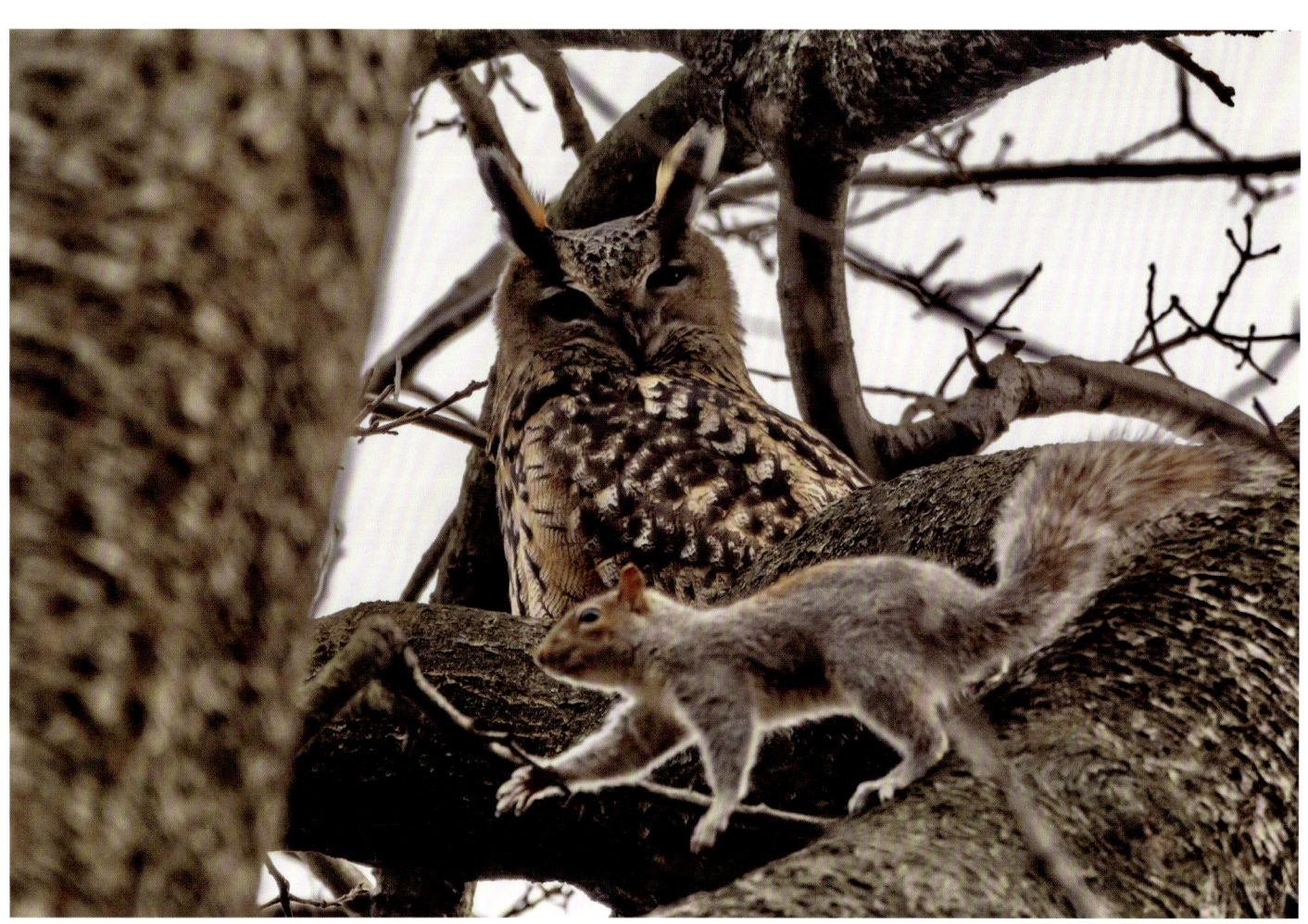

Paul Beiboer, *Flaco and the Squirrel,* Heckscher Playground, 2/23/23, 4:15 p.m.

In the first few weeks of Flaco's freedom, he was still very curious to check out all the animals that came to look him up, like this squirrel near the Heckscher Playground in the late afternoon before flyout. They got up really close and didn't seem to worry about getting eaten up!

Flaco was pretty magnetic to me: his presence, alone . . . he was a really large bird and when he hooted, it sounded to me like he was gathering everybody around him. . . . I know owls do hoot for some reason, whether it's because of some other predatory birds who are present, maybe it's a warning to other birds . . . but to me, it was a calling. *Come over here, listen to what I have to say.* That's what he was telling me, so it always drew me to him. He was saying something more than just a hoot. It wasn't just his natural self, being an owl, it was a message to me. *I'm right here with this microphone. Come hither, I have something to tell you.* It's his way of calling me. This is why I'm so addicted to his messages. I love hearing him. I love hearing his voice. He was an ever-present big huge bird. He had things to say to me, that's how I saw him. It was a message, you know?

STELLA HAMILTON

Venus N. Sallay, *Flaco Hooting,* The Loch, 2/23/23, 4:25 p.m.

This was Flaco's third week of freedom where he spent his days in his favorite tree. I always believed that Flaco chose to roost at this location for many weeks because of the soothing sound of the waterfall just below it. This tree gave Flaco the best view of the people passing through. Many Flaco admirers and curious park-goers enjoyed just watching him up in that tree, remarking how resilient he was and expressing their hopes that he would continue to thrive in the park.

As a photographer, it gave me a great vantage point to observe and take images of him. Here, Flaco shows off his hooting posture . . . calling for a mate he does not know will never come.

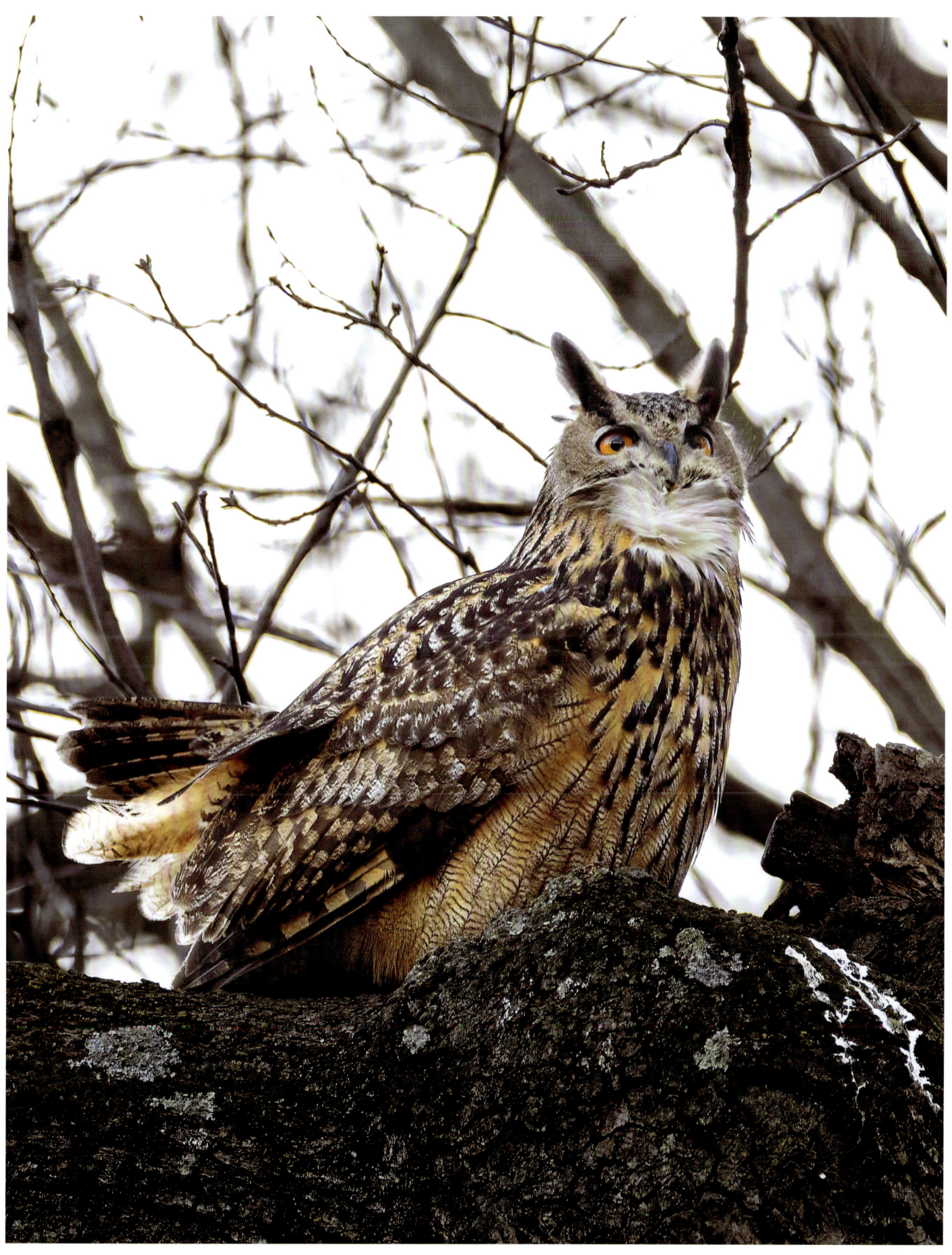

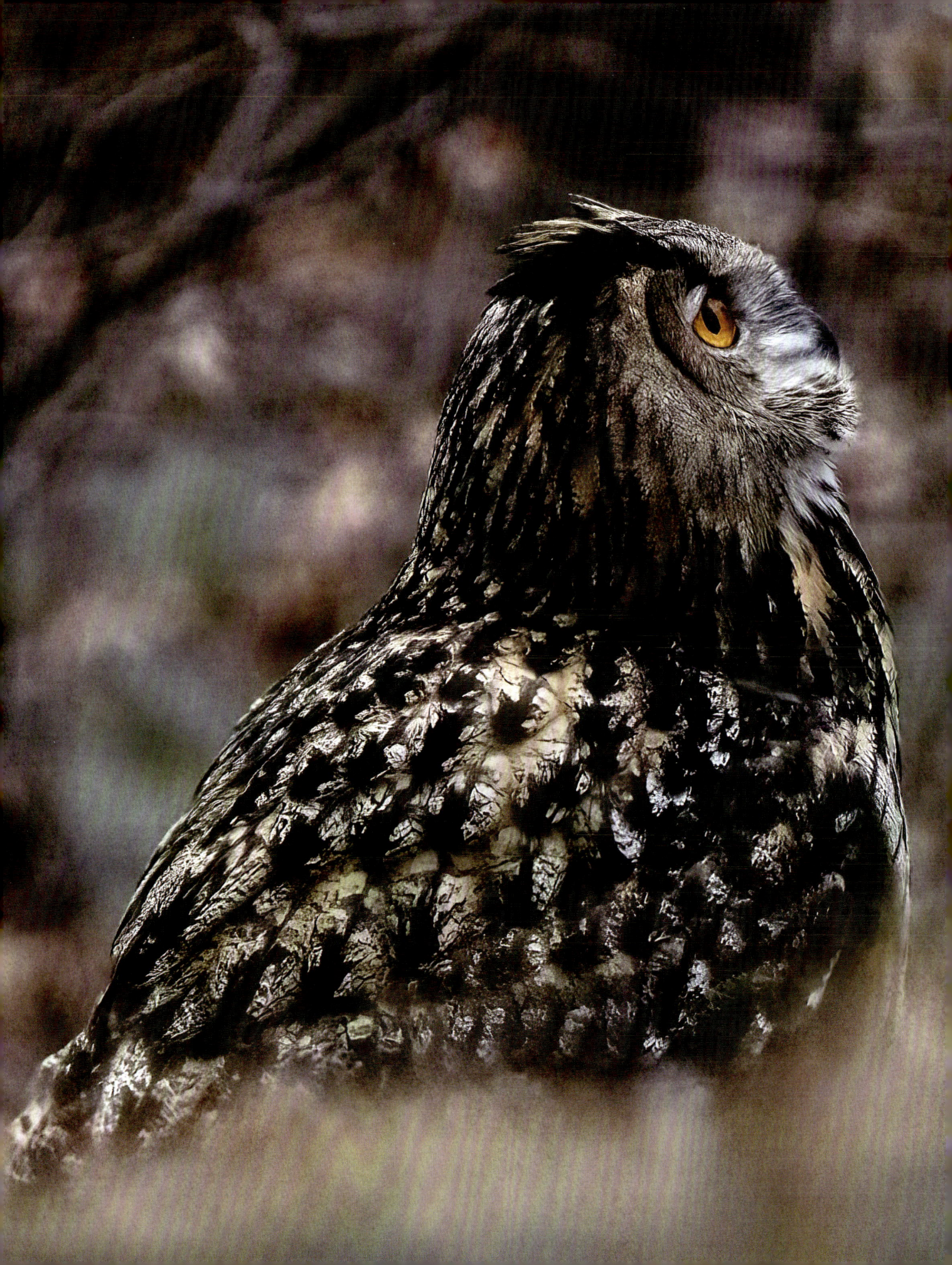

Flaco is free, like all birds should be.

— Philippe Petit, high-wire artist, told *The New York Times*

Paul Beiboer, *Flaco in Profile,* The North Woods, East of West Drive, 2/25/23, 5:40 p.m.

Flaco had been resting in a tree just east of the West Drive in the North Woods all day and flew out around 5:20 p.m. and landed on the ground about 100 yards or so from his rosting spot for the day. He walked around on the ground for about 15 minutes, clearly showing his curiosity to explore the park. Then suddenly, he hopped behind a tree and appeared with a rat shortly afterward, and then went on to eat it in a tree higher up nearby.

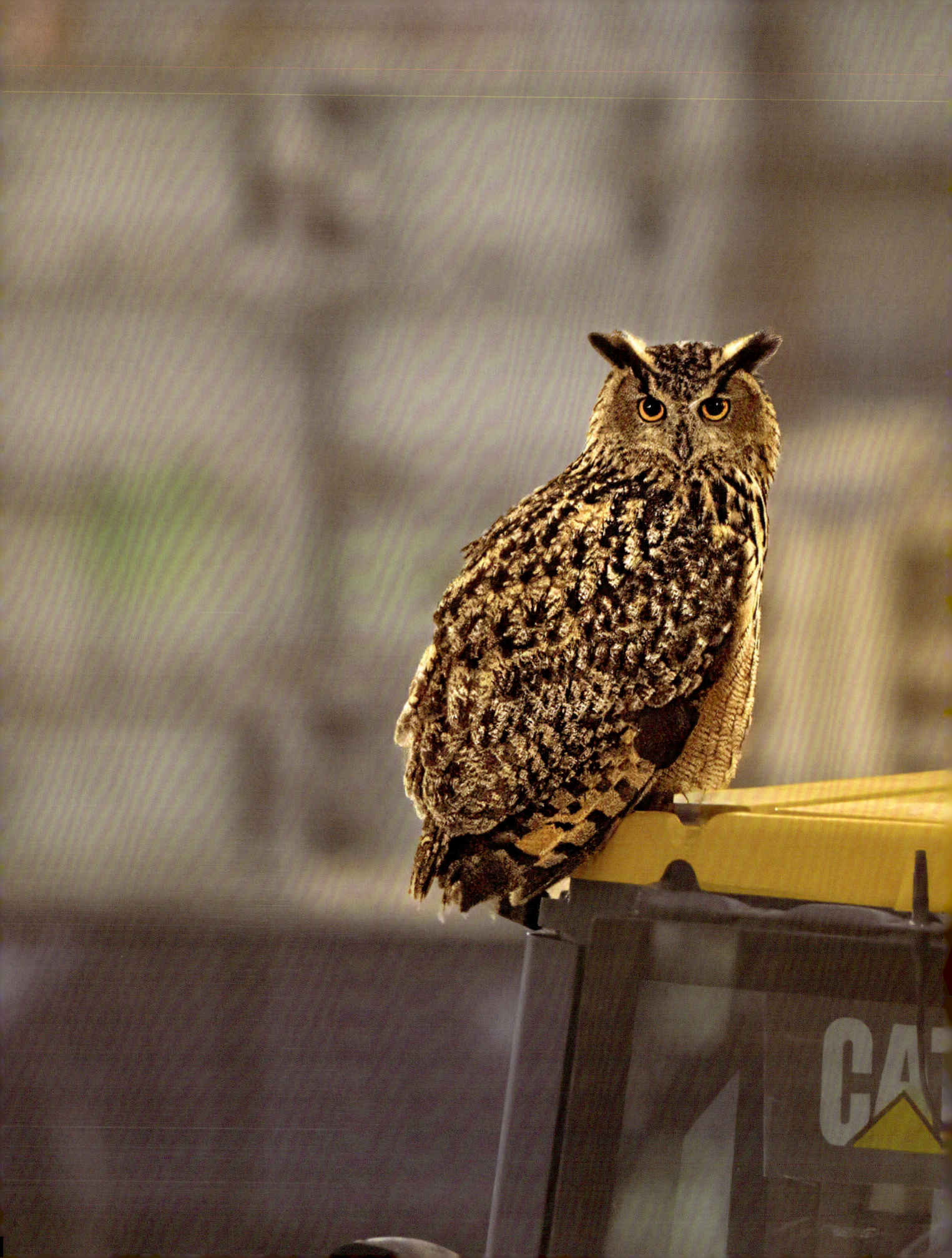

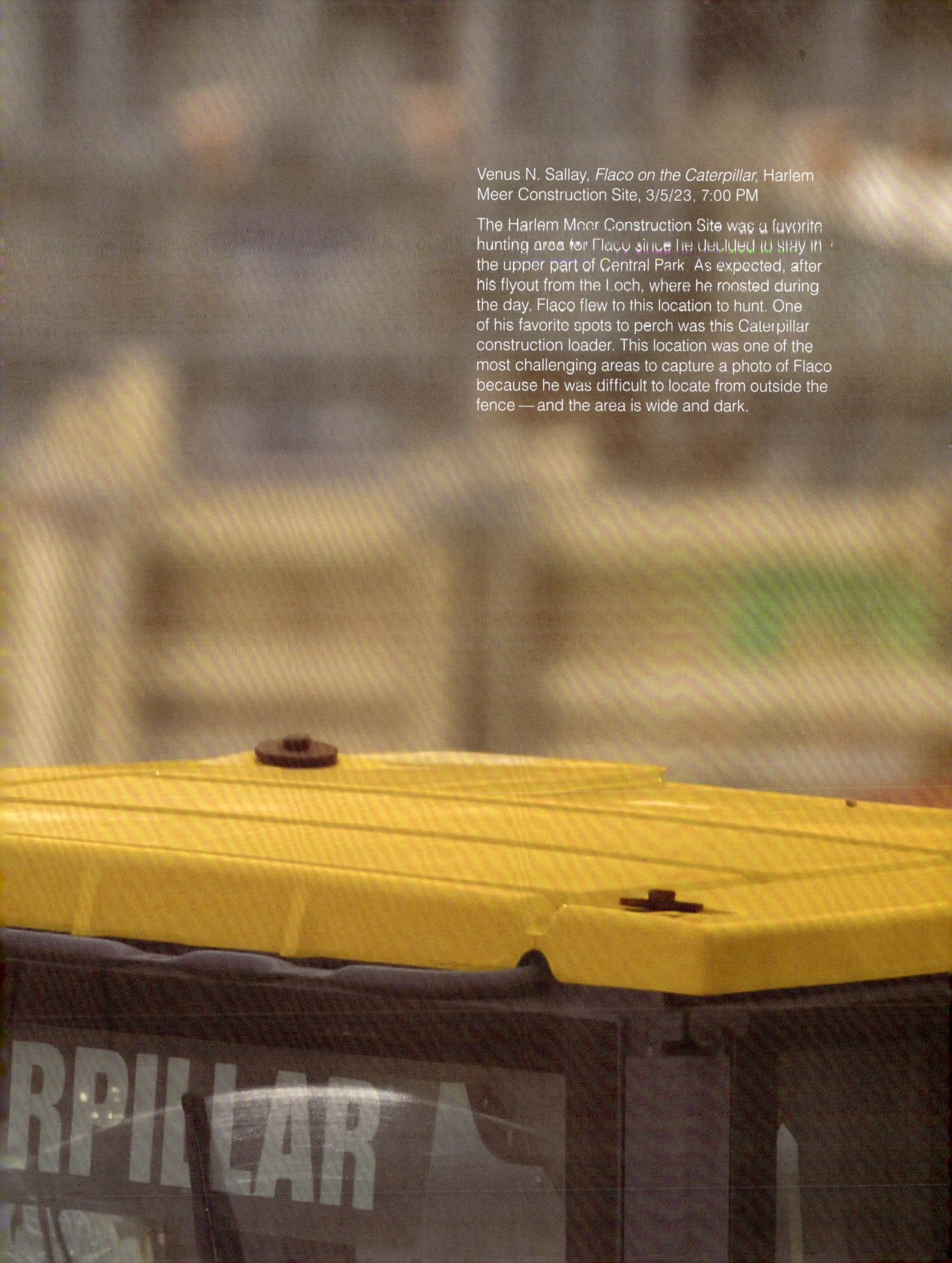

Venus N. Sallay, *Flaco on the Caterpillar*, Harlem Meer Construction Site, 3/5/23, 7:00 PM

The Harlem Meer Construction Site was a favorite hunting area for Flaco since he decided to stay in the upper part of Central Park. As expected, after his flyout from the Loch, where he roosted during the day, Flaco flew to this location to hunt. One of his favorite spots to perch was this Caterpillar construction loader. This location was one of the most challenging areas to capture a photo of Flaco because he was difficult to locate from outside the fence — and the area is wide and dark.

David Barrett, *Flaco Hunting from an Excavator,* Compost Heap, 5/21/23, 9:36 p.m.

We came to the Compost Heap well after sunset because Flaco liked to hunt there—where rats were abundant. Flaco perched in trees, watching and listening, against the relatively bright night sky, so photographing him was straightforward. After Flaco flew off, we rediscovered him with the help of night-vision monoculars—perched on one of his favorite things, a Komatsu excavator.

With Flaco low and in the dark, far away from the streetlamps, we couldn't see him with our eyes alone, but our cameras could, so after some quick trial-and-error, we got acceptable shots before Flaco flew off again.

Following spread Paul Beiboer, *Flaco on the Caterpillar,* Harlem Meer Construction Site, 3/24/23, 6:30 p.m.

This photo was taken shortly after flyout from one of Flaco's favorite trees in the Ramble. He frequently went to hunt in the Harlem Meer Construction Site and seemed to like checking out the various pieces of heavy equipment.

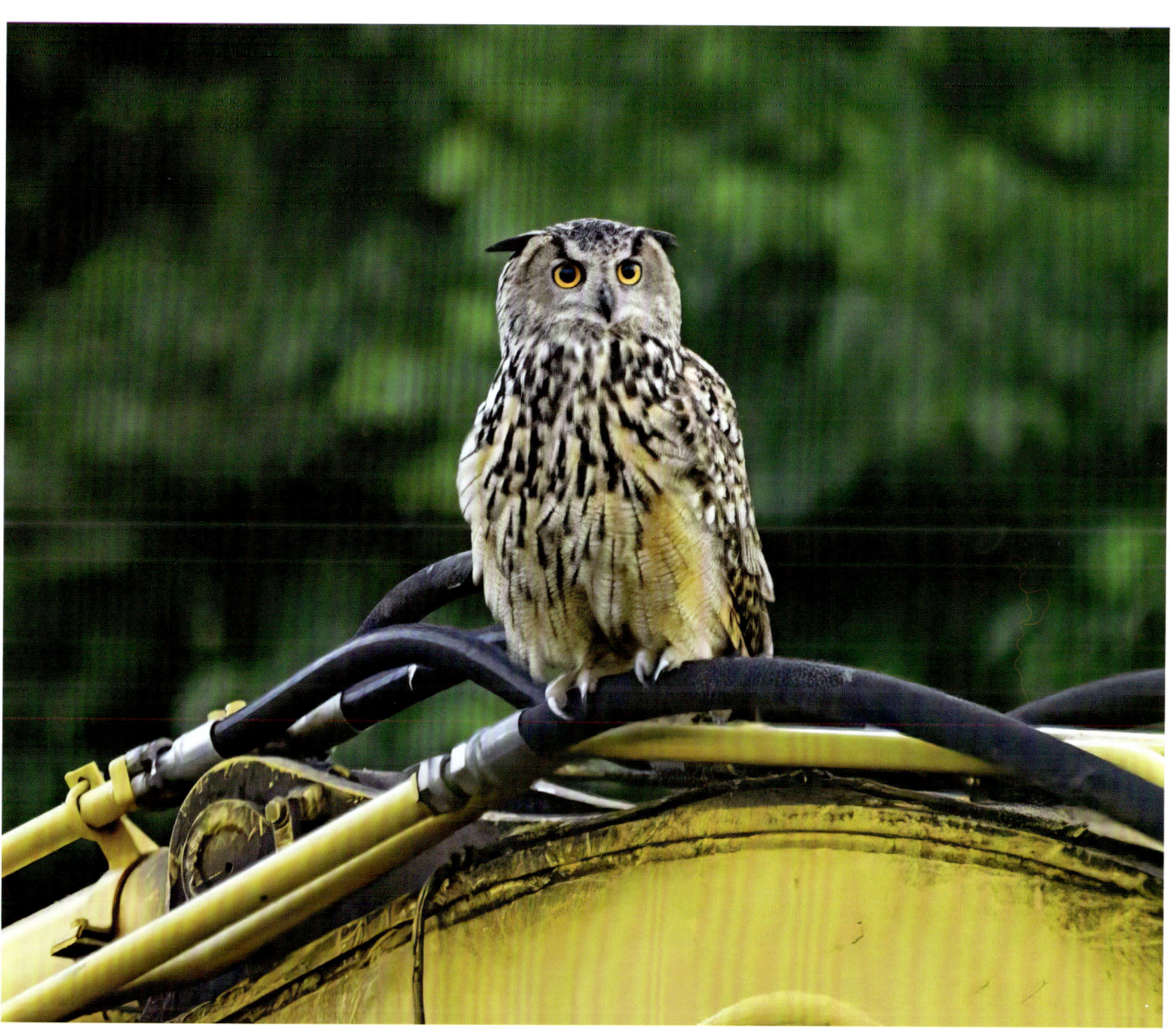

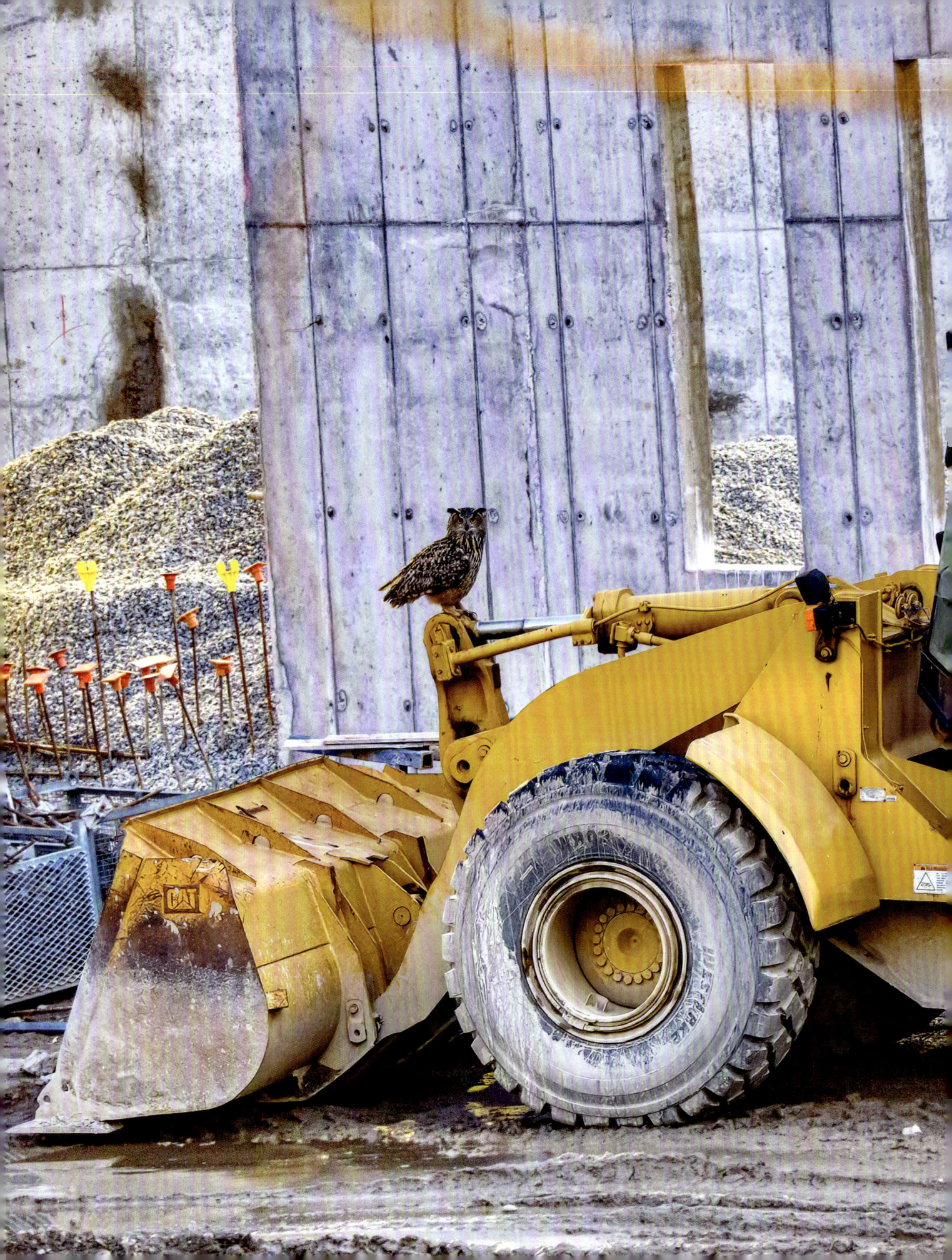

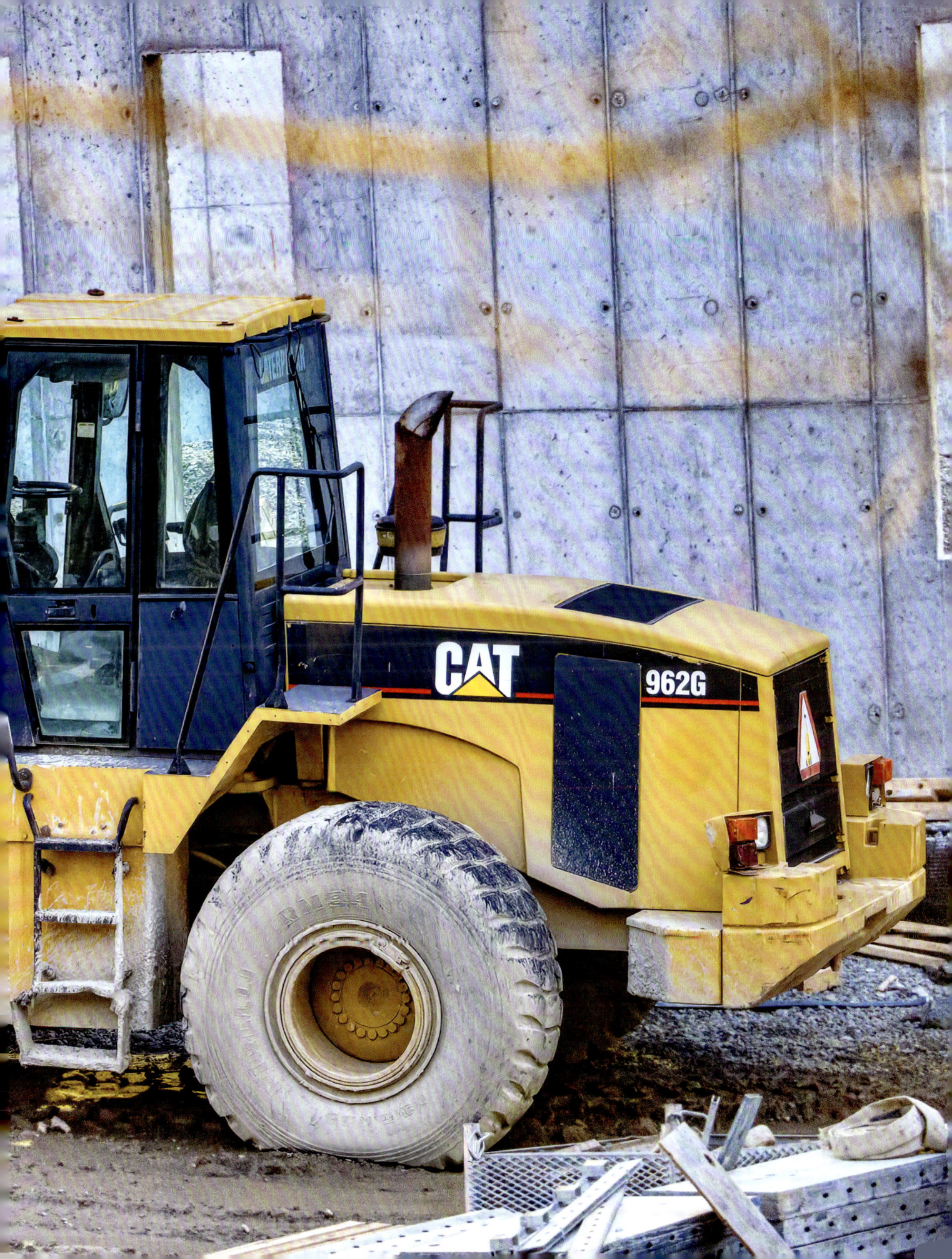

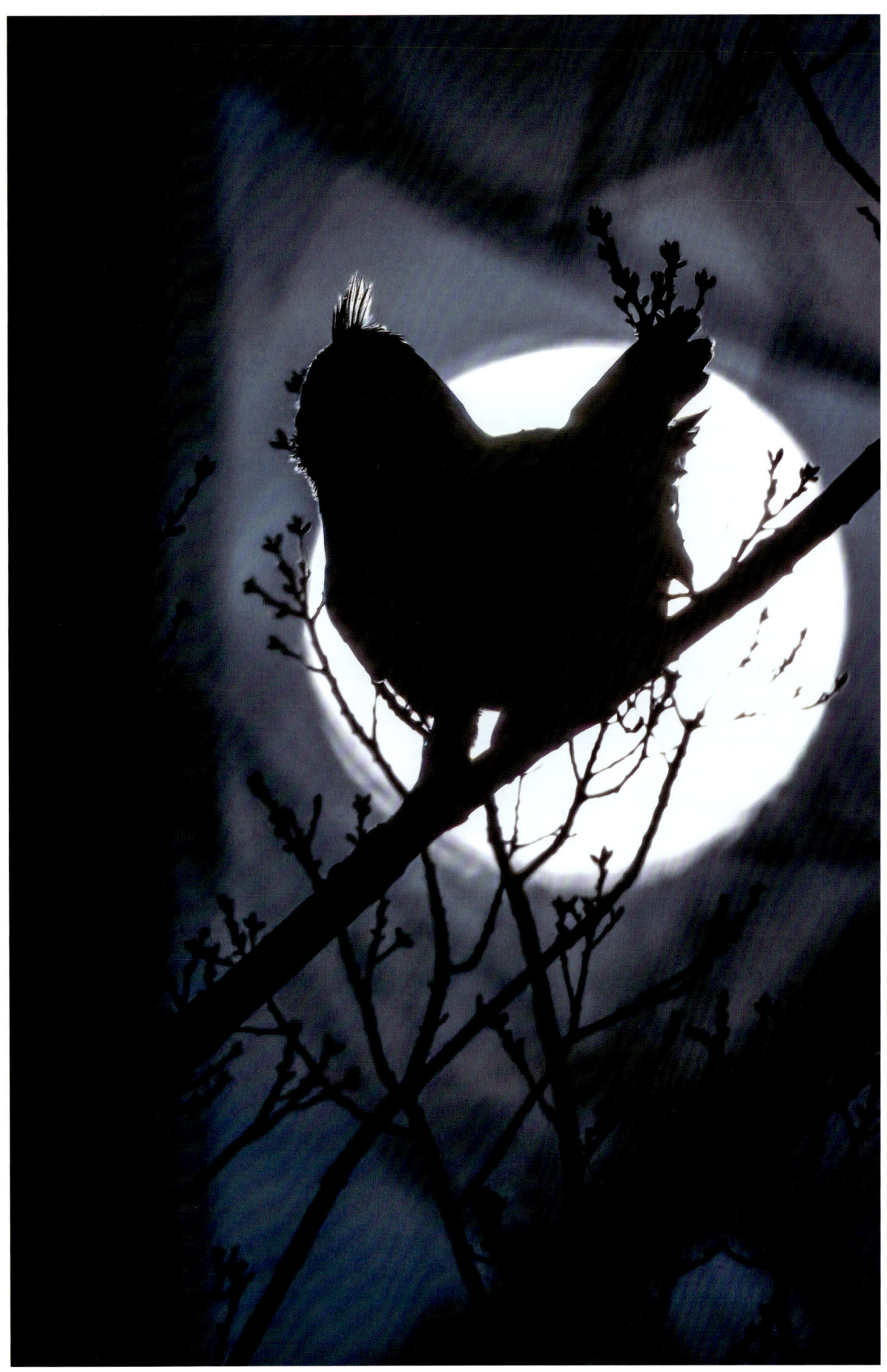

In the night, when the owl is less than exquisitely swift and perfect, the scream of the rabbit is terrible. But the scream of the owl, which is not of pain and hopelessness and the fear of being plucked out of the world, but of the sheer rollicking glory of the death-bringer, is more terrible still. When I hear it resounding through the woods, and then the five black pellets of its song dropping like stones into the air, I know I am standing at the edge of the mystery, in which terror is naturally and abundantly part of life, part of even the most becalmed, intelligent, sunny life as, for example, my own. The world where the owl is endlessly hungry and endlessly on the hunt is the world in which I live too. There is only one world.

MARY OLIVER, Excerpt from "Owls"

Paul Beiboer, *Flaco with Full Moon,* The Ramble, 4/4/23, 7:40 p.m.

I had been watching Flaco since around 7:00 p.m. as he was getting ready for flyout from one of his favorite trees in the Ramble. He flew higher up about half an hour later. I did not see him immediately but did hear his hooting and I started to imagine a picture of Flaco against a bright full moon. I decided to climb up a path on the side of Harlem Hill and was lucky enough to find him there. Flaco continued hooting for about 20 minutes before flying off to hunt.

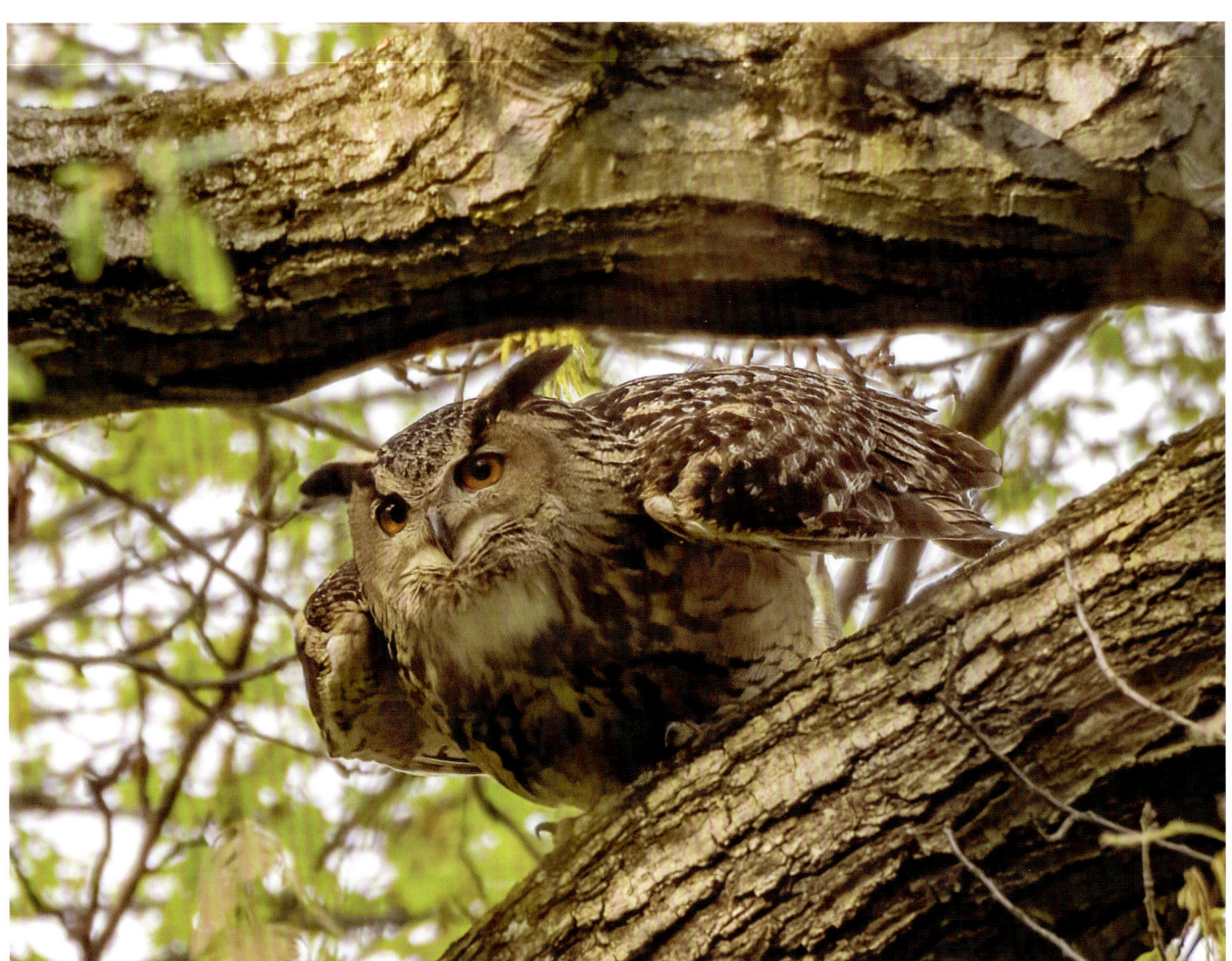

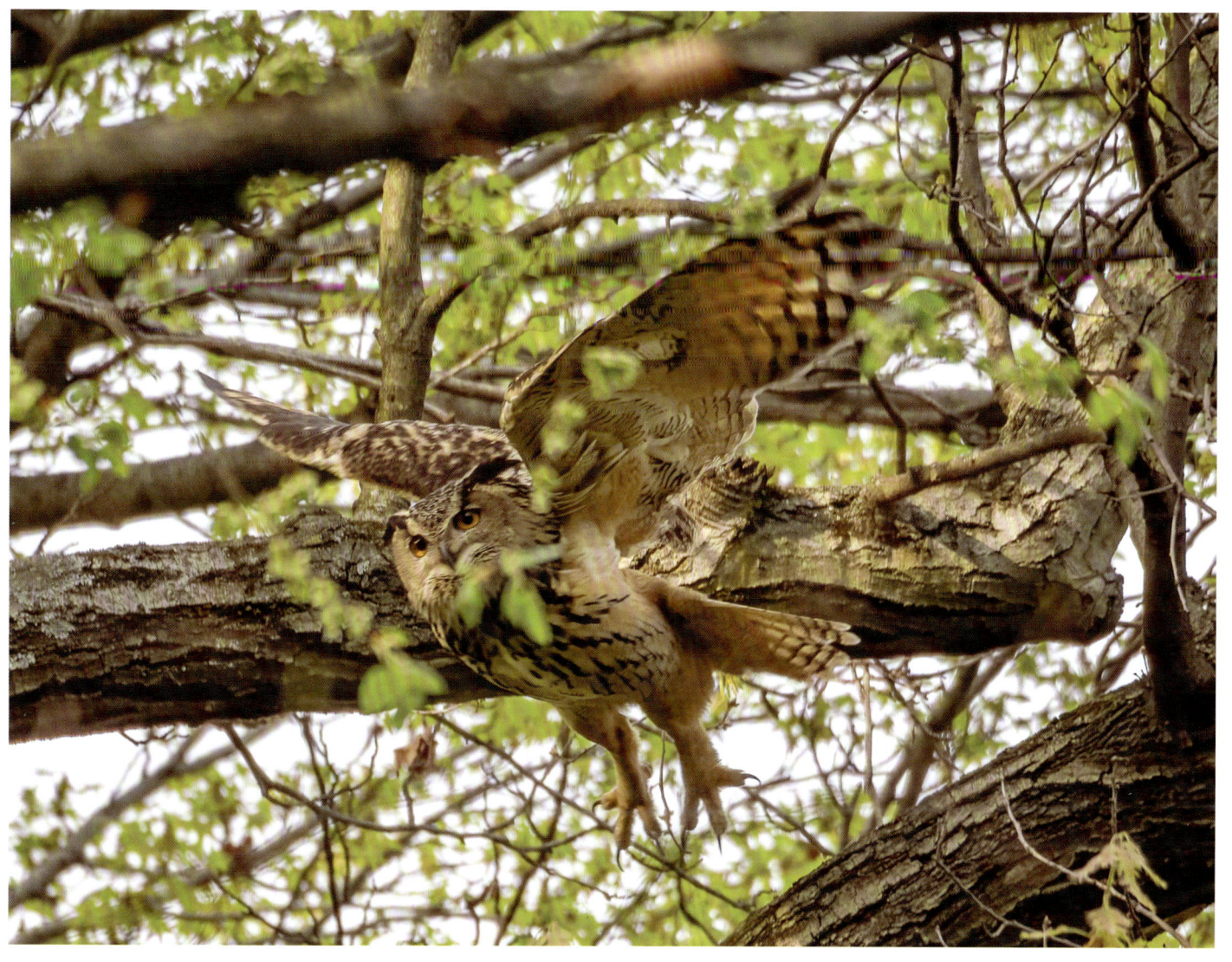

Sheryl Checkman, *Ready for Take-off,* The Loch, 4/16/23, 4:40 p.m.

This photo was taken during Flaco's time spent in the Loch. In this shot, Flaco, framed by two of the tree's branches, is getting ready to fly out for the evening. I remember many late afternoons and evenings spent in the Loch waiting for Flaco to wake up, stretch, and get ready for flyout.

Some days, I stood waiting for several hours. On this particular day, I had my camera set to a high sequential shutter so that once I pressed the shutter, it fired off about 20 frames per second. He had been moving around, and something told me to keep my hand-held camera focused on his eyes, just hoping he would fly. This enabled me to catch the action just as he leapt into the sky.

@chrisangphoto, *Flaco Harassed by a Blue Jay,* The Loch, 4/30/23, 4:30 p.m.

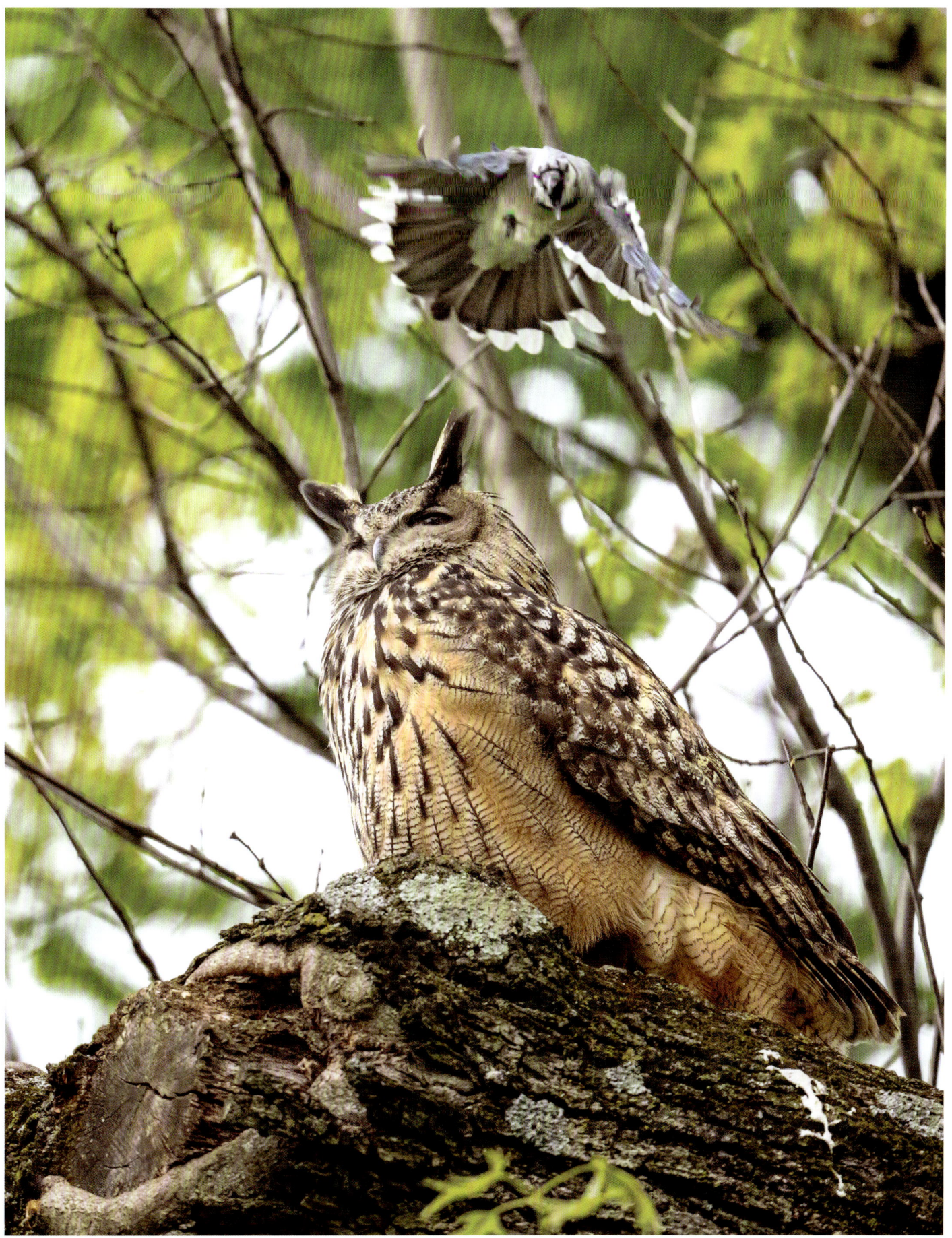

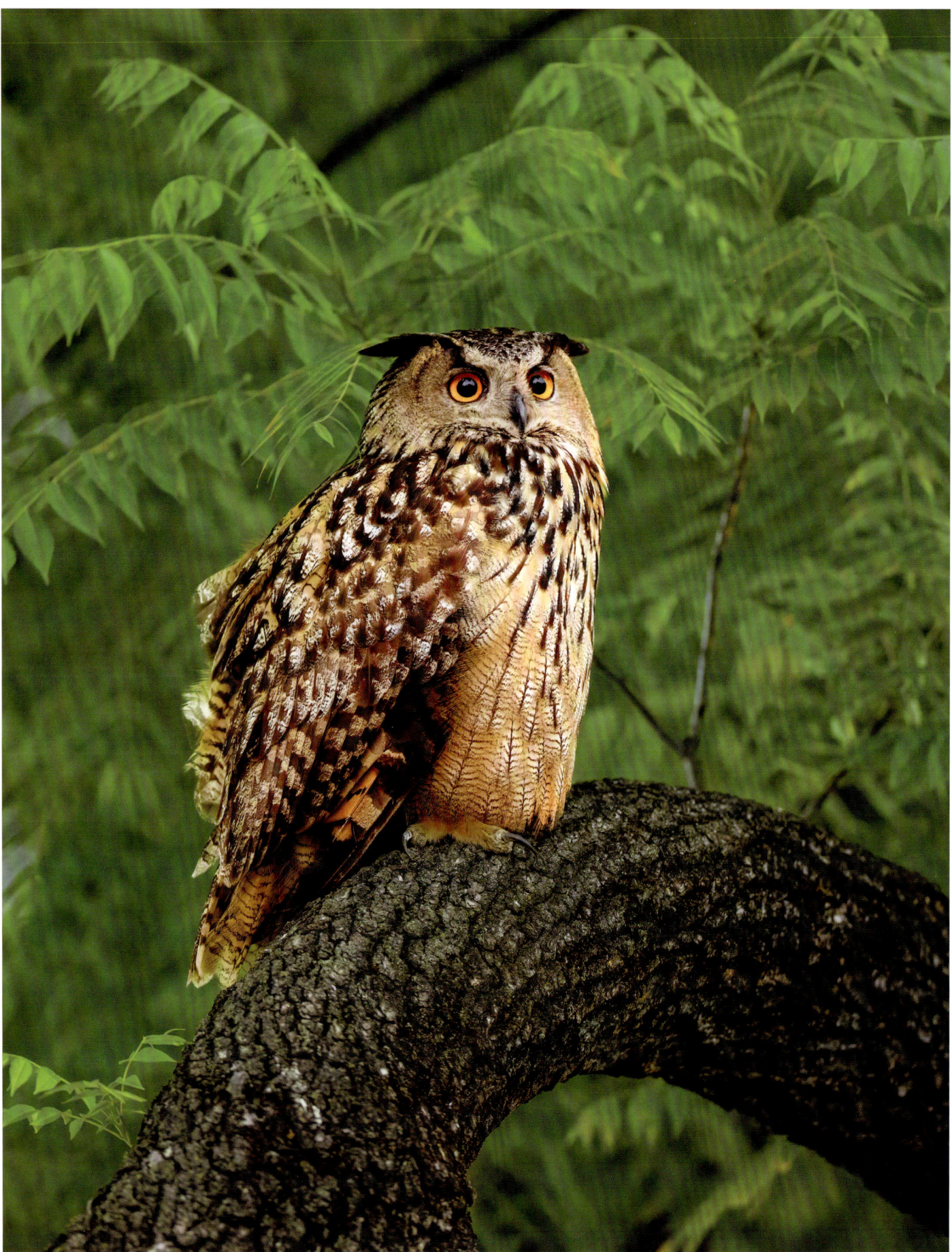

Venus N. Sallay, *Flaco in the Black Walnut Tree,* Compost Heap, 6/4/23, 8:32 p.m.

This image was captured one summer night at the Compost Heap in Central Park. Flaco spent many days now in the nearby black walnut tree by the East Drive, where he enjoyed just roosting and watching people running, walking, riding their bicycles, or pushing little kids in strollers.

This evening after flyout, Flaco stayed in the Compost Heap and on this tree, amazingly, with his attention so focused at a distance, not moving, not even a blink. I even asked myself what was Flaco thinking that night? In this photo, if zoomed close on his eyes, you will see the reflection of what appears to be a nearby building. Image captured using a long exposure in ambient light.

Following spread Anke Frohlich, *A Close Encounter with Flaco at Night,* Compost Heap, 6/5/23

The Compost Heap attracts lots of rats, so Flaco hunted there often. That night, a handful of photographers observed him there in one of his favorite trees. Suddenly, as had happened many times before, he flew off, and we thought we'd lost him.

I turned around and, to my surprise, there he was, perched on a rock, a mere 15 feet away from me! We backed up slowly so as not to spook him. He was relaxed and gave us just enough time to create photos before the headlights of an approaching car scared him off.

The image is illuminated only by a nearby street light and by the city lights reflecting off the cloudy night sky. The photo was brightened in post-production.

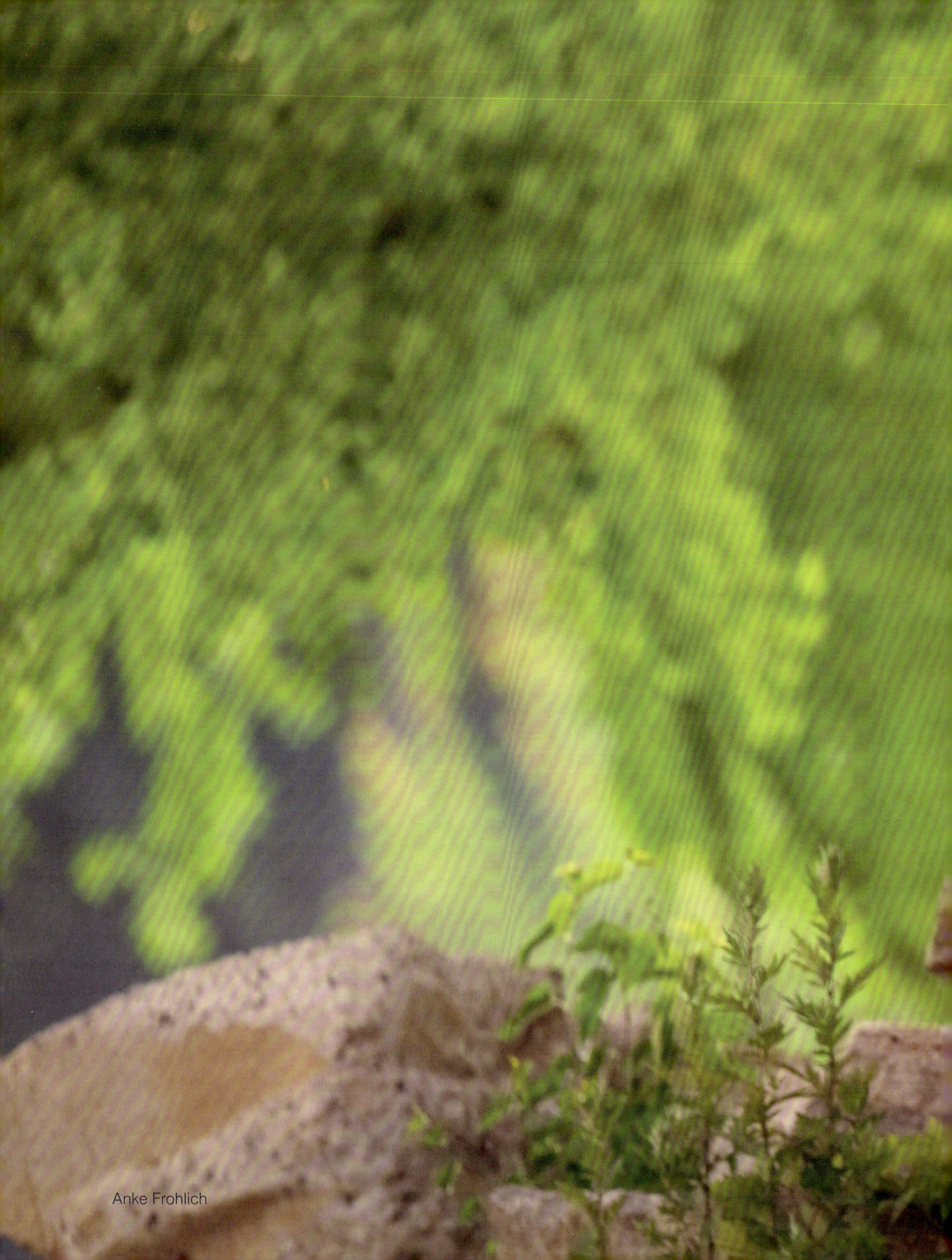

Anke Frohlich

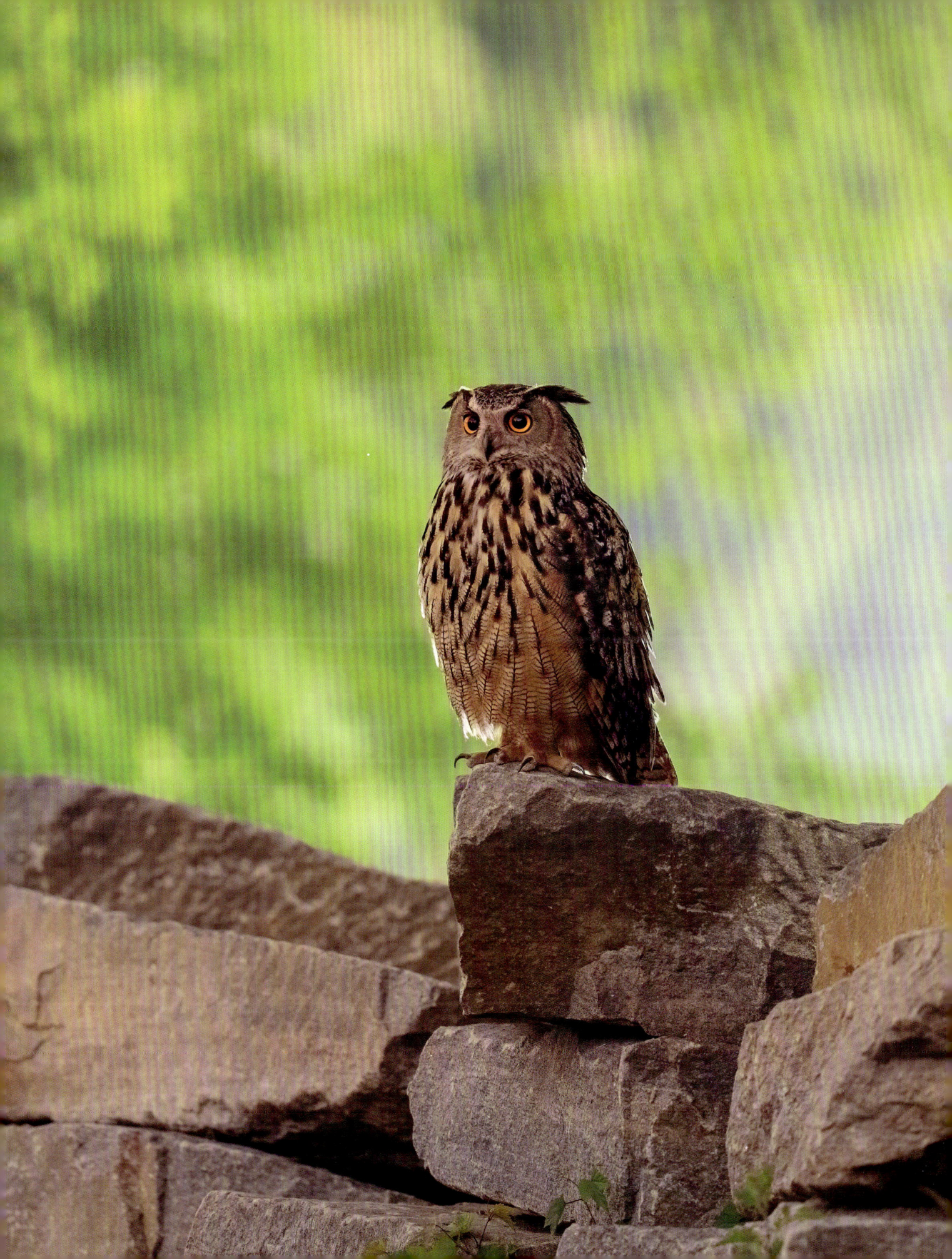

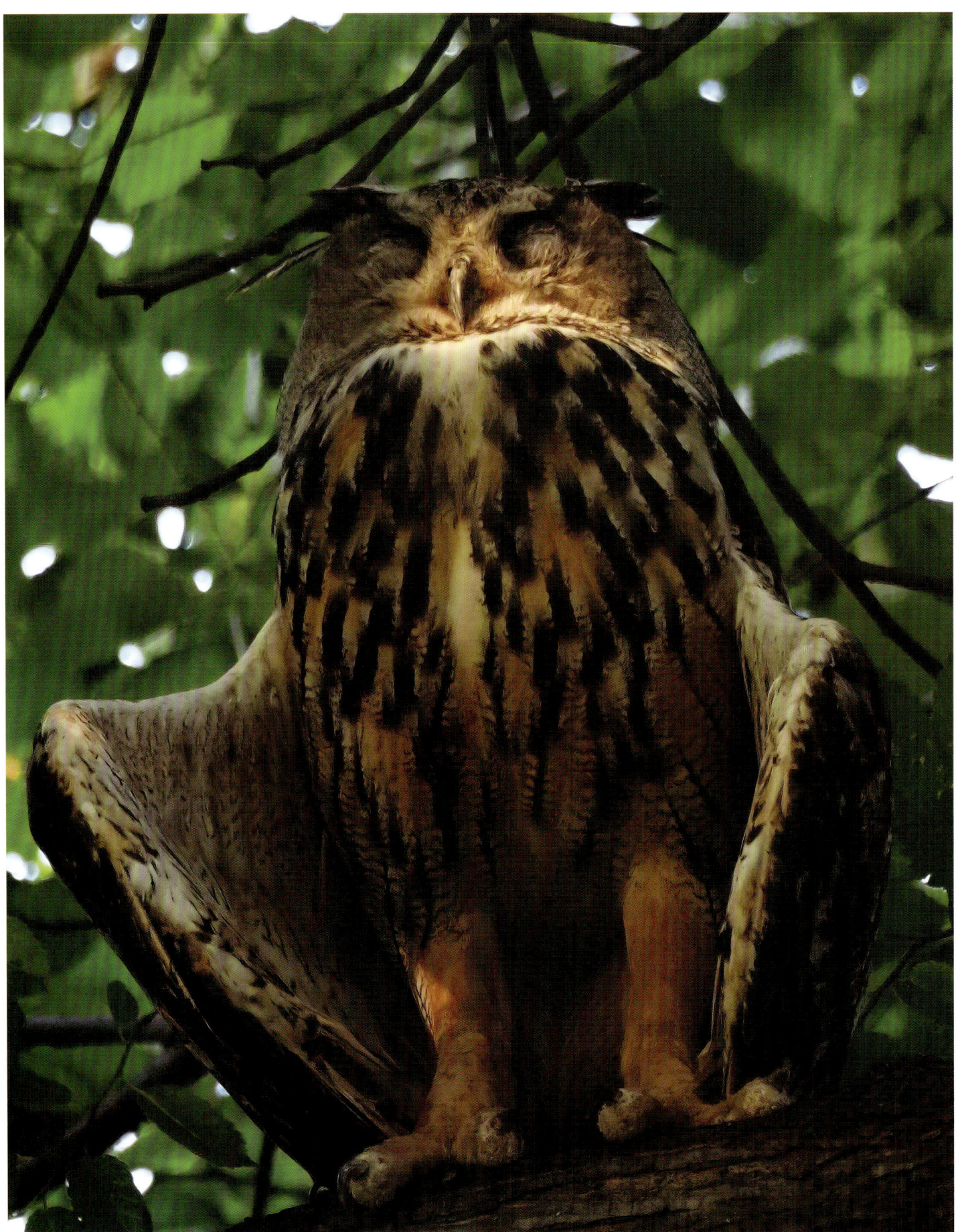

Mark Elliott, *Flaco Keeping Cool,* The Elm, 7/13/23, 6:55 a.m.

We were enduring one of New York City's miserable summer sticky spells when even early morning walks felt like a sauna. And there was Flaco in his favorite elm struggling to get some sleep and stay cool—just like every other New Yorker! I just had to laugh as I took this photograph! And, as I recall, it inspired more comments and reactions than any other of my Flaco posts.

Our salutations list is long,
And filled with a distinguished
　throng:
Flaco the Owl, of Central Park,
"*To-whoo*" the herald angels hark,
We wish him nights of happy ratting
While human owls are Santa-hatting.

IAN FRAZIER

Excerpt from "Greetings, Friends!", Ian Frazier's Annual Holiday Poem Featured in *The New Yorker*, 12/25/23.

Venus N. Sallay, *Flaco with City Lights*, Near the Tennis Courts / Gothic Bridge, 8/5/23, 8:45 p.m.

Flaco frequented this area of Central Park, west of the reservoir near the Gothic Bridge. This evening, Flaco perched on the horizontal branch with the bright city lights from a very distant building shining behind him. Flaco likely chose this perch because it gave him a good 360-degree vantage point while he hunted for rats in the nearby grassy area of the park.

Following spread　Venus N. Sallay, *Flaco in Summer Grass*, North Meadow Ballfield, 8/26/23, 8:25 p.m.

Flaco sat quietly on this night near the fence on the ballfield. This photo was taken not far from where he was, and I, too, observed him quietly as not to scare him off. Flaco flew to several perches in the ballfield as he continued to find his prey.

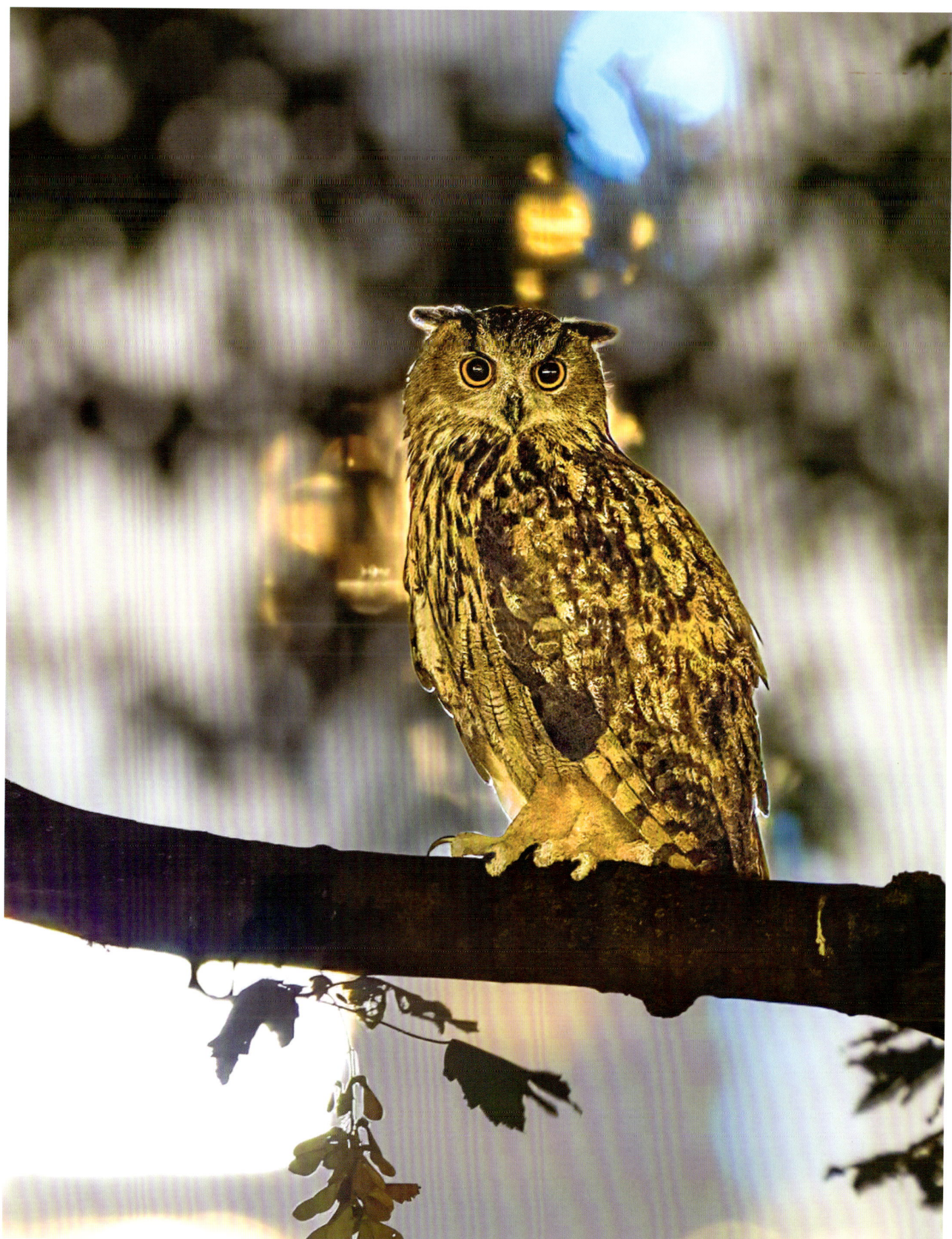

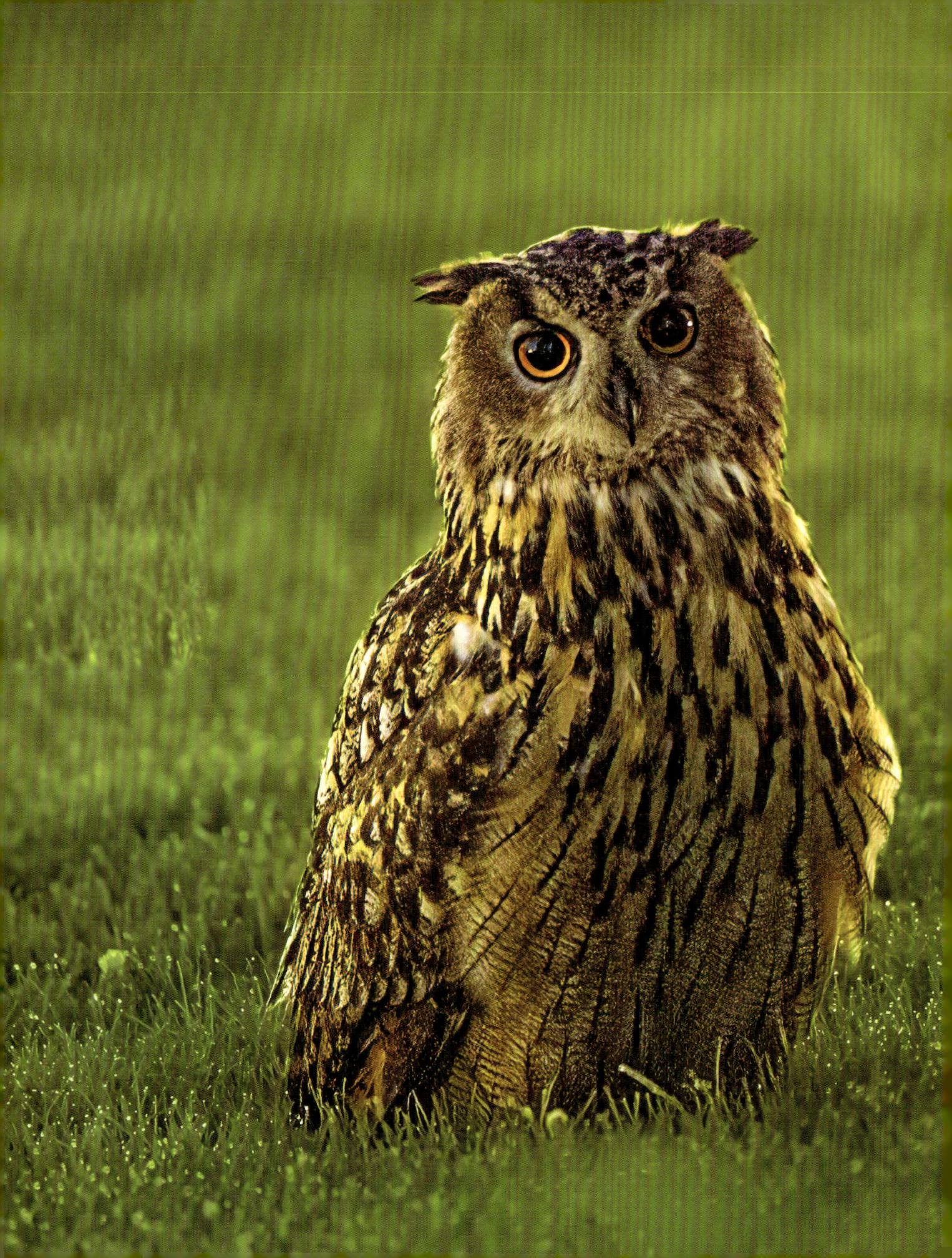

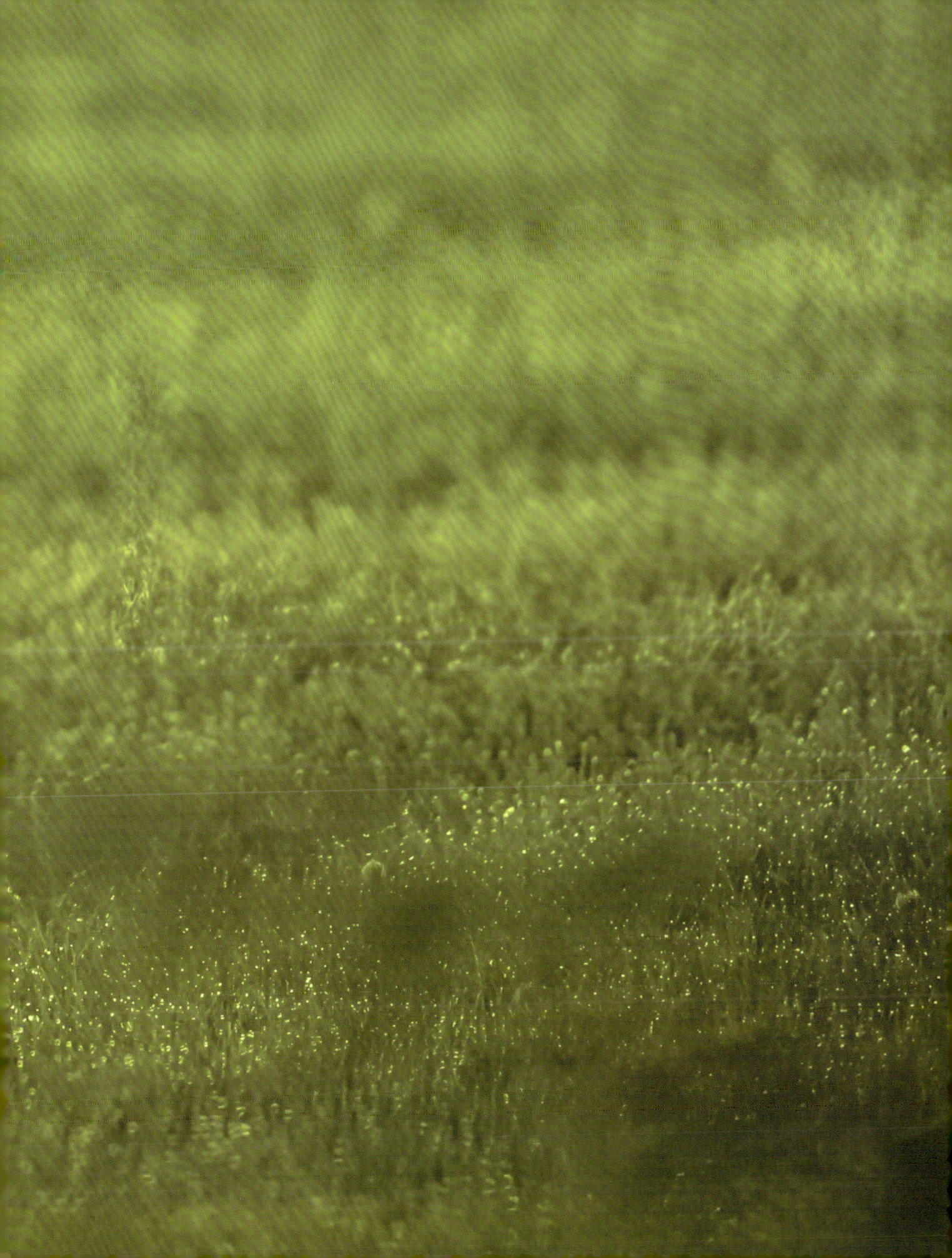

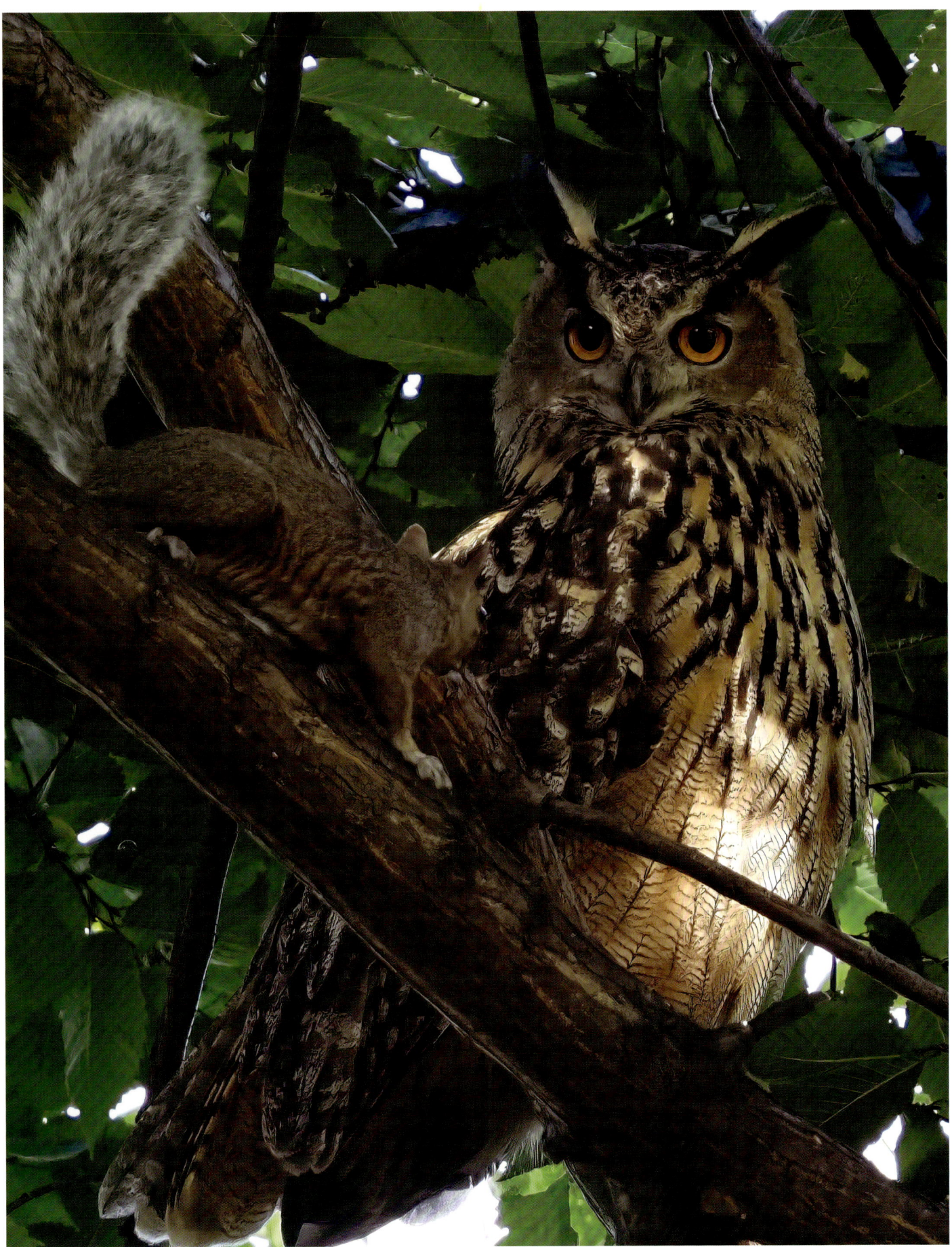

Mark Elliott, *Flaco and the Squirrel Face Off*, The Elm, 9/20/23, 3:26 p.m.

I'm usually in Central Park early. But, occasionally I head out later as well. On a late afternoon jaunt in September I captured Flaco and a squirrel in an epic showdown in his favorite elm. Flaco wasn't known to hunt squirrels, but I don't think the squirrel knew that. And I was unsure what Flaco would do if the squirrel came close. It seemed Flaco was occupying the squirrel's favorite route to a neighboring tree. Neither budged for the longest time. Finally, the squirrel decided it could use a slightly lower branch to get past Flaco on his way next door. And Flaco calmly let it pass!

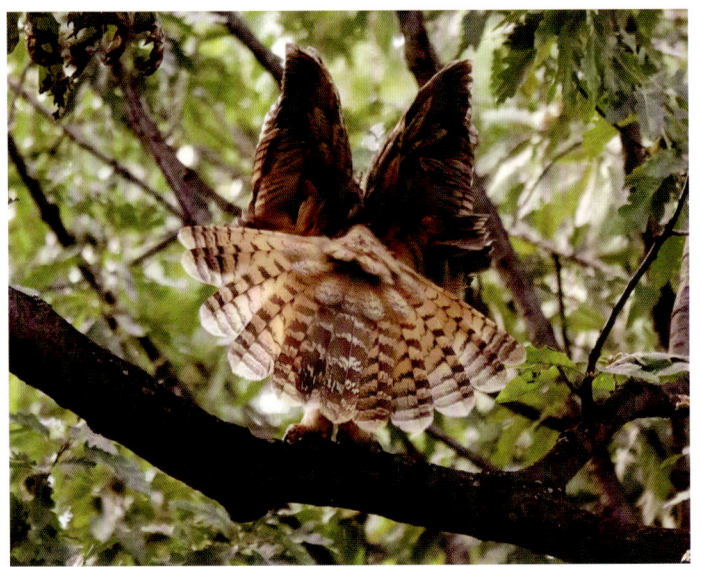 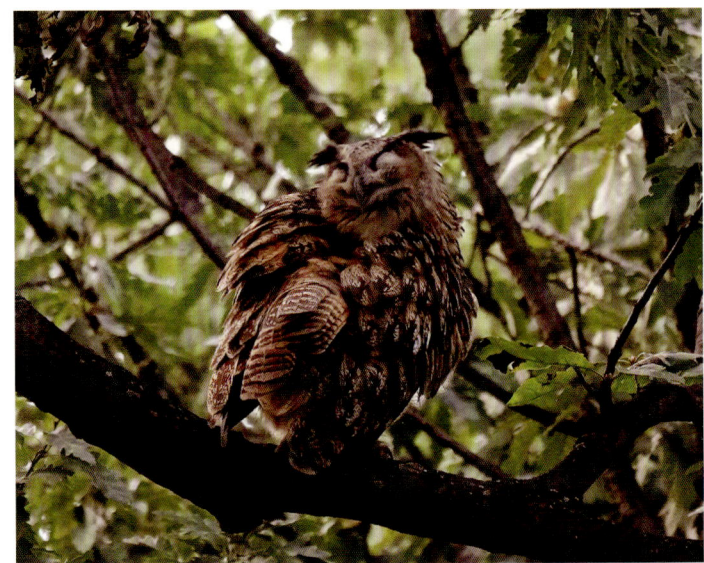

Molly Eustis, *Flaco Preens Before Flyout,* The Oak, East Drive at 104th Street, 9/21/23, 6:49 p.m.

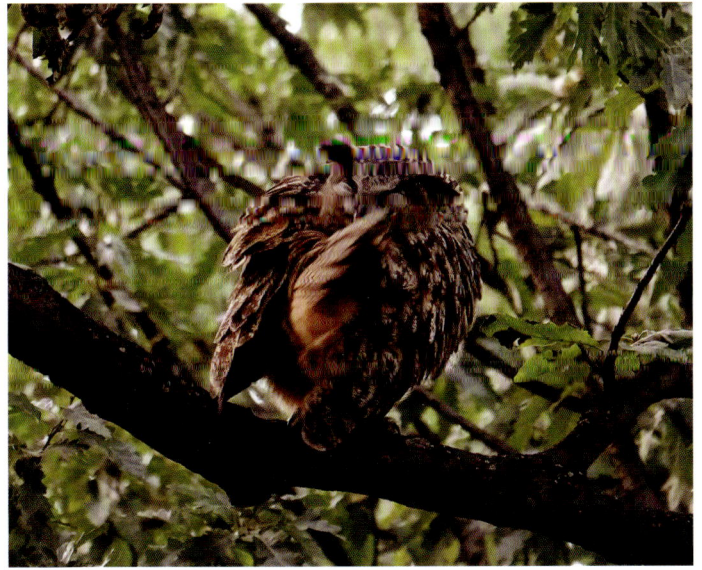 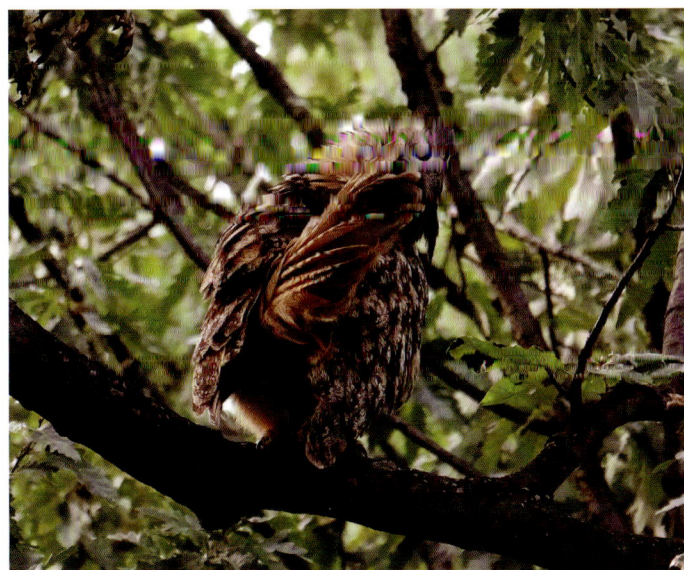

Having spent most of the summer roosting in an elm tree by the North Meadow Recreation Center, Flaco had found a new regular spot at this oak tree by the time September rolled around. It was across East Drive from one of his favorite hunting sites—the Compost Heap. It was a somewhat challenging spot because you either had to stand on East Drive and be subject to bike traffic or stand across the road on a steep slope (I always opted for the latter).

I would show up about 45 minutes before sunset to catch his pre-flyout routine, which always included stretches like this one, which we collectively referred to as the "DeLorean," for obvious reasons.

It was always a real crowd-pleaser, even to those of us who had seen it a hundred times. He was not facing the right direction this day, alas, but it was a view of his beautiful feathers we didn't often get to see.

Flyout was a popular time among the regular owlers—many of us formed this routine together during the days of Barry the Barred Owl back in 2020–21, and that is how I met most of my owling friends. Sunset is one of the best times to watch an owl because you will see them be the most active—waking up, stretching, preening, and ultimately, flying—these are things you are guaranteed to see. Also, you are less likely to disturb an owl, as they are fully awake at that time. Flyout always felt like this sort of exhale at the end of the day, and seeing him take flight never got old.

Flaco was absolutely fastidious about preening. All owls preen, of course, but Flaco seemed to spend more time on it than any other owl I've observed. When he preened, there wasn't usually much to see if he was facing us, but from this angle, we got a great look at the mechanics of it and his gorgeous feathers.

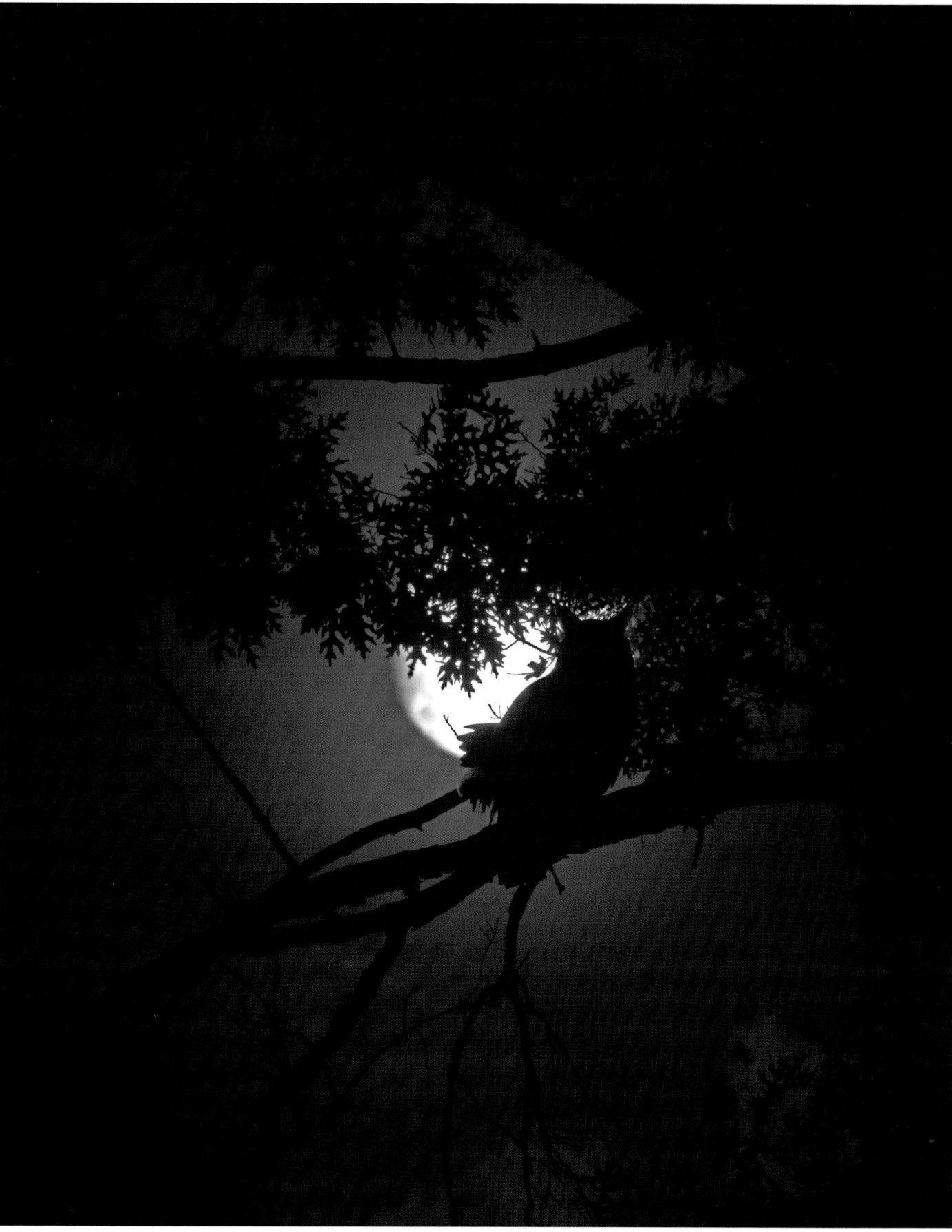

The Owl Who Comes
MARY OLIVER

The owl who comes
through the dark
to sit
in the black boughs of the apple tree

and stare down
the hook of his beak,
dead silent,
and his eyes,

like two moons
in the distance,
soft and shining
under their heavy lashes–

like the most beautiful life–
is thinking
of nothing
as he watches

and waits to see
what might appear,
briskly,
out of the seamless,

deep winter–
out of the teeming
world below–
and if I wish the owl luck,

and I do,
what am I wishing for that other
soft life,
climbing through the snow?

What we must do,
I suppose,
is to hope the world
keeps its balance:

what we are to do, however,
with our hearts
waiting and watching–truly
I do not know.

Photo by Anke Frohlich

Previous spread Anke Frohlich, *Flaco Hooting at the Full Moon,* Compost Heap, 9/26/23, 10:18 p.m.

During full moons, Flaco was often more vocal than usual. Once I heard his hoots, the bright light of the moon on a clear night helped me find him. Then the challenge was to line up my tripod to position Flaco in front of the moon. This was often impossible as branches obscured him or the moon. If the moon was too high, there was simply no suitable angle. On this special night however, it all came together.

I often brighten the images made at night by using long exposure times or later in post-production to give the viewer a clearer and more detailed view of the scene. Many times people mistake those photos for daytime captures. I purposely did not lighten this image to allow you to see what you would have observed with your naked eye had you been in Central Park that night.

Sheryl Checkman, *King of the Hill, Top of the Heap,* Compost Heap, 10/22/2023, 6:25 p.m.

This photo was taken one evening at the Compost Heap, where Flaco, after flying out of his oak tree on East Drive and 104th Street, began his nightly search for dinner. This photo is part of what I like to call my "Table for One" series. Flaco tried a few different "tables" before settling here, on top of a heap of dirt surveying his hunting ground.

On this particular evening, I wasn't expecting to get such wonderful close-up photos of Flaco on the ground, so this was quite a treat. In fact, I had been hoping to catch a photo of him flying out from the tree. I did not have my tripod with me. I missed the flyout since he went in the opposite direction from where I had situated myself. However, the other photographers all ran to the Compost Heap, where it appeared he had flown, and I followed. It was getting dark, and I could barely see him, but I slowed my shutter speed to 1/30 sec and managed to hand-hold my camera to get this shot at a focal length of 800mm.

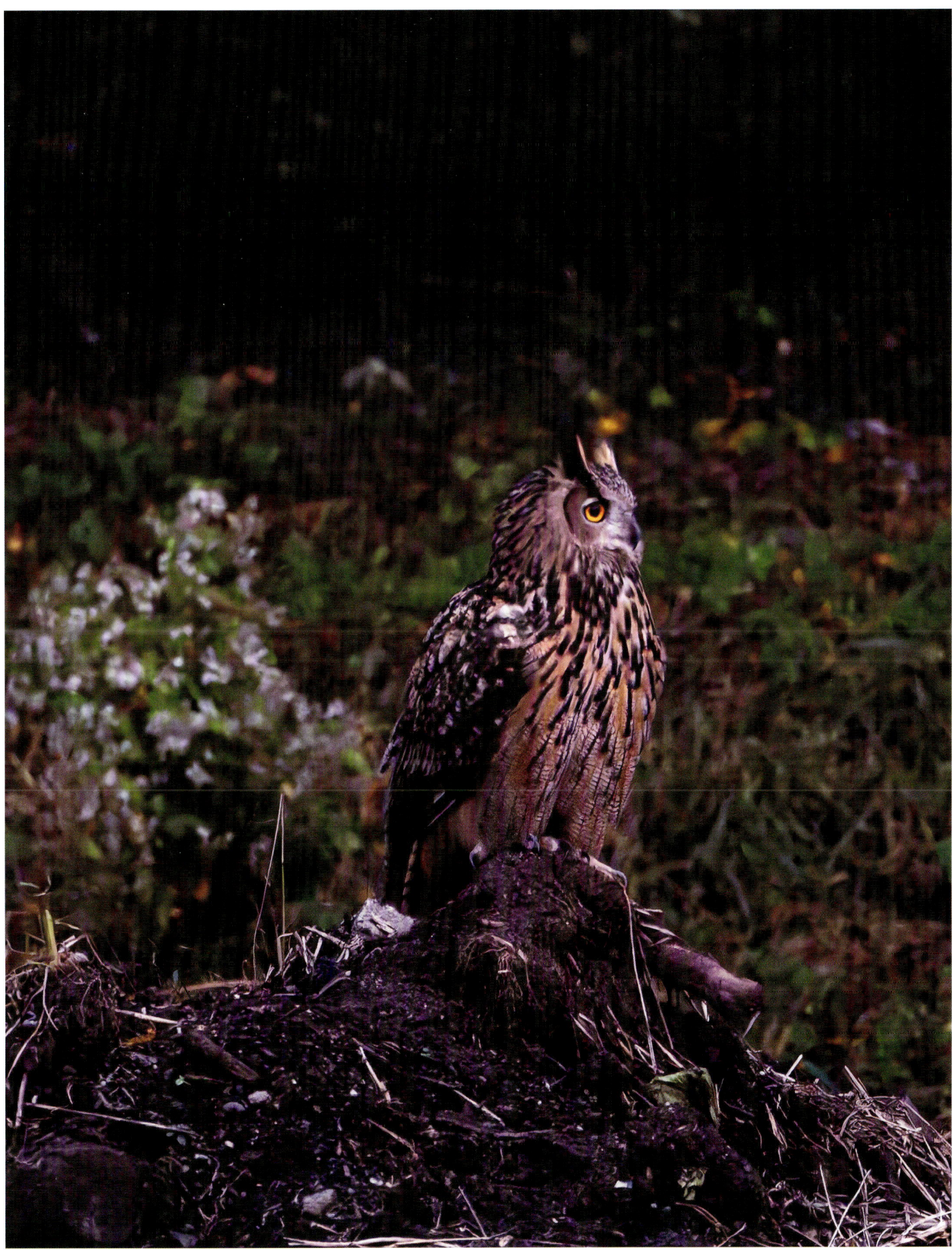

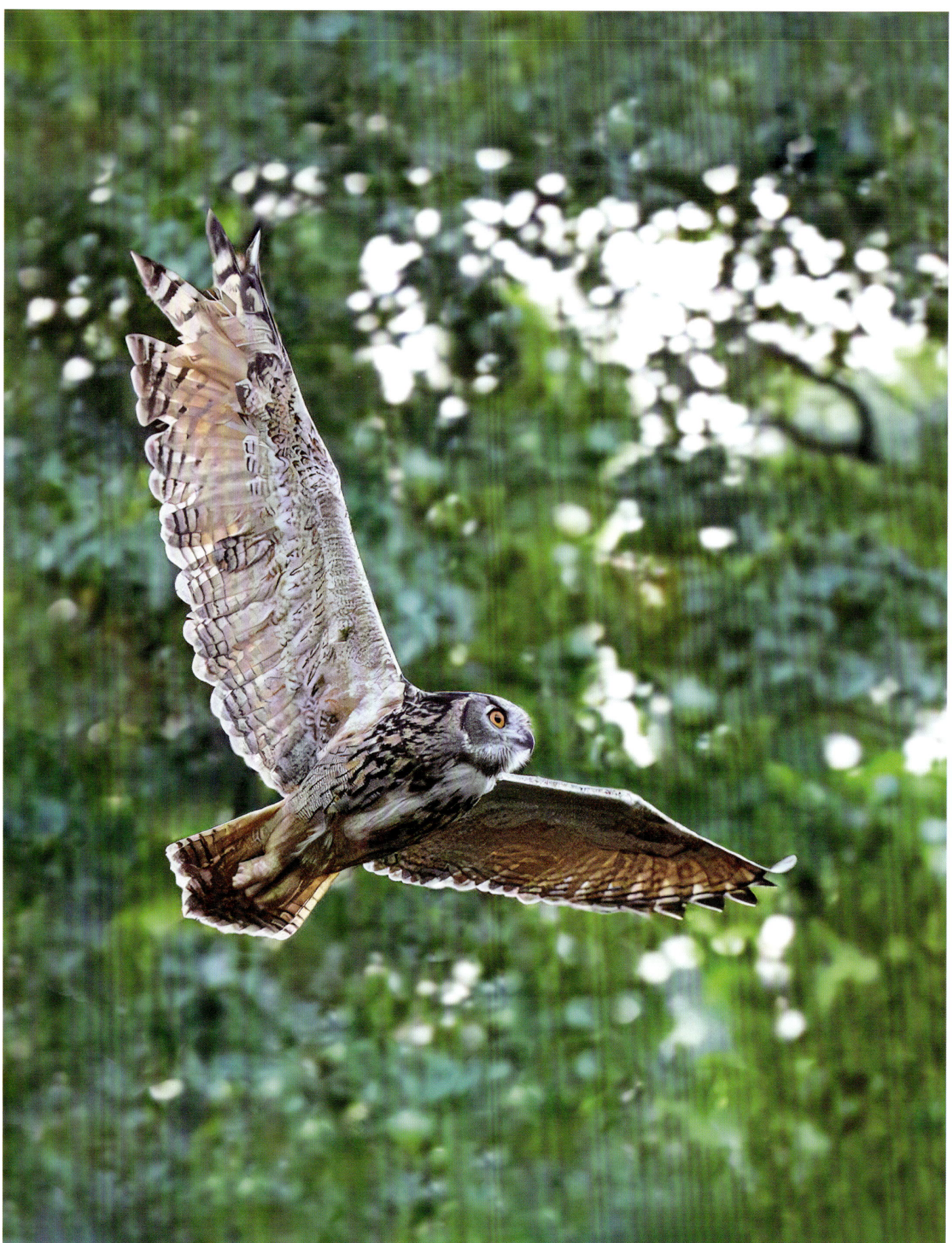

Anke Frohlich, *Flaco Soaring,* East Drive Opposite the Compost Area, 10/5/23, Six Minutes After Sunset

Seeing Flaco fly out was the highlight of the day for many dedicated followers. As this happened after sunset, I thought it impossible to capture this precious moment on camera.

In the fall of 2023, I observed that Flaco often chose the same flight path when leaving his favorite tree for the night, so I grabbed my fastest lens and positioned myself a little north of him on East Drive. Camera in front of my eye, I waited in anticipation. I often stood in that position for a long time, once even for half-an-hour.

As I could not see Flaco from where I was, I could not pre-focus on him. I had to be ready to act at the very first sign of him taking flight. At that point, it was a matter of staying calm and attempting to get the camera to lock focus on him. Due to the low light this was quite difficult. The equipment could not distinguish the owl in flight from the trees in the background. During the three weeks I tried, I succeeded only four times, which makes me cherish these captures all the more.

Paul Beiboer, *Flaco Keeping His Cool While Being "Admired" by Four American Robins,* The Oak, 10/13/23, 5:50 p.m.

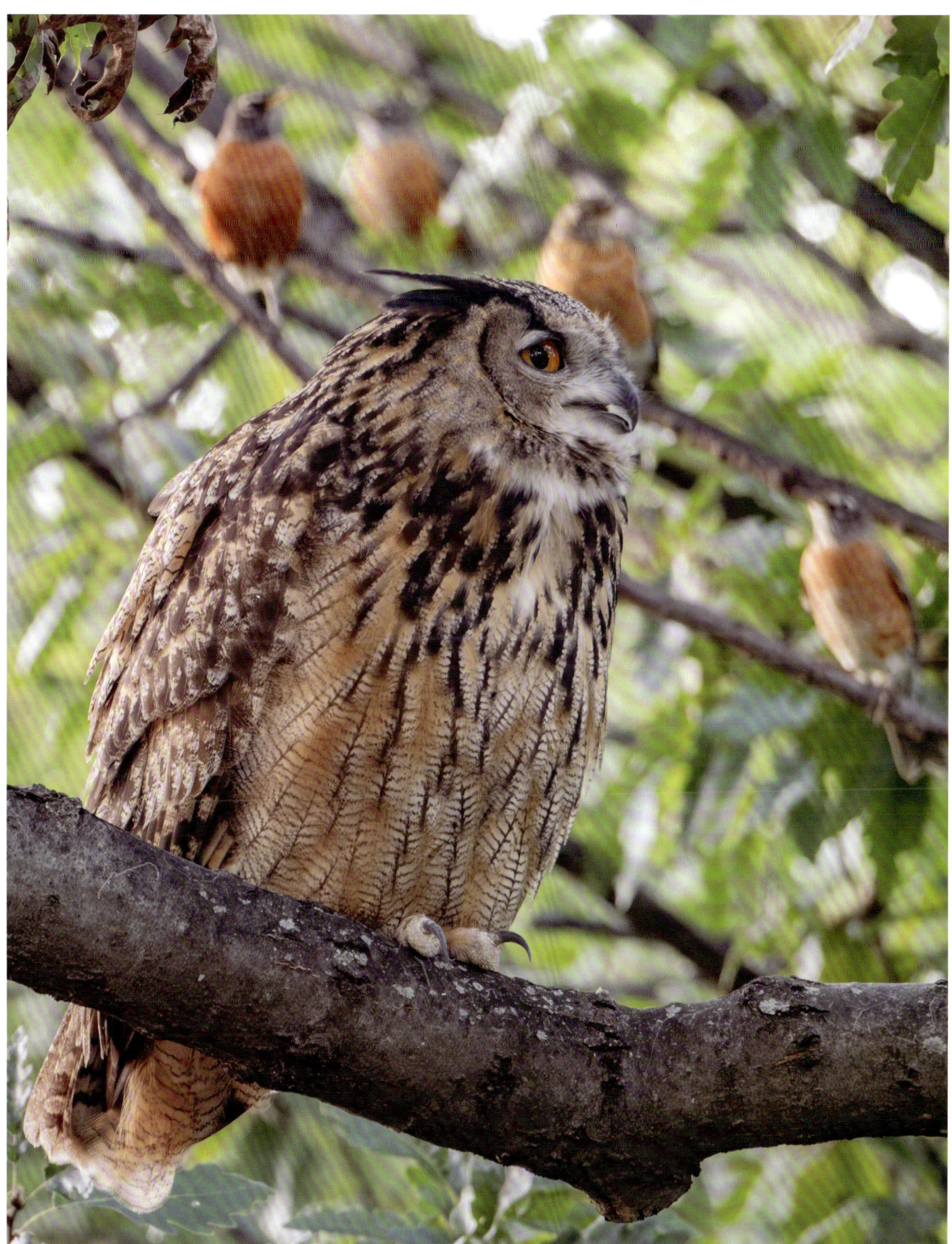

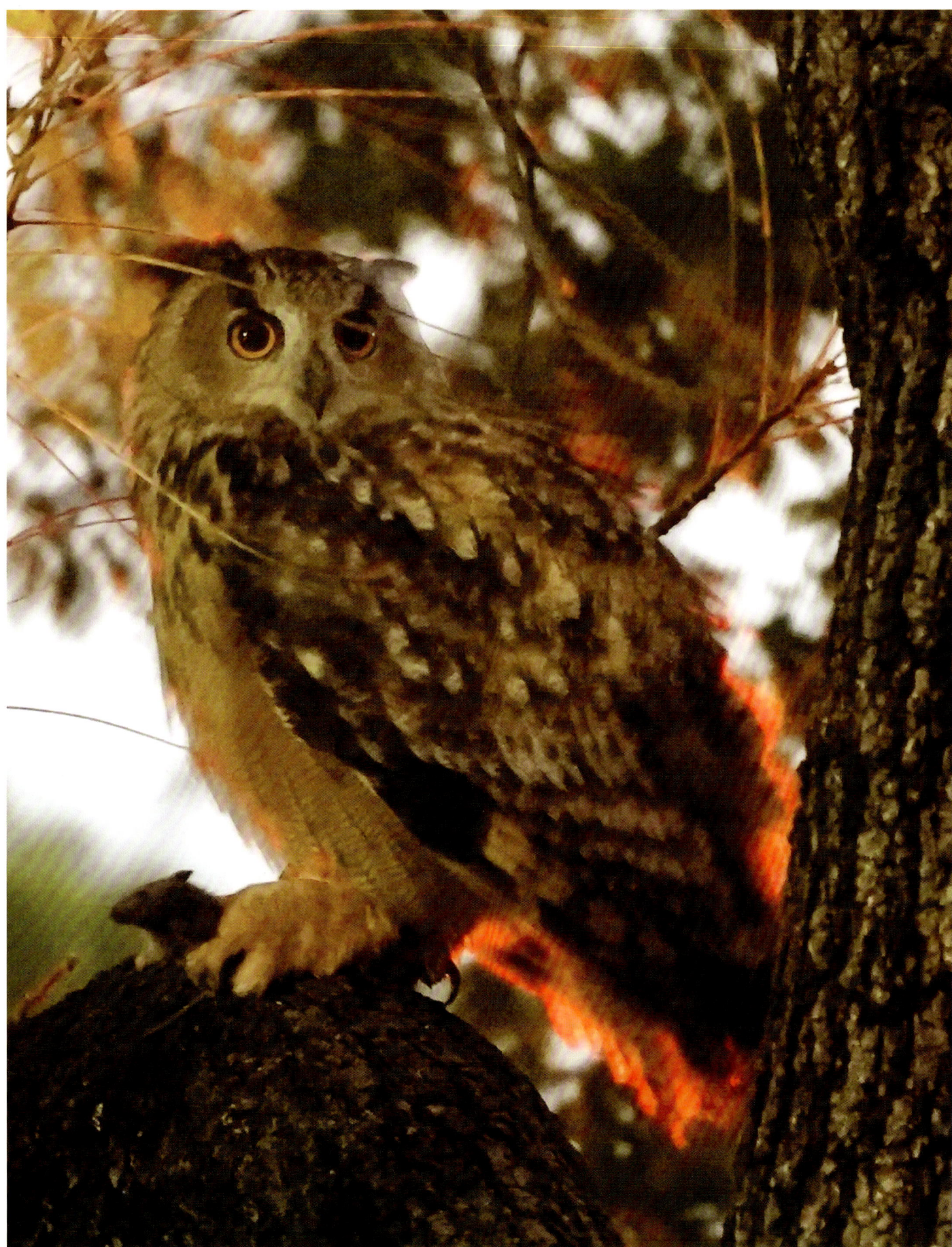

Molly Eustis, *Flaco with a Compost Rat,* Compost Heap, or The Mount, per Central Park, 10/8/23, 9:00 p.m.

The Compost Heap was one of Flaco's regular post-flyout hunting spots. It is teeming with rats and home to two large dumpsters, which often made observing him there a very acute olfactory experience (fortunately for Flaco, owls do not have a great sense of smell).

He had his favorite spots in the various trees there and would occasionally go to the ground on the other side of the heaps of dirt. He also would occasionally swoop low over our heads at Compost in pursuit of his dinner—just exhilarating every time it happened. I think after a certain point, he recognized that we would not interfere with his hunting and thus felt comfortable swooping low and hunting in our presence (this is fairly unusual for wild owls).

On this night there were just three of us there. He caught a rat very quickly near one of the dumpsters and flew up to a tree with it. I was shooting long-exposure, and despite the appearance of this photo, it was actually pretty dark and very hard to see him, so I was essentially blind focusing my camera. Add to that the wind and the fact that he was moving around, and it's basically a miracle I got any semblance of focus on this shot.

Flaco downed the rat in one gulp very shortly after this picture. He had two modes with eating a rat: eat the rat in one take, or take 45-plus minutes to dine. Another challenge of Compost was the nearby traffic light–from frame to frame, Flaco would often change color from yellow to red to green (it was red here).

This location is also notable in its appeal to almost all visiting owls to Central Park in the past 3-plus years. We observed the snowy owl hunt from some of the same perches in 2021, and Geraldine (the former long-time resident Great Horned Owl of Central Park) do the same, as well as a visiting Great Horned Owl in 2022, and the Long-eared Owls in winter 2024.

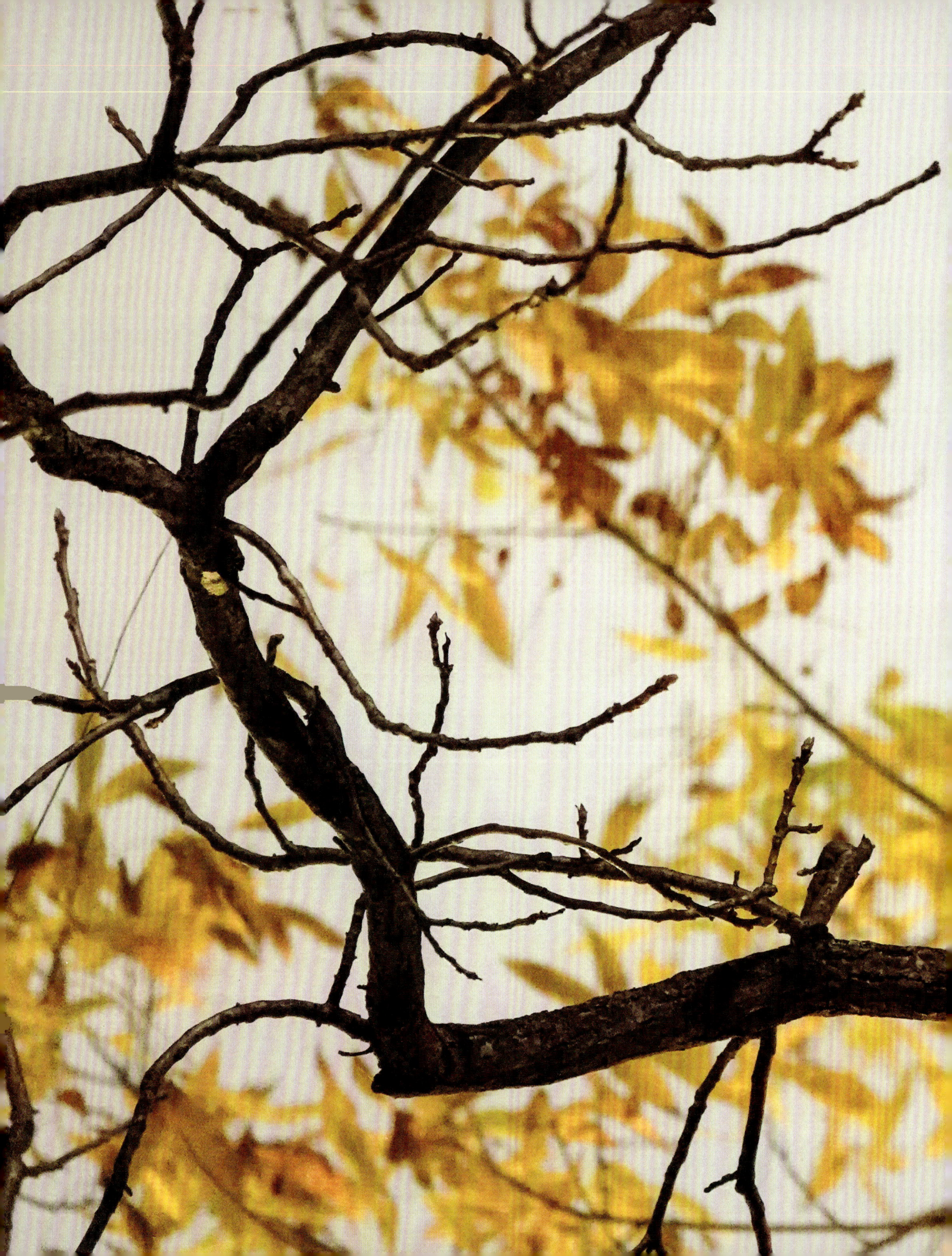

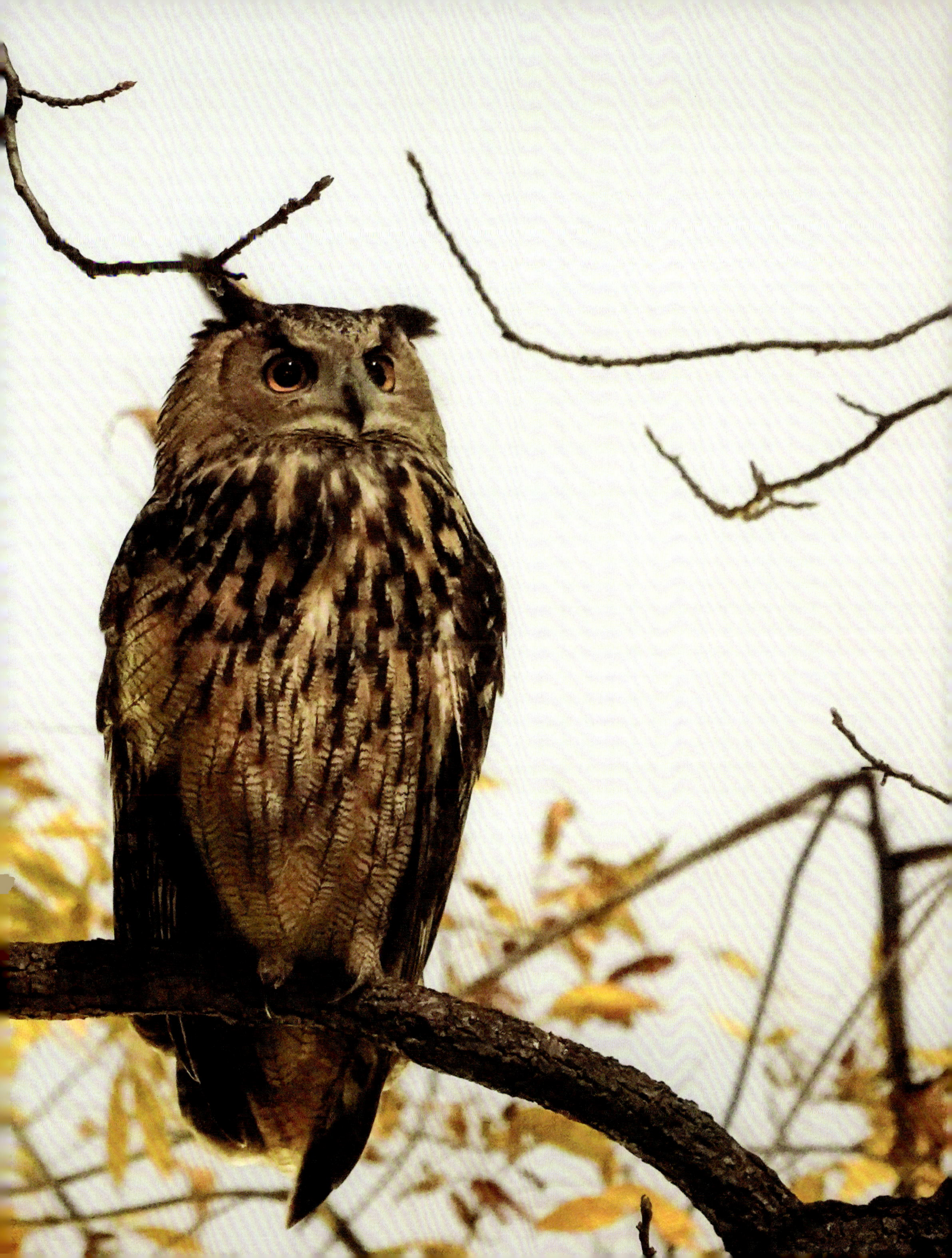

Previous spread   Molly Eustis, *Hunter's Moon,* Compost Heap, 10/27/23, 10:53 p.m.

This was an exceptional night with Flaco. He'd flown out from the oak tree, gone to the construction site for a while, and then eventually to Compost around 10:00 p.m.. Only Anke and I remained at that point. He did not seem to be in a particular hurry to hunt. He perched beautifully among the new fall foliage, occasionally switching trees, watching the rats, us, the sky.

The moon—the full Hunter's Moon—was so bright that it was casting our shadows onto the ground, and from this perch, it was reflected in Flaco's eyes. When night owling in the city, an overcast sky is always preferable, because the cloud layer creates a light bounce from all of the city light, whereas a clear night usually meant difficult light conditions for photography (and finding the owl). However, that was not an issue this night because of the moon.

He was very relaxed that night—he even remained unbothered as the maintenance truck with its bright lights pulled up to transfer garbage into the dumpster underneath the tree where he perched, and later when a police car rolled up with flashing lights on. We had to plead with the officers to turn off the lights; they had just been passing through, but had seen us waving our arms and thought something was wrong.

We eventually left at 1:00 a.m., and Flaco was still at Compost. We didn't know it at the time, but this was the last time we would see him for almost two weeks—until he turned up in the East Village/Lower East Side. He never returned to the park full-time after that. In retrospect, it felt kind of like a farewell to that chapter.

Molly Eustis, *Flaco in Orange,* Compost Heap, 10/28/23, 12:56 a.m.

This picture was a part of the epic Hunter's Moon night (or rather, early morning at this point) at Compost. We'd been remarking all year about how we couldn't wait to see Flaco with the fall foliage, and here we got our wish.

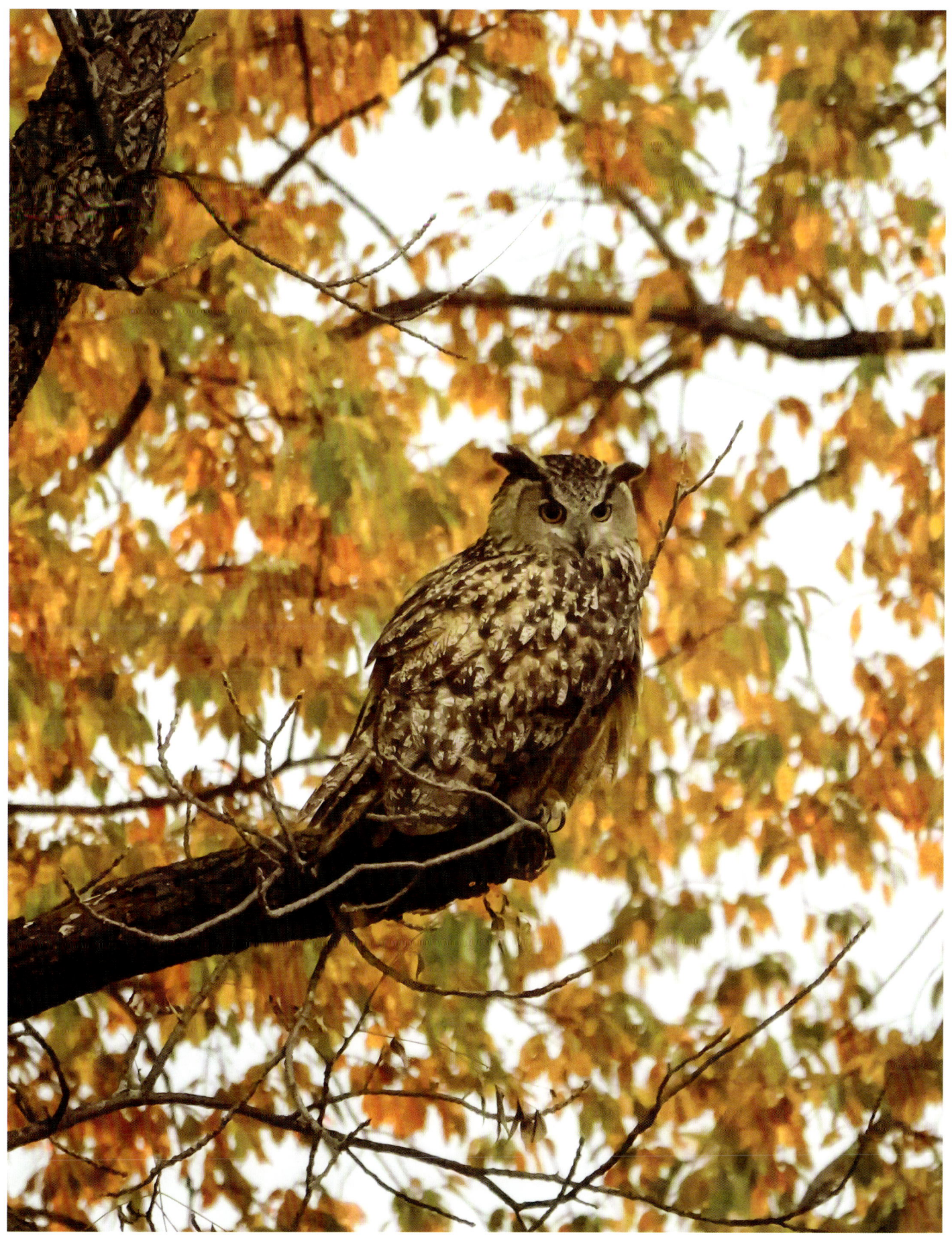

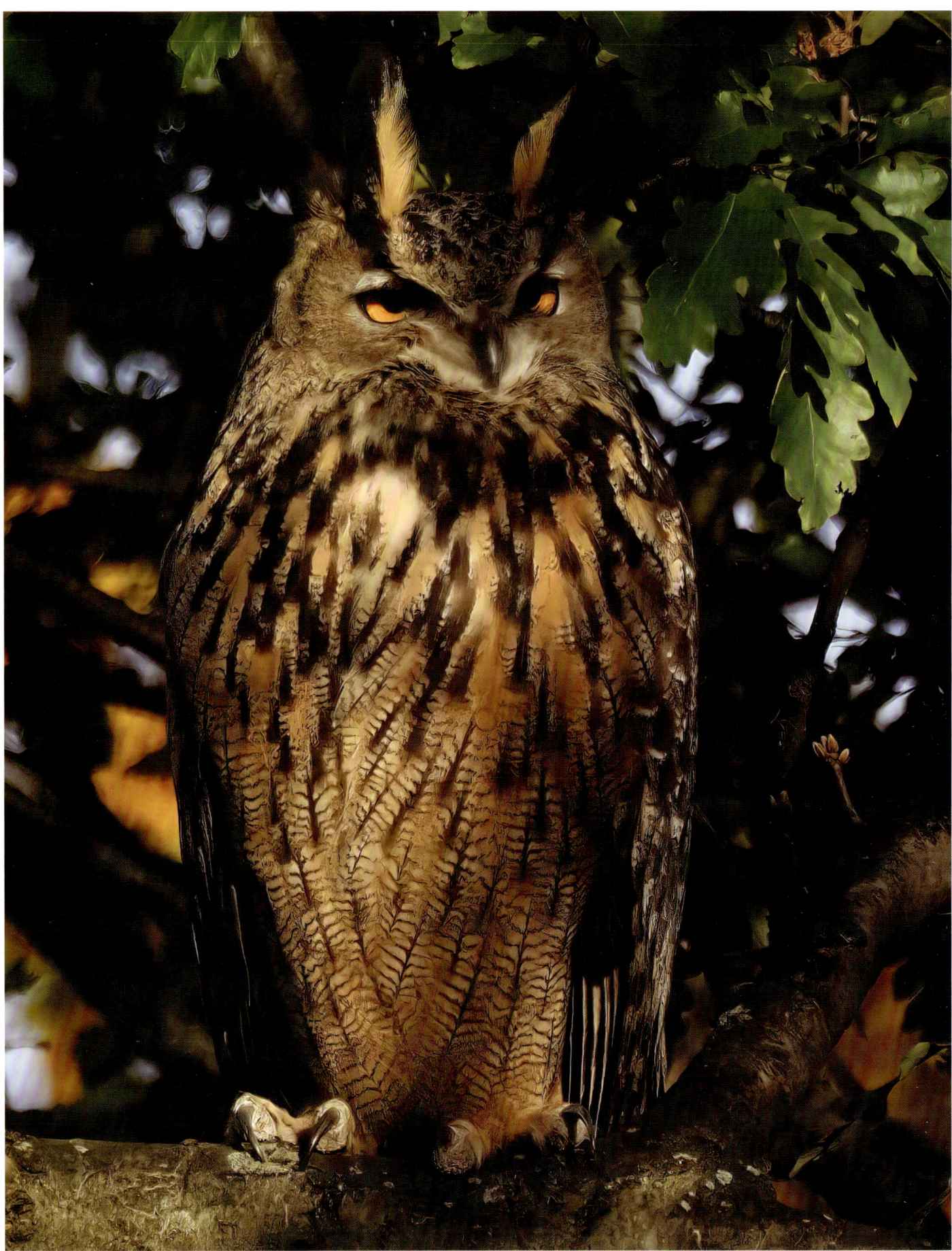

Mark Elliott, *Flaco Returns to the Park,* The Oak, 11/17/23, 7:52 a.m.

Flaco had not been seen in Central Park since late October. I thought it unlikely he'd ever return to the park and hoped for his sake he would depart the city for safer environs. But it turned out that he was still in Manhattan and was seen several times on the Lower East Side. Then he was spotted peering in an apartment window on Fifth Avenue near 96th Street and I thought maybe, just maybe, he would return to the park. So, every day I checked his usual spots on my morning walk, and then, early on the morning of November 17th, there he was in his favorite oak! It dawned clear and blustery, and Flaco was getting buffeted when I took this shot. It was the last time I would ever see him in Central Park.

Venus N. Sallay, *Flaco's Return to Central Park,* The Oak, 11/17/23, 4:00 p.m.

Flaco returned to his favorite oak tree in Central Park after two-and-a-half weeks in downtown Manhattan. Flaco must have missed the crowd that stopped by and gathered around his tree during the day. It always amazed me that Flaco chose locations that gave him the ability to see people around him.

I was reminded of how much he was accustomed to the many people, both young and old, who visited him in the zoo for nearly 13 years. It was wonderful to see him again. I wondered how he found his way back to this part of the park, nonetheless, to this tree.

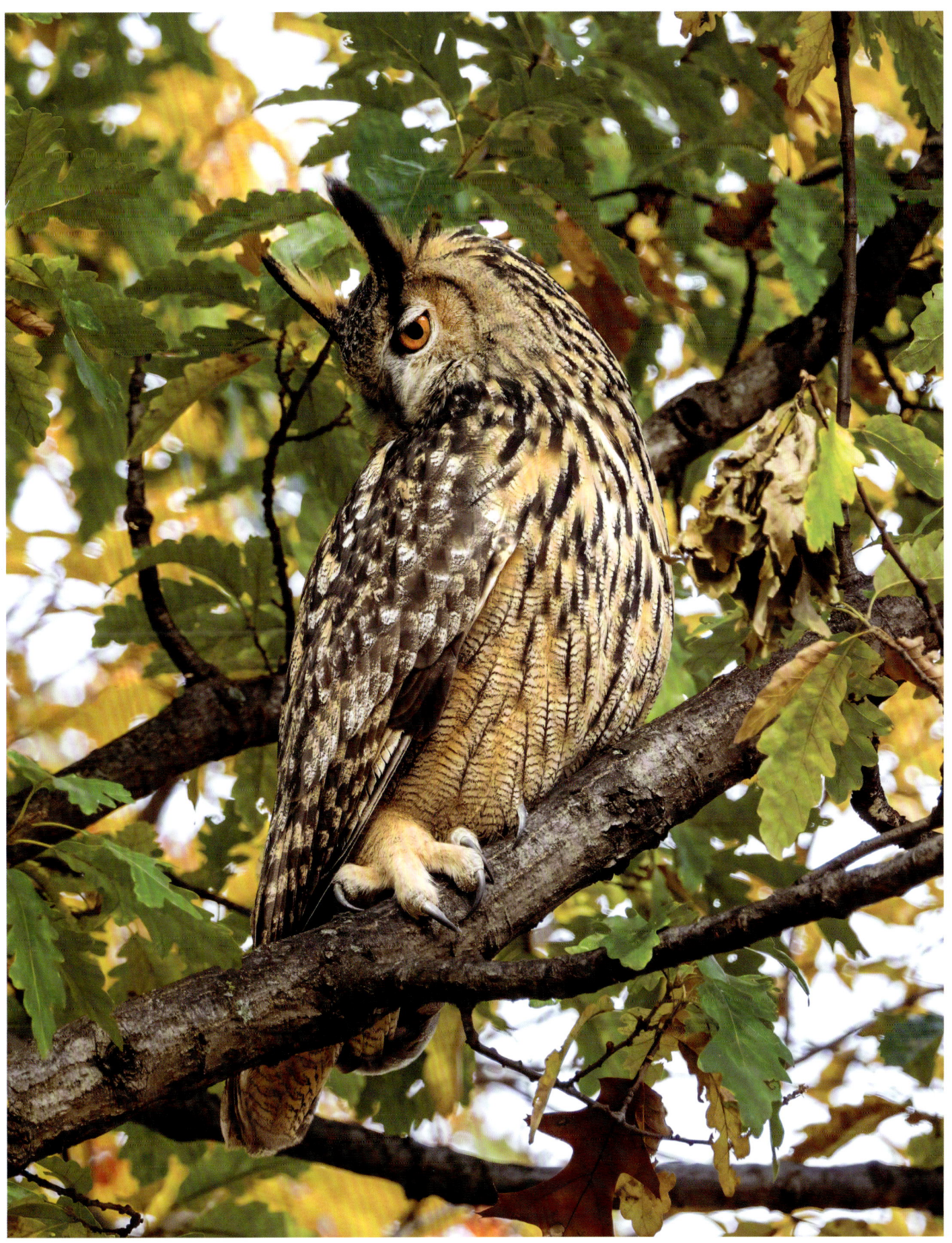

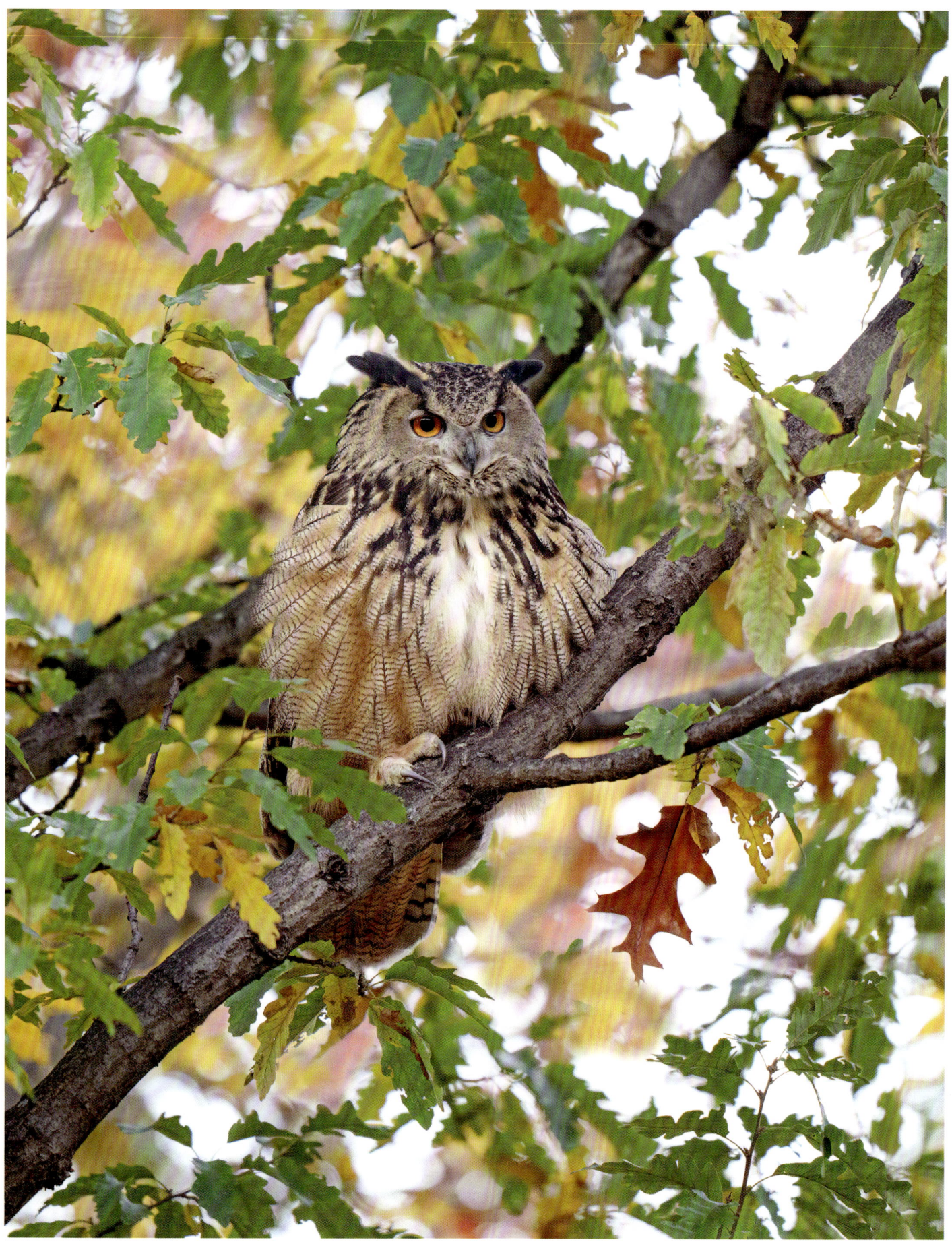

Anke Frohlich, *Flaco in Fall Foliage,* Compost Heap, 11/17/23, 5:45 p.m.

One of my goals was to make photos of Flaco in every season. Once the first signs of fall color appeared in Central Park, I hoped that Flaco would pick a beautiful tree and roost in it. No such luck.

On October 31st, the day of the Halloween parade, I observed Flaco take off and, as we know in hindsight, leave Central Park to explore downtown Manhattan. I thought my chance had passed.

On November 17th, I got word that Flaco was back in Central Park! He was sighted in the Loch. I am happy that I was able to capture him with autumn colors in the frame. I love how his piercing, orange eyes match the leaves. His fluffed feathers even look leaf-like.

Following spread   Venus N. Sallay, *Flaco and Golden Leaves,* The Loch, 11/18/23, 4:45 p.m.

After being missing for more than two weeks, Flaco returned to the Loch not far from where he previously enjoyed most of his days in late winter and early spring of 2023, roosting above the waterfall at the east end of the Loch, soothed by the sound of the flowing water. On this day, Flaco chose to roost on this tree framed with the most beautiful, radiant fall colors. This was the only time I saw Flaco surrounded by this bright color. I remember I felt so happy and excited to find him back in the Loch. I didn't even realize then that this would be the very last time I would see Flaco in the North Woods of Central Park.

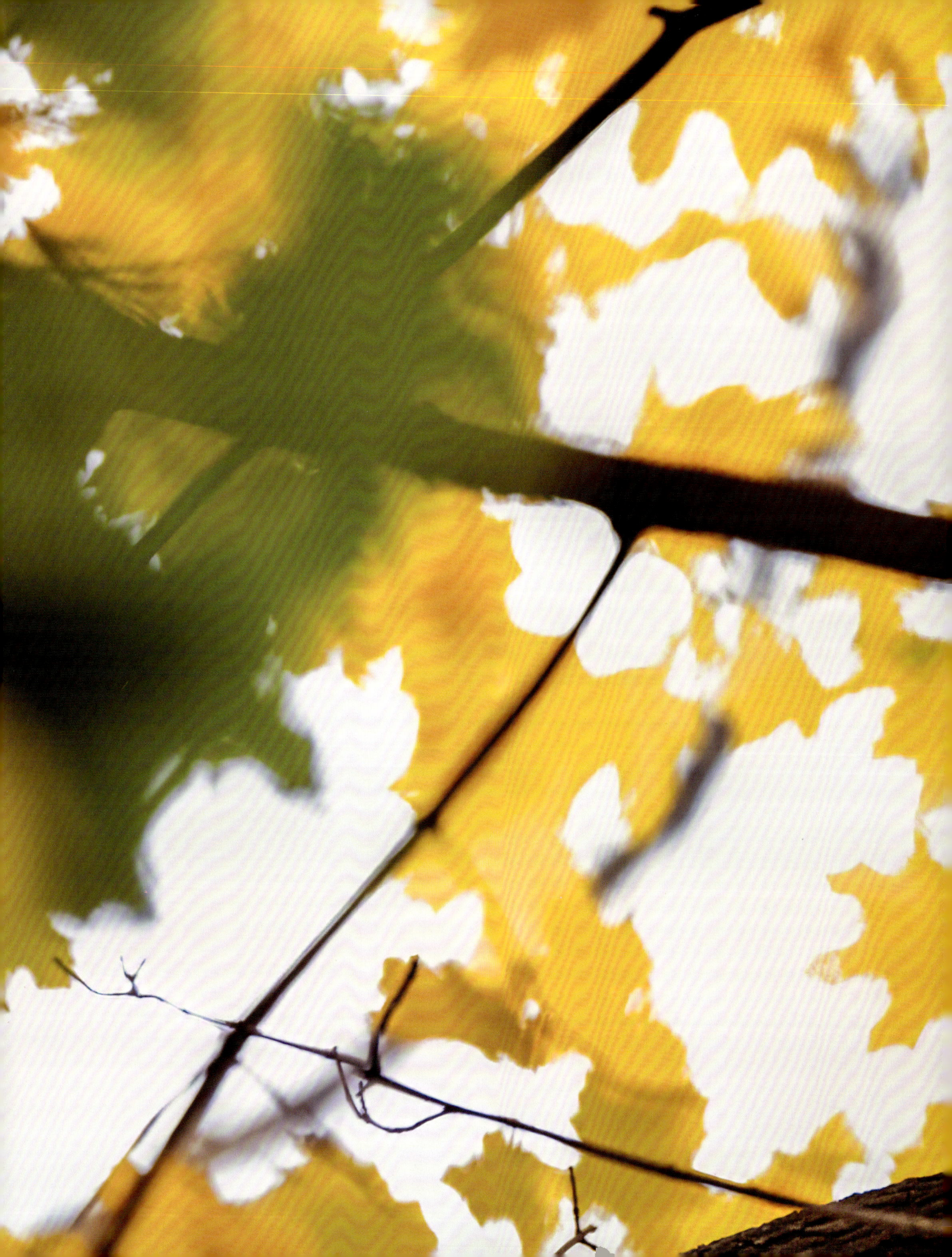

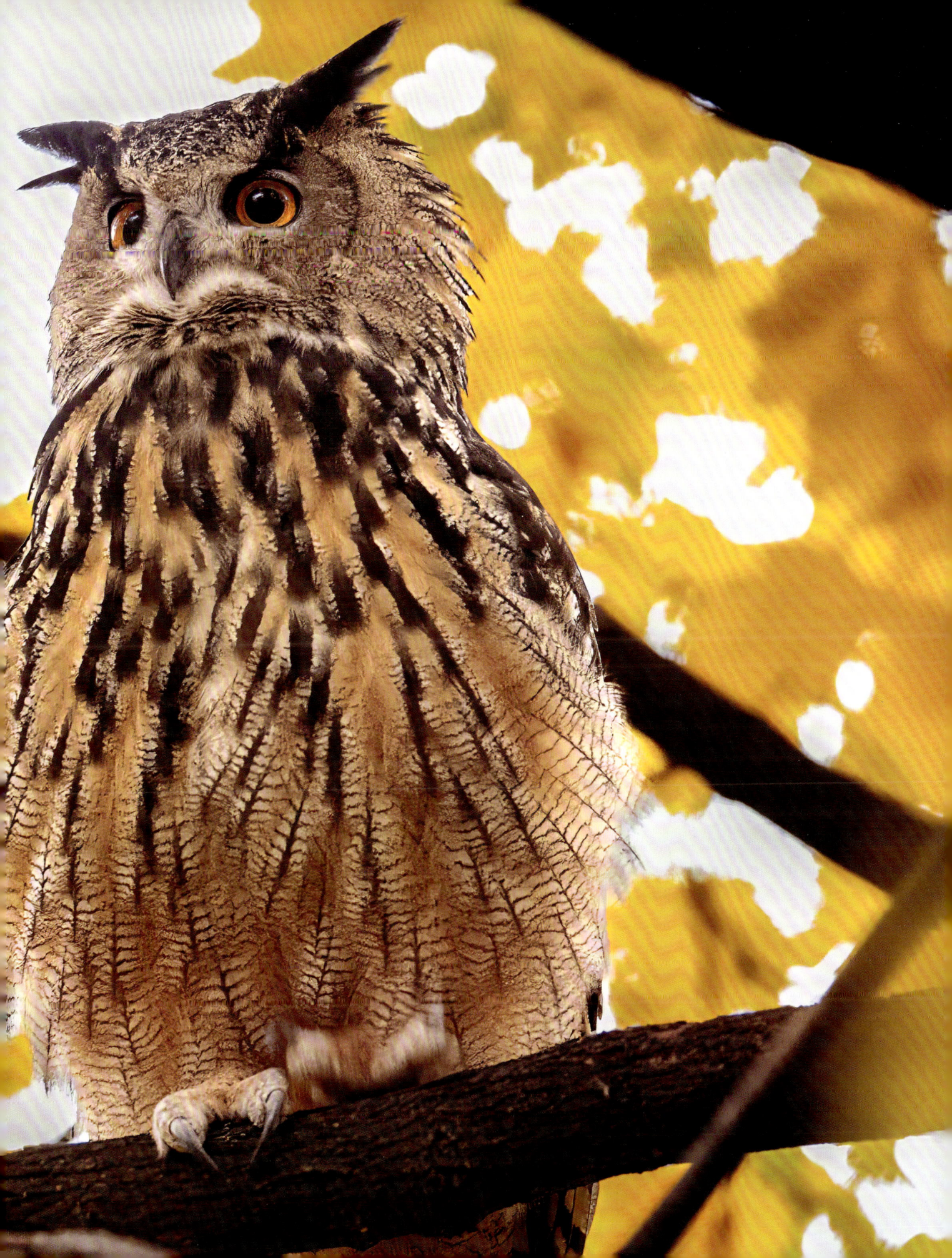

David Barrett, *Flaco Roosting on a Fire Escape,* Upper West Side, 11/27/23, 4:45 p.m.

We had not seen Flaco since his last appearance in Central Park on November 18th, though we had received a report that he was on the Upper West Side. We were delighted to get a tip—and an invitation to visit—from a follower who'd discovered Flaco roosting on their fire escape not far from Central Park in the West 80s. This was our first of many looks at Flaco inside an Upper West Side courtyard. He seemed relaxed and well as he looked down at us from his third-story perch. Then, he quietly flew off into the night.

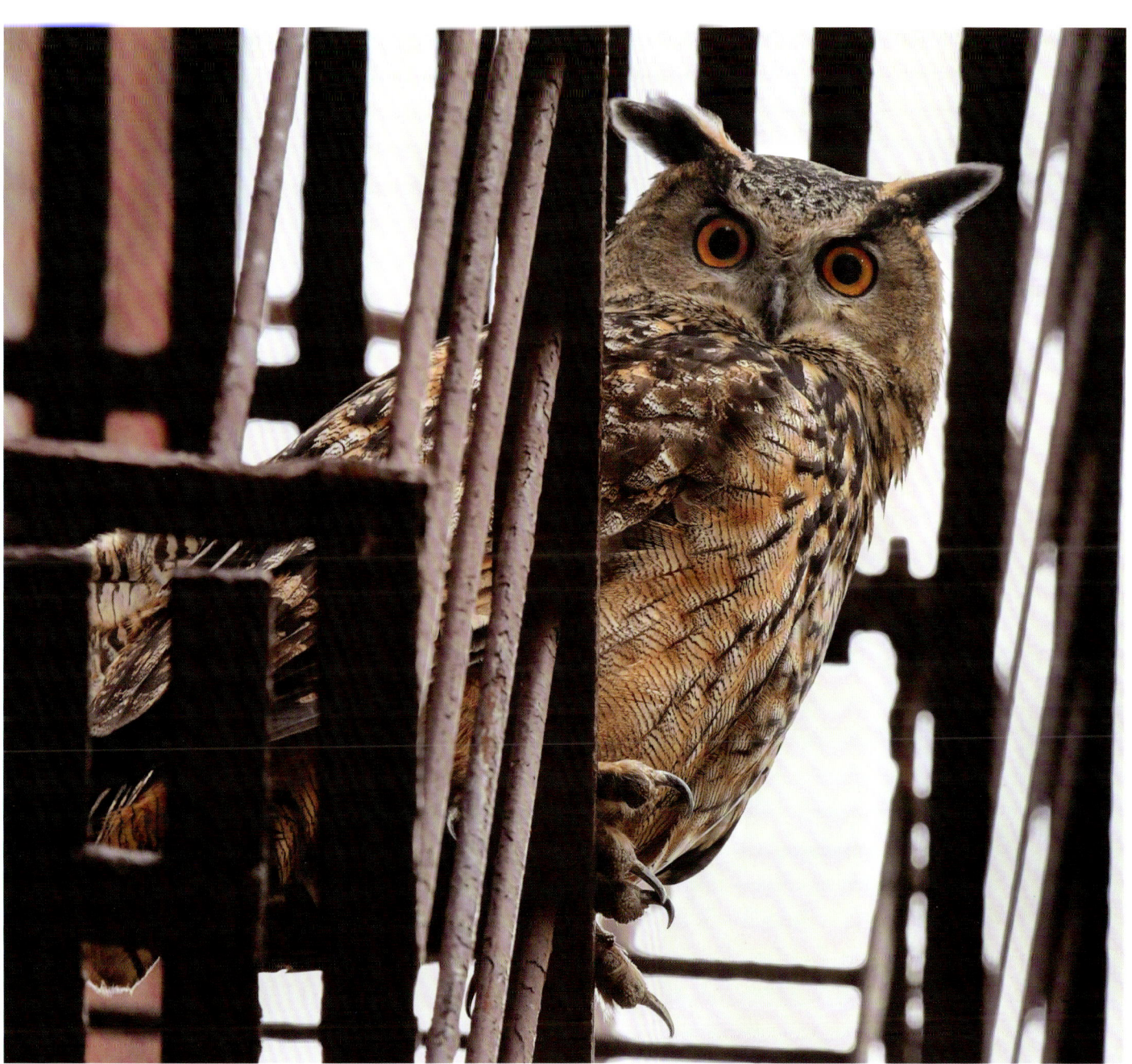

Paul Beiboer, *Flaco on 5 West 86th Street,* Upper West Side, 12/2/23, 9:00 p.m.

As I was watching TV on a Saturday night, I casually checked X to see if there had been any Flaco sighting. Much to my delight, I saw a picture posted of Flaco sitting on a cage on top of the building I lived in! On my apartment building! I was so excited, and went up to the roof and observed Flaco for about 20 minutes from close by as he was hooting and looking around. After that, he flew off to a nearby water tower (86th Street and Columbus Avenue), where he stayed for hours, hooting continuously.

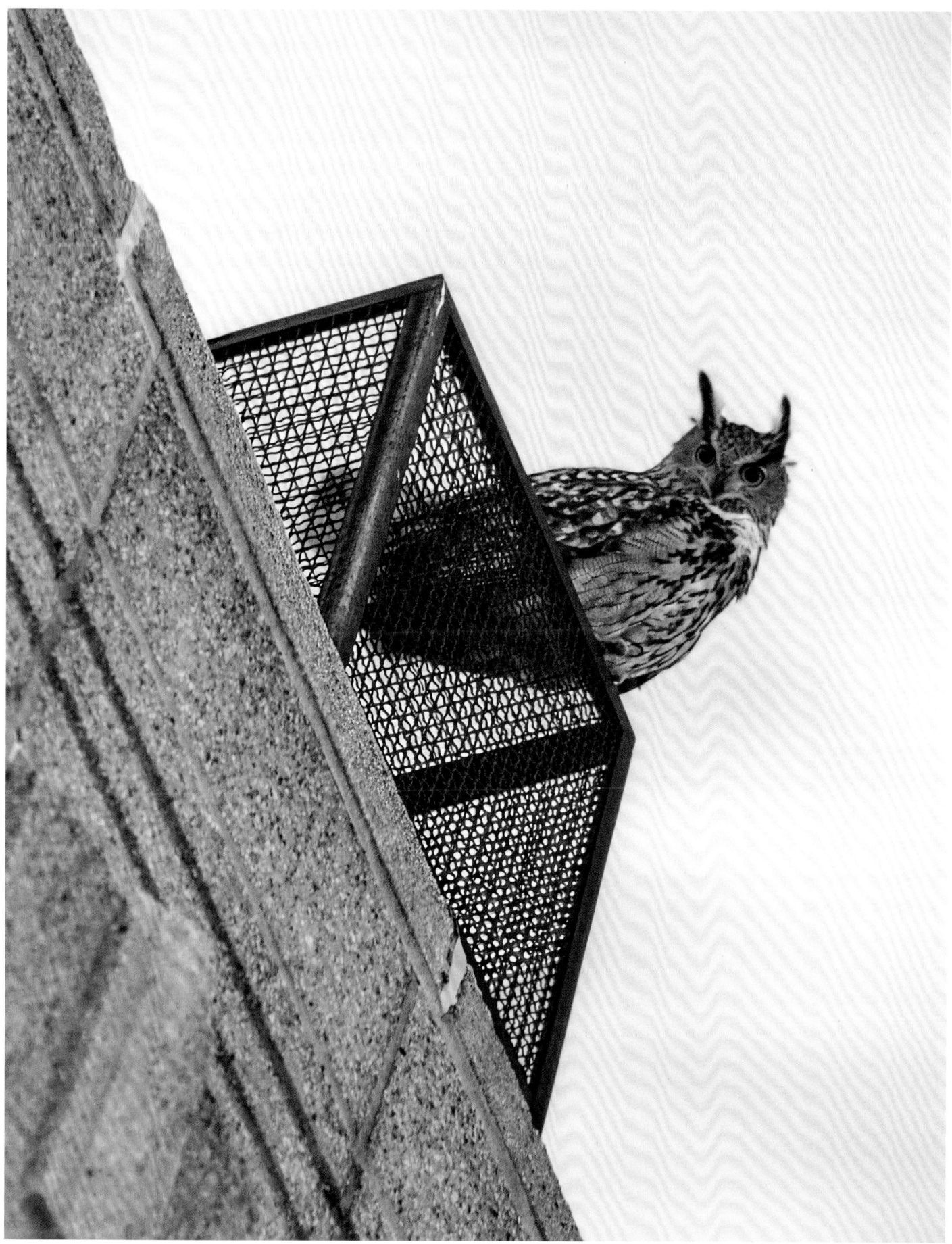

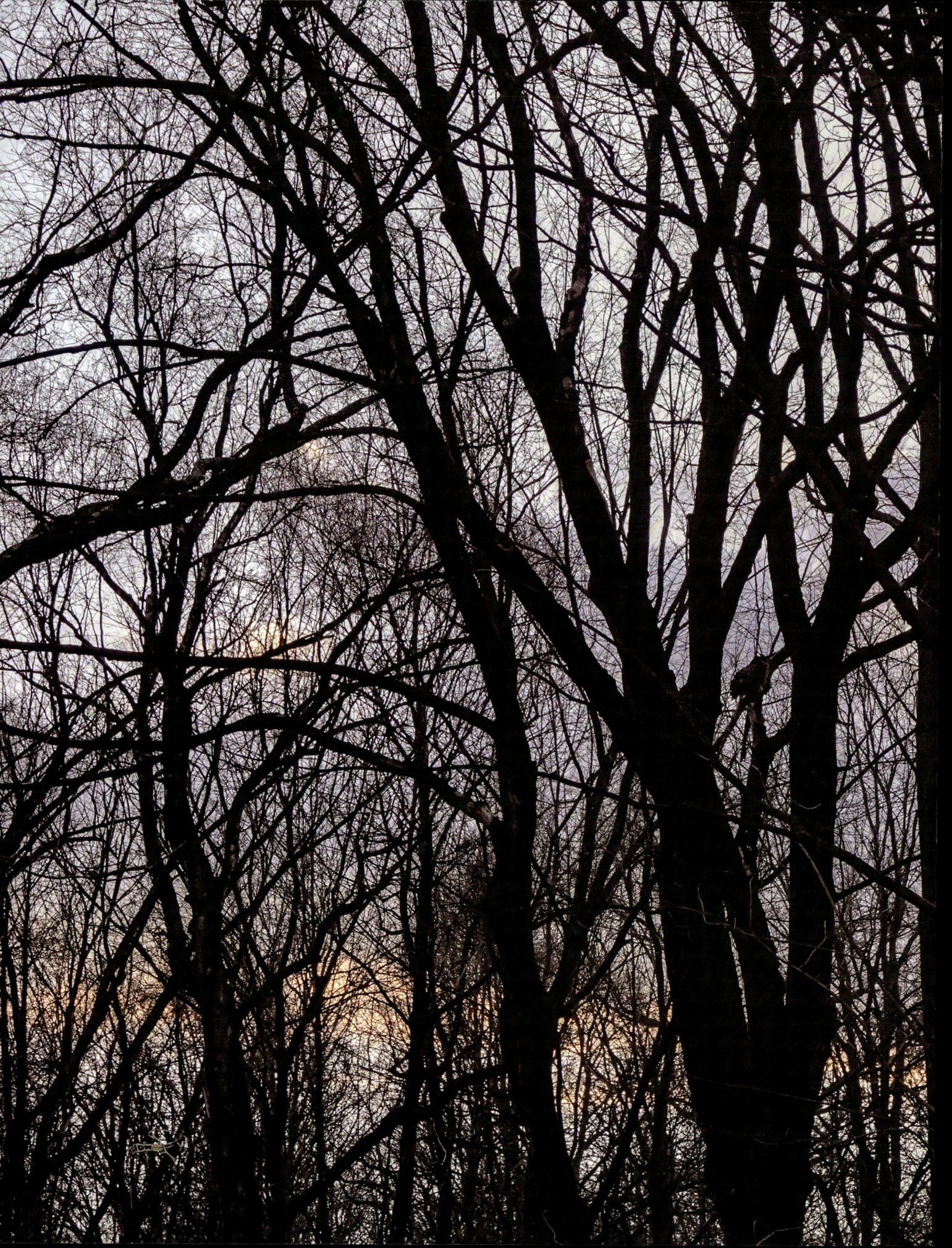

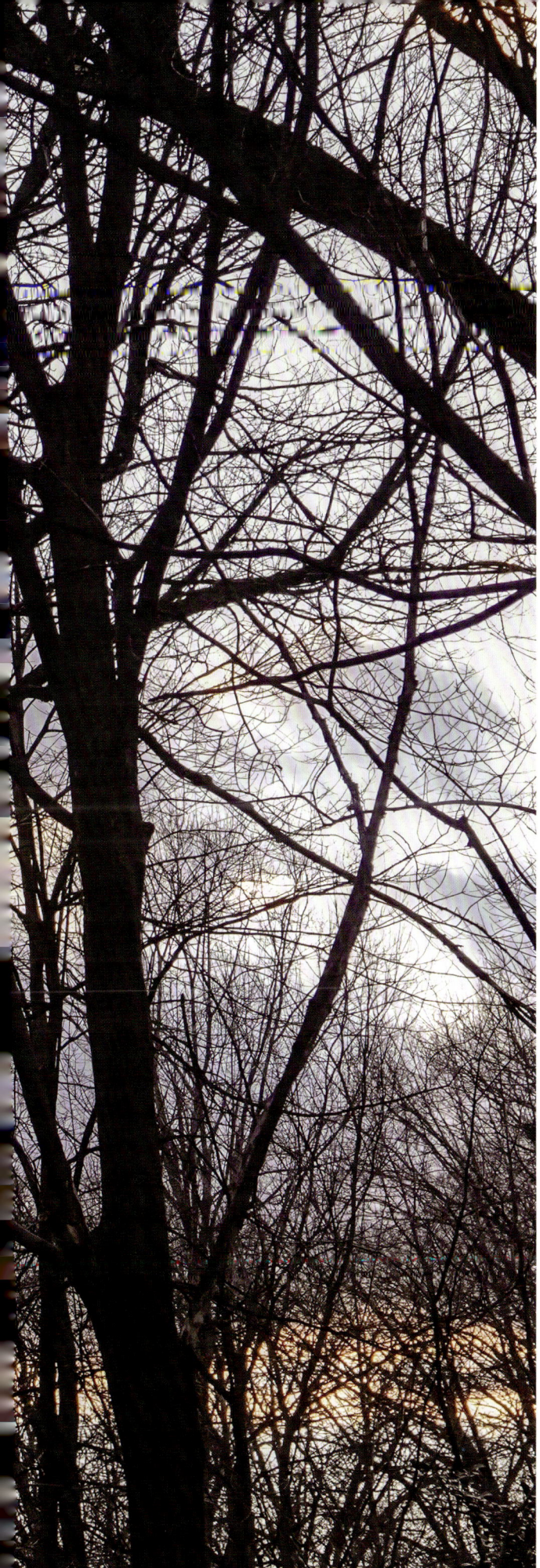

Molly Eustis, *Flaco in the Loch at Dusk,* 1/13/24, 4:30 p.m.

This was the last time anyone saw Flaco in Central Park, to my knowledge (or at least during the day). The Loch was one of his regular roosting spots from early 2023. I saw the photographers first, then looked up and spotted his silhouette almost immediately. I was indescribably happy to see him back in the park—and in general, as I hadn't seen much of Flaco in the weeks prior. It was very windy, but the light was beautiful late-afternoon winter light through the bare trees—my favorite. Most of our old flyout group was there, and we watched him fly out, ultimately making his way to the Construction Site, where he perched in many of his old favorite spots, including the Komatsu. We were all elated.

Following spread Paul Beiboer, *Flaco on the Chimney, on the One-Year Anniversary of His Freedom,* Upper West Side, 2/2/24, 9:50 p.m.

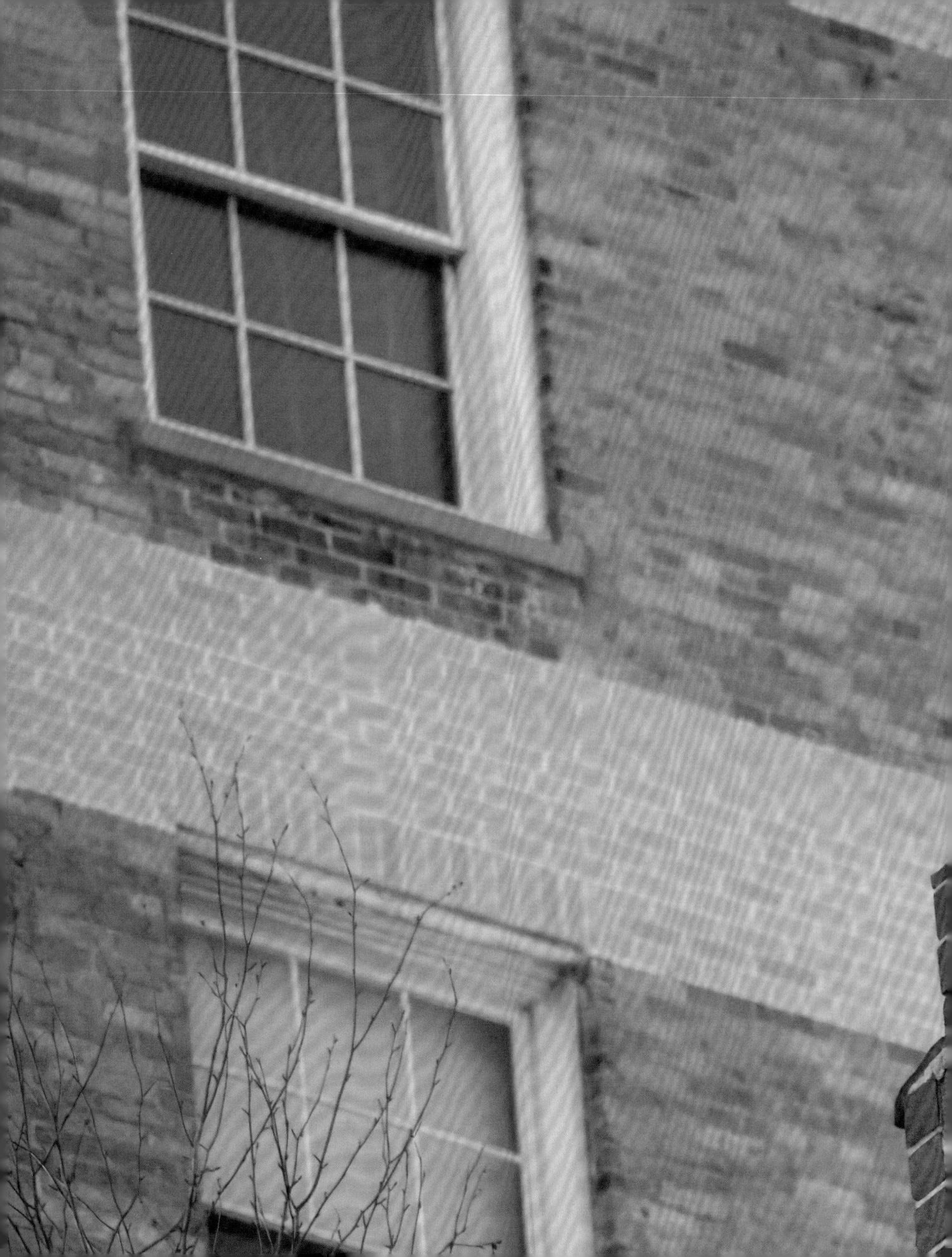

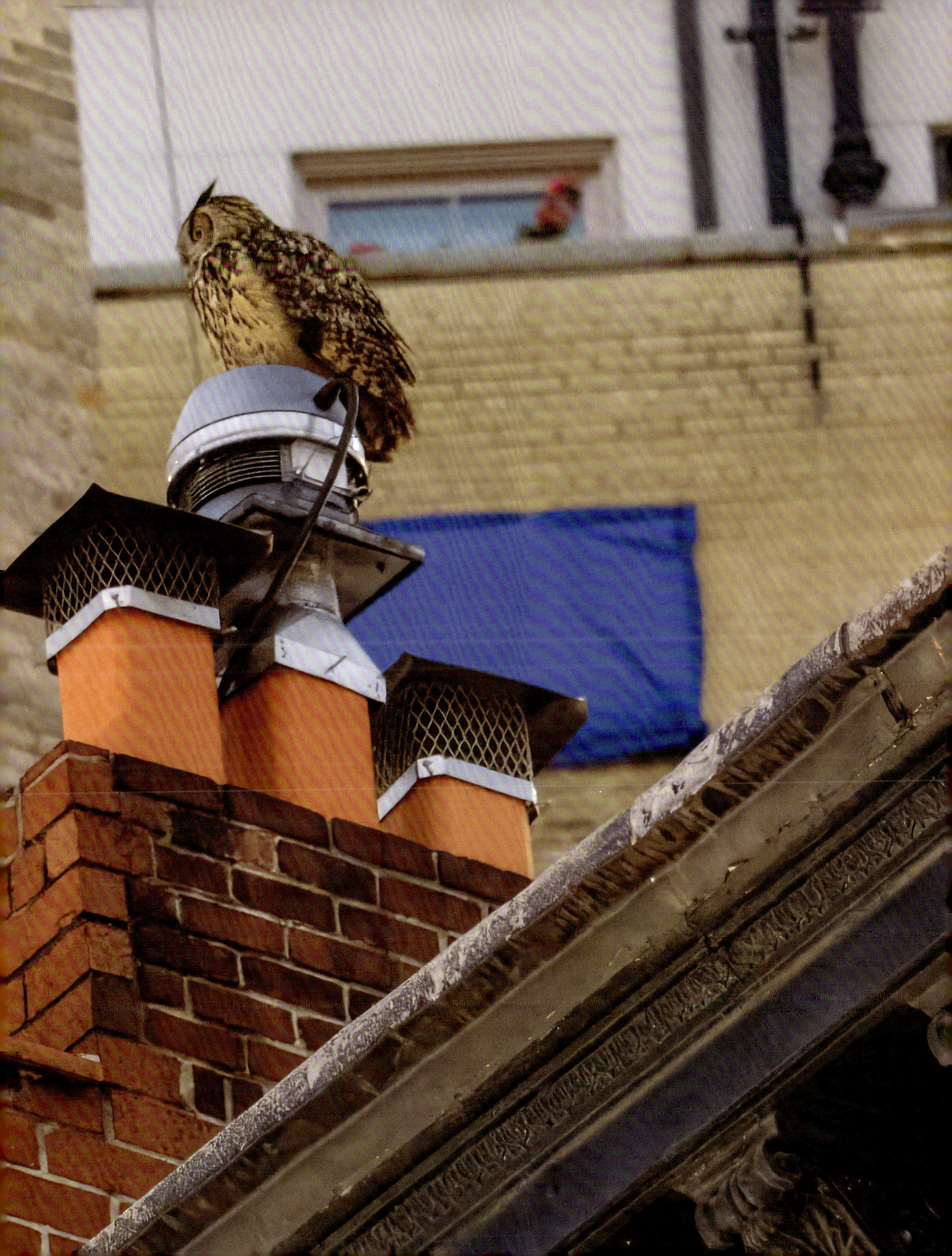

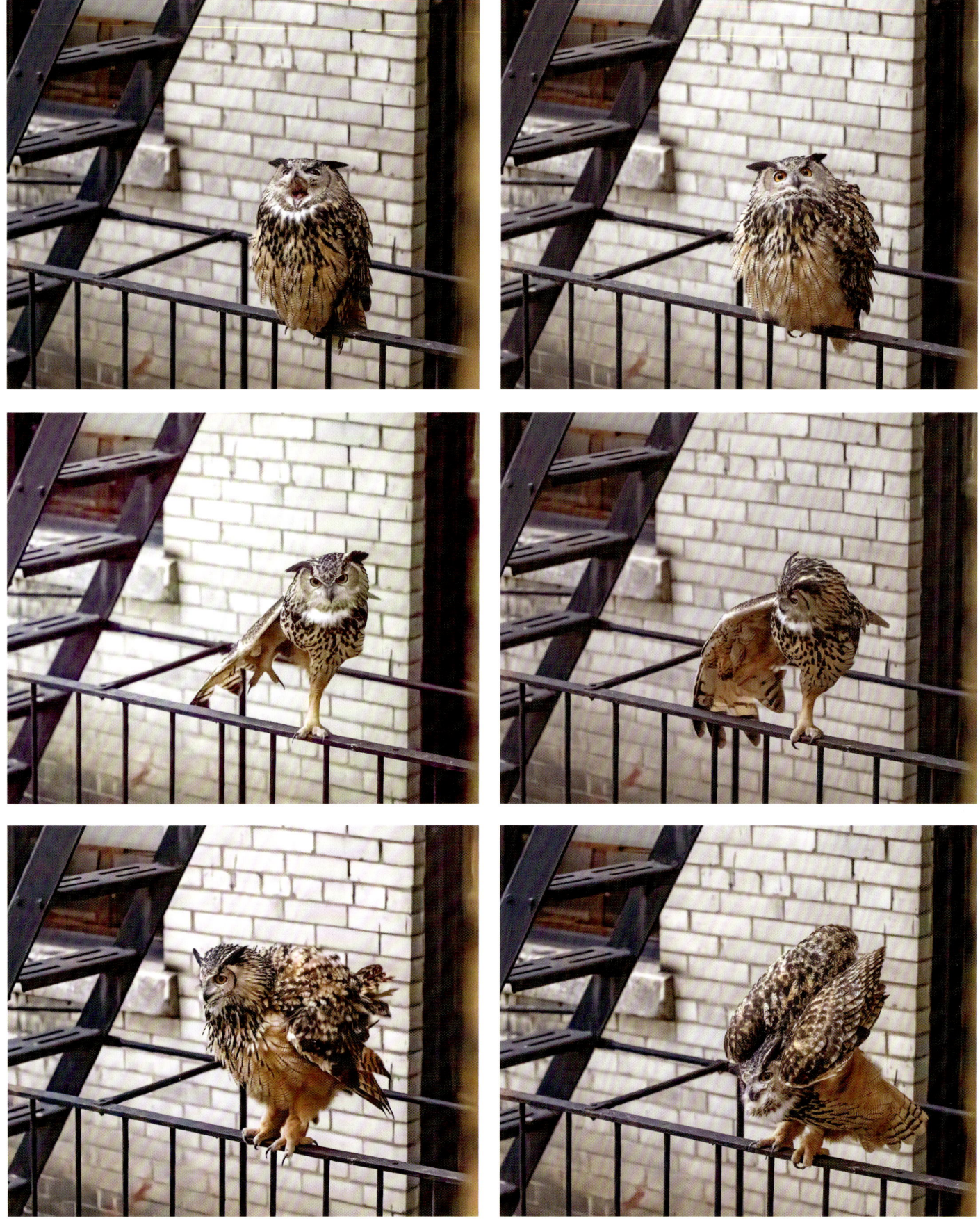

When a 75-pound dog wakes you at 3:00 a.m. with a bathroom emergency — you walk him no matter how groggily.

On an Upper West Side weeknight, it can actually be a lovely hour for a walk. West End Avenue is empty but well-lit. Doormen acknowledge you with a sleepy nod and smile as you pass. Occasionally, you encounter another shuffling owner imploring their pup to do their business. And it's wonderfully quiet. Cars zooming up the West Side Highway sound like waves breaking on the shore if you listen carefully.

And suddenly, in the silence, there was a loud but gentle *WHOOOO*.

Of course, I knew about Flaco, the outlaw owl. I photographed him soon after his escape when he was still staying in Central Park. I'd often see him in "Flaco's Tree." But it wasn't until a year later that I heard him. And he was on our building.

I found his feather outside the next day, but it turned out I didn't need the evidence. The building was buzzing with the news: "Did you hear the owl last night?" "So and so saw him!" "Was it really Flaco?"

Flaco had chosen a perch in our courtyard, poignantly located outside the window of the now-empty apartment of a long-time resident who had just passed.

Residents I had hardly spoken to in my 20 years here became fast friends, texting when he showed up and when he flew out. Generous neighbors let me into their apartment to photograph through their windows. He brought us together, excited that this avian underdog continued to choose our fire escapes and windowsills every day.

Watching him was an experience in paradoxes. It was exciting but meditative. He was solitary but brought us together. He exuded fortitude, yet we worried for him.

Flaco would get us to stop scrolling and fretting to instead quiet ourselves, stay still, and focus on appreciating what was right in front of us, for hours at a time, every day. Until the day he didn't.

We all knew how unlikely it was that this dream would last for as long as we hoped it would. There were just too many odds against him. The last time he flew off our fire escape was the last time he was seen before the dream ended.

But Flaco's magic still lingers. We might have had to wake up from our lovely dream, but we're still so lucky to have had it at all.

MARIANNE DeMARCO

Marianne DeMarco, *Flaco Preening Before Flyout*, Upper West Side, 2/10/24, 6:24–6:31 p.m.

Marianne DeMarco, *Weegee Flaco (Infrared),* Upper West Side, 2/12/24, 5:35 p.m.

You could always tell when it was approaching time for Flaco to fly off to his nighttime adventures as he would start his meticulous grooming.

As there was less light at this hour, I wanted to use a flash—but I feared that using such a bright light would discomfit Flaco. I decided to use an infrared system. While owls have exceptional night vision, they aren't able to see the infrared wavelength.

Happily, it worked. I was able to use flash to photograph Flaco without interrupting his preening. In infrared, the photos reminded me of the legendary photojournalist Weegee's stark black-and-white photos from the 1930s and 40s.

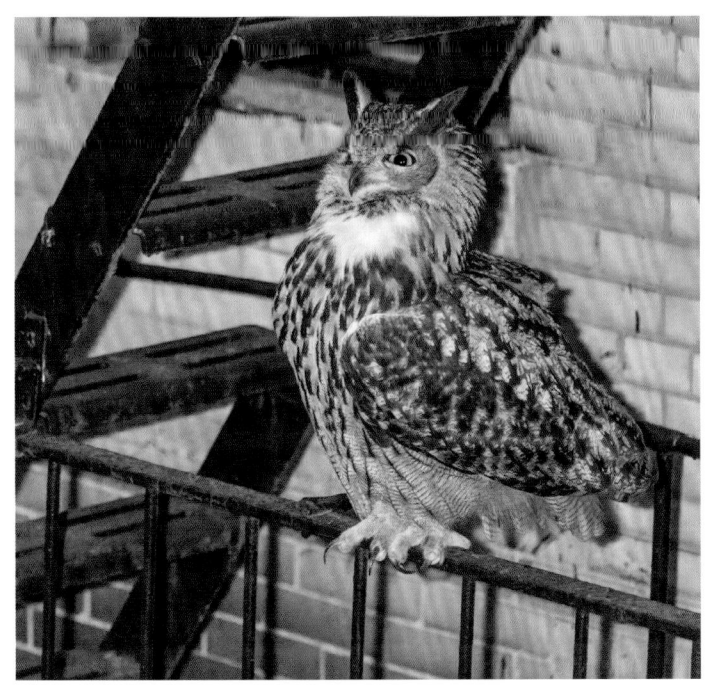
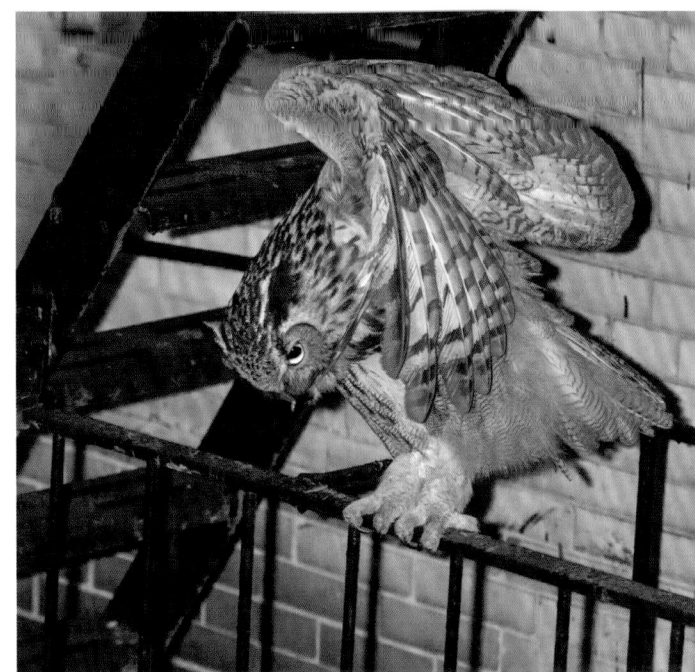
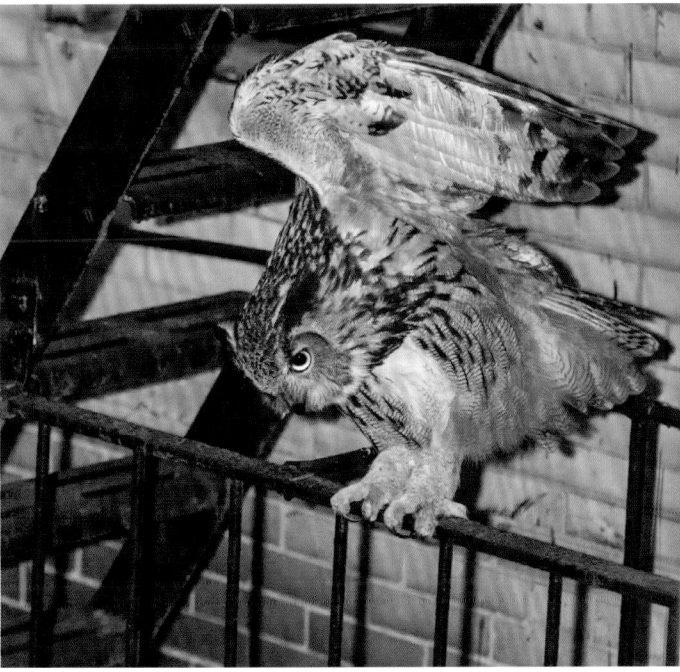
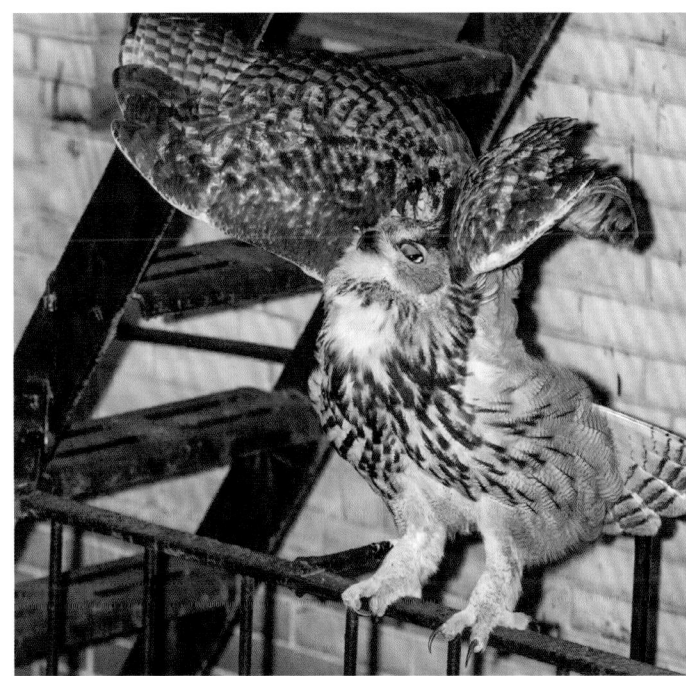

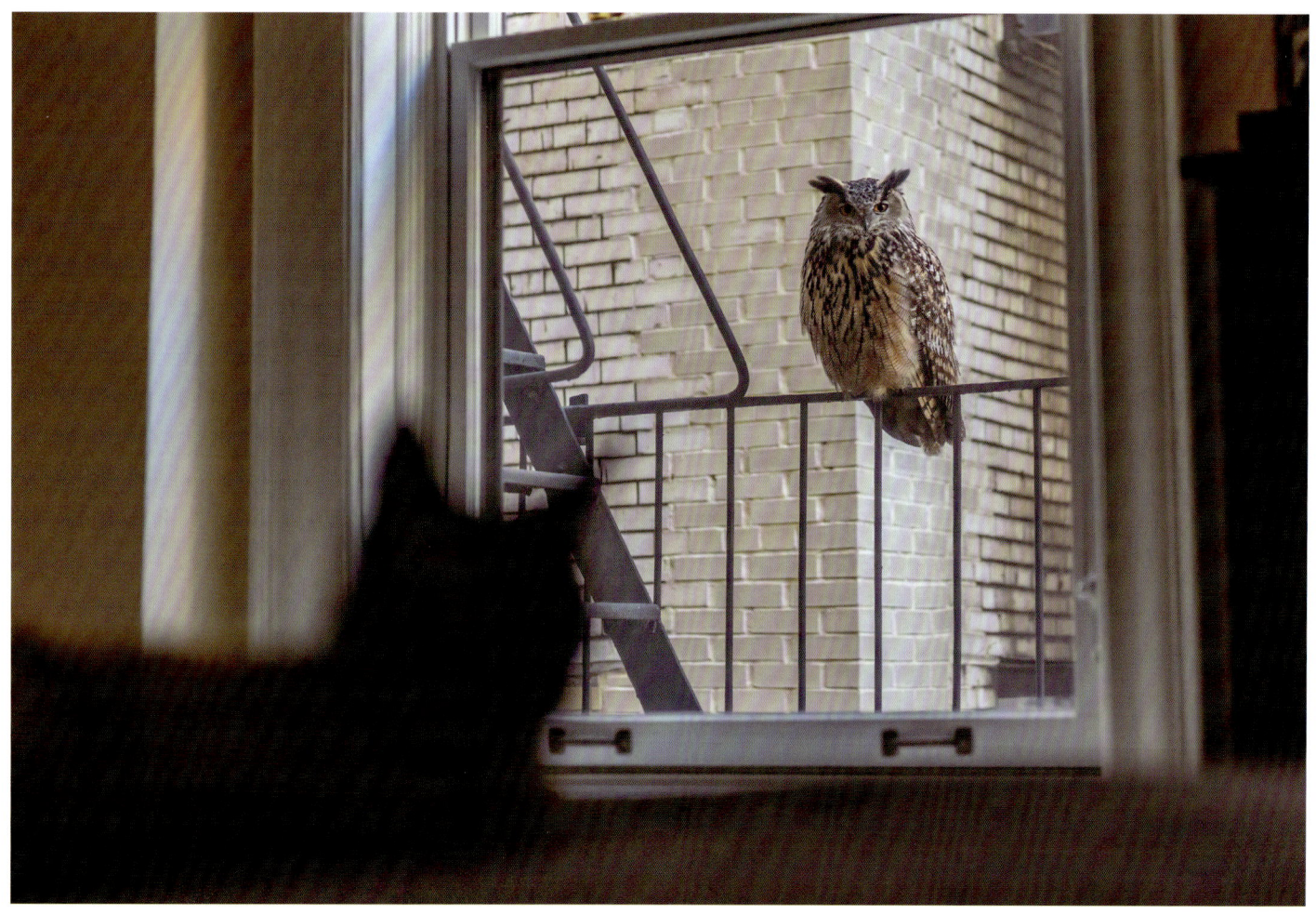

Marianne DeMarco, *Flaco & Indie the Cat,* Upper West Side, 2/16/24, 5:07 p.m.

One of the times Flaco found a new perch on our building was this evening when he roosted outside my neighbors' bedroom. Both the cat "Indie" and Flaco were unbothered by each other. After taking a moment to appreciate each other's style, they spent several contented hours alternating between grooming and sleeping.

Right   Marianne DeMarco, *Flaco in a Snowstorm,* Upper West Side, 2/13/24, 9:30 a.m.

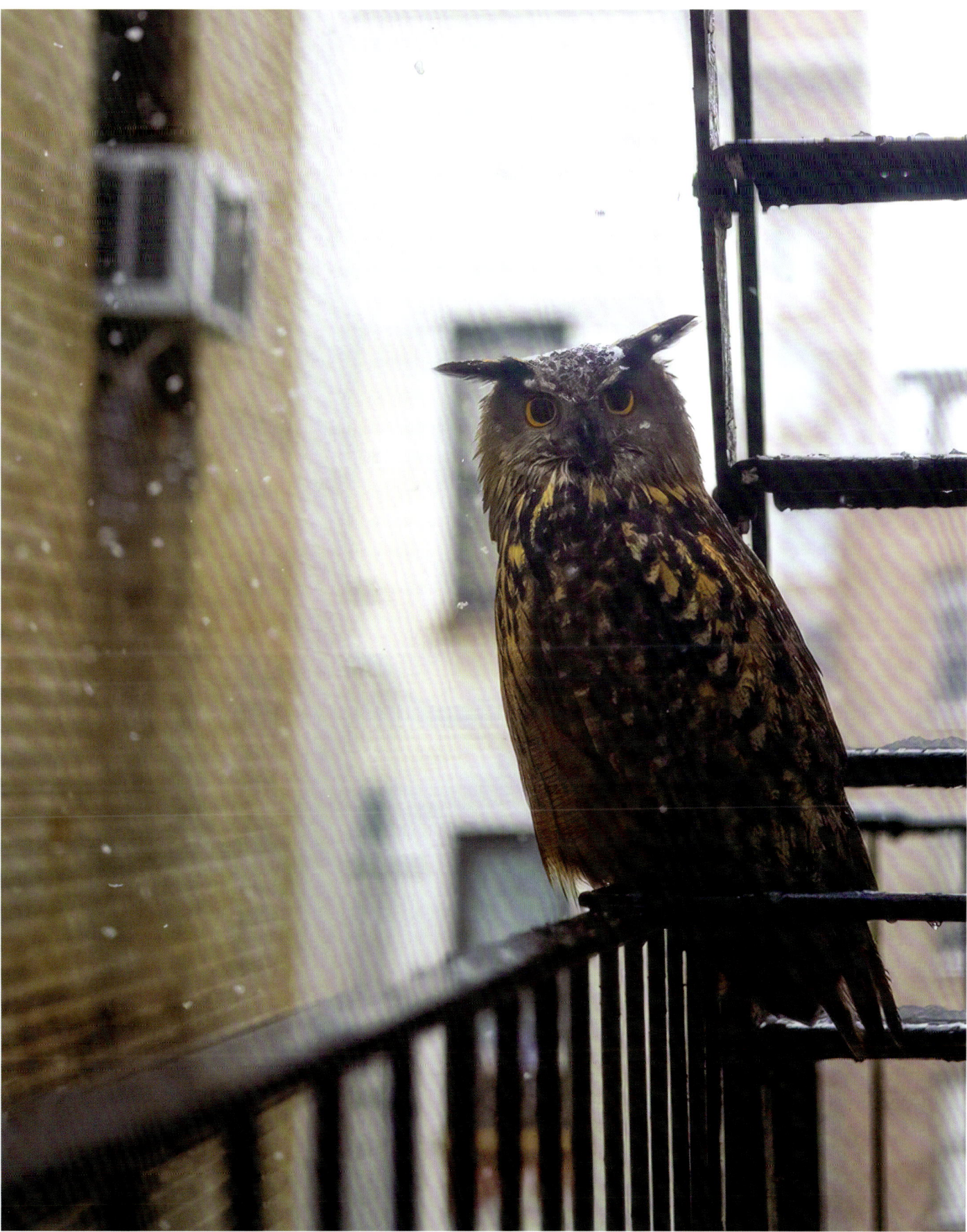

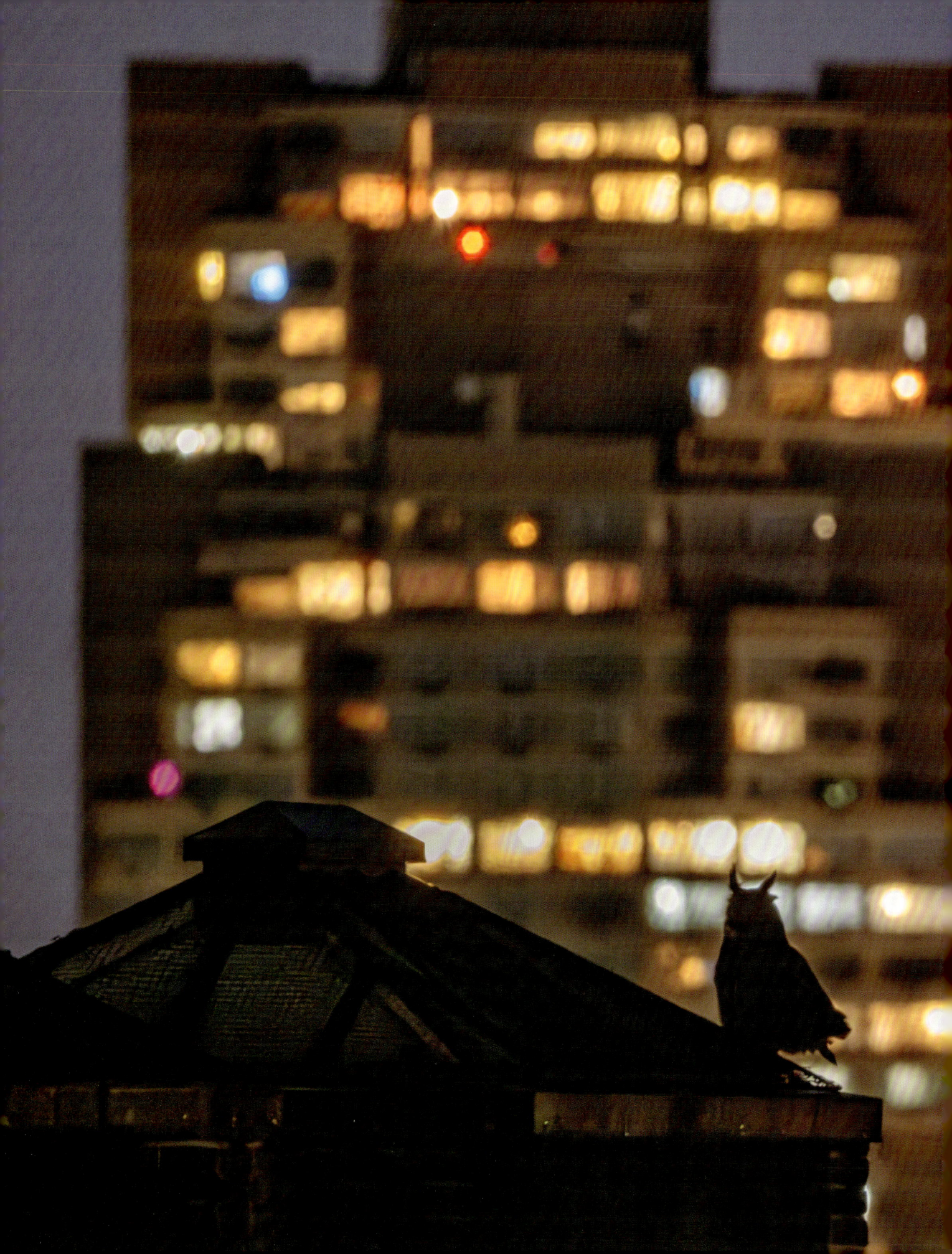

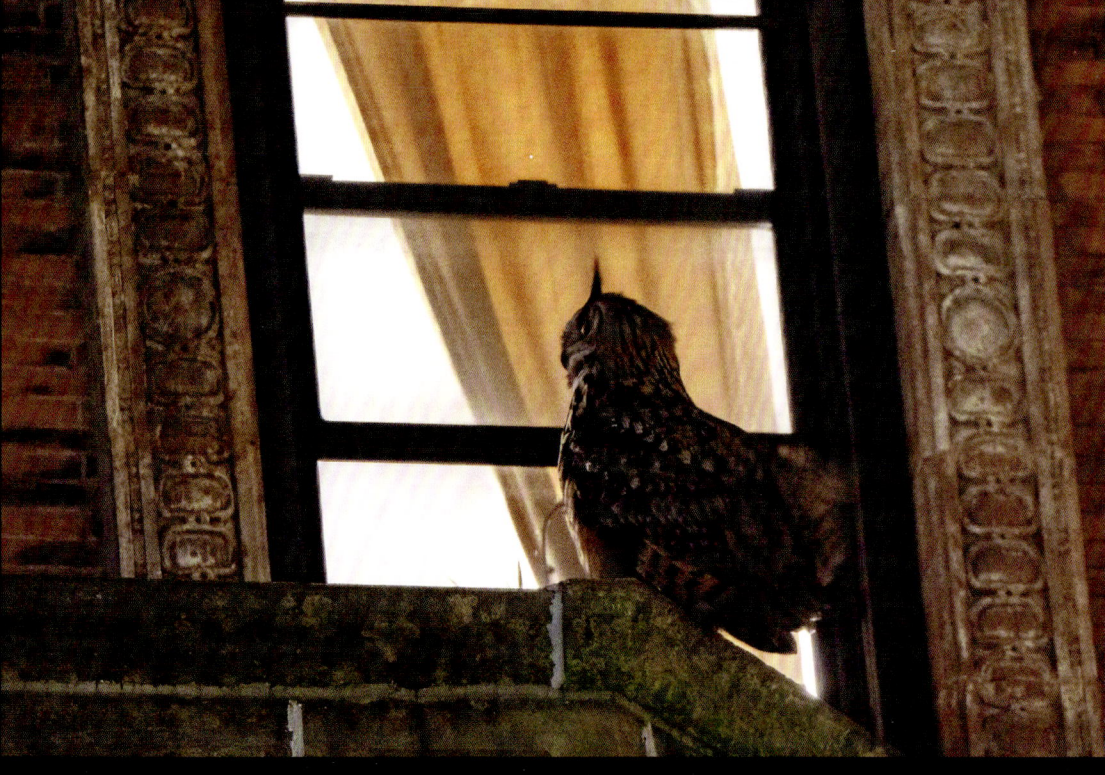

[Penny Lane, a filmmaker, and her crew, working on a Flaco documentary] arranged for a get-together on the one-year anniversary of Flaco being free on February 2nd, 2024. And they called me up and said, "Hey, do you want to join? We're getting some people together. We're going to meet at, let's say, 90th and Broadway and see if we can find Flaco."

It's a Friday night and I'm like, "Hey, yeah, I'll be there," but at the same time, I thought there is no way we're going to see him. Hello, what are the chances? We're just standing on Broadway and 90th. What are the chances we're actually going to see Flaco? There had been sightings—fire escapes, water towers, whatever, but he wasn't consistently in one place at that time. He was moving around a lot.

We're standing there: I think it was 89th Street between Broadway and West End Avenue, heading west, like fifteen people, including film crew and Flaco's most loyal fans . . . and there's Flaco! And he's sitting on one of these brownstones, like, maybe twenty yards away, and he's sitting on the balcony. This was on the day there was quite a lot of news coverage: Flaco's one year of freedom. And it was funny because Flaco is sitting on the balcony of a brownstone, again fifteen to twenty yards away, and he's literally looking inside the building—and then he flies across the street, and he's looking inside another window. It was almost like he was seeing himself on the TV.

That's what it felt like.

And then he popped up and he sits on a chimney. Here we are, fifteen people celebrating his one year of freedom, and out of nowhere he just comes to say, "Hi," and flies across the street and hangs around a bit before disappearing and flying up to some higher building.

That's just an incredible moment. Incredible.

PAUL BEIBOER

Previous spread   Paul Beiboer, *Flaco and City Lights,* Upper West Side, 2/17/24, 10:40 p.m.

This is one of the last photos of Flaco. That evening, I observed him from around 10:00 till 11:30 p.m. He still seemed fine that evening as he perched on this rooftop and moved between two different water towers on 86th Street, hooting frequently.

Paul Beiboer, *Flaco on the One-Year Anniversary of His Release,* West 89th Street, 2/2/24, 9:55 p.m.

"Do you like

our owl?"

— Rachael Tyrell, a Nexus-7 replicant, asks Rick Deckard, referencing "Eden," the Tyrell Corporation's "animoid" owl, played by a Eurasian eagle-owl in Ridley Scott's *Blade Runner* (1982)

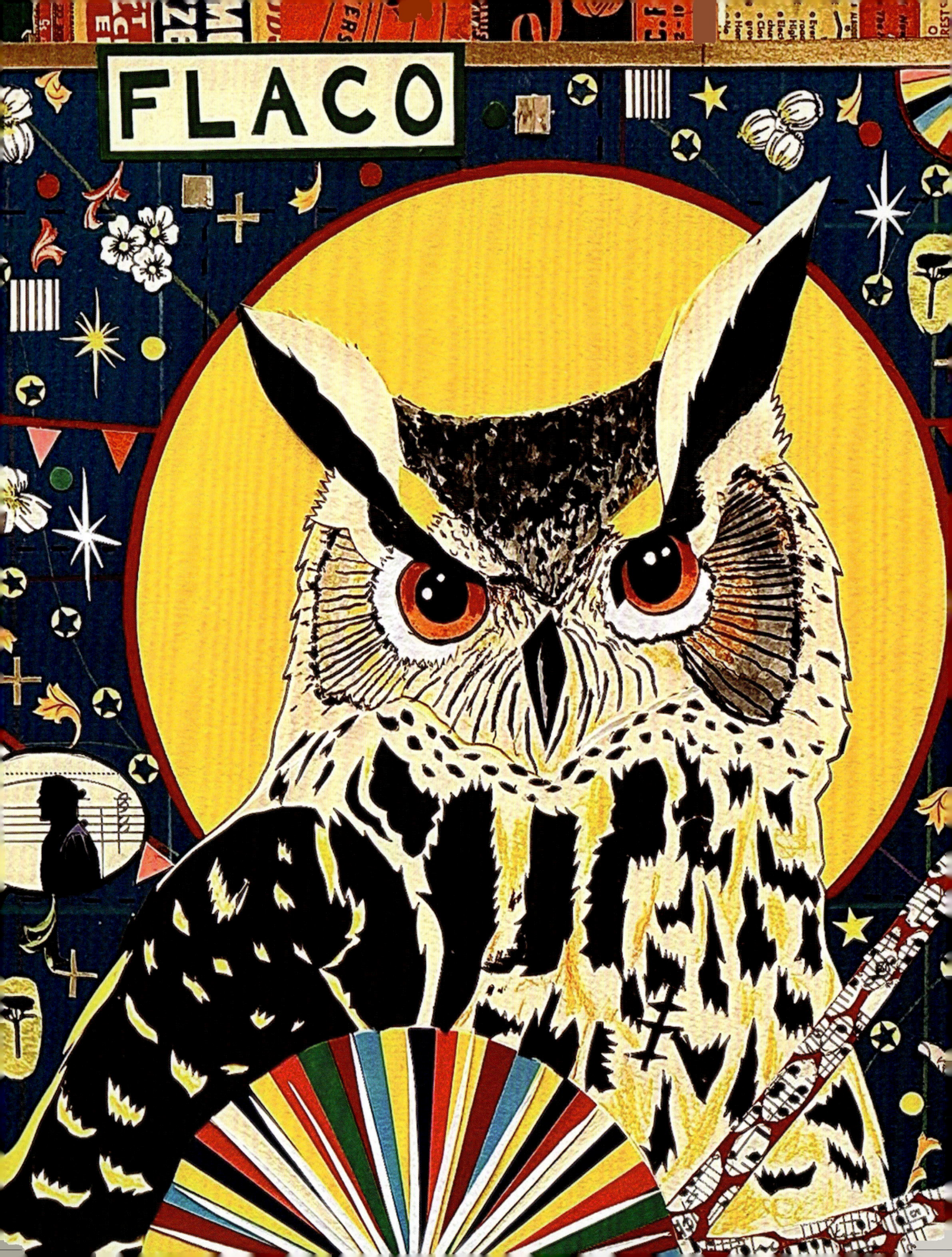

Flaco and the Artists' Vision

Flaco's story inspired a broad swath of creative output, with many works begun or finished on the anniversary dates of his release or passing. Media included a thirteen-foot totem pole, drawing on linen, stitchwork, mixed media, ink and graphite on paper, watercolors, acrylic on canvas, layered collages, tattoos, poetry, songs for acoustic guitar, saxophone solos, and street-art spray painted with limited time. The artists are not just New York-based but work across the country. Some are well-known figures in the Flaco community, while others pivoted within their creative practice or stepped away from other professions to create what was often a singular Flaco-inspired work. Fortunately, in our age where a hashtag is the secret knock to larger creative communities, this rich range of artwork was waiting to be discovered.

Tony Fitzpatrick, Detail from *Flaco (When Everyday Was a 4th of July)*, 2023, drawing/collage, ink, gouache, watercolor, & paper ephemera, 24 x 24 in.

Bill Hutchinson

In September 2023, I said goodbye to my 95-year-old mother, Sumiko, for good. It was one of those tear-drenched Facebook farewells, like the ones we grew accustomed to seeing in the darkest days of the pandemic. My mom was in her West Coast hospital death bed, while I was on the Upper West Side of Manhattan, staring into my tear-drenched cell phone screen, telling her it was okay to let go.

Well, she fooled us all and, like Lazareth, came back from the dead, at least in my mind, having already begun the grieving process. While helping to nurse her back to health, relieved to have more time with her, I regaled her with stories of Flaco and encounters my wife, Lisa, and I had with him in our neighborhood park, which just happens to be Central Park. I showed her the portraits I had made of the Eurasian Eagle-owl and the news stories I had written about.

Having survived World War II dodging American bullets and bombs on Okinawa, she related to the apex predator's survival skills to the point her health dramatically improved. I promised to make her a totem pole topped with Flaco's likeness if she vowed to make it to her 96th birthday. With a chainsaw and a ladder, I brought a dead 13-foot-tall palm stump back to life in a self-portrait with Flaco sitting on my head. And on her 96th birthday, I presented it to her, and we toasted our beloved feathered friend.

Bill Hutchinson, *Flaco's Perch,* 2023, chainsaw-carved totem pole from palm stump, 13 x 2½ ft.

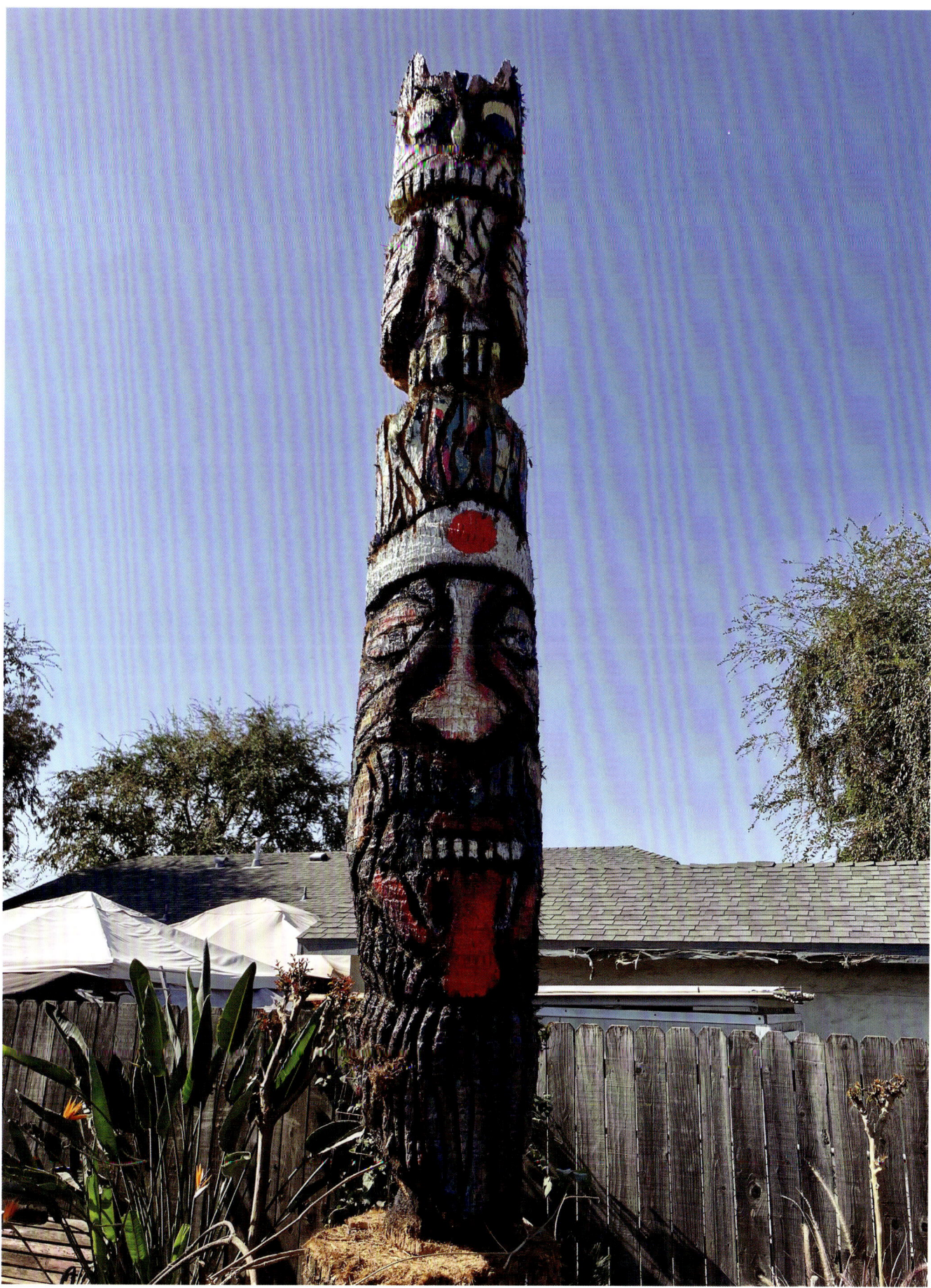

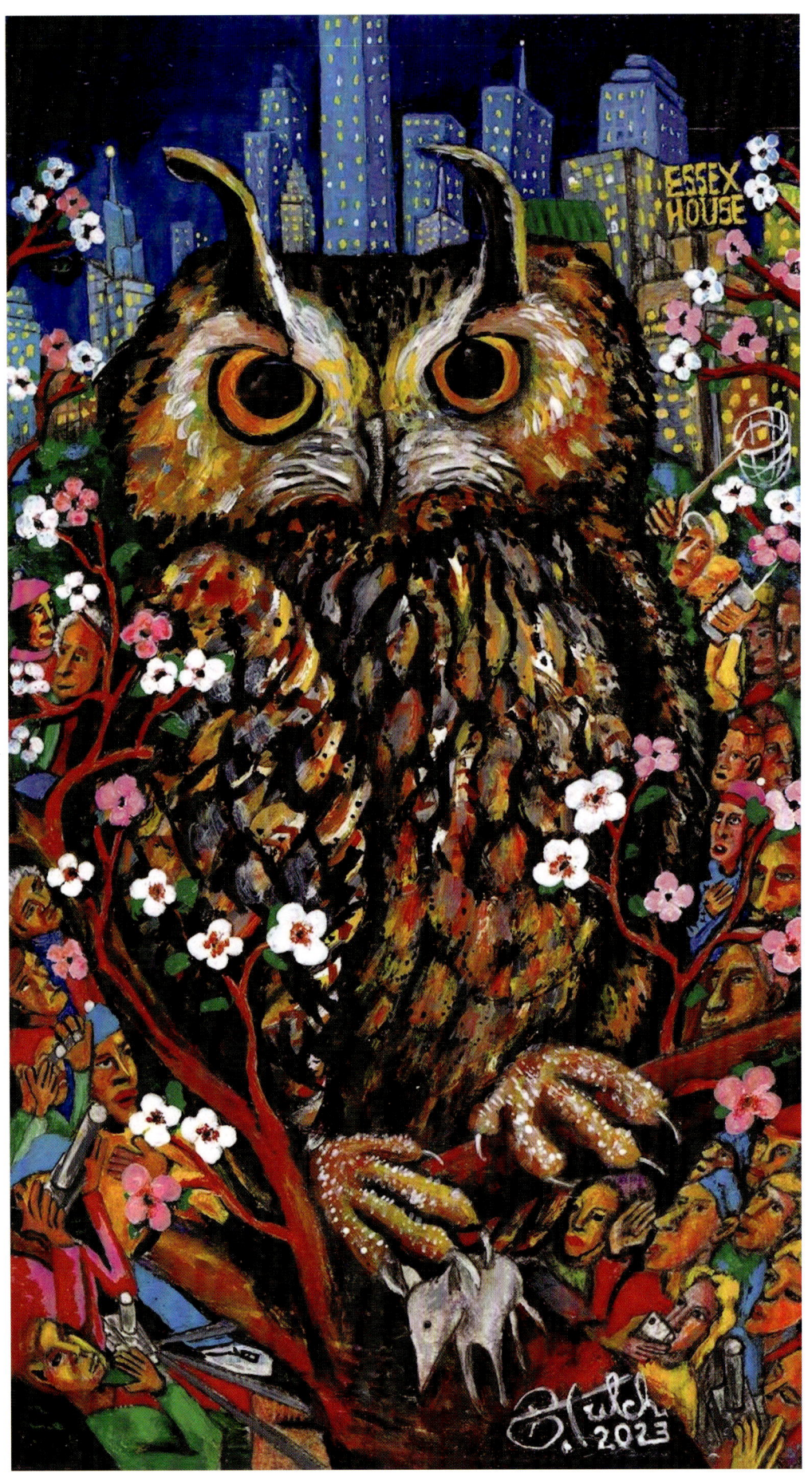

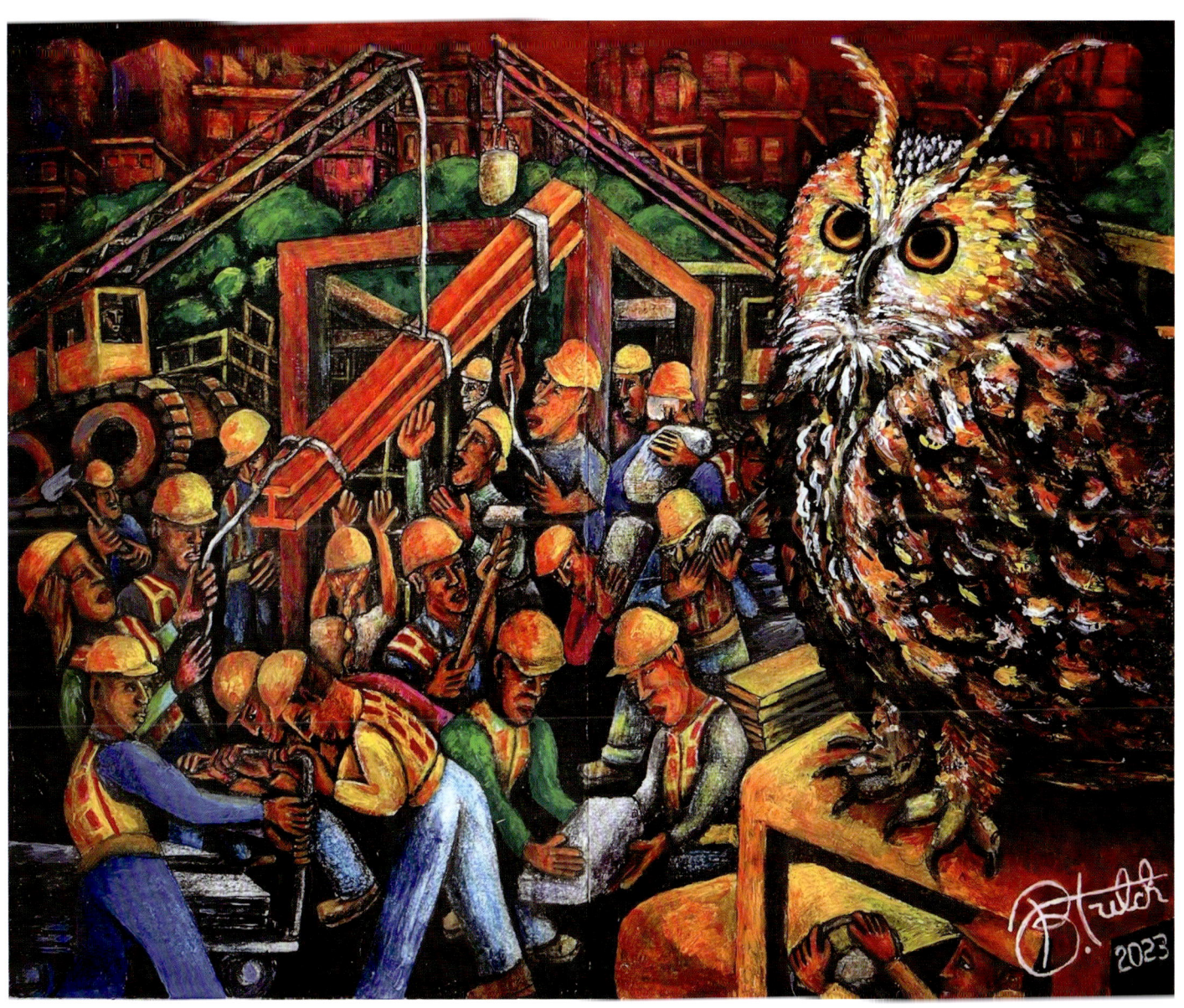

Left Bill Hutchinson, *Flaco the Owl,* 2023, acrylic on paper, 9½ x 6 in.

Above Bill Hutchinson, *Flaco the Foreman,* 2023, acrylic on paper, 11 x 9 in.

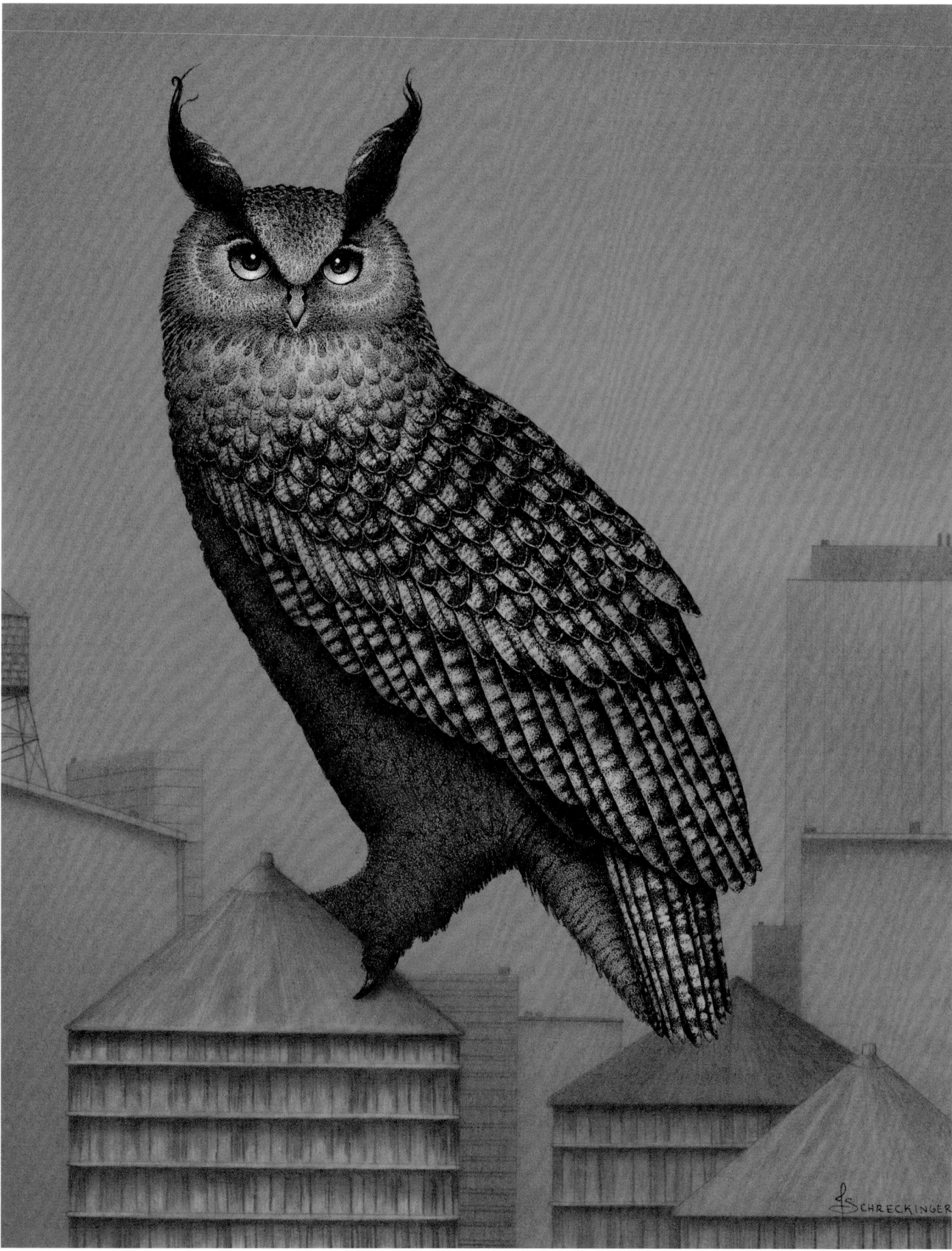

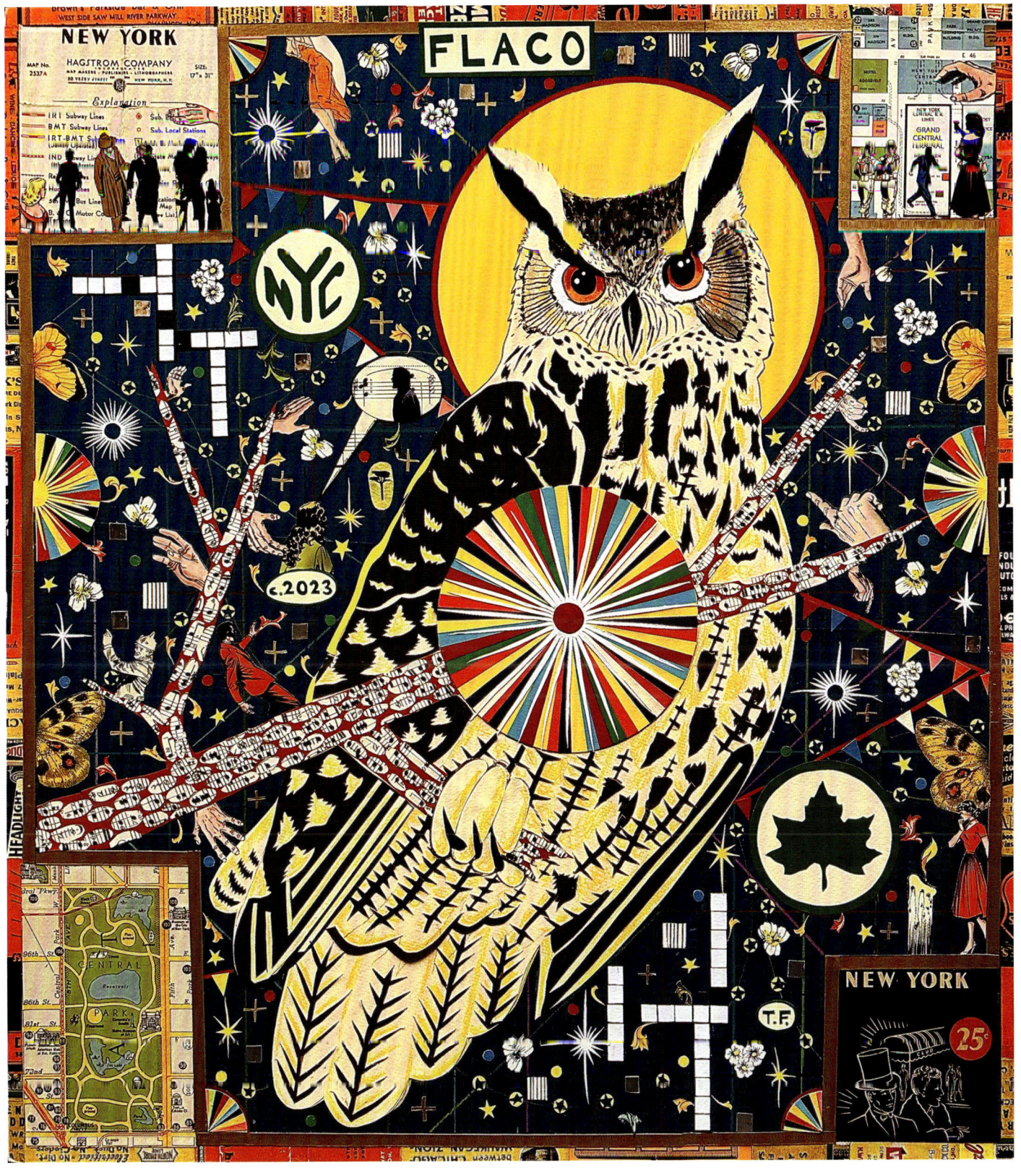

Left Juliet Schreckinger, *Flaco,* 2023, ink and graphite on Arches paper, 8 x 10 in.

Above Tony Fitzpatrick, *Flaco (When Everyday Was a 4th of July),* 2023, drawing/collage, ink, gouache, watercolor, & paper ephemera, 24 x 24 in.

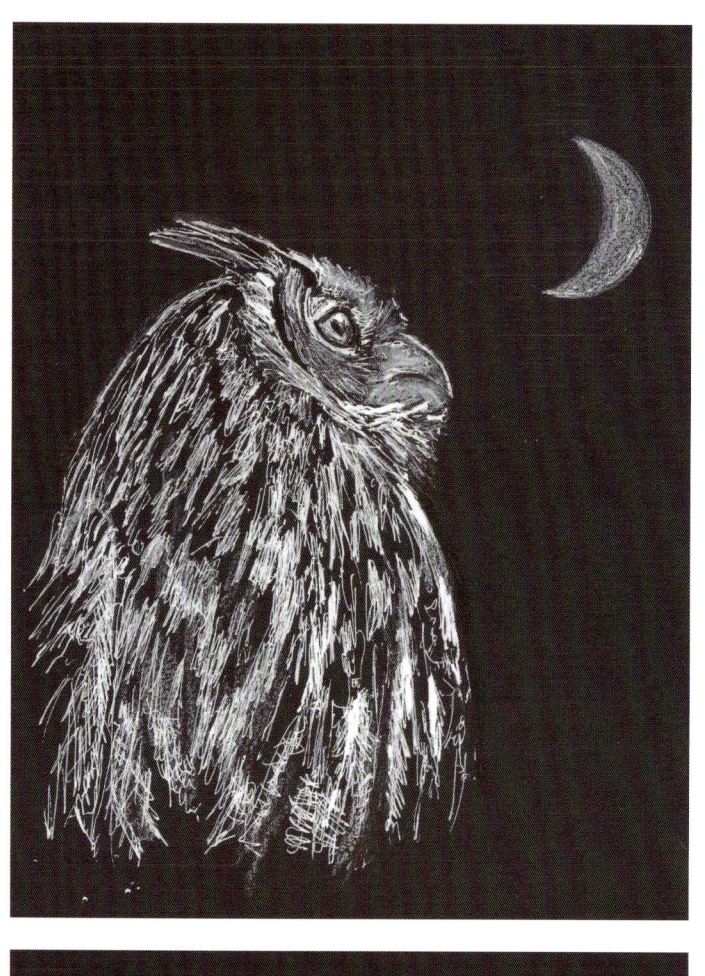
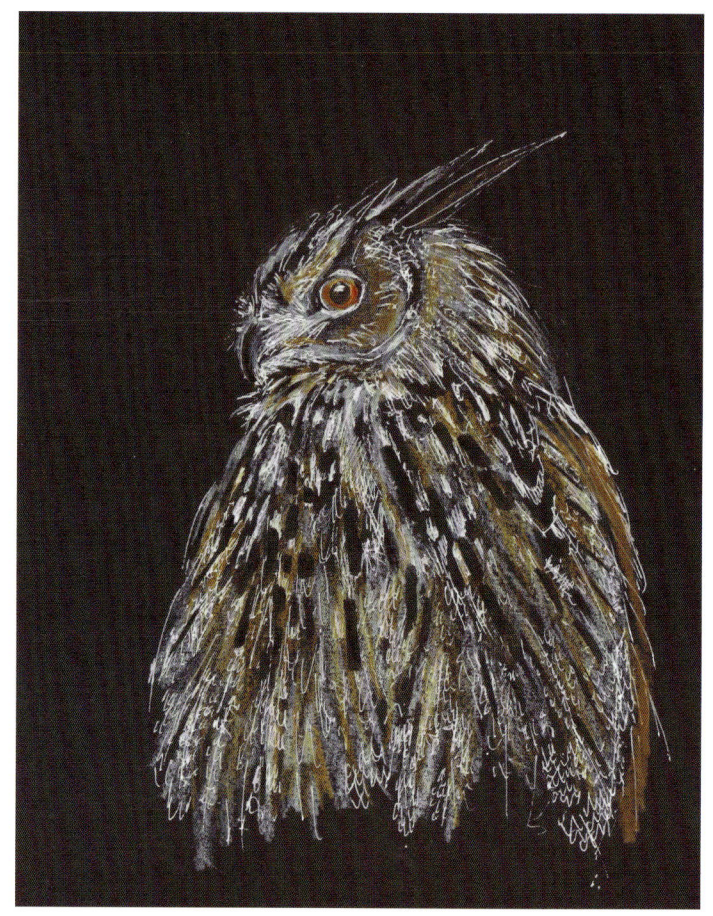
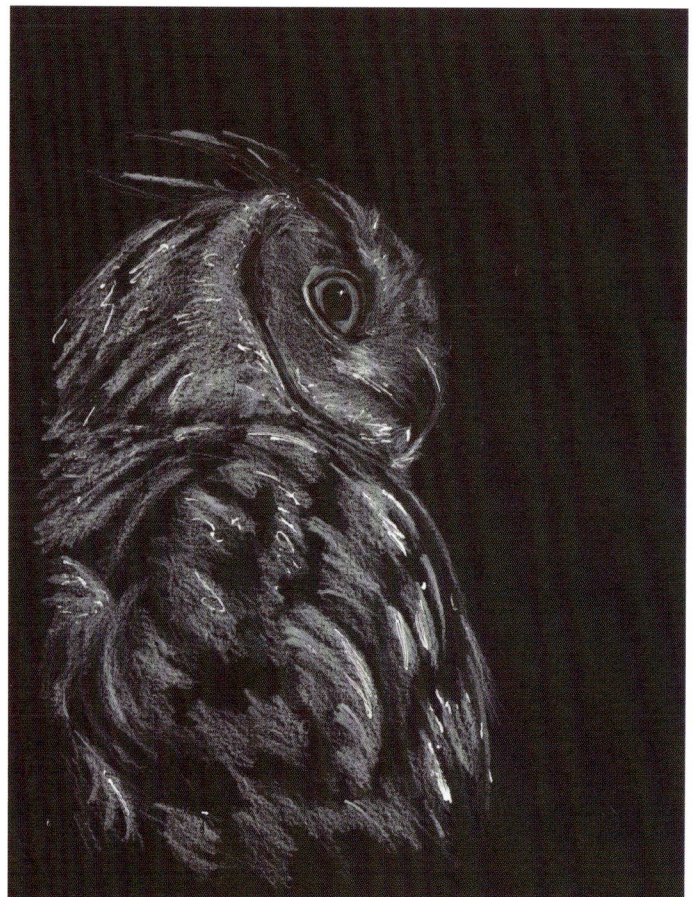
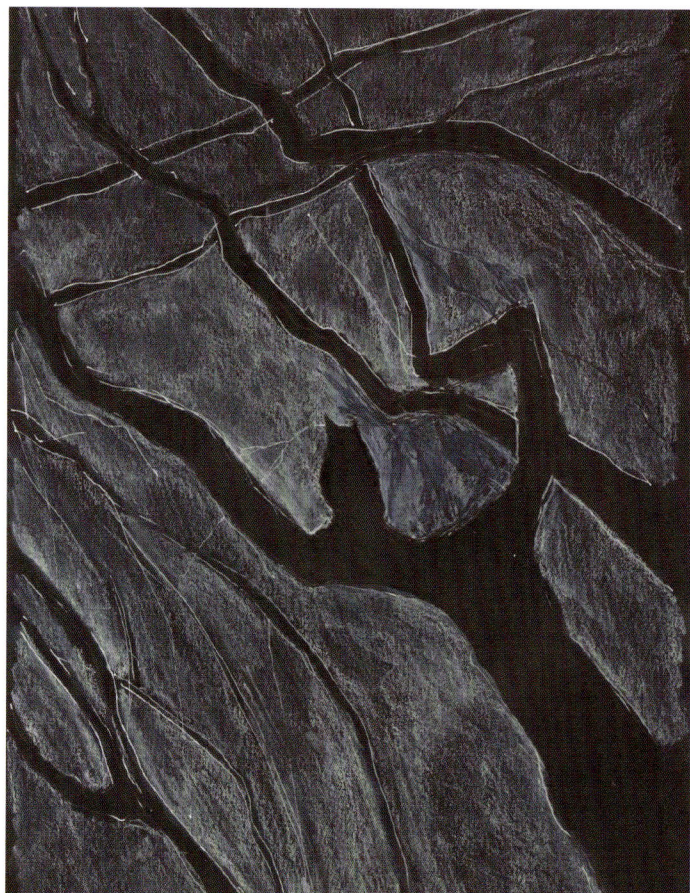

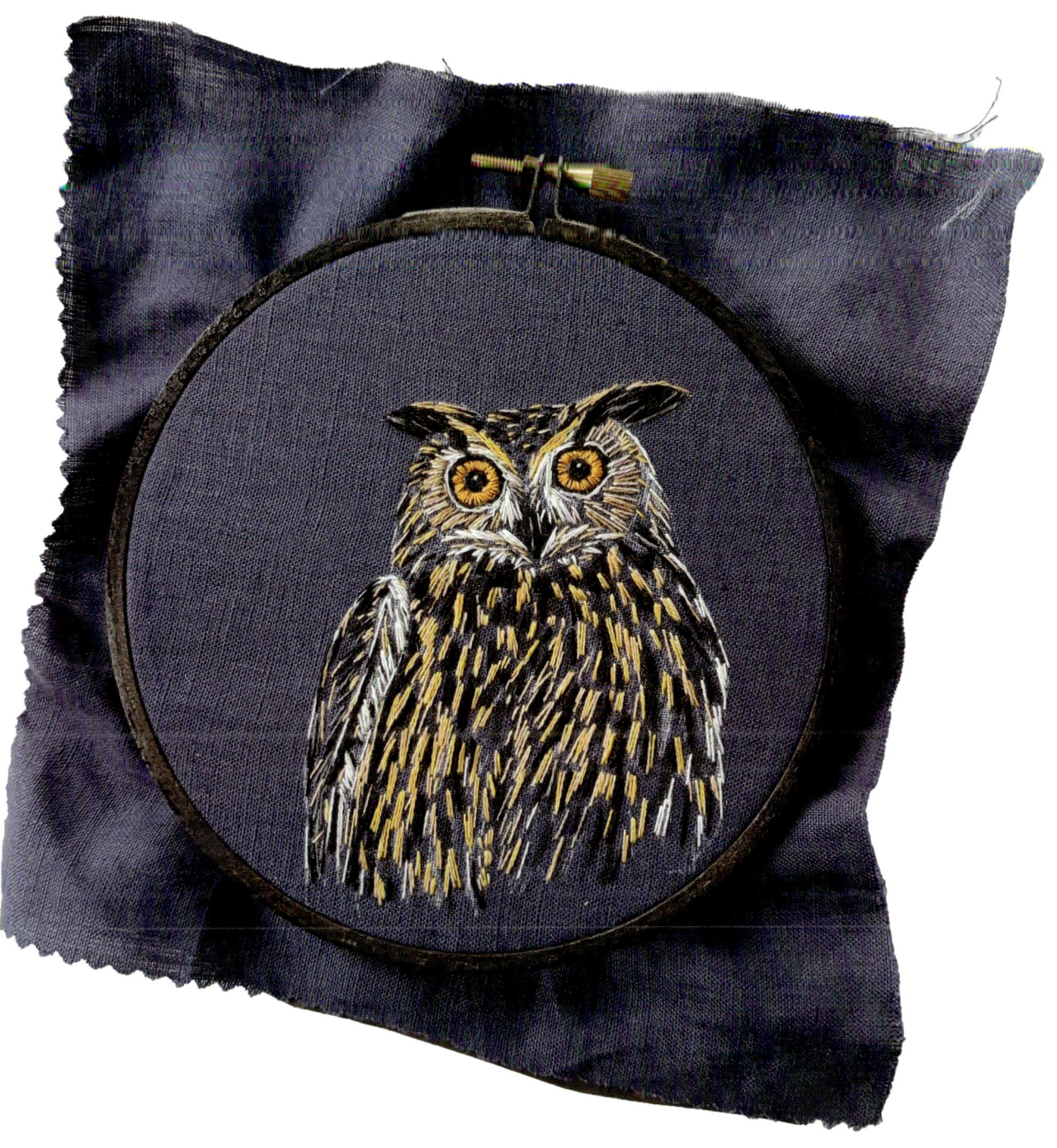

Left Martha Nishida, *Flaco Variations,* 2023, white/colored pencil and Sakura Gelly Roll Pen on paper, 8 x 6 in. Drawings based on photographs by Mark Elliott (top left) and Jacqueline Emery (top right).

Above Martha Nishida, *Untitled,* 2024, wool thread on linen, created expressly for this publication, the first time Nishida had created a Flaco piece since his death, 5¼ in. diameter.

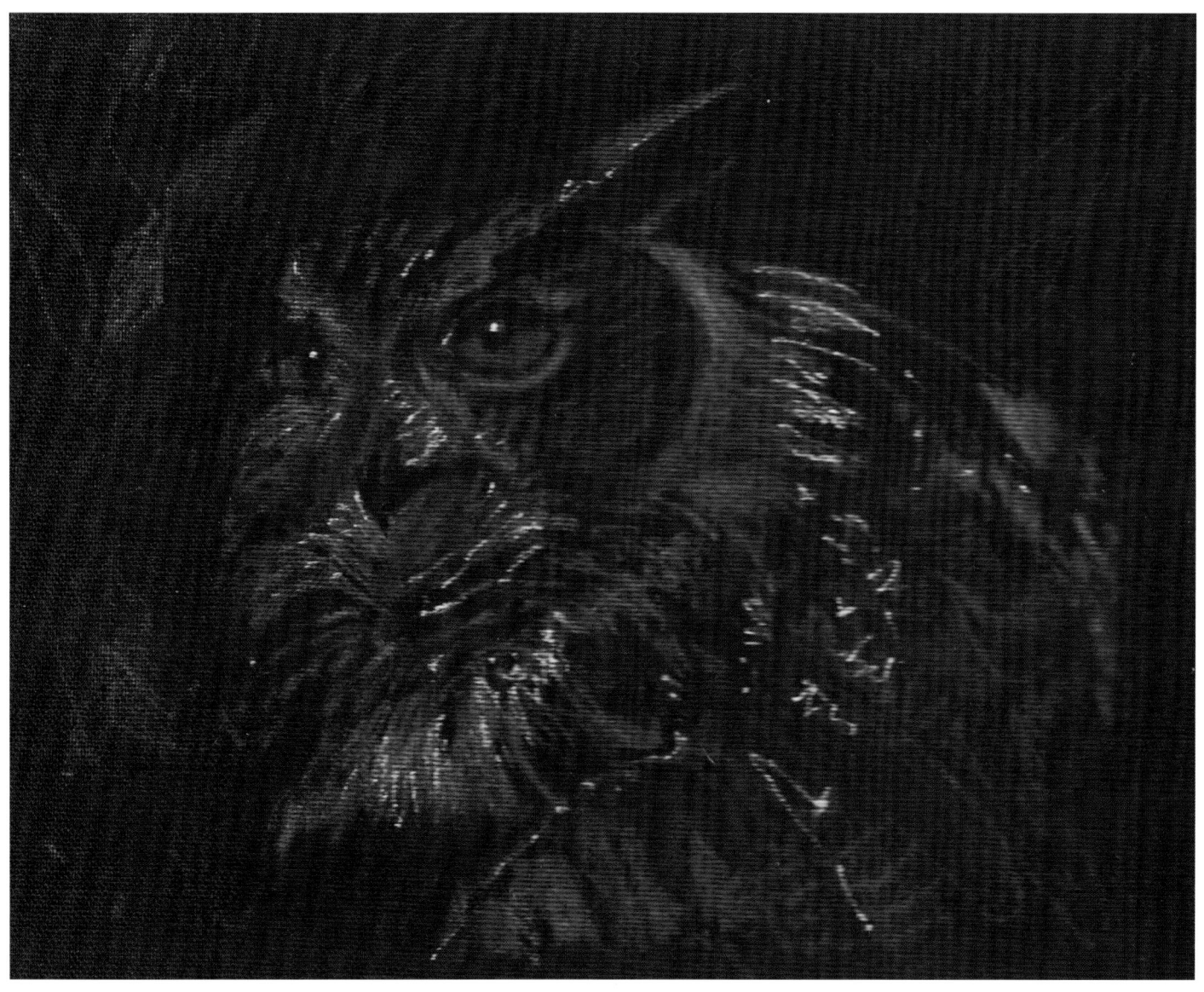

Martha Nishida

As the seasons changed, Flaco experienced each one for the first time. What a joy it was to know that. On a magic morning in early summer, I stood with my husband beneath the elm tree, about 30 feet from Flaco while he preened. A feather fell and wafted slowly down toward us. We didn't move, but my husband held out his hand and the feather landed in his palm.

Above Martha Nishida, *Flaco in the Elm,* 2023, white/colored pencil and Sakura Gelly Roll Pen on linen, 5½ x 7 in. Drawing based on a photograph by Mark Elliott.

Right Martha Nishida, *Flaco Faces,* 2023, wool yarn on wool felt, 2½ x 1½ in.

Following spread Fred Tomaselli, Detail of *February 25, 2024,* 2024, gouache and collage on archival inkjet print, 11 x 14 in.

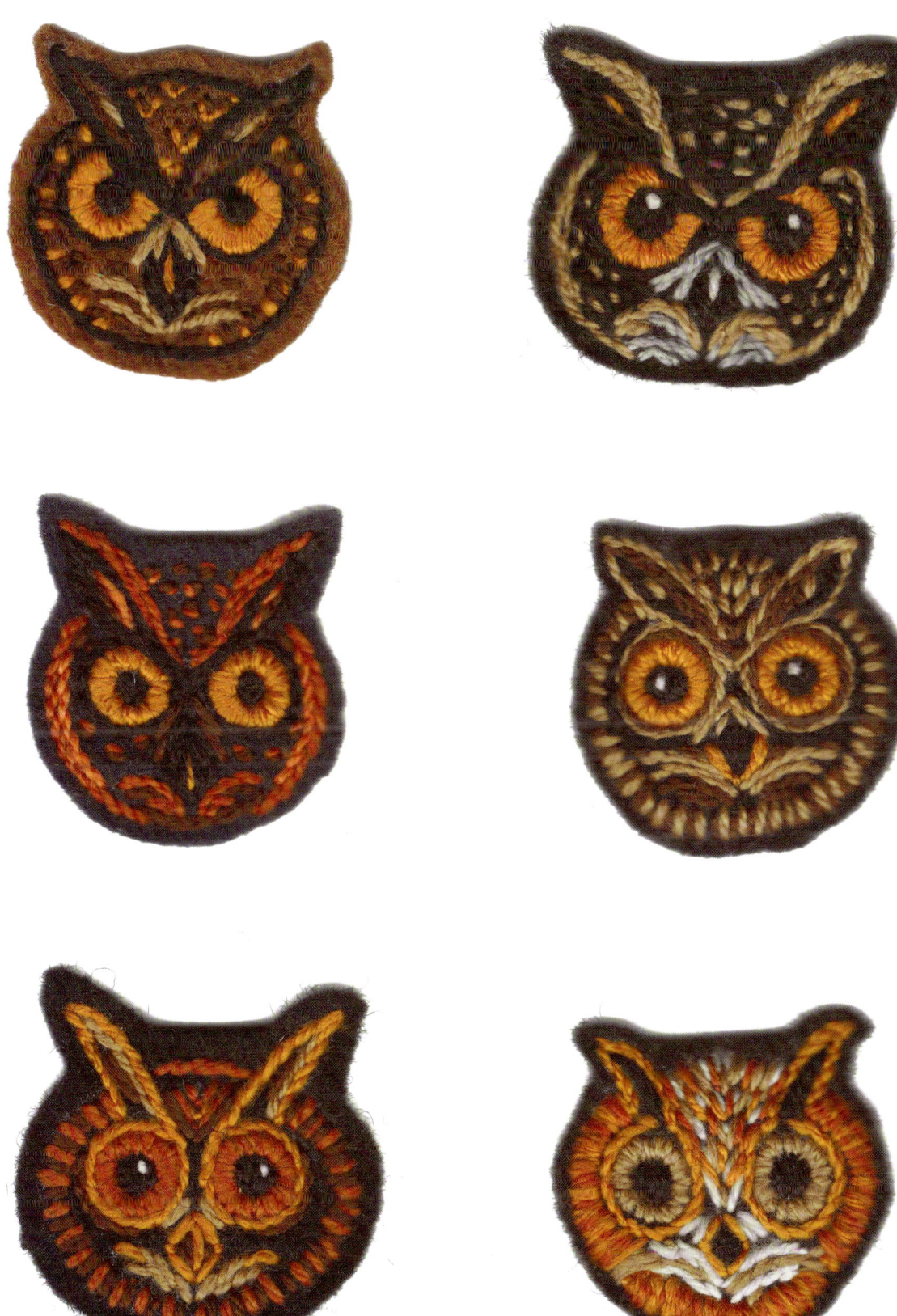

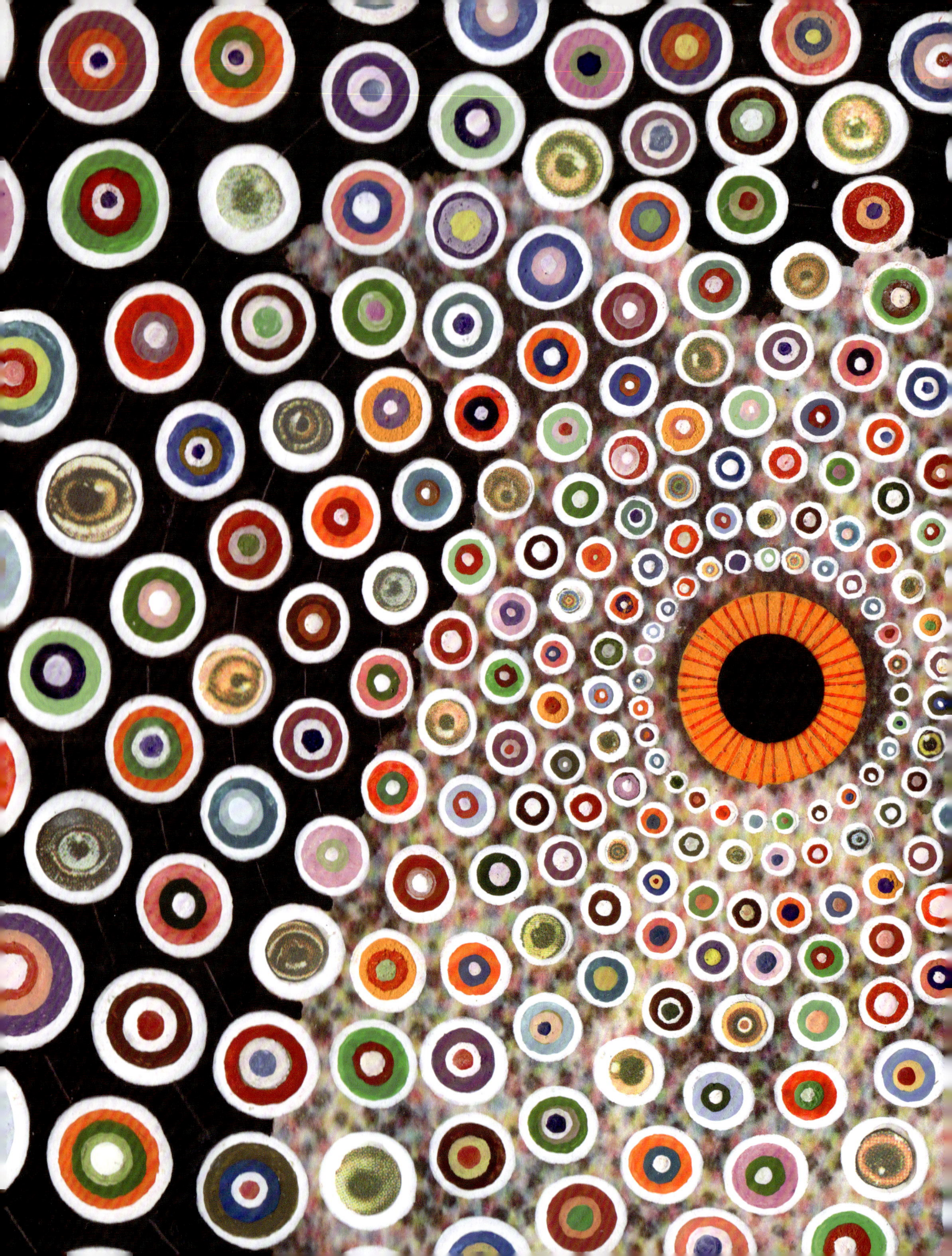

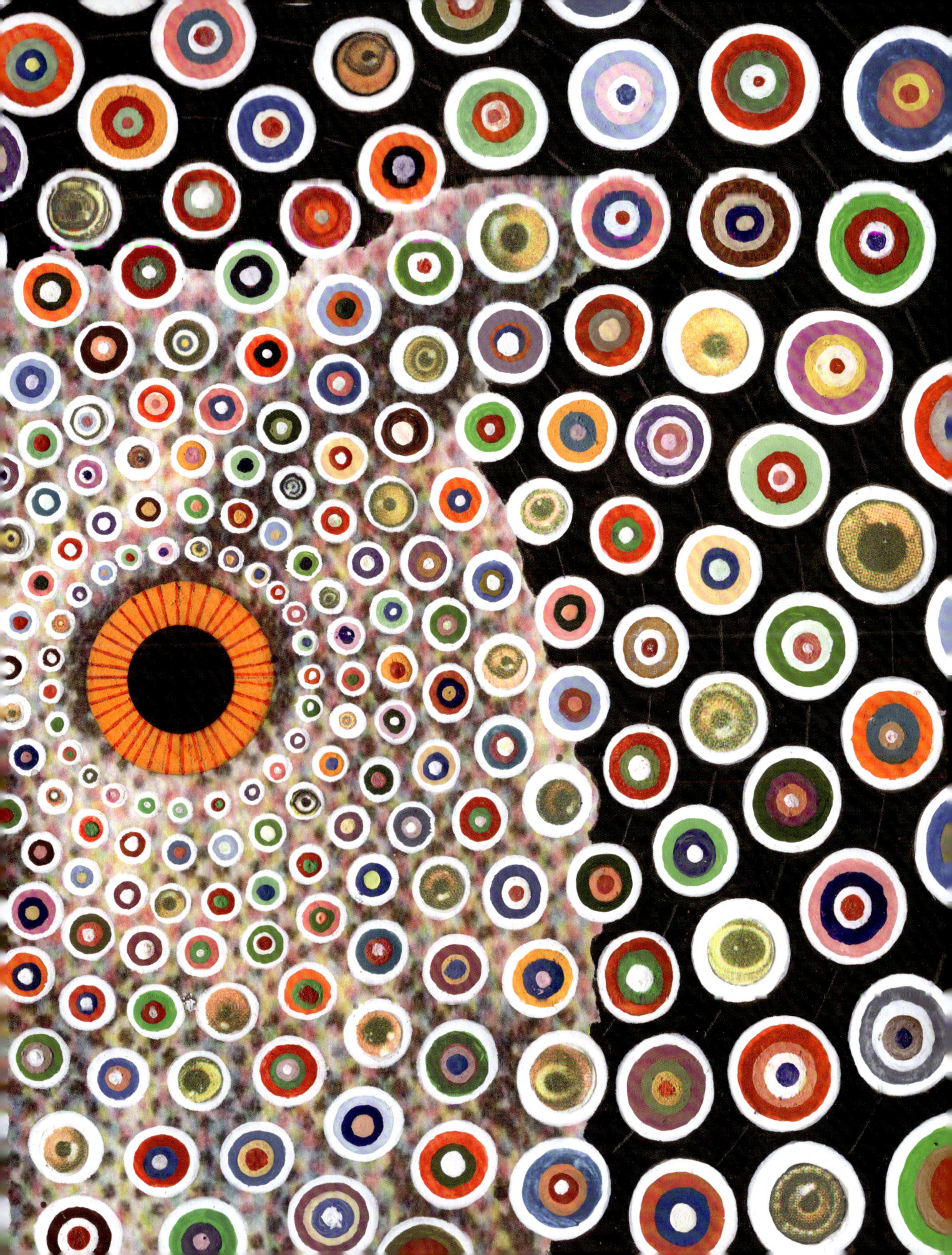

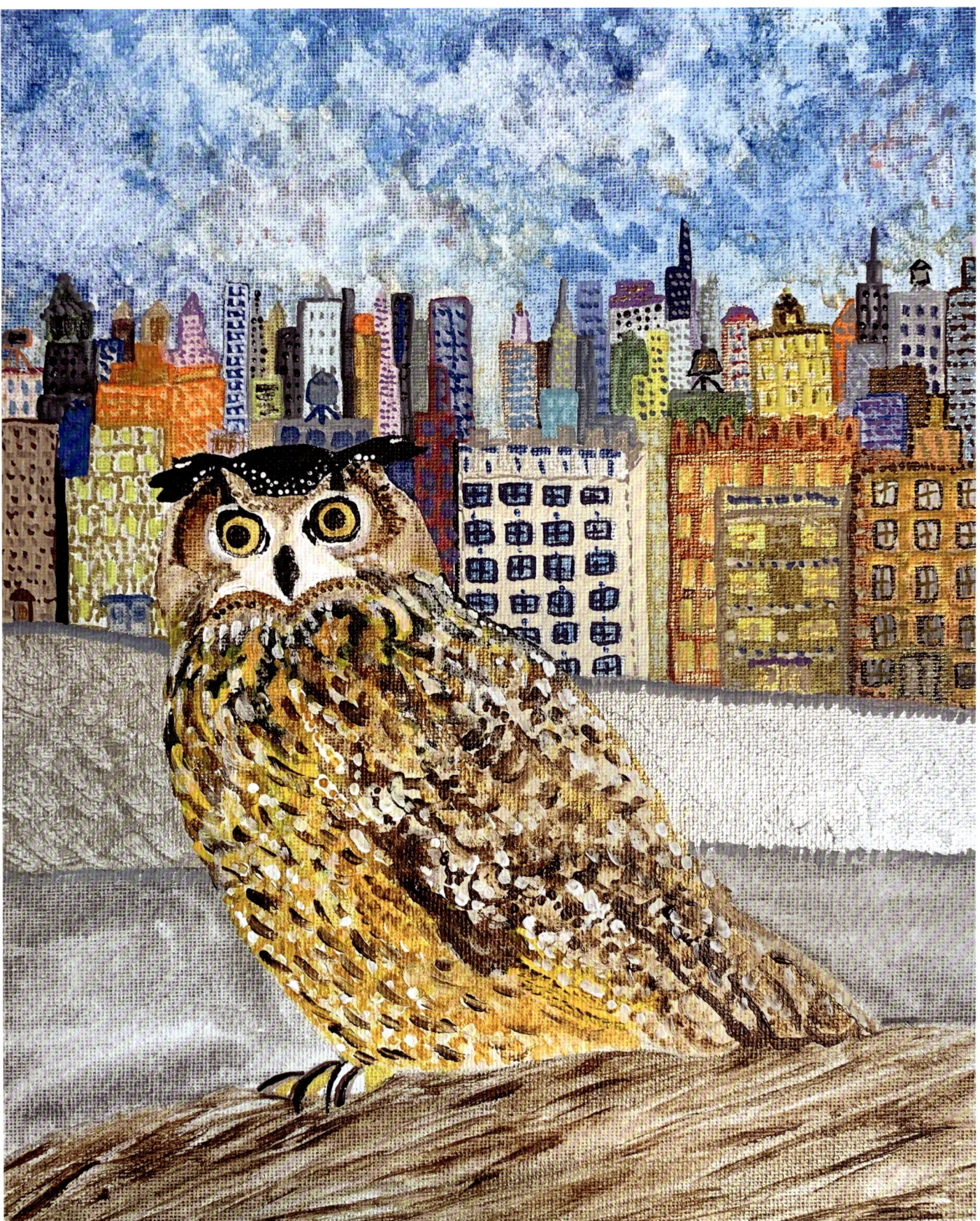

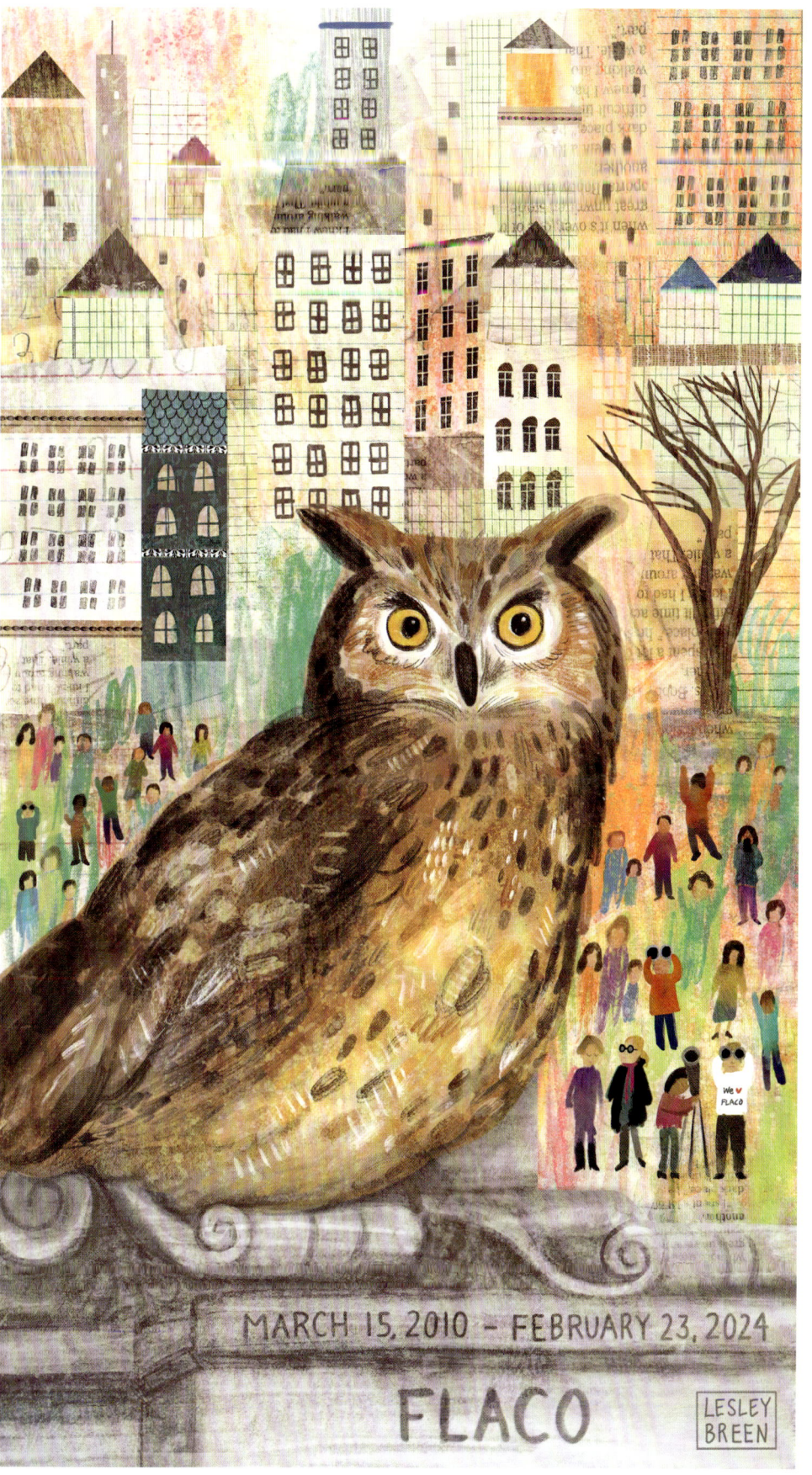

Heide Hatry

From the moment I heard about Flaco's escape, I was captivated. I rushed to the zoo area, eager to see him for myself. When I first laid eyes on him, I thought, there's a bobcat in that tree! He was so out of scale.

As I followed his life in the wild, I was astonished that, despite a lifetime of captivity, his native instincts told him how to survive. It felt like a reminder of nature's resilience.

I visited him often, each encounter a quiet and mediative, somehow primordial, exchange between two beings, and, I might add, two aliens in New York. I wanted others to be able to have that experience as well, and posted his (and my) favorite location: just a bit southwest of the North Meadow Softball Field 12, near 98th Street.

When I learned that owls vomit the indigestible parts of their prey—hair, feathers, bones, claws, beaks, teeth, and tiny skulls—in compact pellets averaging 3.5 x 1.5 inches, I'd keep my eyes open beneath his favorite perch to collect them.

One evening at dusk I followed him to a rocky area where the sky was still bright above but the rocks completely dark. He had somehow merged with the shadows of the landscape, and I lost sight of him. I had given up looking when suddenly an enormous, silent shadow swept past me and shocked me to the core. It was utterly terrifying, a brush with the wild so close I could have touched him; he certainly could have touched me had he so chosen. I followed him to a tree where he'd perched on a low branch. "You scared the life out of me," I said. And I swear he smiled.

After his death I found out that billions of birds die crashing into windows each year. I also learned that their preen or uropygial gland, located near the base of their tail produces oil, that the birds spread with their beaks over their feathers to waterproof them, keep them flexible, and maintain insulation. When a bird crashes into a window, that protective layer, leaves a shockingly and incredibly exact print, akin to a fingerprint, on the window.

To honor his spirit, I began making unique artist's and miniature books, recreating imprints of his body on plastic sheets and inserting them like windows into hollowed-out books, ghostly reminders of everything we fail to see, no matter how keen our vision. Other books contain the very bones of Flaco's prey, which he sometimes spat out right in front of me and which of course I took as confirmation that, in recognition of our connection, he wanted me to have them as gifts.

Previous spread left   Erika Bleiberg, *Flaco on Upper West Side Roof,* February 24th, 2024, acrylic paint and marker on textured canvas, 9 x 12 in. Painting completed upon the news of Flaco's death.

Previous spread right   Lesley Breen, *Flaco,* February 2024, digital/mixed media, 15 x 8¾ in.

Right   Heide Hatry, *On the Nature of Things,* 2024, altered book with rodent bones from Flaco's actual prey. 7½ x 4½ x 1½ in.

On the Nature of Things

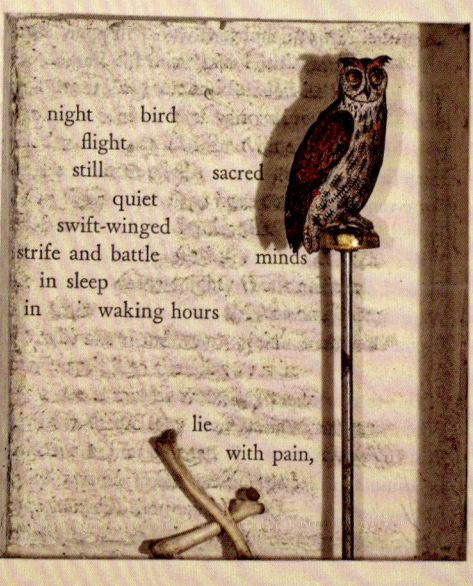

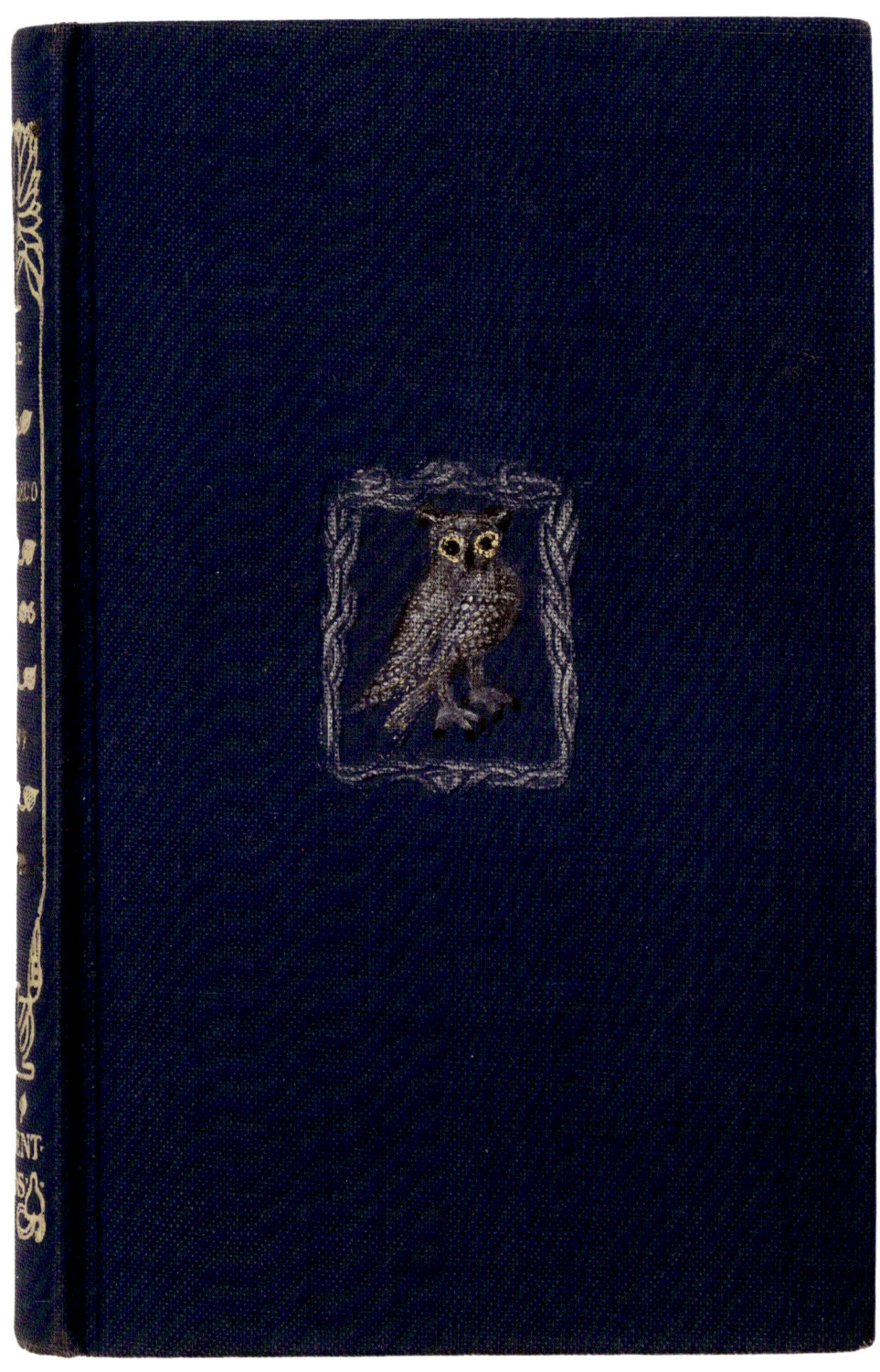

Heide Hatry, *Flaco XX (Flaco Agonistes)*, 2024, cover of altered book, 6 x 4 x ¾ in.

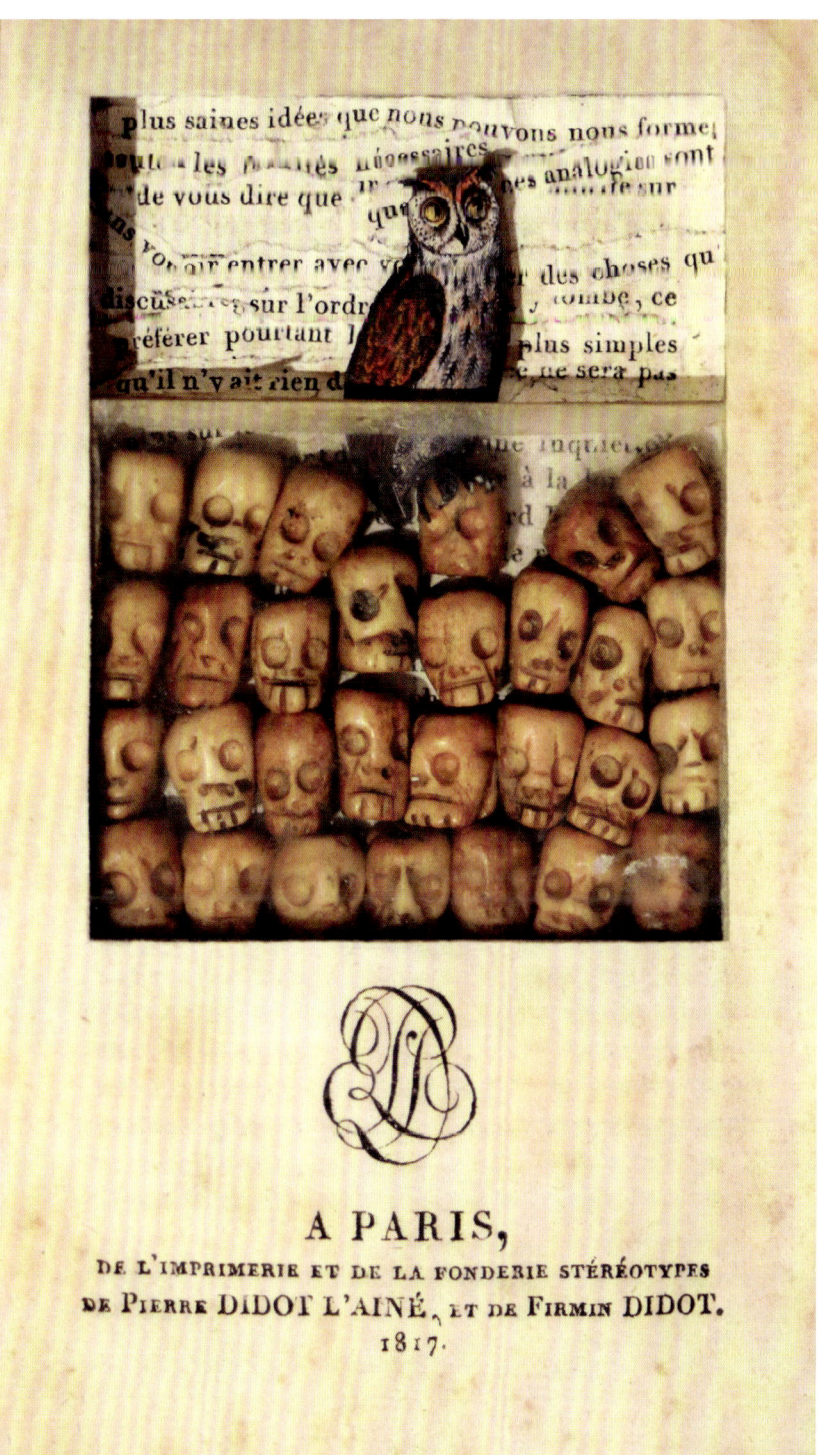

Heide Hatry, *Flaco XII (The Burden of Conformity)*, 2024, altered book with owl cutout and bone skulls, 5½ x 3½ x 1 in.

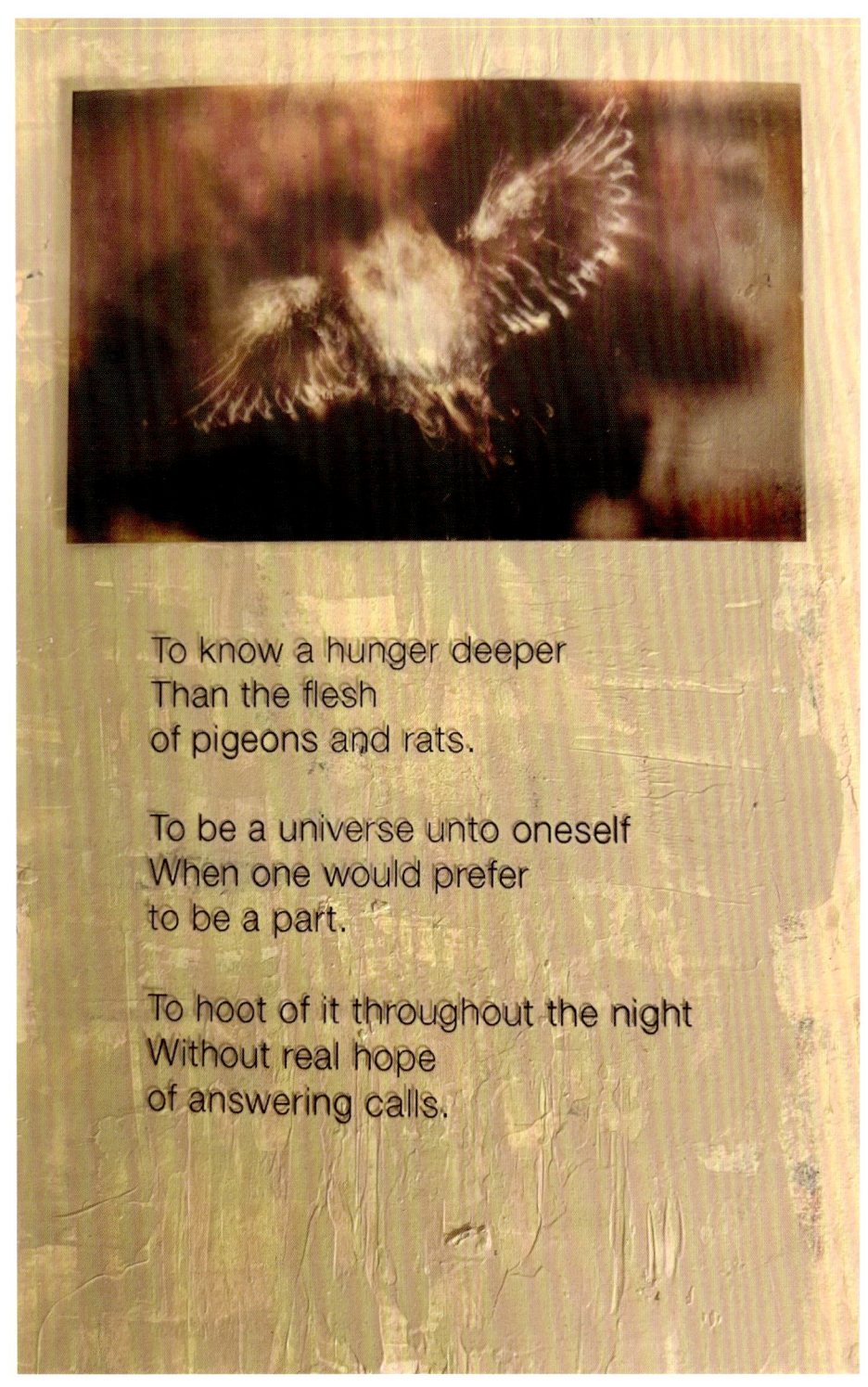

To know a hunger deeper
Than the flesh
of pigeons and rats.

To be a universe unto oneself
When one would prefer
to be a part.

To hoot of it throughout the night
Without real hope
of answering calls.

Heide Hatry, *Coop and Cosmos,* 2024, altered book with text by Leonard Schwartz, 7¼ x 4¾ x ¼ in.

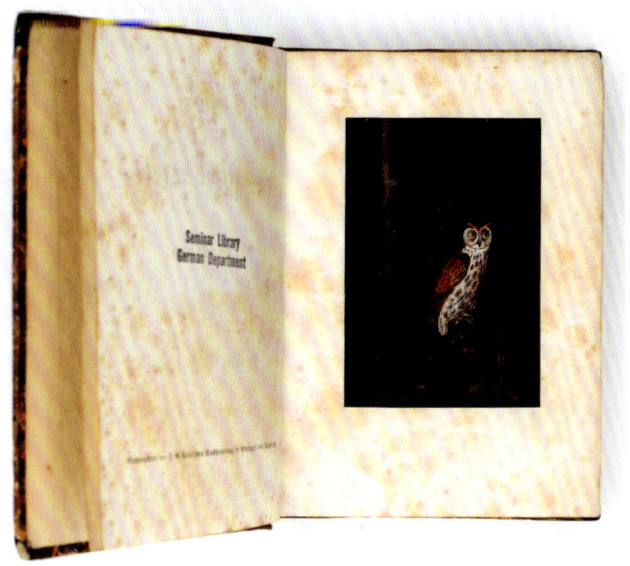
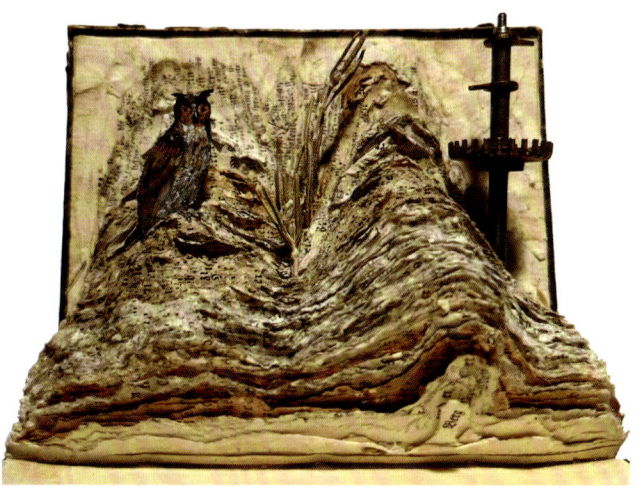

Above left Heide Hatry, *Flaco VII (And the Lion Shall Lie Down with the Lamb)*, 2024, altered book with cutouts and branches, 6 x 4¾ x 1½ in.

Above right Heide Hatry, *Der Berg,* 2024, sculptural assemblage, 5¼ x 3¾ x 1½ in. (Courtesy of the University of Miami Libraries: Richter Library.)

Following spread left Kamila Zmrzla, *Saint Flaco,* 2024, mixed media, ink, watercolor, gouache, pencil, 20 x 14 in.

Following spread right Elizabeth Kennen, *Flaco the Eurasian Eagle-Owl of NYC,* 2024, watercolor, 16 x 12 in., completed February 24th, inspired by a photograph by Jacqueline Emery.

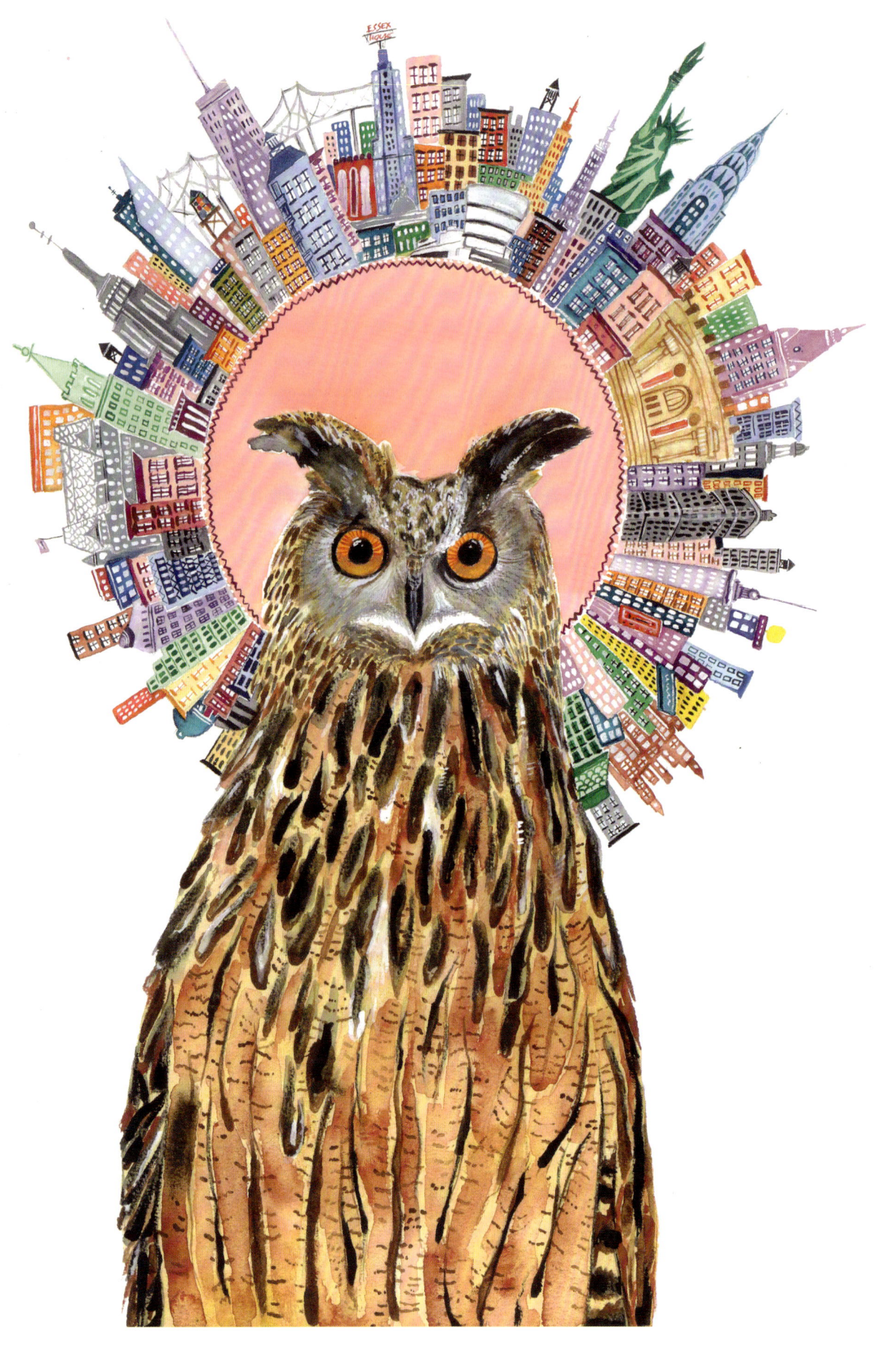

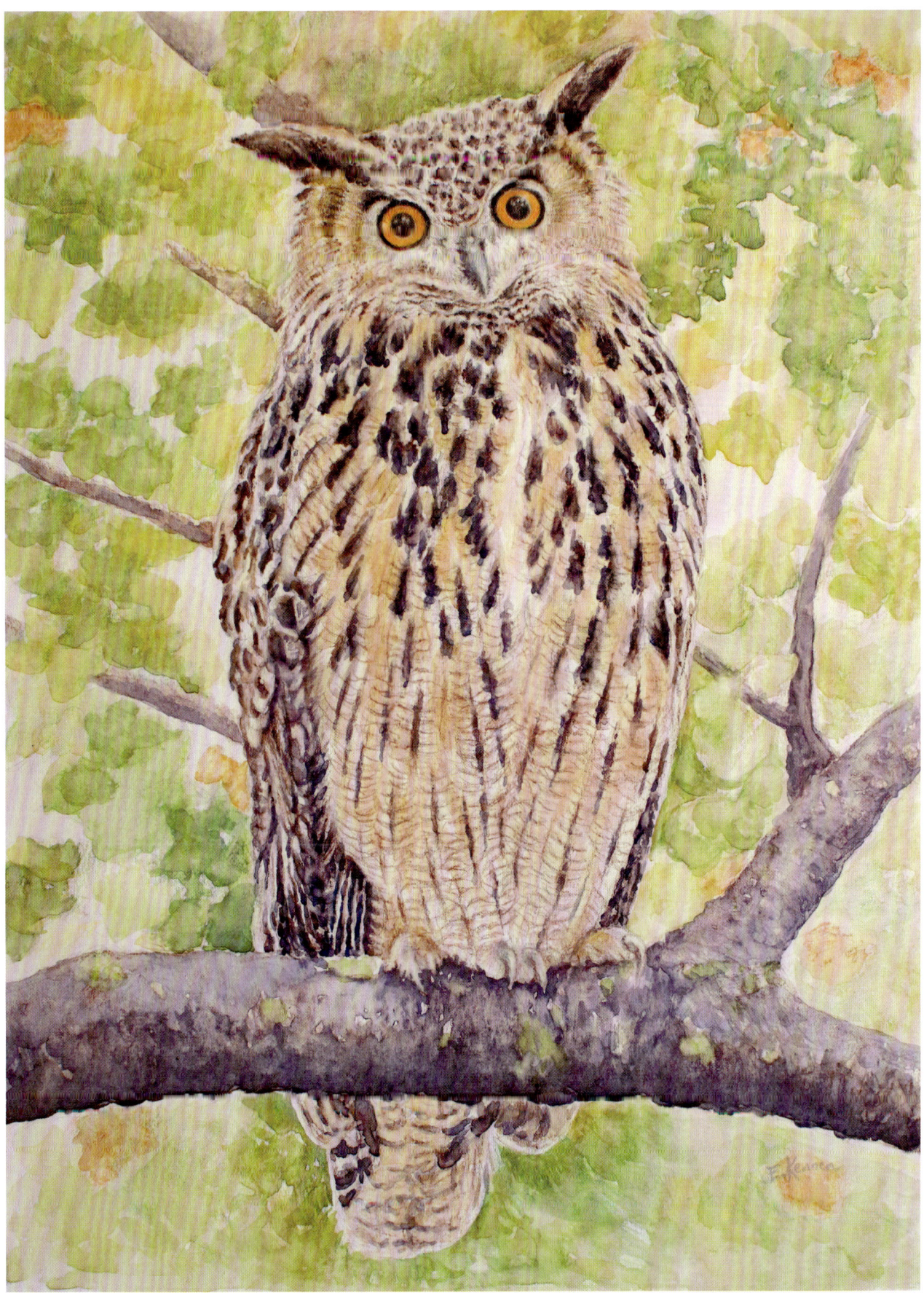

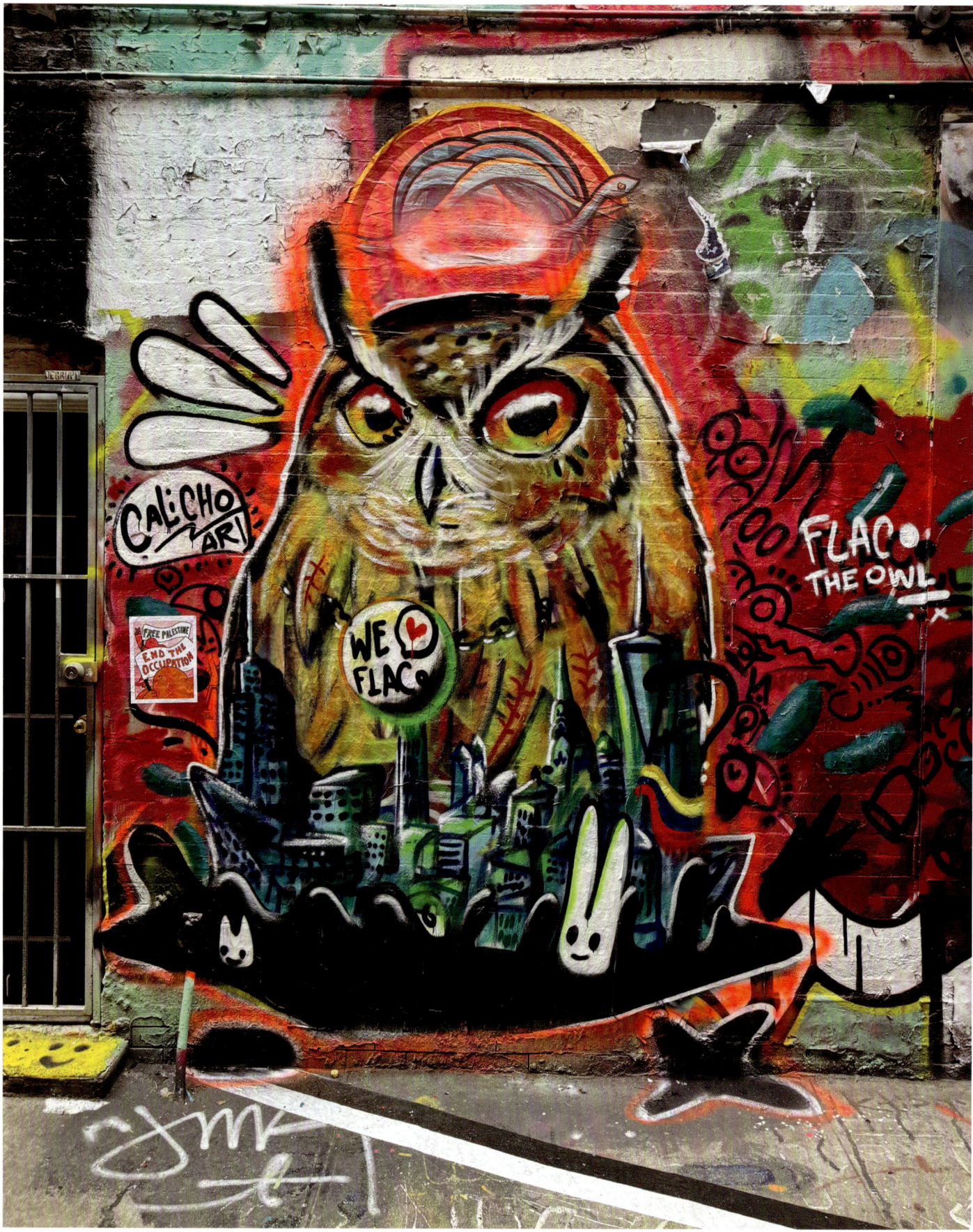

Calicho Arevalo

Colombian artist and architect Calicho Arevalo first encountered Flaco when the escaped Eurasian eagle owl landed on one of his buildings on the Lower East Side. The story of the stranger in a strange land tapped into the artist's own feelings of being an outsider in New York, and inspired him to create a series of murals in Lower Manhattan, along with lithographs and spray-painted Flaco-themed clothing. Inspired by Flaco's year living on his own terms, Arevalo has subsequently stepped away from his architectural practice to pursue his dream of being a full-time visual artist.

After Flaco's passing, Calicho announced on X that he would be painting a final memorial mural with a location still to be determined, which would be his most iconic. The next morning (Saturday), "I went there to Freeman Alley to paint"—a well-established space for street art—"and I remember when I was on the way, I received an email from *The New York Times,* saying 'We are interested in covering your painting. What time are you going to be there? We are on the way.' And I was like, *whoa.* We arrived almost at the same time, and they said, "You have an hour to do this wall," which Calicho completed in 90 minutes.

The next day the painting was vandalized, which brought about another wave of media coverage and personal messages. "That was when I realized how many people really loved the [owl], because I received a lot of messages of support . . . from kids and grandmas, people of all ages and races about how much they loved the owl and identify with [him]. So, I realized I was not alone in this purpose of making Flaco a symbol for the city. It was beautiful to know that New Yorkers could join each other for a simple cause. Something that was a sparkle in the day—it was beautiful to talk about something that was pure love."

Calicho Arevalo, *Flaco Memorial, Final Tribute,* February 24th, 2024, Freeman Alley, spray paint on brick.

Following spread left Calicho Arevalo, *Flaco the Owl,* May 2023, The Bowery, Lower East Side, spray paint on plywood.

Following spread right Calicho Arevalo, *Flaco in NYC,* 2023–2024, digital media.

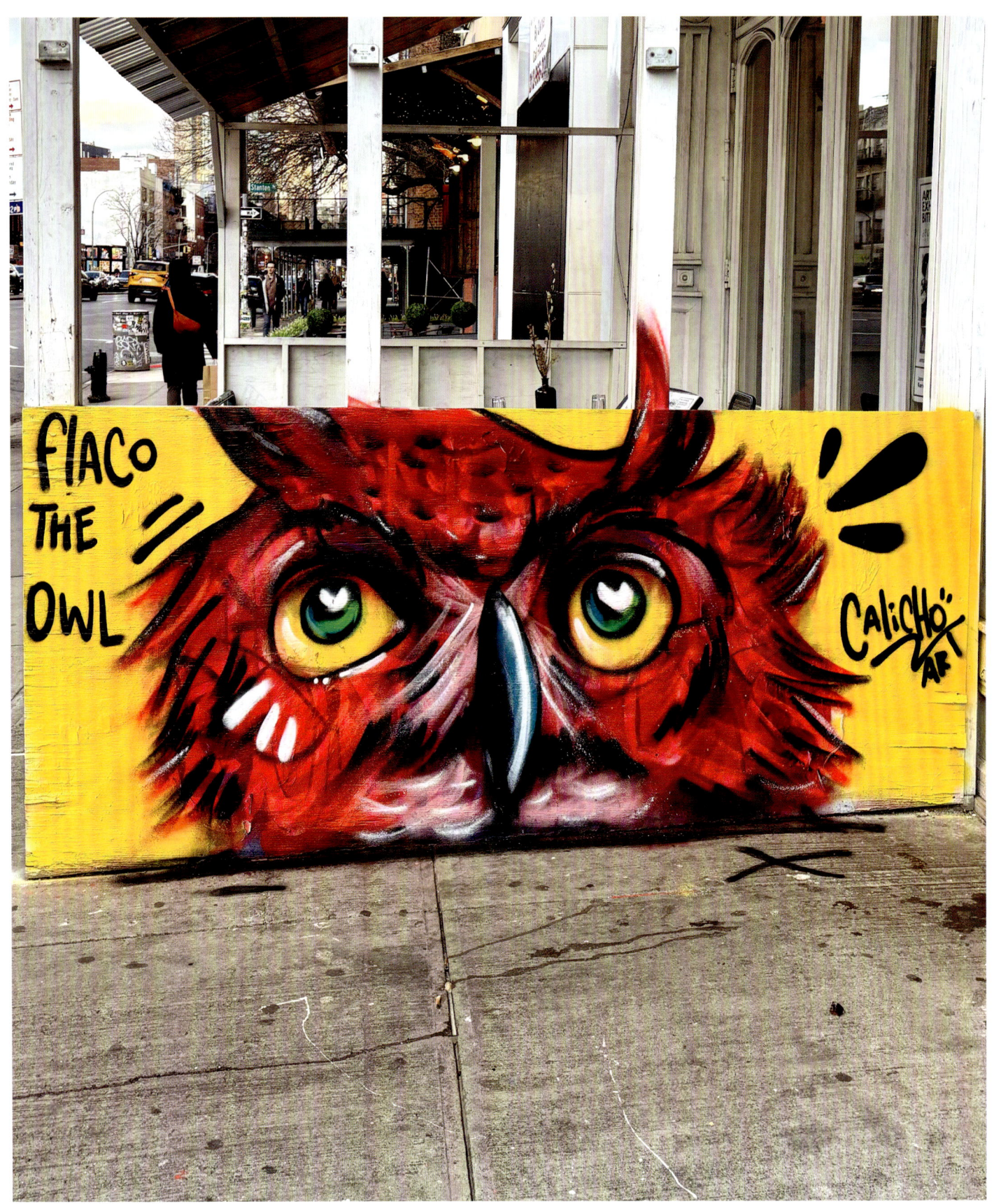

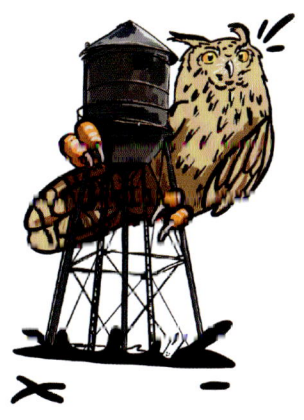
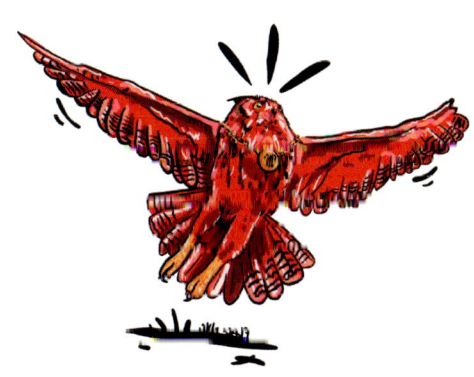
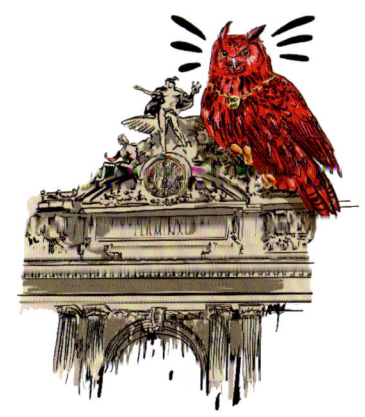
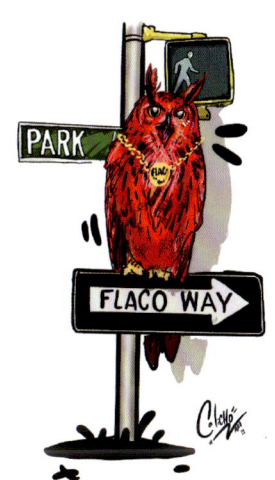

We ♥ Flaco

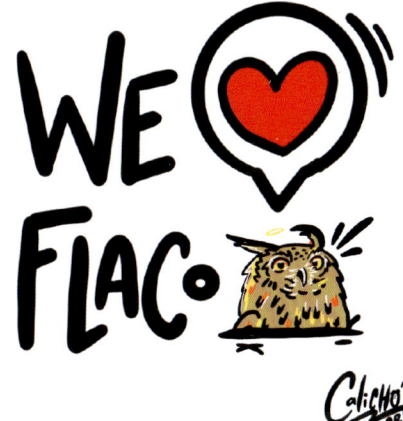
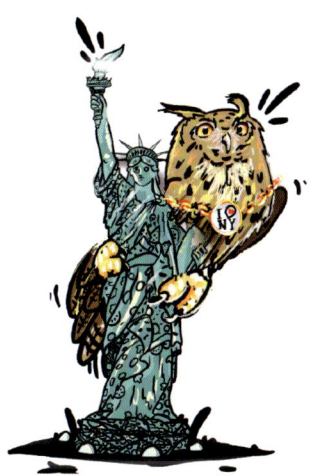
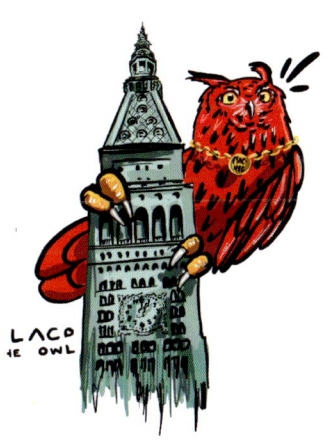
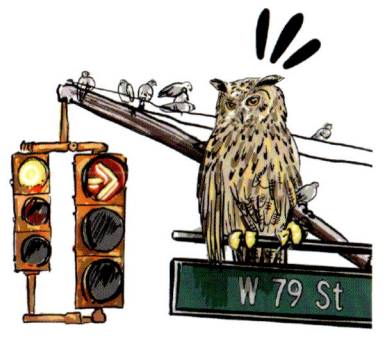
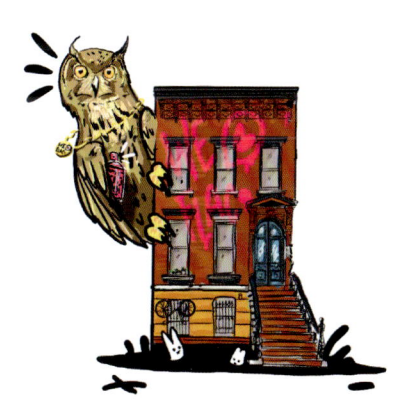
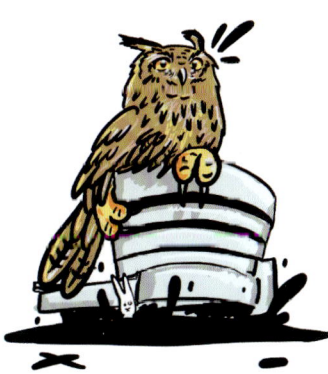
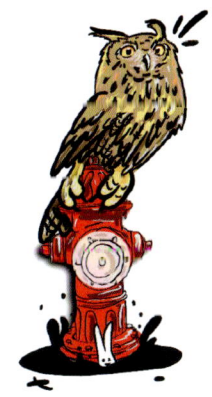
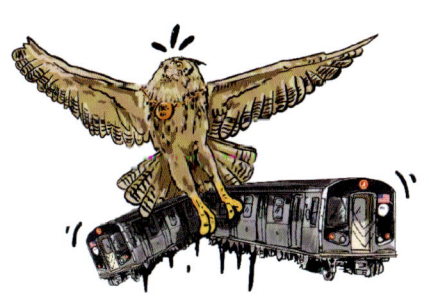

Flaco as Muse

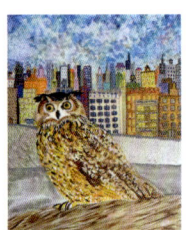

Erika Bleiberg:
Flaco was an inspiration in his quest for freedom and survival. When I heard he had departed his zoo cage and was living at large in NYC, I was concerned for his safety but exhilarated by the idea that he was now at liberty to pursue his natural life. Reports of him stretching his wings over Manhattan brought joy, and he became a sort of avian superhero. I had always hoped to catch a glimpse of him, and though I never did, I liked to think of him soaring above the intensity of the city as I went about my day. I envisioned him looking down through his binocular eyes with compassion and sympathy. For his tribute portrait, I decided to position Flaco on a rooftop in the West 80s—the neighborhood where he was often seen and ultimately where his life concluded. RIP, Flaco. May you forever fly free.

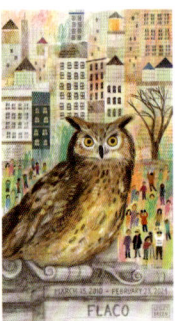

Lesley Breen:
I was deeply moved by the story of Flaco, the Eurasian Eagle-Owl, and I was inspired to create art based on his journey. Despite being born in captivity and not expected to survive, he embraced his newfound freedom and made the busy streets of New York his home. Flaco brought joy and wonder to all who saw him, becoming a symbol of resilience and freedom. In my art, I wanted to capture the feeling of togetherness and connection people experienced during the time Flaco was flying free, as well as the hope he inspired in those who saw their own experiences reflected in his story.

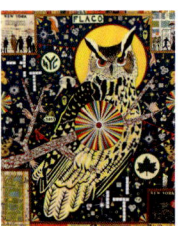

Tony Fitzpatrick:
He belongs in Central Park—free—he came to NYC for the same reason every immigrant did—to realize his better self in a new world—to live among the wonder—the reason he is so popular is that New Yorkers see themselves in him—he needed more room—a bigger world and a more expansive place to become more…he is one of my heroes—I hope I do him justice…he's beautiful, he gives me hope…if you've ever been in a place against your will—you understand and pull for Flaco.

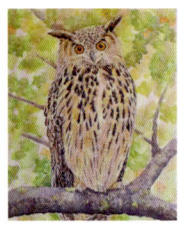

Elizabeth Kennen:
I found such a sense of joy and wonder as I followed the story of Flaco. As an artist and nature lover in California, I was drawn to the images shared by New York bird lovers. This was the first time I'd ever seen an Eurasian eagle owl and was captivated by beautiful Flaco. At the start of the new year, I was inspired to paint this amazing owl in watercolor. My painting was finished on February 2, the date that marked his one year of flying free. This is one of the most meaningful art projects I've ever had. I loved every moment of working on this composition.

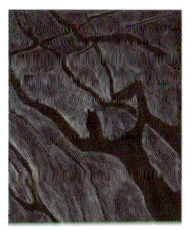

Martha Nishida:
How woven into our lives was Flaco during his time in Central Park and the city! I enjoyed visiting his various roosts regularly during that year — whether just strolling by or enjoying a longer visit while I, too, perched nearby. I often enjoyed photographing the areas that were his neck of the woods, or the trees where he roosted. A number of crafting projects were part of the picture too — but mostly I enjoyed sketching Flaco.

The drawing above was based on a photo of Flaco perched on a bare limb overlooking the Loch, taken on the first day of spring just before sunset. There was no one else in sight and standing there I was struck by the thought that while he looked all alone in a cold landscape—he was part of the landscape. And I thought—it's a new road, Flaco. I'm so glad to have been near him for his journey.

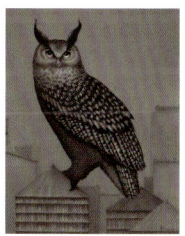

Juliet Schreckinger:
My passion for art has always been centered around the idea of telling visual narratives. Flaco is a real-life superhero, an icon that captured the hearts of so many not just in the concrete jungle, but far beyond as well. Flaco wrote his own story, and as an illustrator, I knew it was one I wanted to help share visually. He became larger-than-life in a way; the magnificence of this beautiful wild creature roaming the streets of New York was apparent to all who heard his story. I chose to depict him as grand and proud atop the water tower to illustrate the astronomical effect he had on the people of this city. His courage gave us hope, one small bird taking on the entire city, and I hope my illustration of this incredible creature depicts this courage to all who see it.

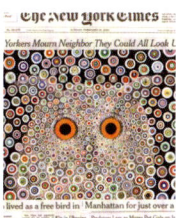

Fred Tomaselli:
Watching Flaco flying free in Central Park was extra thrilling, coming as it did, not long after COVID lockdowns were lifted. Somehow a crazy story of a 'liberated' owl became the embodiment of a sense of regained freedom. But more than that, Flaco was beautiful and alert. We thought we were looking at him but he was also looking at us.

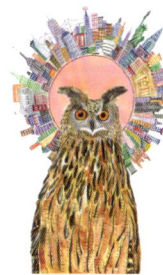

Kamilla Zmrzla:
As many New Yorkers and nature lovers, I followed Flaco's story closely and was very much rooting for him. For me, he was a little speck of hope in this crazy world and his freedom was something that many of us are searching for. I made this painting of him as a saint owl of NYC with the city skyline as his halo; the city will belong to Flaco for some time.

Flaco Day:
East River
Tattoo
Greenpoint,
Brooklyn

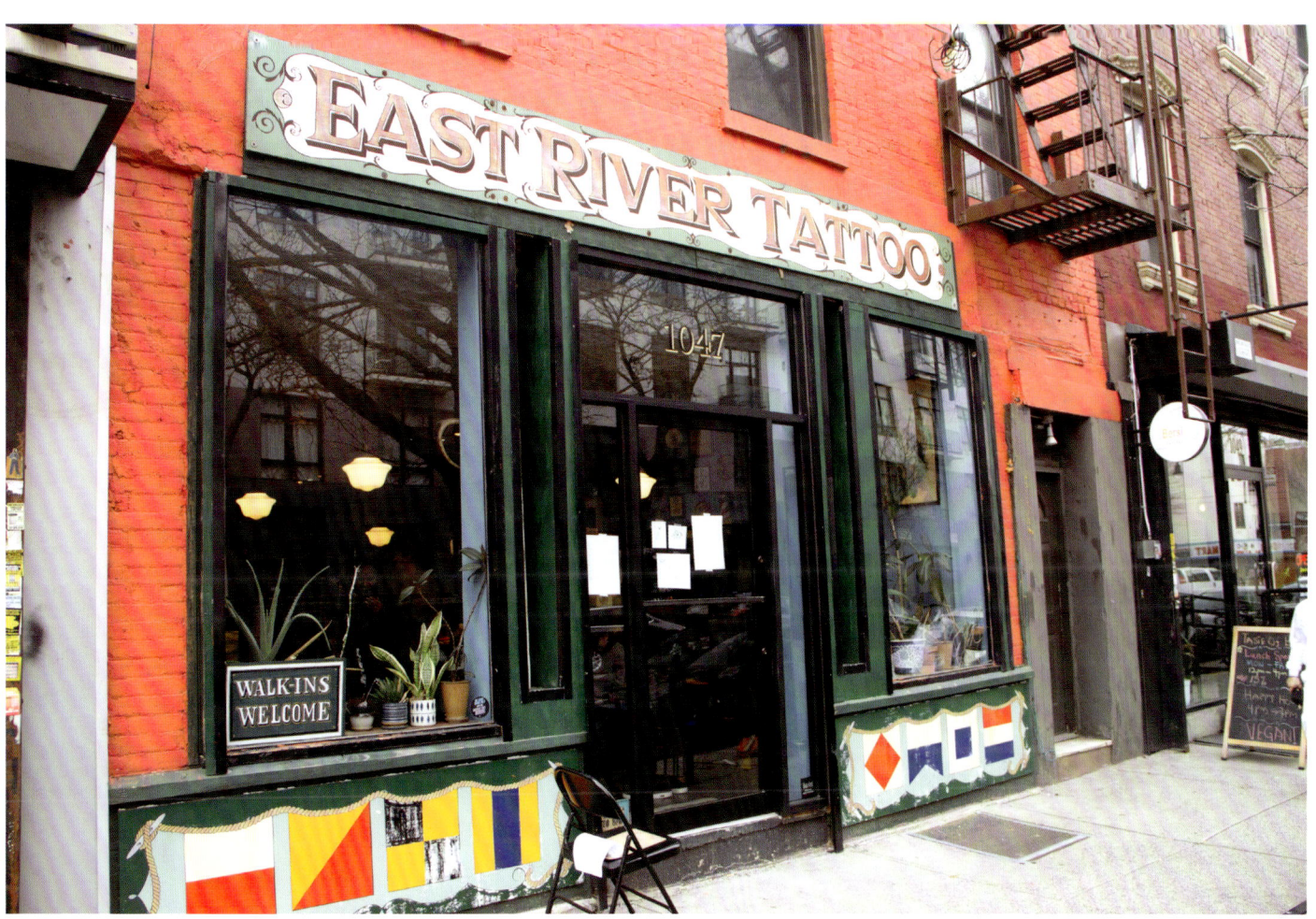

Tattoo parlors across the city had already experienced an uptick in demand for Flaco tattoos after Flaco's death, but on April 11th, East River Tattoo hosted a Flaco flash sale, in which Flaco aficionados could get a specially-designed Flaco tattoo by visual artist Duke Riley, whose work focuses upon human impact on the environment.

Photos by Jonathan Hollingsworth

Following spread left   Duke Riley's Flaco Design

Following spread right   Duke Riley at East River Tattoo, on Flaco Day

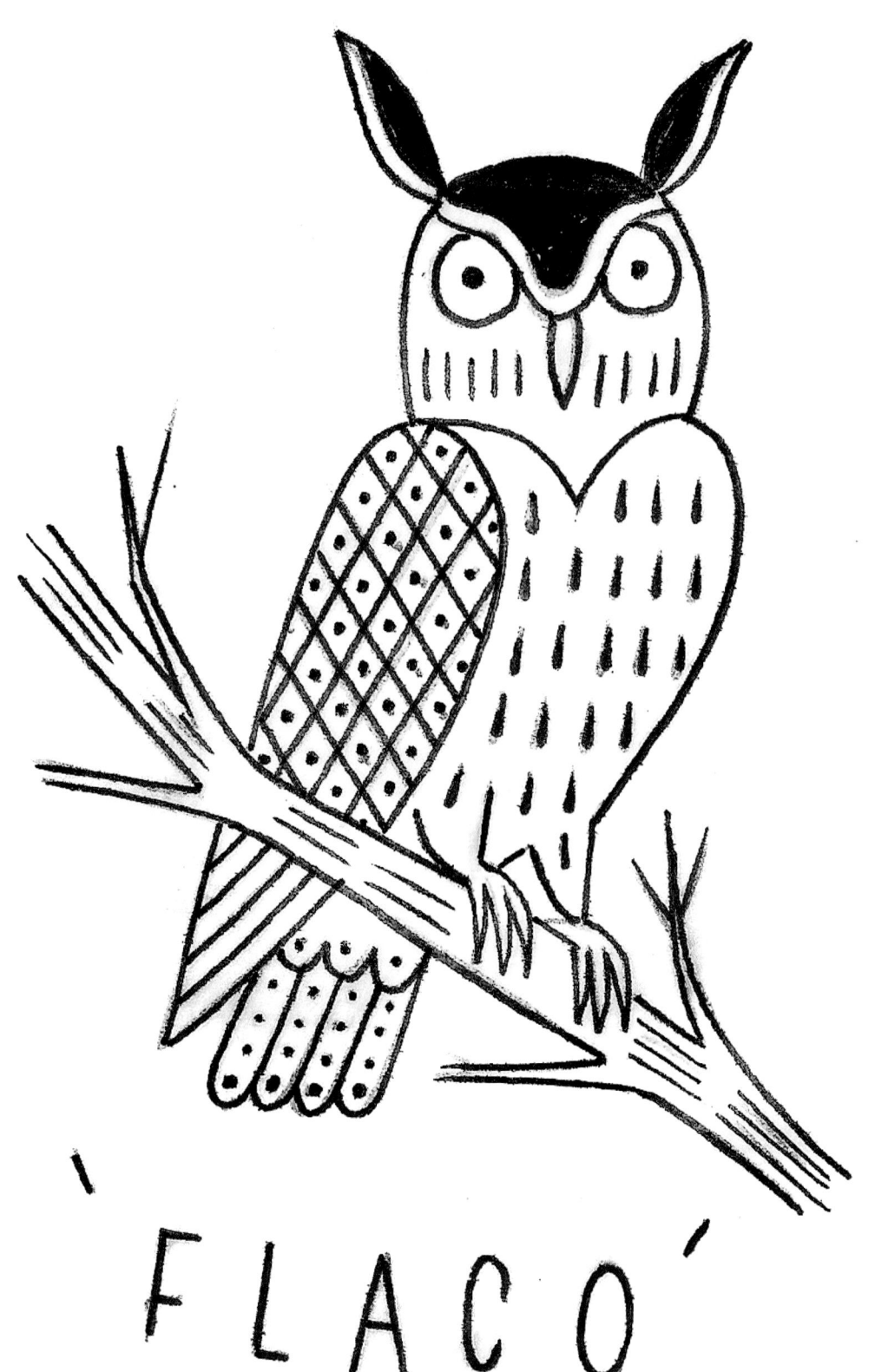

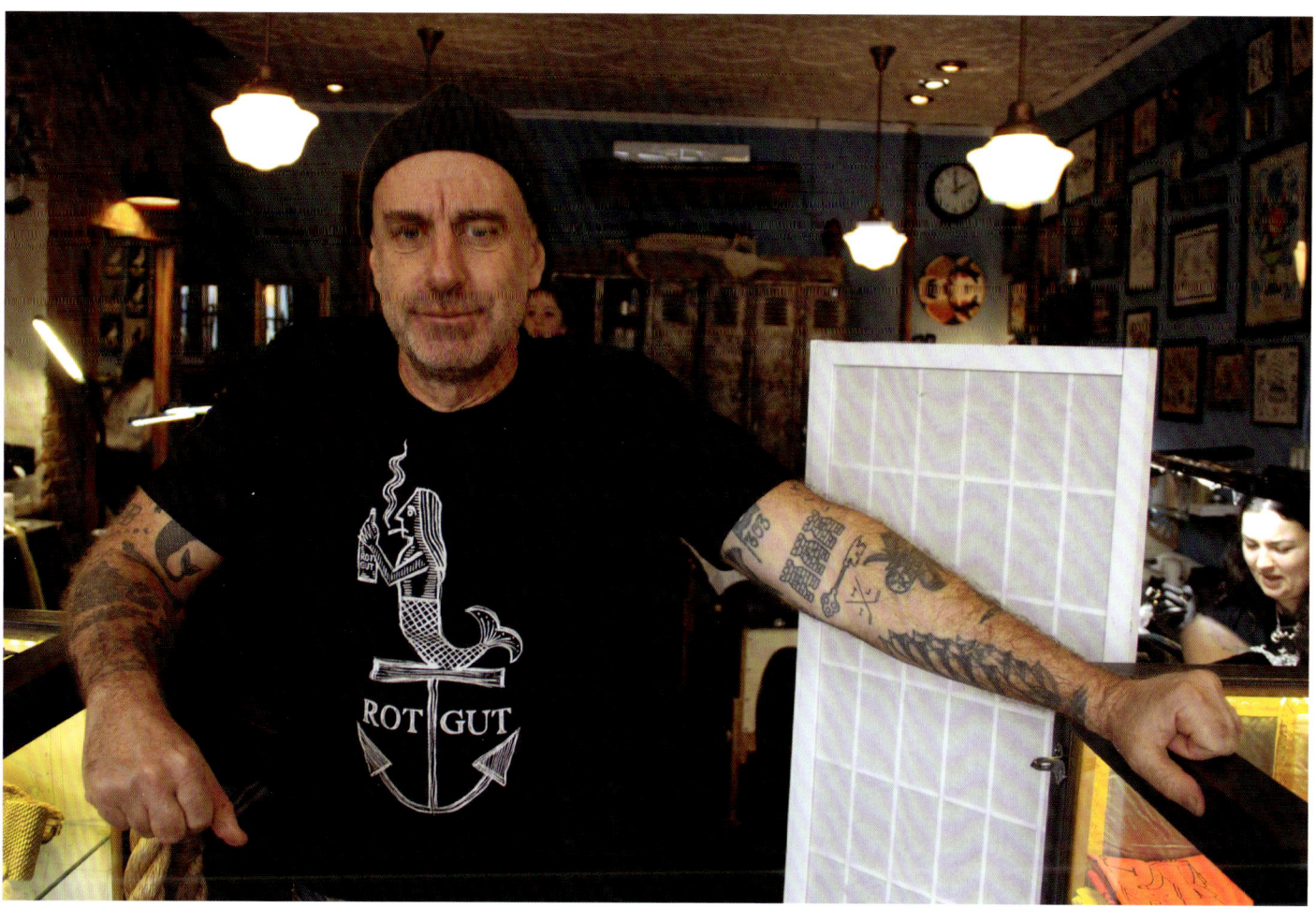

Jonathan Hollingsworth

How does Flaco's story intersect with the themes that you explore in your work, e.g., human impact on the environment?

Duke Riley

My work generally addresses the conflict between nature and institutional power, often focusing on birds within the urban environment, so a story about an owl escaping from the zoo and trying to carve out an unshackled life for itself in New York City just naturally drew my attention.

Is the tattoo meant to be a long-term emissary of the Flaco legacy and the lessons we learned?

With anything that I do, I'm not ever trying to impose my thoughts or ideas on other people. I think that everyone who came in to get the tattoo had very different reasons for getting it, relationships to Flaco, and takeaways from his legacy. I learned a lot.

Could you speak about the choice for the design? Did it evolve, or did you have a clear vision from the beginning?

I did a very quick drawing of Flaco that was the first thing that came to my mind. I decided not to edit it in any way. I felt like I wanted it to be a spontaneous reaction.

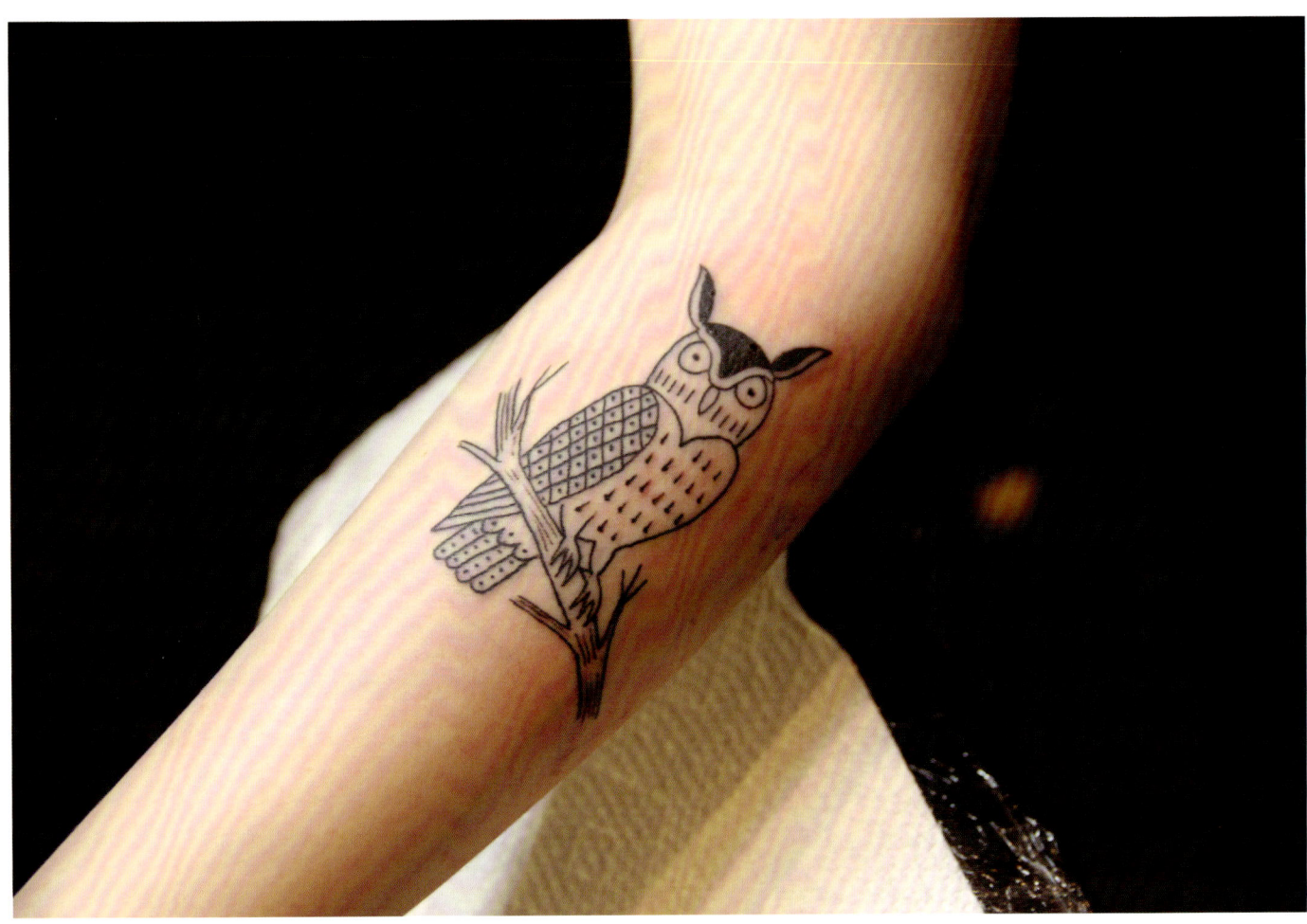

Kari Nicolaisen, 29, resident of the Bedford
—Stuyvesant neighborhood of Brooklyn.

Above   Kari Nicolaisen's completed tattoo, the first of the day.

Right   Duke Riley at work, inking Flaco's feathers.

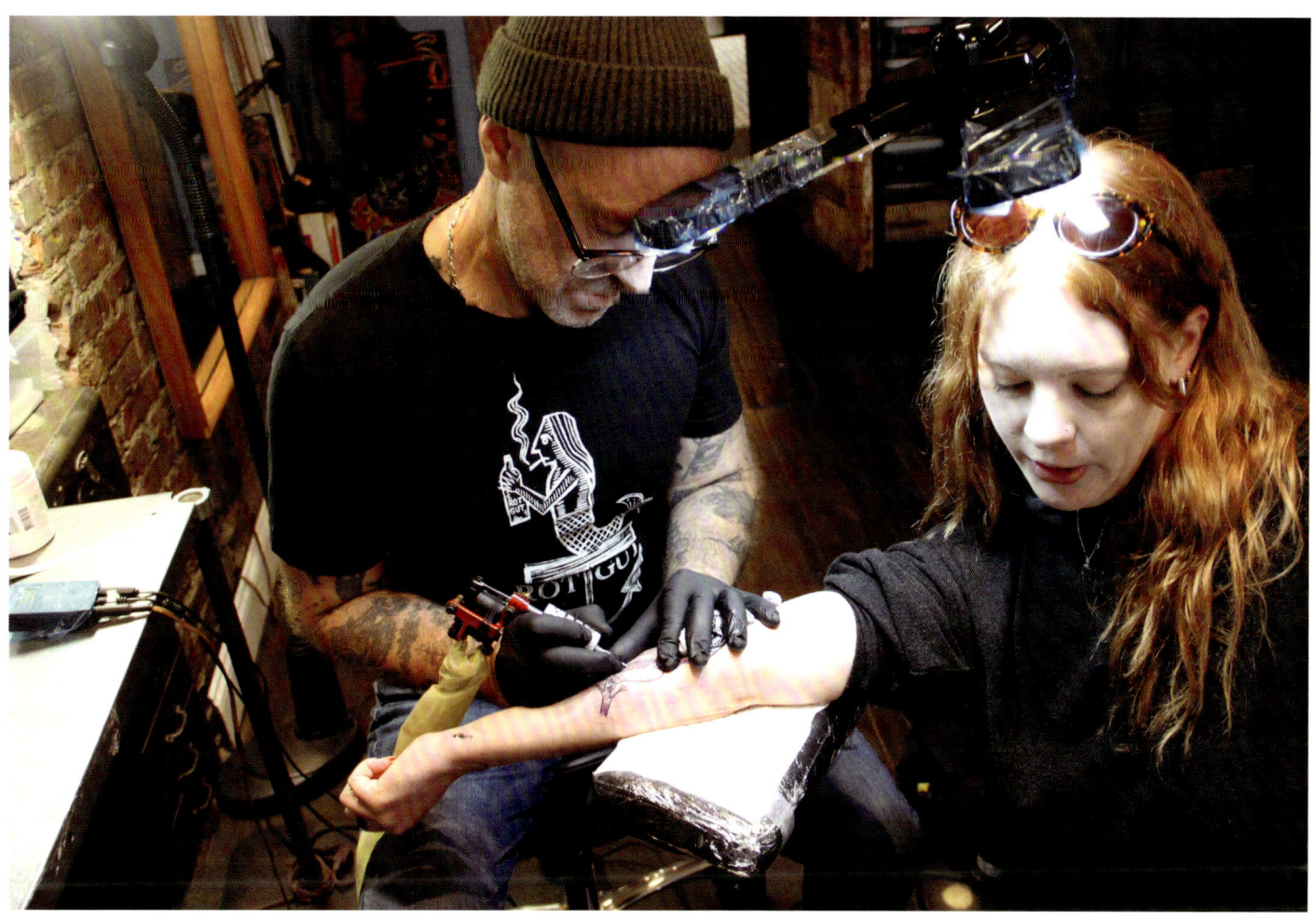

What is your personal connection to Flaco?

Kari Nicolaisen

I used to work over near Central Park Zoo, and soon after [Flaco] got out, I was on a break walking through the park, and I saw him — and I was just struck — he's very majestic.

How did Flaco's story inspire you?

I quit my job recently and I'm thinking about doing some traveling next month — just kind of a pivot in life when I eventually come back. He has definitely inspired me — his story has stuck with me. I was really sad when I heard he had passed.

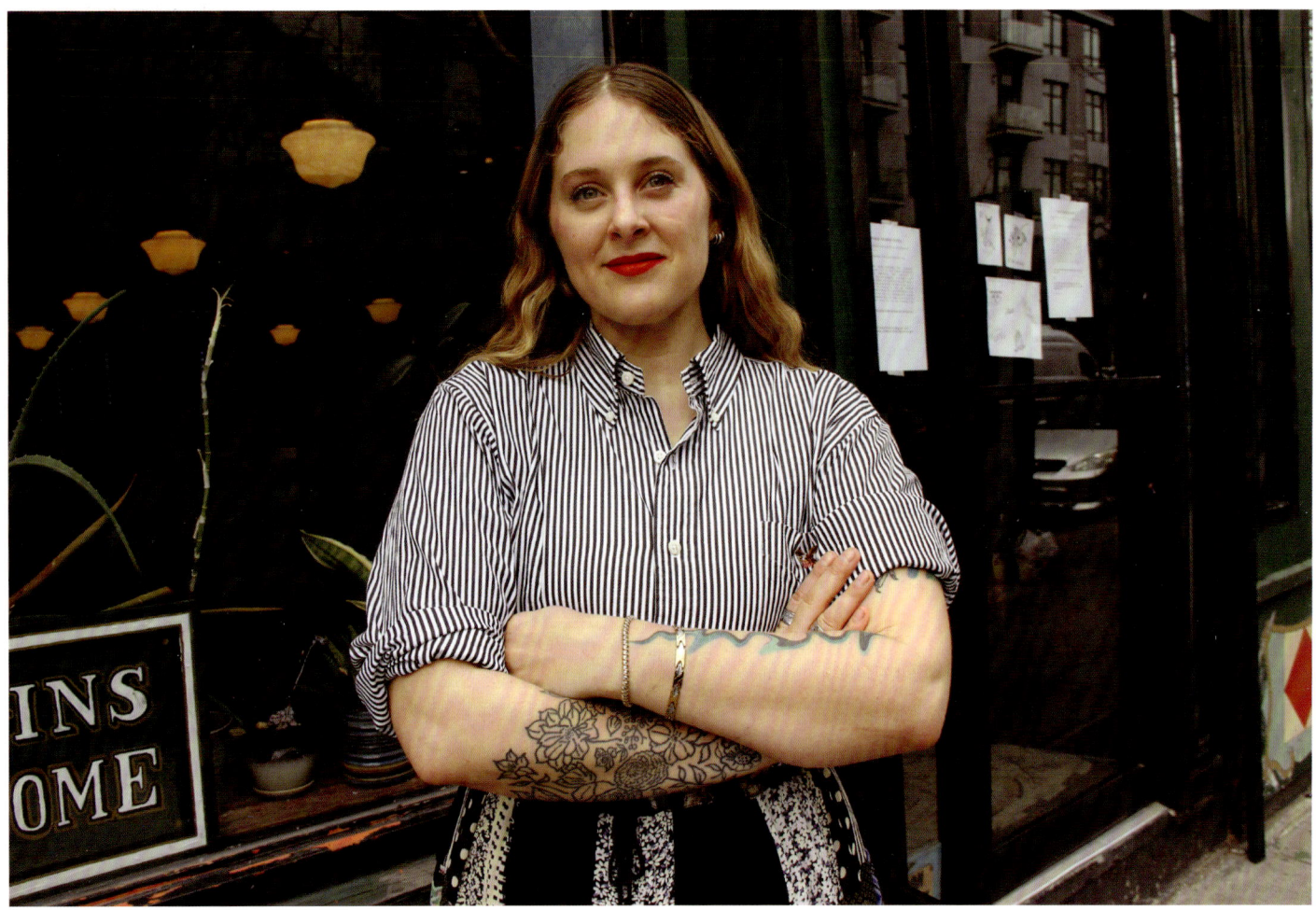

What's your personal connection to the Flaco story?

Kelly Fritz

I've been following it from the beginning. His death was tragic but also predictable. I found the whole [story] not only very entertaining but also sweet and lovely how the whole city became fascinated with him.

Do you think this is a New York story — or is it something bigger?

I think New York is a home of a lot of people who've been transplanted, who feel lonely, a home of immigrants, a home of people who are looking for others of their kind, and I think Flaco — whether people realize it or not — embodies that symbolism. I'm crying talking about this!

Kelly Fritz, 33, Bushwick, Brooklyn.

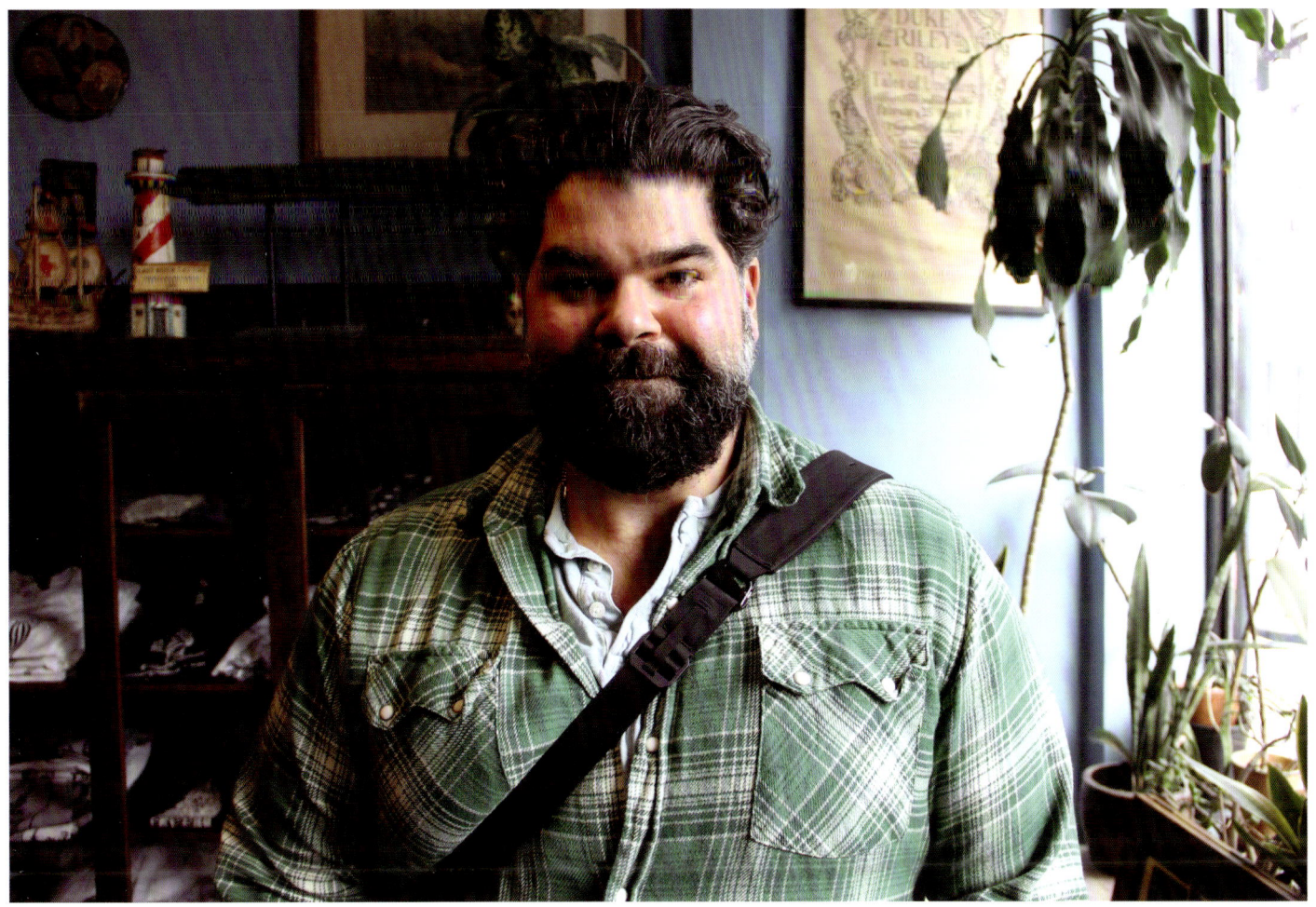

So many people perceive this as a New York story. As a Bostonian, what was your connection to Flaco?

Ion Sokhos

Well, I love owls and it was national news. It was almost like Flaco was a folk hero to a lot of people. Just the symbolism of how he was in captivity and then he was free. I loved how he then became the observer, flying up to people's windows, peering into their homes. It was pretty remarkable, and tragic how he passed, but amazing that he was able to be free for a year.

Why do you think Flaco inspired so many people?

I think especially in a place like New York it's a pretty anonymous city. Everyone's kind of doing their best just to get by. I think something like his story can inspire hope in people… You could look at it a lot of ways: he's the embodiment of freedom and I think that's something we all want and try to achieve.

Ion Sokhos, 45, Boston MA, who drove to NYC for the Flaco tattoo.

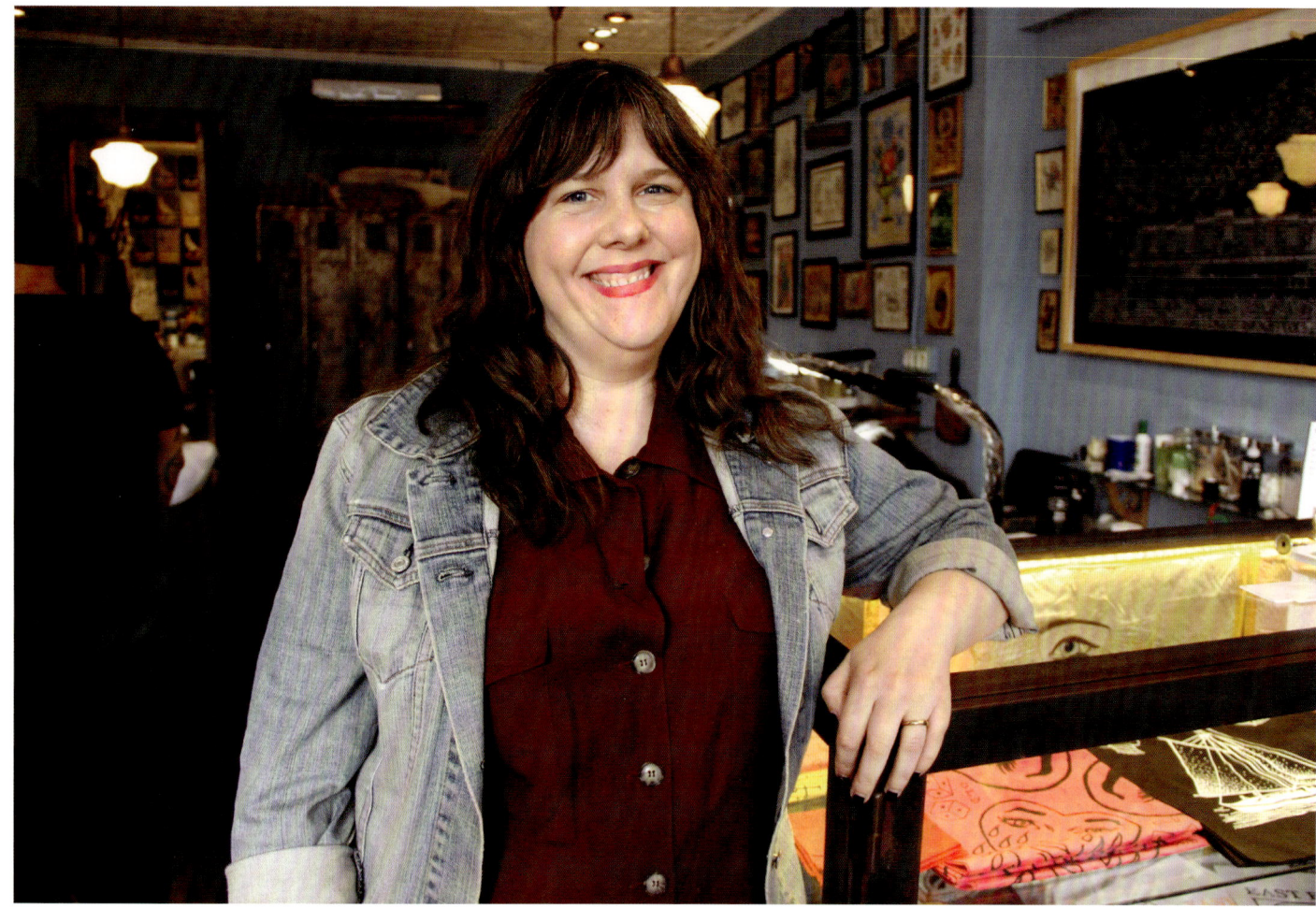

What inspired you to get the Flaco tattoo here at East River?

Emily Gallagher

It was a combination of things. 1) I live and work in this district. 2) I was already thinking about getting a Flaco tattoo because I felt a really — especially with his escape and then his ability to survive on his own despite everything against him — I really felt a connection to that story, even though I know he was experiencing it completely differently way than we were. I am a Democratic Socialist, and I am trying to escape the confines of the system we've created — and I believe that there is a whole other world that we could be in, that we could create and be a part of. The skepticism of that other world, the fear of it, is what holds a lot of us back. For me, Flaco has become a symbol of the creature who dares to — either by his own volition or someone else opening the gate — who is exploring a different way to live, and to me, that is a real touchstone.

Emily Gallagher, 40, New York State Assembly member & Greenpoint, Brooklyn resident.

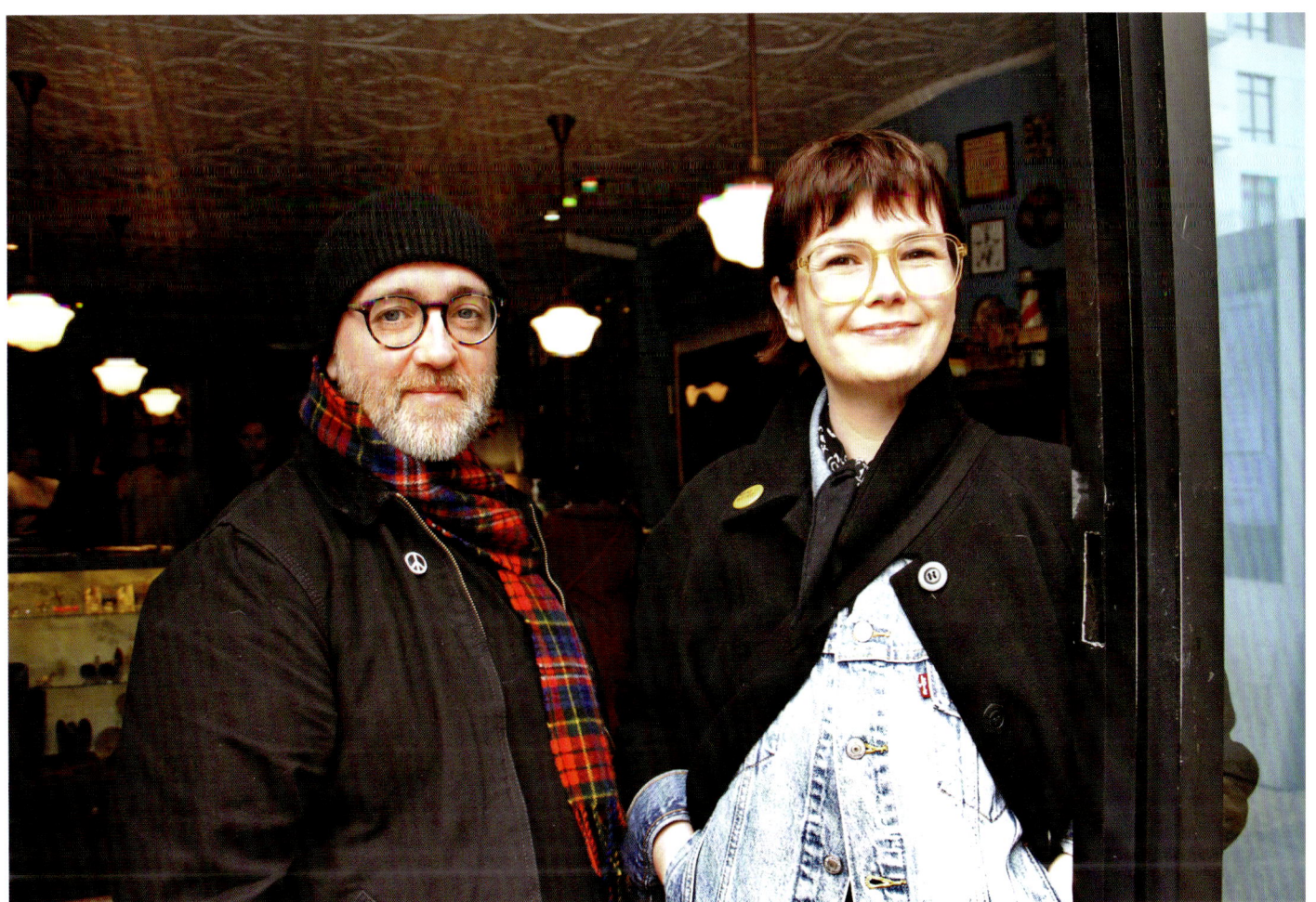

I'm really grateful to be talking to you because we're getting an international perspective here: When did you first hear about Flaco, and how did he come to mean something to you?

Sean Welsh

We follow the late-night shows, like, on YouTube, so we kind of religiously watch those every day... and it just caught our imaginations.

A lot of us think of Flaco as an inherently New York story, but how do you think it's also a global story?

Certain aspects of Flaco just transcend national boundaries. In Scotland, we like to spread our wings, and we're also quite riddled with disease, so that's something we can relate to.

Sean Welsh, 42, and Megan Mitchell, 29, from Glasgow, Scotland, who were on a holiday in NYC and had just gotten married two days before.

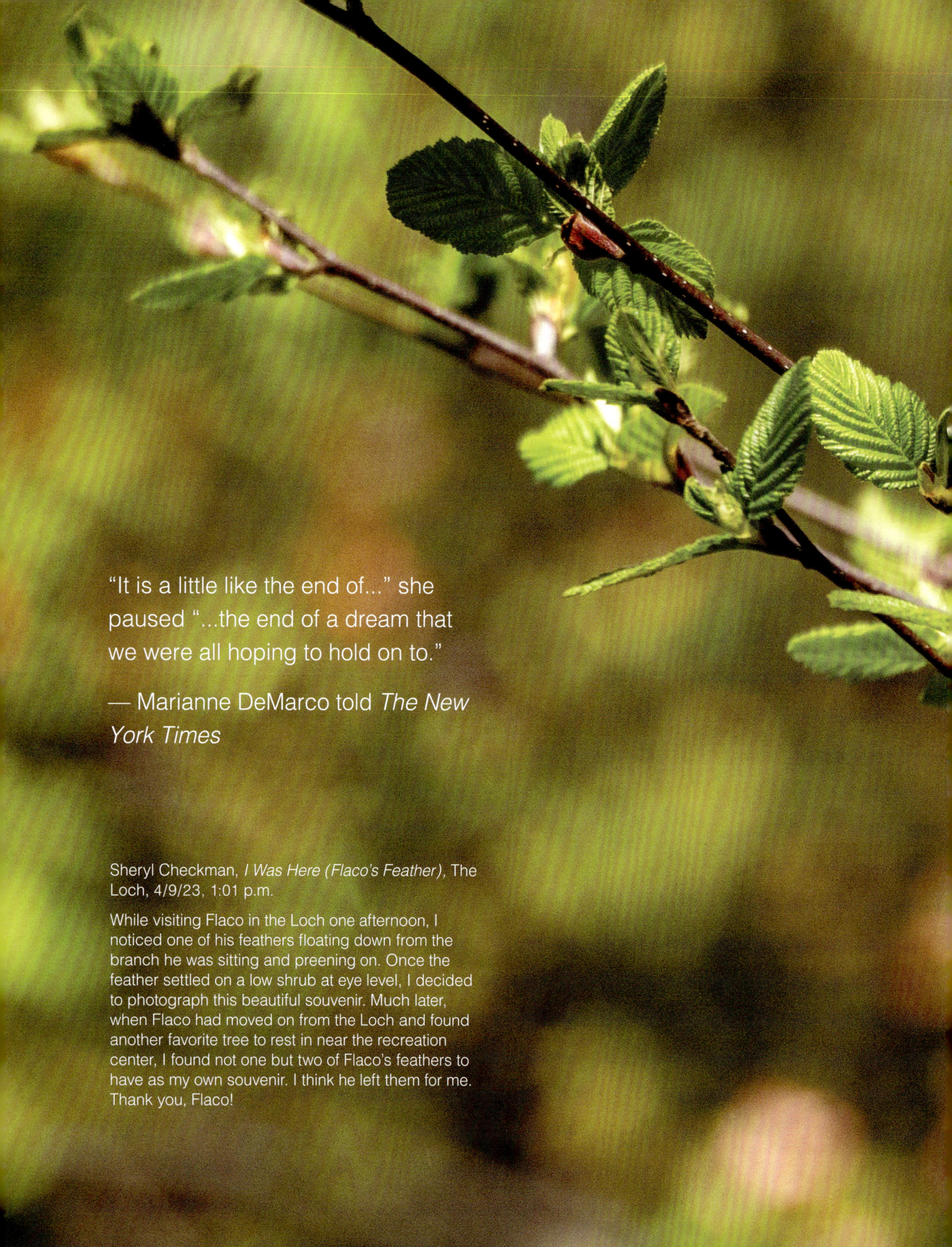

"It is a little like the end of…" she paused "…the end of a dream that we were all hoping to hold on to."

— Marianne DeMarco told *The New York Times*

Sheryl Checkman, *I Was Here (Flaco's Feather)*, The Loch, 4/9/23, 1:01 p.m.

While visiting Flaco in the Loch one afternoon, I noticed one of his feathers floating down from the branch he was sitting and preening on. Once the feather settled on a low shrub at eye level, I decided to photograph this beautiful souvenir. Much later, when Flaco had moved on from the Loch and found another favorite tree to rest in near the recreation center, I found not one but two of Flaco's feathers to have as my own souvenir. I think he left them for me. Thank you, Flaco!

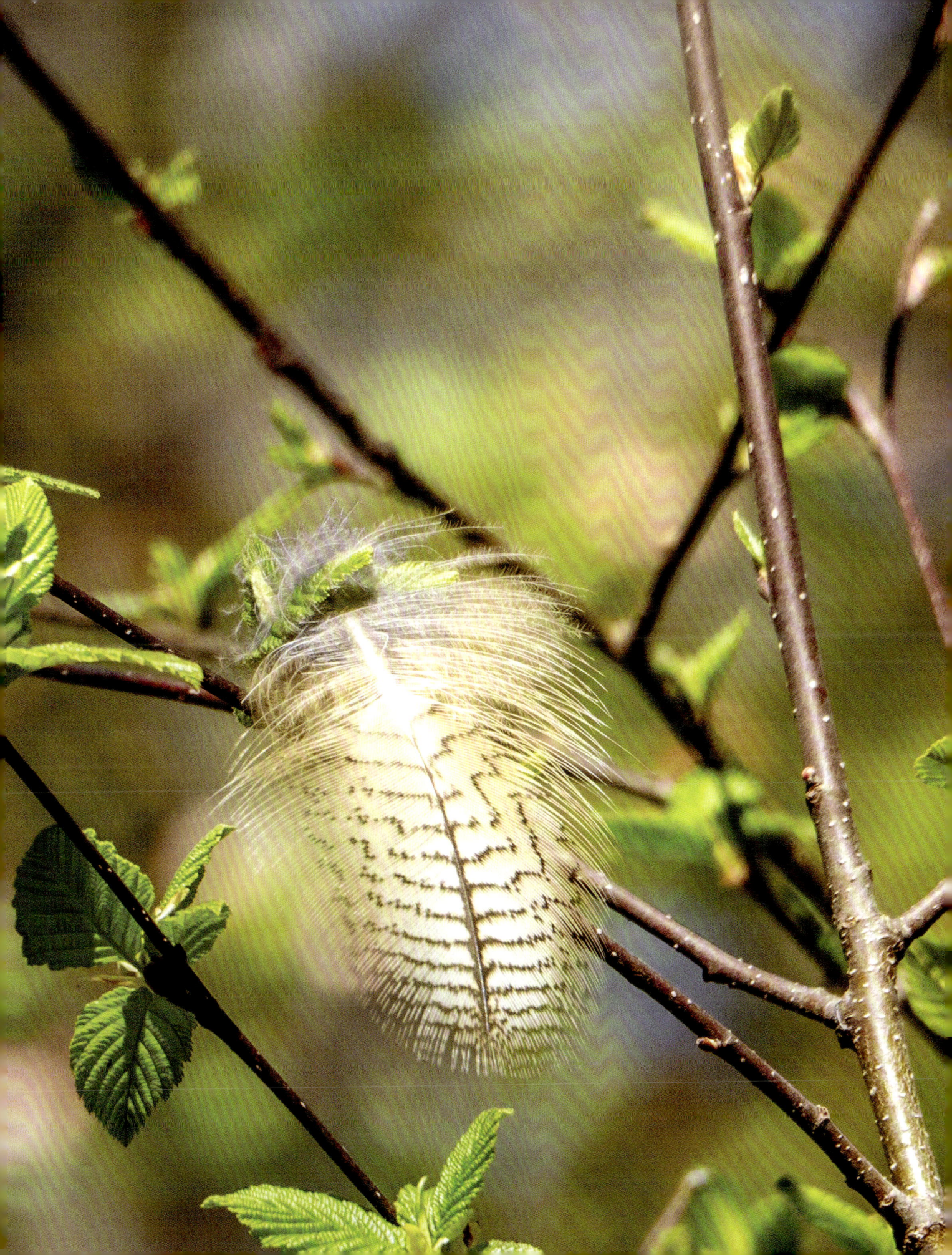

'A fabulous ambassador' Flaco, the beloved New York owl, died after building collision — NPR, 2/24/24

Flaco ist tot: New York trauert um seinen liebsten Uhu
—*Neue Zürcher Zeitung*, 2/25/24

Central Park memorial service for Flaco the owl draws huge crowd
— *ABC News,* 3/3/24

Flaco, Escaped Central Park Zoo

Flaco, New York City's beloved owl, dies after striking a building
— *Le Monde,* 2/24/24

Flaco the owl, New York City's favourite flying fugitive, found dead
— *CBC News,* 2/24/24

New York in lutto per Flaco, il gufo scappato dallo zoo e metafora di libertà –*la Repubblica,* 2/25/24

Beloved NYC owl Flaco dies after colliding with Upper West side building one year after vandals helped him stage great escape from Central Park Zoo – *Daily Mail, 2/24/24*

Parts of Flaco the Owl are being housed at the American Museum of Natural History – *Gothamist, 5/28/24*

Fans Call for Statue in Honor of Beloved Owl Flaco
– *Art & Object Magazine, 3/6/24*

Owl and Defier of Doubts, Is Dead
– *The New York Times, 2/23/24*

'It's a tragic loss': New Yorkers mourn Flaco, the owl the city took to its heart – *The Guardian, 2/27/24*

Poisoning by Rodenticide Played a Part in Flaco the Owl's Death
– *American Bird Conservancy, 3/26/24*

Flaco the owl had pigeon herpes, 4 kinds of rat poison in his system when he tragically died
– *New York Post, 3/25/24*

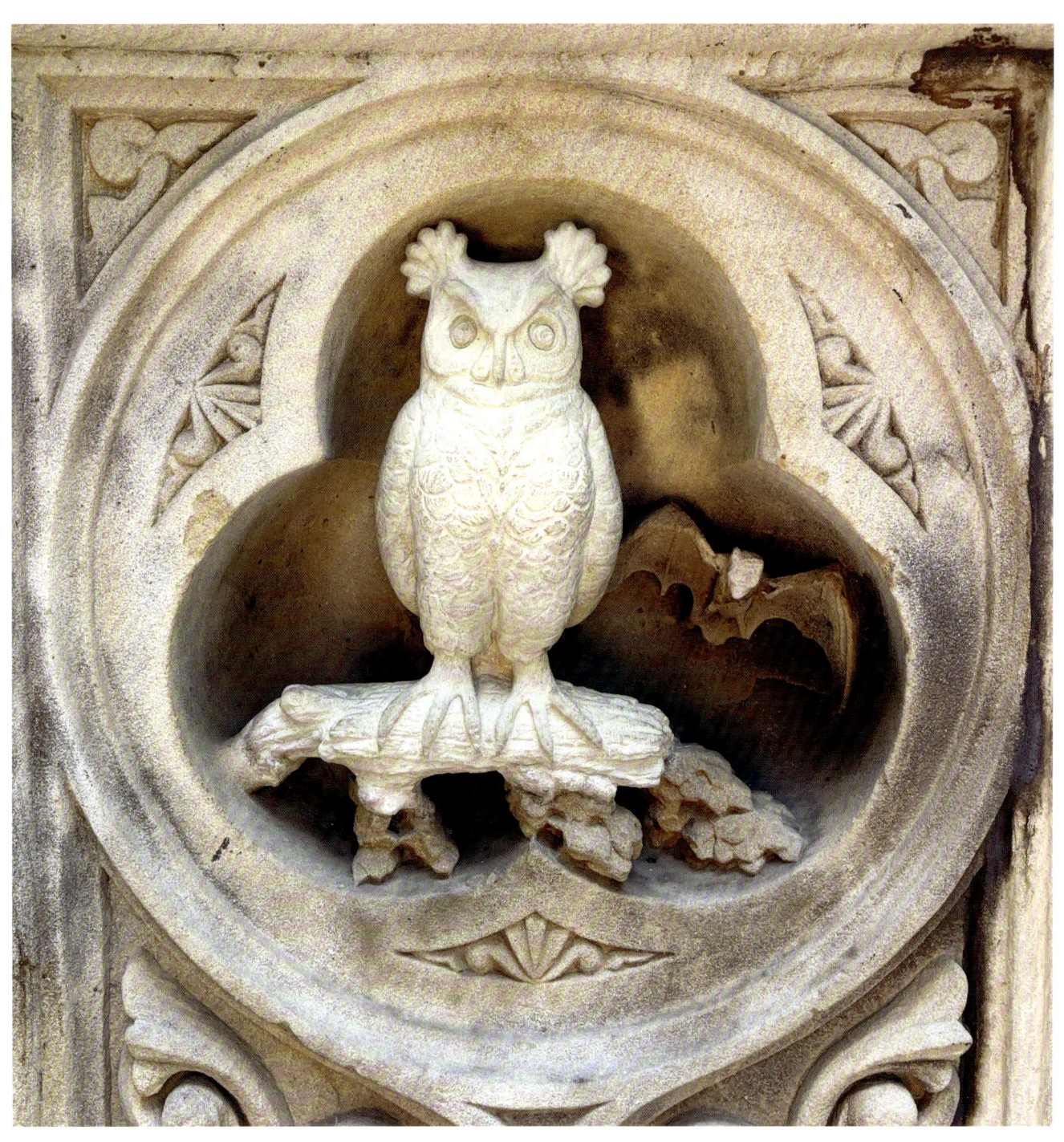

Jonathan Hollingsworth, Owl Sculpture on the Terrace Above the Bethesda Fountain, Central Park, 9/11/24, 8:37 a.m.

Flaco, a Reckoning

In the late afternoon of Friday, February 23rd, 2024, three weeks after Flaco's one-year anniversary of freedom and the bonanza of media coverage that accompanied it, Pjetar Nikaj, a building superintendent at 267 West 89th Street, an eight-story building near Riverside Park, discovered a feathery heap in the building's courtyard.

Building resident and birder Alan Drogin reported to the NYS Birds listserv that the super had found Flaco still alive, lying face down with wings spread, outside the building's basement door. The building had been among the lucky hosts to Flaco, having seen him roosting on the fire escape adjacent to their courtyard and heard him hooting at night. Drogin contacted the Wild Bird Fund a few blocks away, which sent two rescue volunteers who pronounced Flaco dead shortly thereafter.

The following day, the Central Park Zoo announced the initial findings of the Bronx Zoo pathologists' necropsy: the acute traumatic collision had yielded no evidence of head trauma or bone fractures, but there was significant bleeding behind the sternum and in the back of the body cavity and minor bleeding behind the left eye. Otherwise, the zoo announced, "Flaco was in good body condition at the time of death, with good muscling and adequate fat stores." He'd lost a tenth of a pound between the last time his weight was taken at the zoo and the time of his necropsy, weighing in at 4.1lb.

But as with the death of Barry the Barred Owl, who also suffered an acute traumatic injury, the question remained whether there were other factors that had contributed to Flaco's death. And there were. On March 25th, the Central Park Zoo announced the final set of findings from the necropsy:

"[Flaco] had a severe pigeon herpesvirus from eating feral pigeons that had become part of his diet," and the virus had caused "severe tissue damage and inflammation in many organs, including the spleen, liver, gastrointestinal tract, bone marrow, and brain." Flaco suffered "exposure to four different anticoagulant rodenticides that are commonly used for rat control in New York City. These factors would have been debilitating and ultimately fatal, even without a traumatic injury, and may have predisposed him to flying into or falling from the building."

The photographers who documented Flaco had expressed concern about what would happen when he left the park. The Central Park Conservancy reported that they had stopped their usage of rodenticide, but the rest of the city was another matter, with its nearly 300-year-old rat problem, courtesy of the ships that had brought "Old World" diseases and vermin from Europe and Asia. New York is home to an estimated three million rats, which is at least a head or a tail for each of the city's eight million human residents. So far, the city's most common method for stymying the rats' population growth is poison, which affects species well beyond the rodenticide's target.

And then there were the pigeons, who can carry the herpesvirus with no detrimental effect on themselves. No one had seen Flaco dismantling a pigeon in the park, but he developed an appetite for them while on the Lower East Side, and later, while moving between the Upper East and Upper West Side. On her Instagram account, Anke Frohlich posted an image of Flaco looking down from the top of a building, with a green arrow pointing to the two pigeon legs extending over the building's edge.

The departure from the relative safety of the park might have been Flaco's undoing, where he was exposed to an exponential increase of danger, risking a collision with a building, window, or car, and subsisting on a toxic diet.

After the final necropsy was published, *Saturday Night Live* (which had already made a cringe-worthy "Flaco's last words" joke—inducing a groan from its live audience—the month prior) made hay of "pigeon herpes." Cast member Sarah Sherman appeared as Flaco's weepy, feathery widow—the irony being that Flaco had no chance of finding a mate—devastated by Flaco's infidelity more than his death.

The domestic and international media, which had covered Flaco's liberation and the subsequent marvel at his survival, published the final coverage of his death and its causes.

Dissenters in the NYC birding community—who never gave up their position that Flaco should have been captured and that the Central Park Zoo had shrugged and given up too easily to avoid a public relations disaster and risk being further cast as the Big Bad Zoo—wagged their fingers and excoriated the entire Flaco movement, taking to task the media, journalists, photographers, social media followers, artists, bloggers, documentarians and filmmakers, who, to paraphrase, used Flaco for the sensational story, cheap inspiration and fuzzy feelings he induced.

"We selfishly ignored the truth and simply let him die. We did not love him," D. Bruce Yolton wrote in his "Science Denial Killed Flaco" post (February 29th, 2024) on UrbanHawks.com.

Following the necropsy, the Bronx Zoo donated Flaco's wings and frozen tissue samples to the scientific collection of the American Museum of Natural History, while the rest of his remains have been archived at the Bronx Zoo's Wildlife Health Center. The Museum of Natural History's Flaco holdings will not be on view to the public but will be used by scientists and artists for educational materials and field guides.

With Flaco's death came petitions. On ThePetitionSite.com, 63,000 people (so far) have signed a petition "to urge the NYPD and Central Park Zoo officials to relaunch the investigation into the vandalism of Flaco's habitat to prevent any further zoo inhabitant escapes." At Flaco's memorial service, a speaker wearing aviator sunglasses said, "Flaco's story does not have to end here. It does not have to end in tragedy," asking those gathered to sign a petition for the placement of a bronze memorial in Central Park. Three separate petitions begun by Mike Hubbard, Jesse McGraw, and David X have accrued more than 5,000 signatures.

Flaco would be in excellent company among the park's long history of animal monuments and sculptures, including *Balto*, the Siberian husky and life-saving Alaskan sled dog (1925), *Still Hunt*, the American panther posed in a low crouch sculpted by Edward Kemeys (1883), or *Eagles and Prey* depicting two eagles attacking a goat in gruesome detail, by the French artist Christopher Fratin, installed in 1863. But the bureaucracy of placing a monument in Central Park can be years in the making and the park's complicated relationship with Flaco might not be one they'd like to commemorate in bronze.

The Monday after Flaco's death, two pieces of New York State legislation resurfaced with the aim of creating safer skies for birds: The Bird Safe Buildings Act, S.7098/A.7808, was renamed the FLACO "Feathered Lives Also Count" Act, which requires new or significantly updated buildings to incorporate bird-friendly design, most importantly in their windows. The Audubon Society estimates that up to one billion birds die in the U.S. annually from window collisions, particularly with the increased use of highly glazed or ultra-clear glass and the confusing effects of light pollution.

The Dark Skies Protection Act, S.7663/A5632, first introduced in the New York State Senate in January 2022 and sponsored by State Senator Brad Hoylman-Sigal, would aim to reduce light pollution in New York, requiring that non-essential outdoor lighting be shielded, motion activated, or turned off between 11:00 p.m. and 5:00 a.m.. Light pollution disrupts birds' natural sense of their environment, drawing them to the lethal dangers of urban centers which can be devastating for the 80% of birds who migrate at night.

The New York Historical Society acquired a selection of memorial objects left at the base of the oak and featured them in an exhibition, *The Year of Flaco,* from January to July 2025, curated by Rebecca Klassen and miraculously produced in the museum world where exhibitions can be years in the making.

Despite initial enthusiasm, more than a dozen publishers rejected this manuscript on the basis that the Flaco parade would have passed by the time they could have brought the book to market, that it wouldn't backlist well (publishing lingo for selling beyond the first year of publication), that niche audience demand couldn't meet the inevitable glut of Flaco books to come, and lastly, perhaps the real reason, that the story was just too sad.

But here we are.

There will never be a safe way to talk about Flaco's narrative, the same way there are no easy ways to discuss the roles of zoos in our society. Perception tends to be in black or white, with little patience for the murky gray between.

Was New York City good for Flaco? In the end, no. But New York is where the story happened — and in a very public way. Flaco's was a life — and death — that received a blinding degree of attention and care that few other animals, or species, ever receive — even though they are just as deserving.

That we've failed to give the same attention to other wildlife is perhaps the greater tragedy of the Flaco story.

Signage for Flaco Remembrance Ceremony, Hung on Flaco's Oak After His Passing, Design by Breanne Delgado

Following spread left Photos by Stella Hamilton, Memorial Objects at the Base of Flaco's Oak, 3/3/24

Following spread right Photos by Stella Hamilton. Bottom left photo: by Jonathan Hollingsworth. Bottom right: T-shirt designed by Calicho Arevalo.

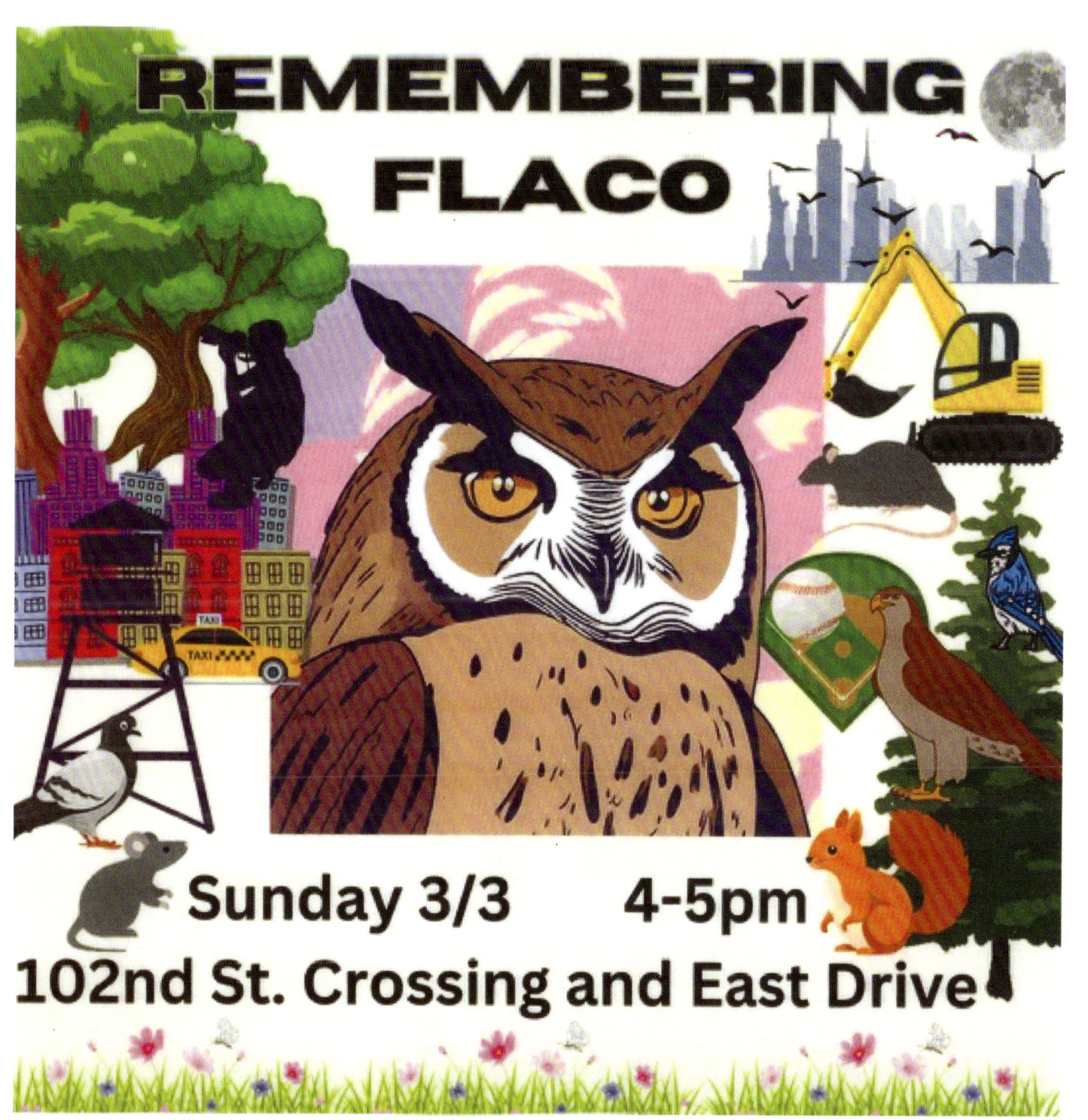

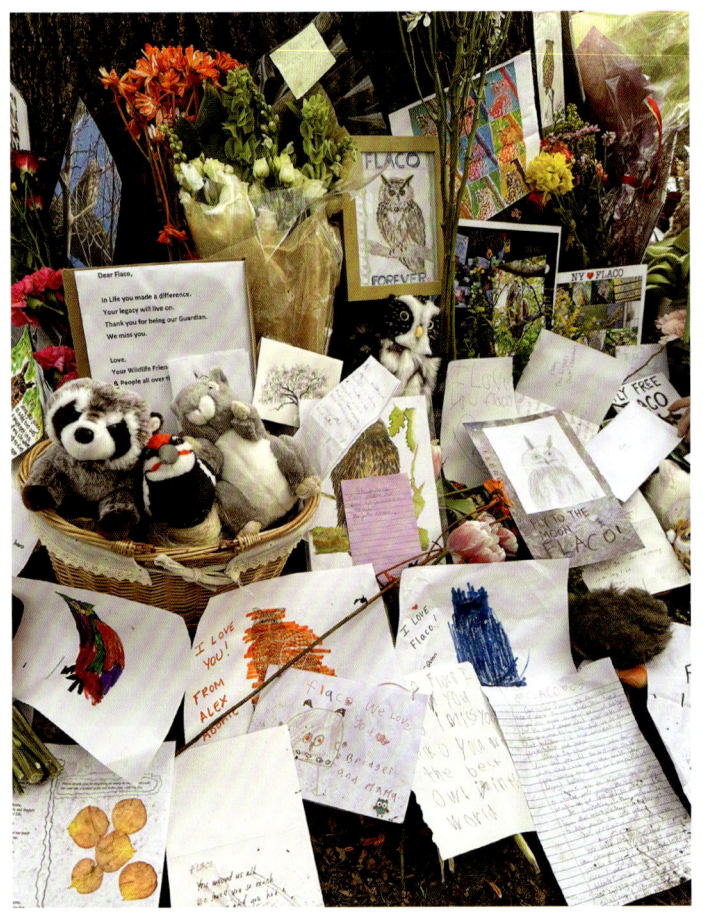
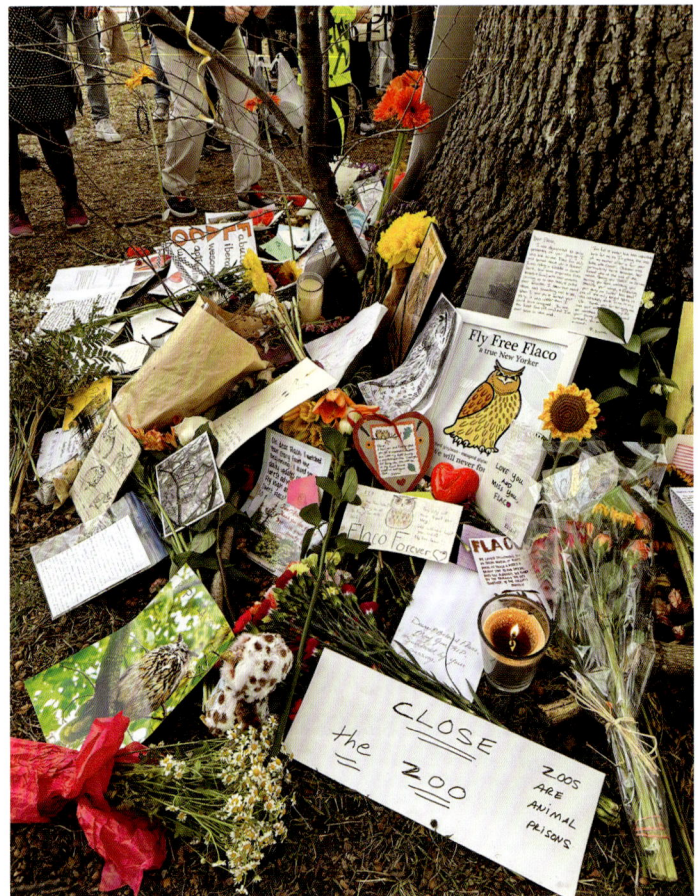
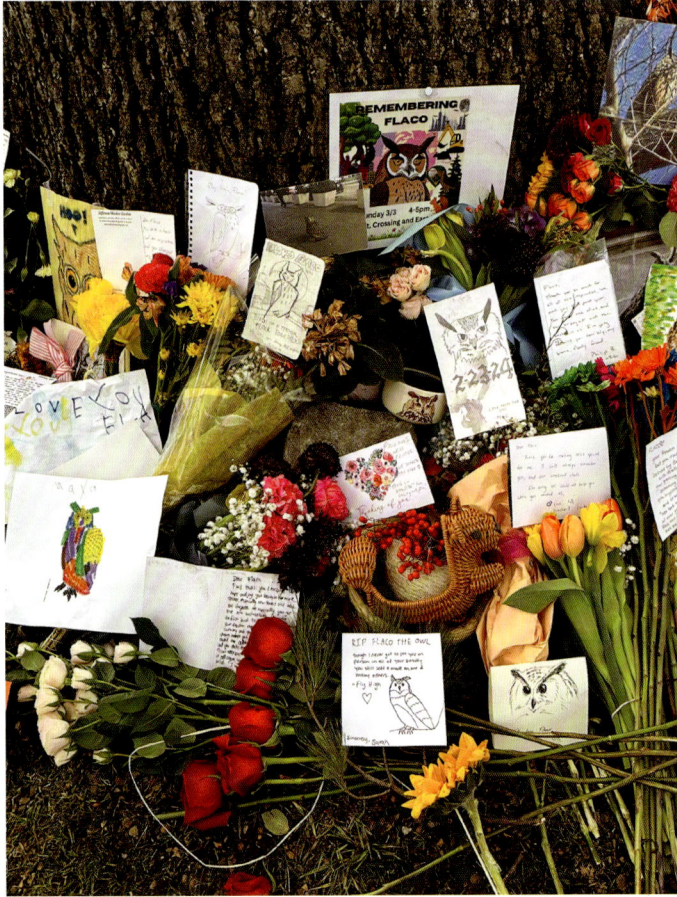
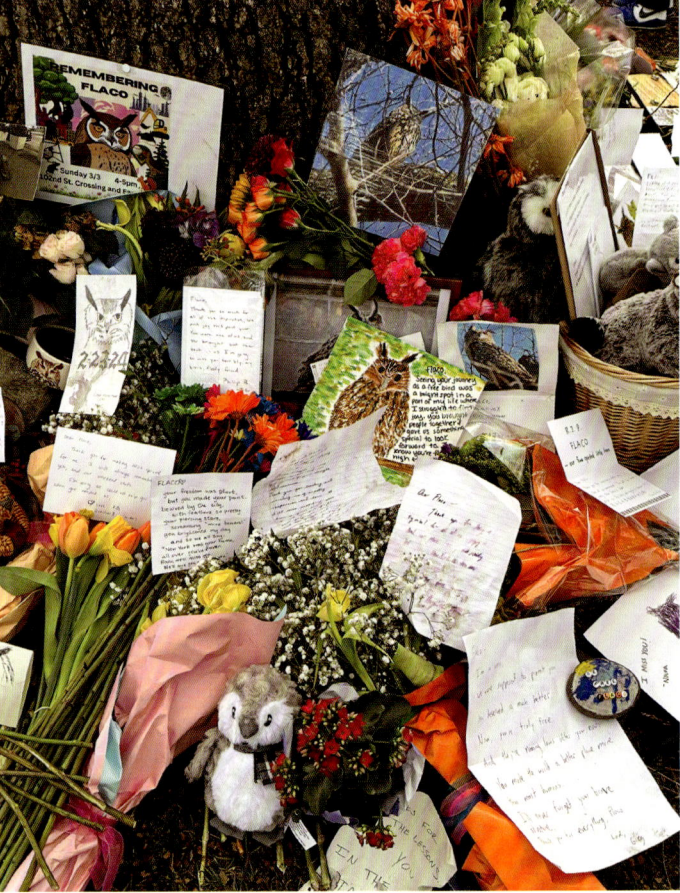

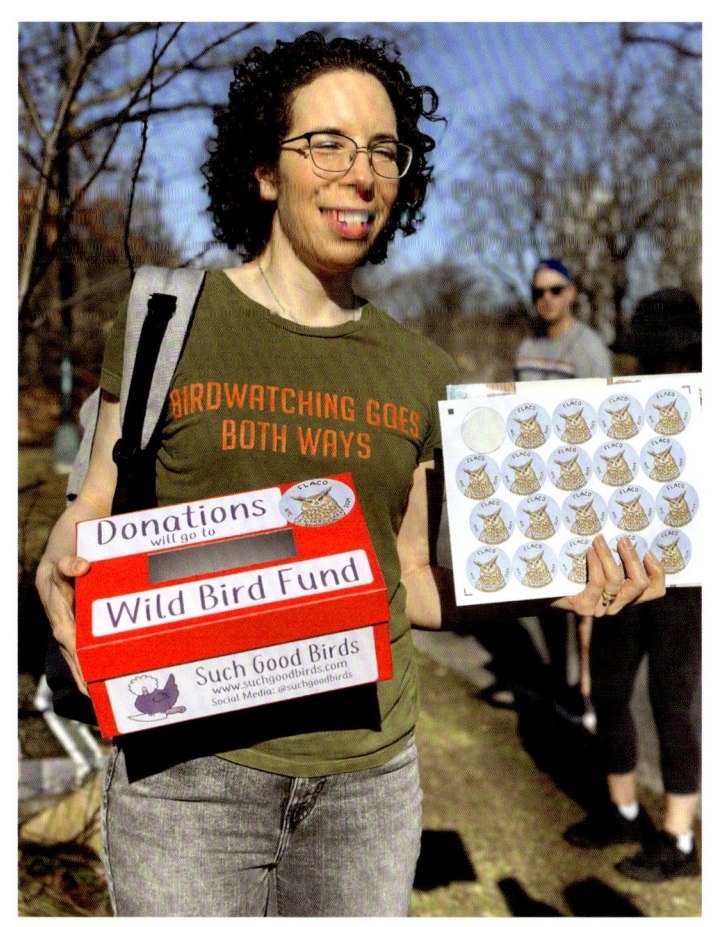
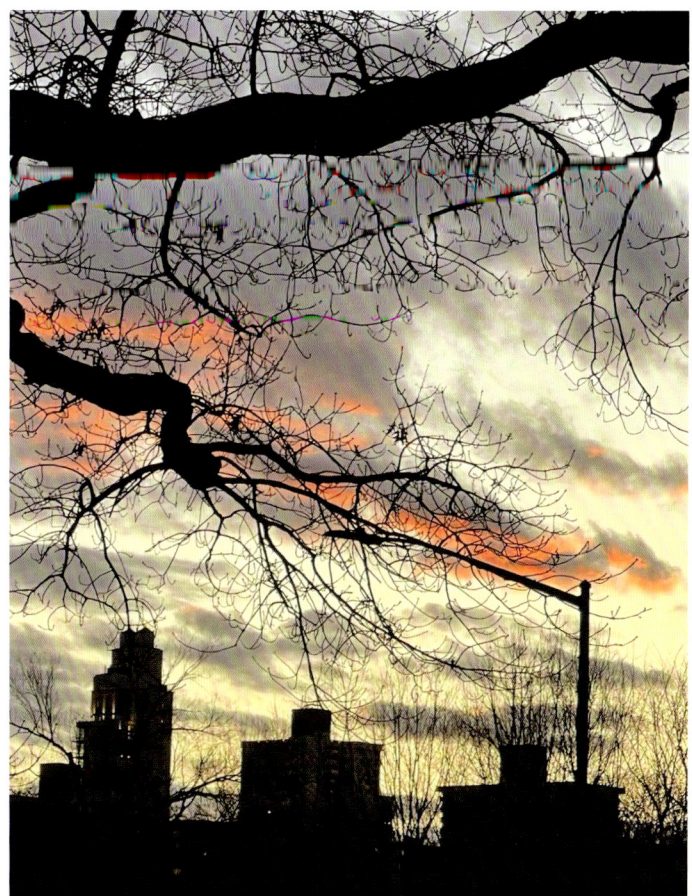
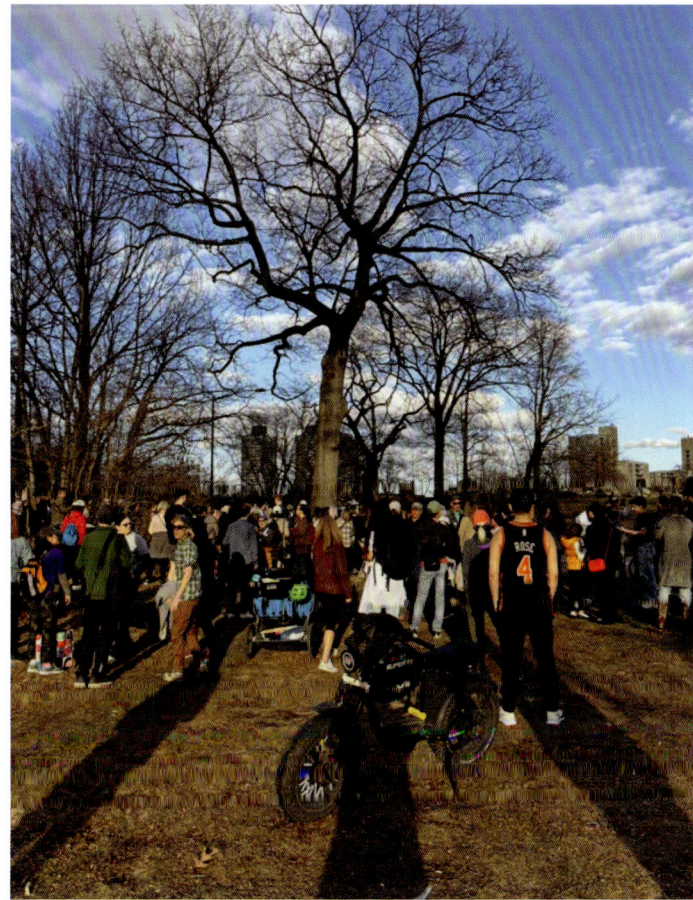
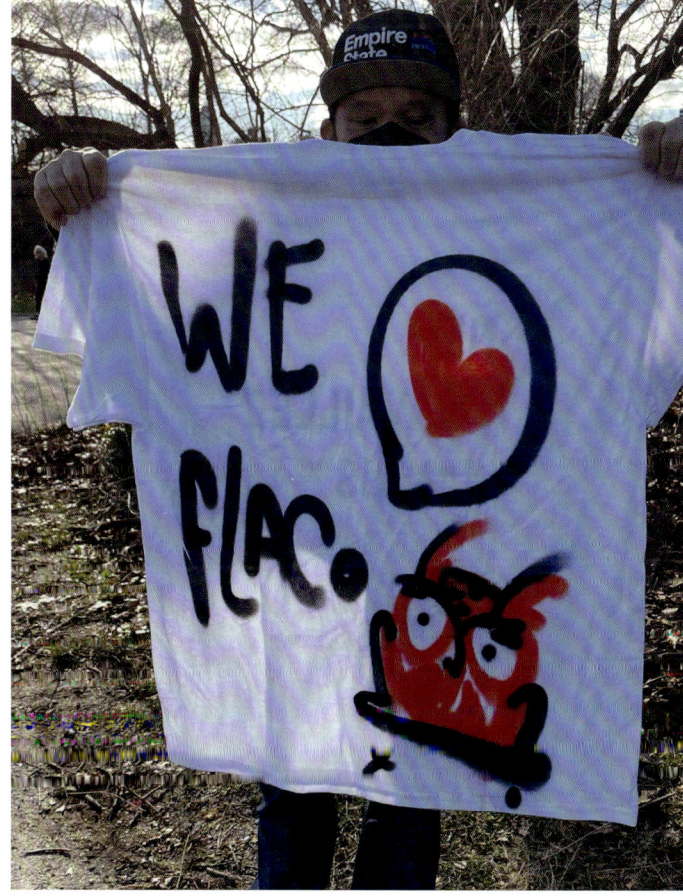

In Memoriam: Remembering Flaco

After the news of Flaco's death on February 23rd, 2024, David Barrett announced via Manhattan Bird Alert that Flaco's oak at 104th Street and East Drive would be the designated spot for remembrances. On that first day, a Saturday, mourners placed a handful of bouquets and notes at the base of the tree—but not enough to cover every inch of ground as would be the case in the following days. The same day, Stella Hamilton, an avid birder and Flaco devotee who had visited the owl almost every day of the previous year, began planning a remembrance ceremony for the following weekend. In addition to fellow Flaco fans, there were photographers, writers, musicians, and singer-songwriters who volunteered to contribute to the ceremony.

On Tuesday, February 27th, when weather reports predicted rain, Hamilton and Valerie Hartman, a fellow Flaco follower, collected the materials that could be damaged by rain—most of it paper—for safekeeping. In the following days, even in inclement weather, more objects arrived at the tree, collected and preserved at the end of each day. Despite their best efforts to save them from rain, some of the drawings and notes are marked by the elements, with ink smeared and paper rumpled, as if someone had deliberately cried on each one. (The remembrance objects left at the base of Barry the Barred Owl's tree after her fatal collision with a Central Park Conservancy maintenance vehicle in August 2021, had not been so fortunate: the Central Park grounds crew had gathered them up and thrown everything away. No one had thought to preserve it.)

At the memorial service in the late afternoon of Sunday, March 3rd, the objects were returned, like a revelation, and carefully laid out among the flowers. There was no official count of the mourners in attendance, but the number was in the hundreds, with people surrounding the tree and spilling onto the pavement on East Drive. News crews, with their cameras and fuzzy-headed sound equipment, lined up in a phalanx at the front, reminding us that Flaco's story had always been a media event for public consumption. Within hours, the *Isn't-that-so-New-York* owl funeral would be packaged into a tidy two-minute segment, broadcast into the living rooms of America. The passing bikes slowed to observe the crowd and shouted to each other, irreverently, "It's for that owl."

The feelings of grief and devastation were palpable, even before the ceremony began.

It can be difficult to contextualize our human impact on the environment. The icecaps melt on our smartphones; the summers are hotter, the winters milder; sea levels are rising, and the planet's temperature increases by degrees . . . we know about these things, but they are seldom an immediate part of our daily lives. But the poisoning of an owl—a majestic creature among the most beloved and mysterious in the avian family—killed in our own backyard, on our watch, struck deep. In addition to the feelings of loss, there was culpability, too. Our prophets, our saints—and our beloved owls—never last as long as we might like them to, because we always kill them in the end.

Breanne Delgado officiated the ceremony. David Lei and Jacqueline Emery, both among the core Flaco photographers, brought the microphone and sound equipment and spoke to the crowd. The capacity of the equipment couldn't quite accommodate the masses, so those in the outer orbits strained to hear and hushed peripheral conversations. Nan Knighton, who'd had a three-hour Flaco visitation at her kitchen window, read a poem. Singer-songwriter Jonathan Green performed his Flaco tribute, "Orange Eyes," on acoustic guitar, accompanied by Elijah Shiffer. Shiffer also performed "Postscript for Flaco," a piece he'd composed for alto saxophone. A boy, maybe 10 years old, began his remembrance by saying he "wasn't a superfan," but the tears in his eyes later in the ceremony suggested otherwise. Flaco muralist Calicho Arevalo spray painted "We Love Flaco" on T-shirts and jackets at no charge. A graphic designer sold Flaco stickers to benefit the Wild Bird Fund. On the activist front, representatives from the Wild Bird Fund and the Coalition for City Lights (which is lobbying to implement legislation to mitigate light pollution that leads to millions of urban bird deaths each year) were in attendance.

As speaker after speaker took the mic and stood in the middle of the great circle, some in the crowd maintained their composure, gracefully wiping tears from their cheeks. For others, the intensity of their sorrow could not be so neatly contained, and swelled their faces with crying. The ceremony was like theater, not the stuff on 42nd Street, but theater as the ancient Greeks had conceived it—an event of catharsis and transformation.

After the ceremony, in the golden afternoon light of late winter, the crowd broke into smaller groups, speaking softly, consoling each other. In addition to the sense of grief, something else was happening, too: a sense of celebration and grace. In a city that's famous for its aversion to eye contact or familiarity among strangers, there were hugs among people who didn't know each other, reunions among friends, and unexpected meetings between those who had followed each other on social media for years, but had never met in person.

In this sea of kindness, to be human seemed like such a lovely thing. Maybe that was one of Flaco's greatest gifts. He gave us back our humanity and reminded us of our great power and responsibility to be stewards and caretakers, not just for owls, but all animals and this gem of a planet–our only home.

That was Flaco's gift and his sacrifice.

Elijah Shiffer
City of Birds: Postscript for Flaco

New York City-based composer and alto saxophonist Elijah Shiffer began conceiving his "City of Birds" project in 2021. Inspired by the songs, characteristics, and habitats of the city's indigenous birds that he'd encountered in the wild—mourning doves, bank swallows, and Wilson's Phalarope, among others—he created compositions devoted to each bird, which often debuted in public spaces during the pandemic and were released in 2023, in the first of a series of albums.

Flaco didn't fit the mold for "City of Birds," though: he wasn't indigenous, but instead, an accidental interloper and surprise guest in the city's rich bird ecosystem. Even so, owls had been a musical inspiration as Shiffer had been considering a musical interpretation of Edward Lear's infectiously rhythmic children's poem, "The Owl and the Pussy-Cat," written in 1867.

When Shiffer learned of Flaco's death and saw signage at the base of the owl's favorite oak in Central Park announcing a remembrance ceremony, he knew he wanted to be a part of it and wrote the composition "Postscript for Flaco," performed as a saxophone solo, utilizing the Edward Lear melody that had never been committed to paper. Though he'd seen Flaco once in the wild, he had never heard his haunting call, so Shiffer listened to recordings of Eurasian eagle-owls and noticed their two-tone calls, in the notes A and F, which he recreated in our conversation.

E flat minor, a close neighbor to the A/F call, captured the somber nature of Flaco's death and, for Shiffer, felt like a key that evoked the dark, foreboding mysteries of forests at night. When he debuted the piece at Flaco's remembrance ceremony, the sound carried up into the bare branches of the winter oak, into the crisp blue sky of early March, and stopped even those who'd casually happened upon the hundreds who'd gathered to mourn for an owl.

Postscript For Flaco

Elijah Shiffer

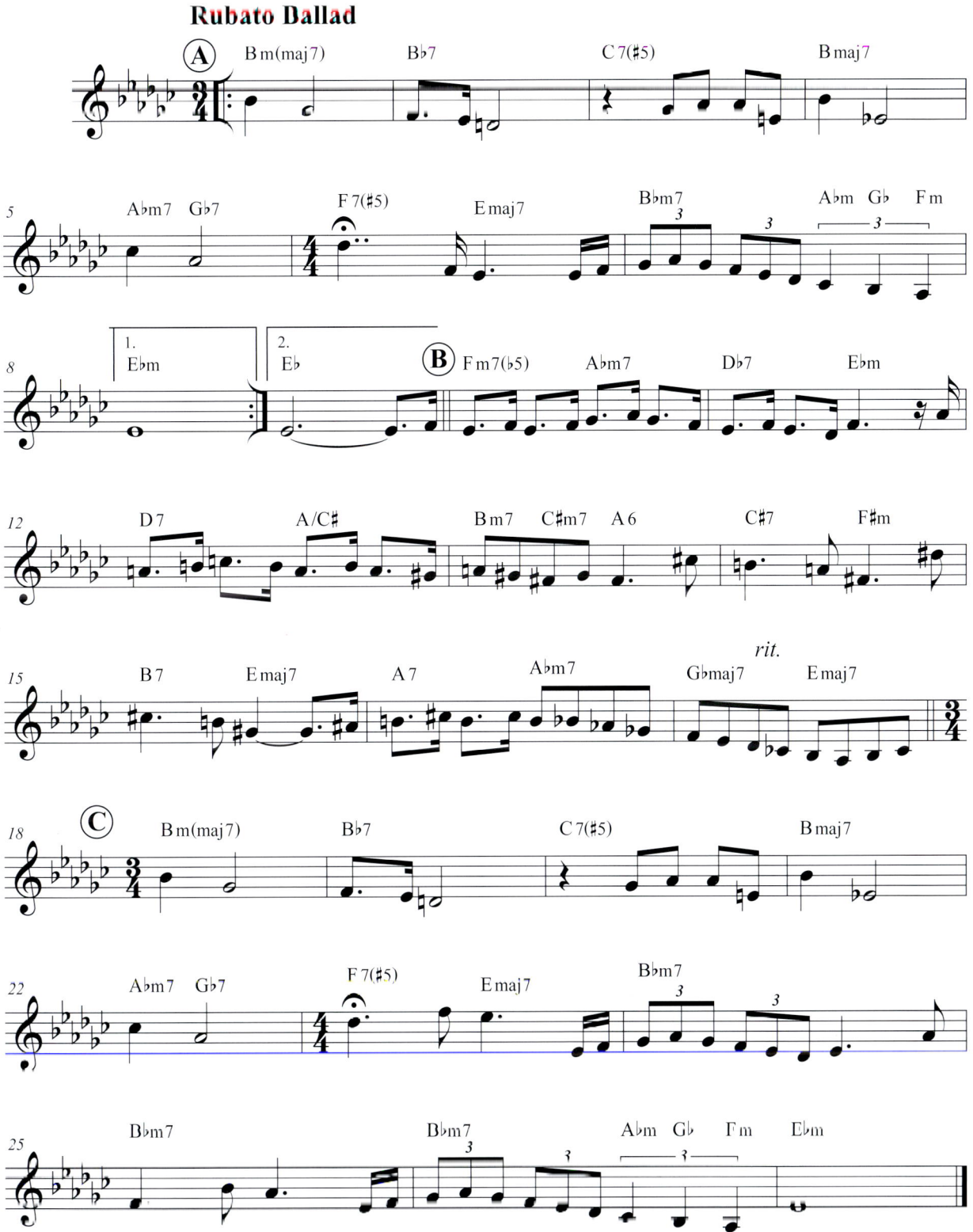

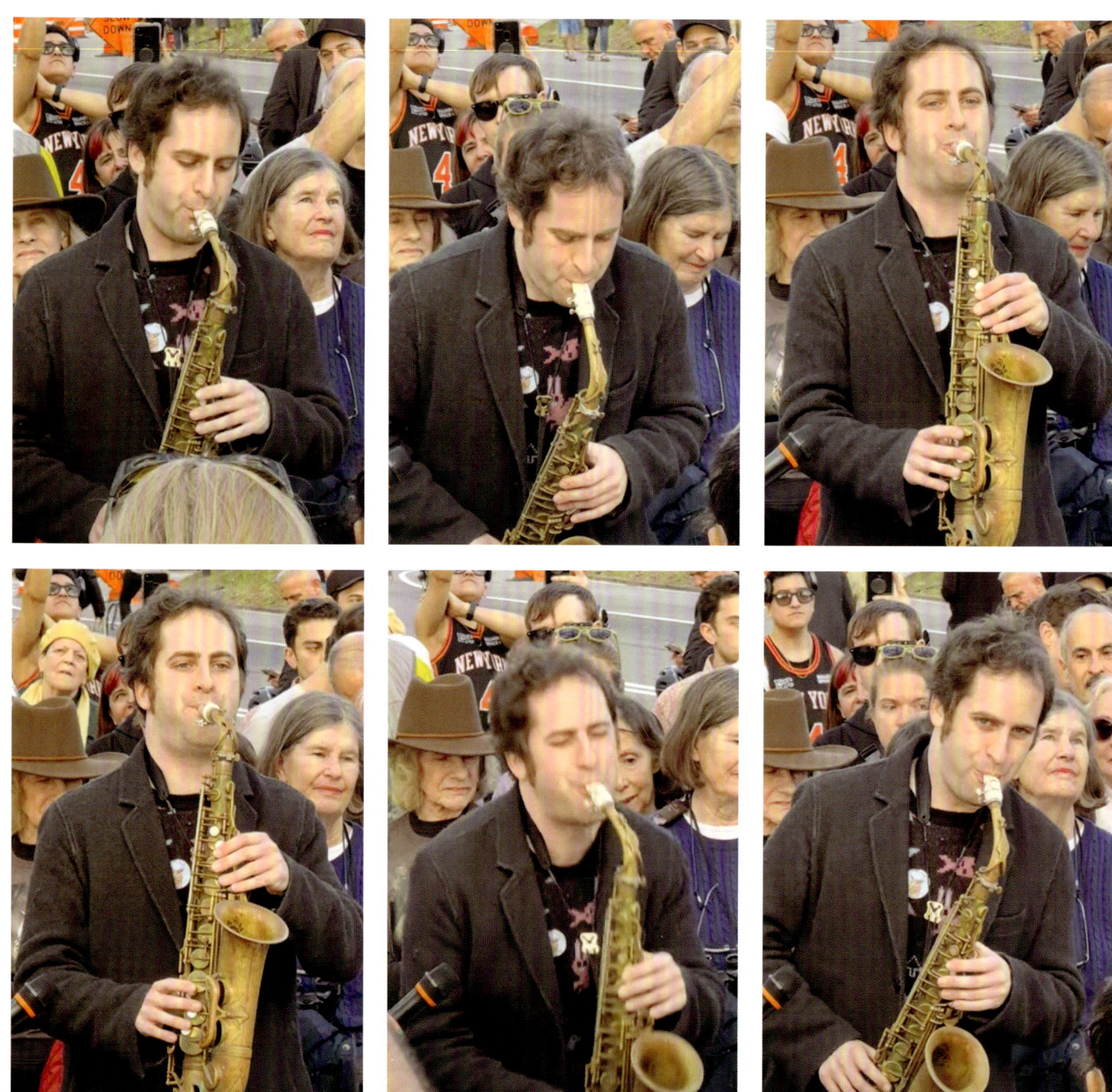

Elijah Shiffer performing "Postscript for Flaco" at the Flaco remembrance ceremony, March 3rd, 2024.

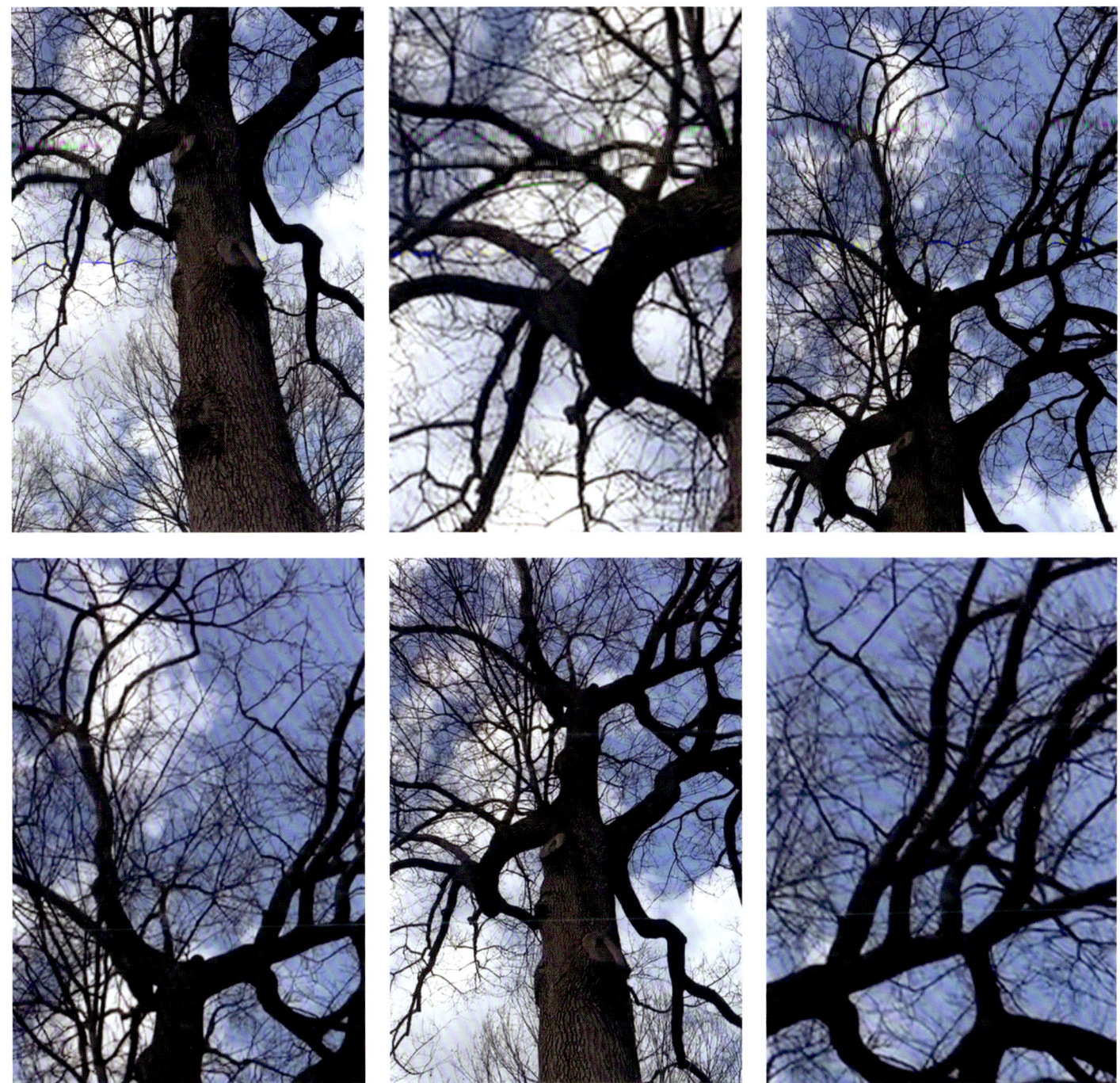

Branches of Flaco's oak, filmed by Stefan Shanni during Shiffer's solo.

FLY HIGH FLACO!

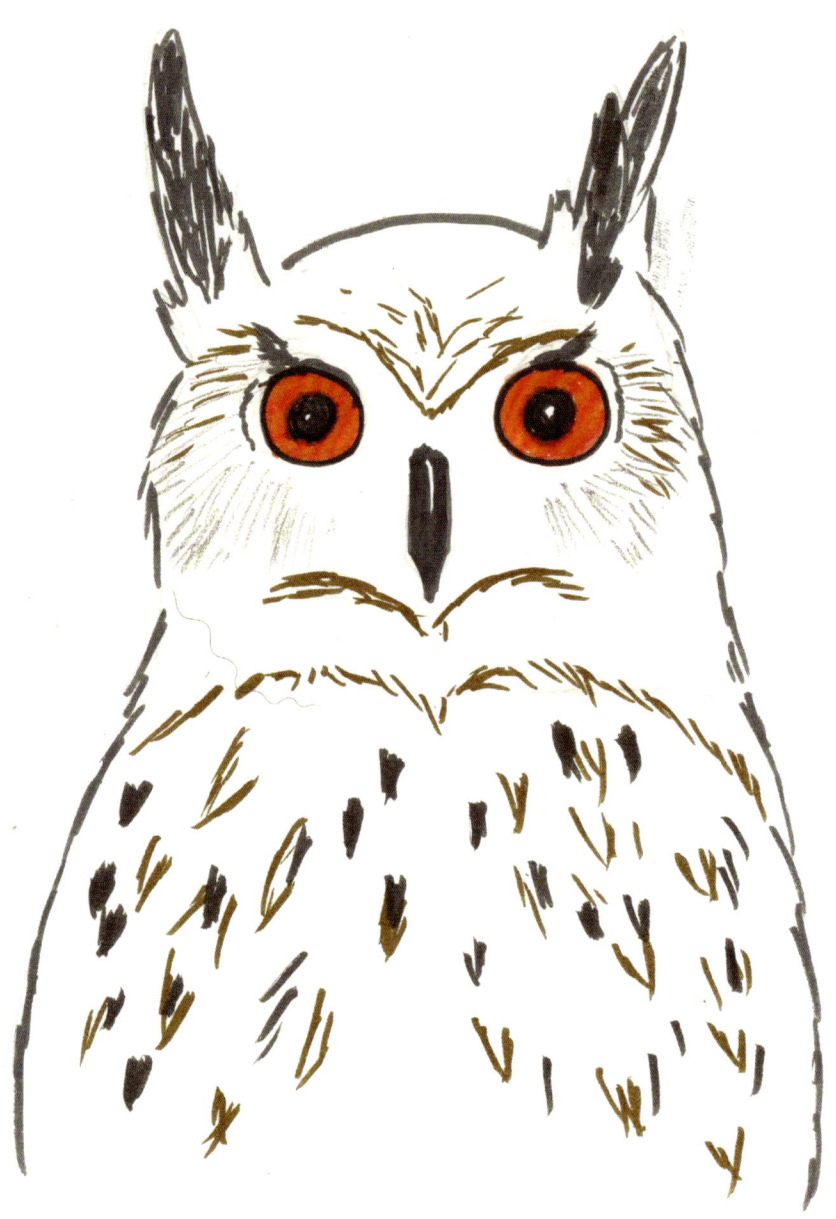

I have been worrying about you since your escape a year ago, but have been inspired, dazzled, and joyful about how you overcame the doubts and made it on your own. Hope your year was amazing... your memory will live on!! ♡ ♡ ♡   -T.L.

Memorial Objects

Baskets: 4
Heart-shaped box: 1
Bracelets: 3
Brochure: 1
Candle: 1
Cards: 39
Collages: 2
Coloring pages: 6
Coral: 1
Currency (Peso): 1
Digital print: 1
Drawings: 27
Flaco feather: 1
Figurines: 2
Flyer: 1
Illustrated cards/notes: 12
Illustrations: 5
Letters: 32
Magnets: 2

Mug: 1
Notes: 49
Origami: 1
Ornaments: 3
Rocks: 2
Paper (designed, no note): 1
Pennant: 1
Photographs: 10
Photographs with letters: 3
Poems: 4
Postcards: 2
Poster: 1
Prints: 6
Shells: 2
Signs: 6
Sculpture: 1
Stickers: 2 sets
Stuffed animals: 15
Toy car: 1

T.L., *Fly High Flaco!*, pencil and marker on paper, 11 x 8½ in.

About the Collection

In addition to the layers of flowers, mourners left 257 objects at the base of the oak.

Most were notes, letters, and cards, but the arrangement included drawings, photographs, and paintings, too; then the odd ephemera of painted rocks, shells, ornaments, and figurines. Some of the most touching objects were made by children, of course, with their uncertain handwriting and anatomically questionable owls, but it was the letters and cards where the heart of the story was laid bare, revealing deep vulnerabilities and why Flaco had been a beacon of hope and inspiration during seasons of darkness. Regardless of the memento, everyone had left a part of themselves under that tree.

Some had given thought to their presentation — and preservation — placing them inside Ziploc bags, maybe anticipating rain. Others encased their notes/drawings in clear packing tape, not as aesthetically pleasing, but functional. Inside the plastic heart-shaped box, there was a note. A Cuban peso was inscribed "We Love Flaco." Beautifully produced watercolors and drawings were laminated or placed in glassine pouches and left with modest indications of who had created them. Some of the letter-writers closed with a name or an initial, but most were unsigned in an expression that was deeply personal yet public and anonymous. To step back from the tree and study the objects was not just to witness our grief but to study a portrait of ourselves.

The business of choosing which objects to include in the following pages was not an easy one, because the entire collection warrants its own book. ("Charlotte," if your parents ever buy a copy of this book, you got three well-deserved pages, more than anyone else, including the multi-colored feathers that fluttered out of the "I Love You Flaco" envelope, accompanying the four stapled pages each emphatically marked with your name.) Sorting through them all, item by item, while carefully brushing the dirt off, carried an emotional weight that was a little overwhelming at times. The objects I was handling felt sacred: they had left the hands of their creators for an unknown destination.

Most of the objects were created between the news of Flaco's death on February 23rd and the memorial ceremony on March 3rd, but there were other tribute objects that had been created during Flaco's year of freedom, dated before his death. The captions in the following pages include dates only in instances in which it was noted by the work's creator.

After the ceremony ended, when even most of the stragglers had gone home, a small group lingered, crouching over the objects and taking pictures in the last light of the day. For those of us there, the question remained: what to do with the objects because no one else had claimed responsibility for them. It would have been like leaving a stray kitten by the side of the road — unconscionable. Someone suggested leaving the collection overnight, then offered to gather it up the next morning, but we could see what exposure to the elements could do, from the watermarks and smudges of dirt on white paper.

The box and tote bags on hand didn't seem adequate to carry everything, but our little group managed, working in silence, carefully stacking each item. The collection belongs to everyone and no one. It is public domain, but now a selection of the items has found a permanent home, fittingly, at the New York Historical Society where they will be exhibited in 2025, a year after Flaco's death, and preserved for future generations to understand Flaco's cultural impact.

When it was done, there was a quiet solidarity among our little group, most who did not know each other (yet). We had done something good—and from that moment, this book was born.

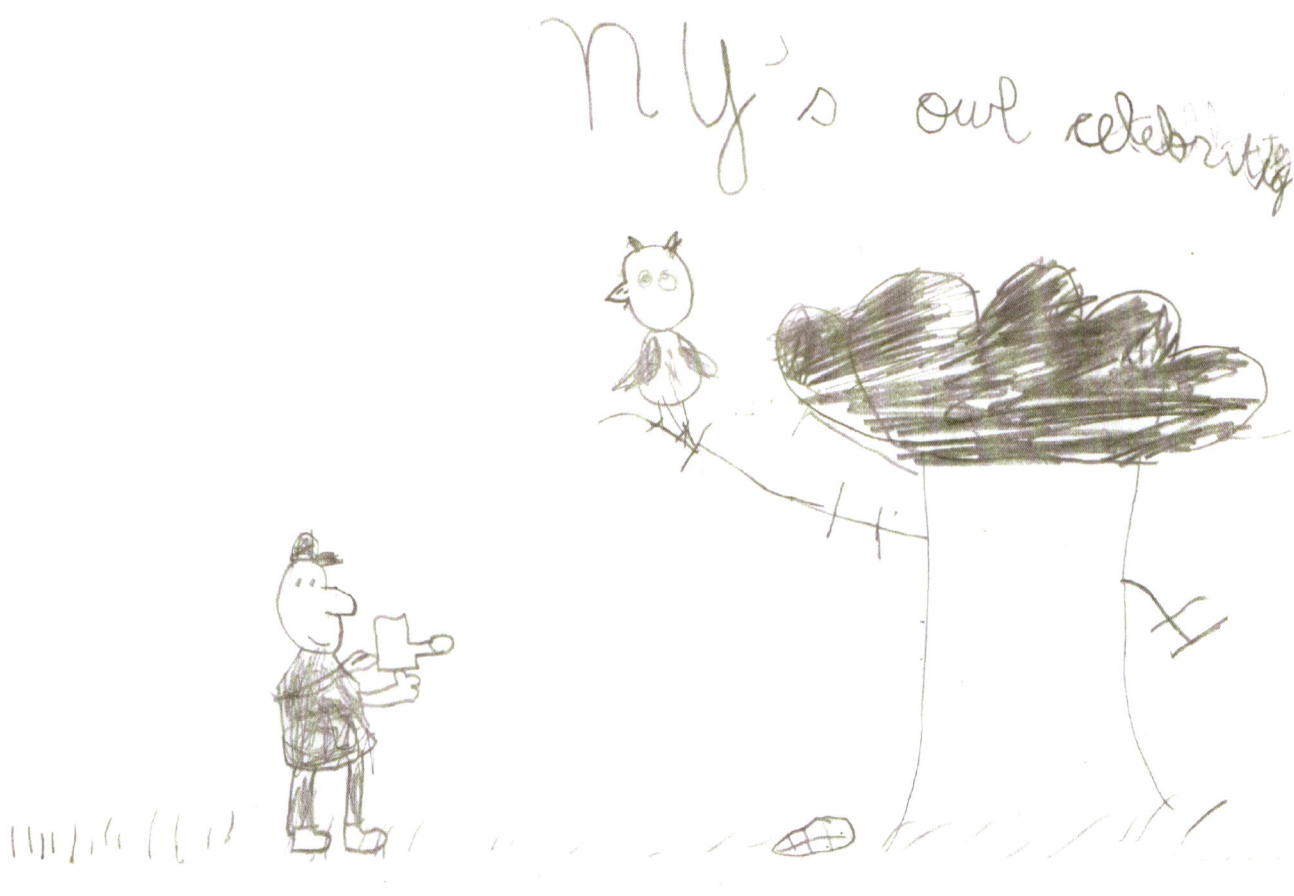

Fly Free Flaco: NY's Owl Celebrity, pencil on paper, 8½ × 11 in.

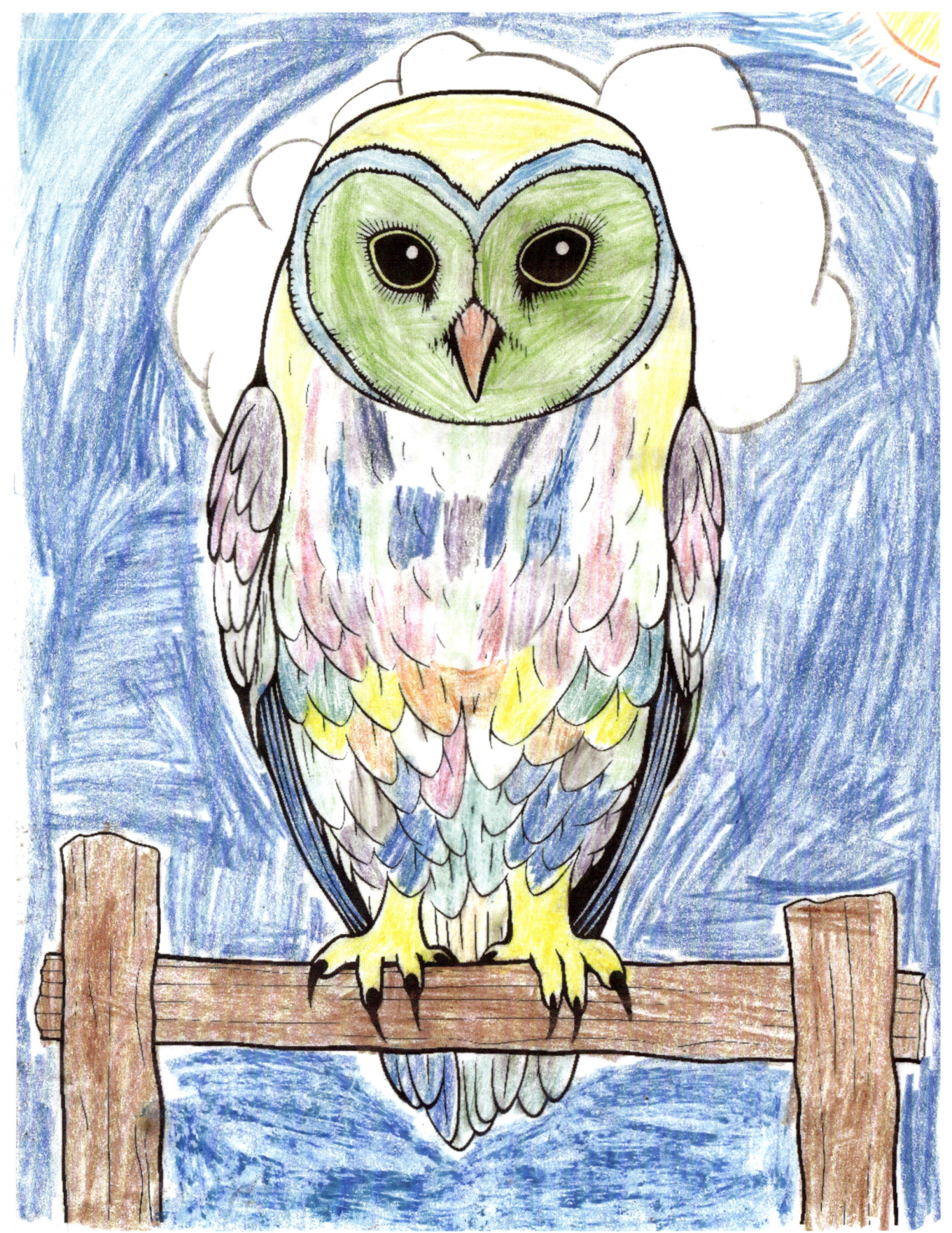

Flaco on Fence, crayon on inkjet facsimile, 11 x 8½ in.

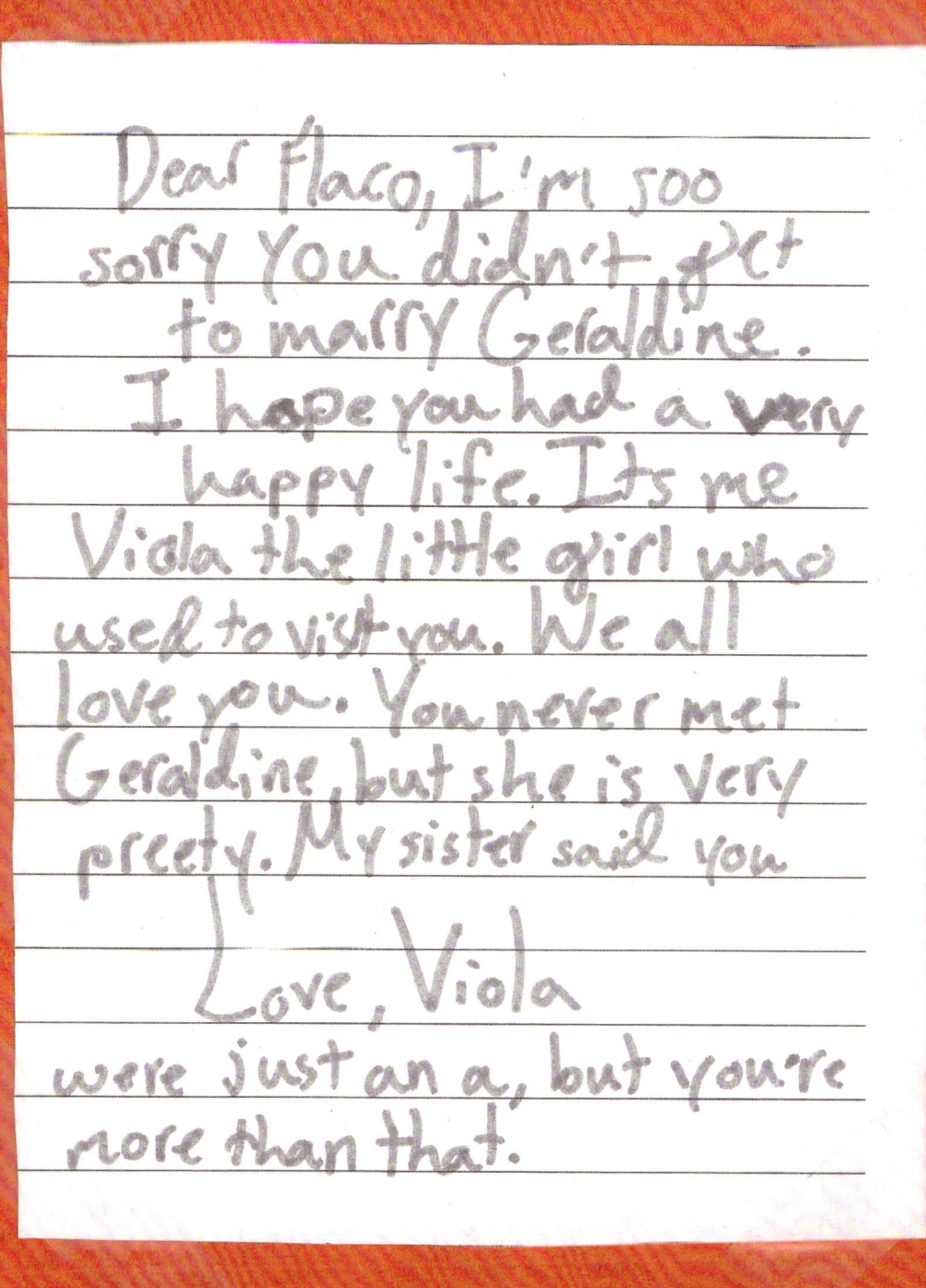

Dear Flaco, I'm soo sorry you didn't get to marry Geraldine. I hope you had a very happy life. Its me Viola the little girl who used to vist you. We all love you. You never met Geraldine, but she is very preety. My sister said you were just an a, but you're more than that.

Love, Viola

Viola, *Dear Flaco*, construction paper, notebook paper, marker and tape, 7 x 6 in.

Dear Flaco,

I am sorry that your life was so tragically cut short and that you only had 1 year as a free bird. But your story touched thousands, if not millions of people all around the world. You first escaped your enclosure during a tough time for me, when I was battling crippling depression before getting the right treatment. You got me out of my apartment when getting up was the last thing I wanted to do. Seeing you peacefully rest in your tree turned the worst days around. And when I applied to law schools, I thought of you every time I felt like I would fail. You were the good luck charm I needed to succeed in that process. Your story inspired me and my family members 3,000 miles away. When I go to law school and conquer the unknown, I will always think of you and be inspired!
Fly high in heaven ♡

—O

O., *Dear Flaco*, marker on paper, 11 x 8½ in.

Right K., *Flaco the Owl,* Central Park, NYC, 2023, watercolor, colored pencil, and ink on watercolor paper, laminated, 10½ x 7½ in.

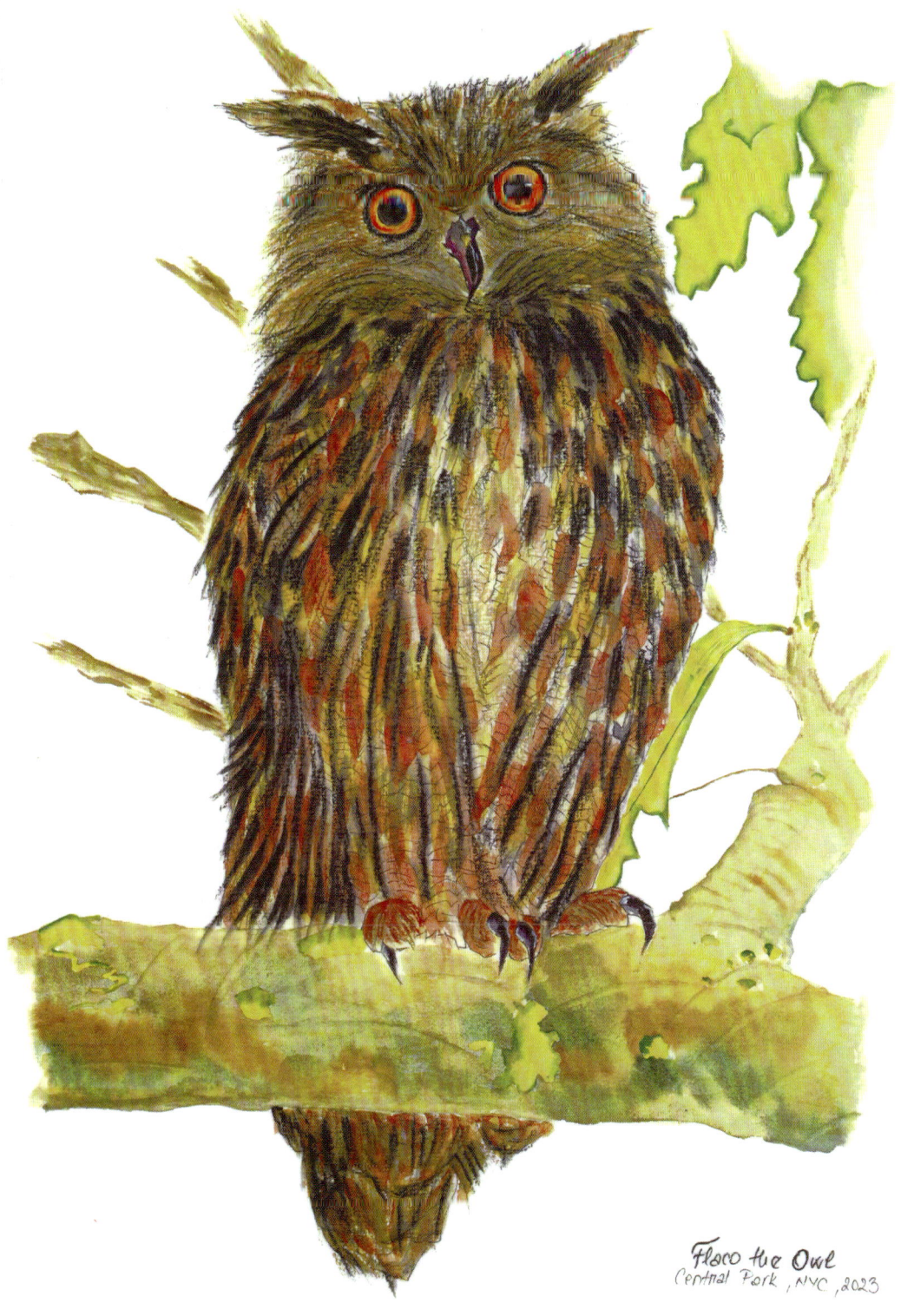

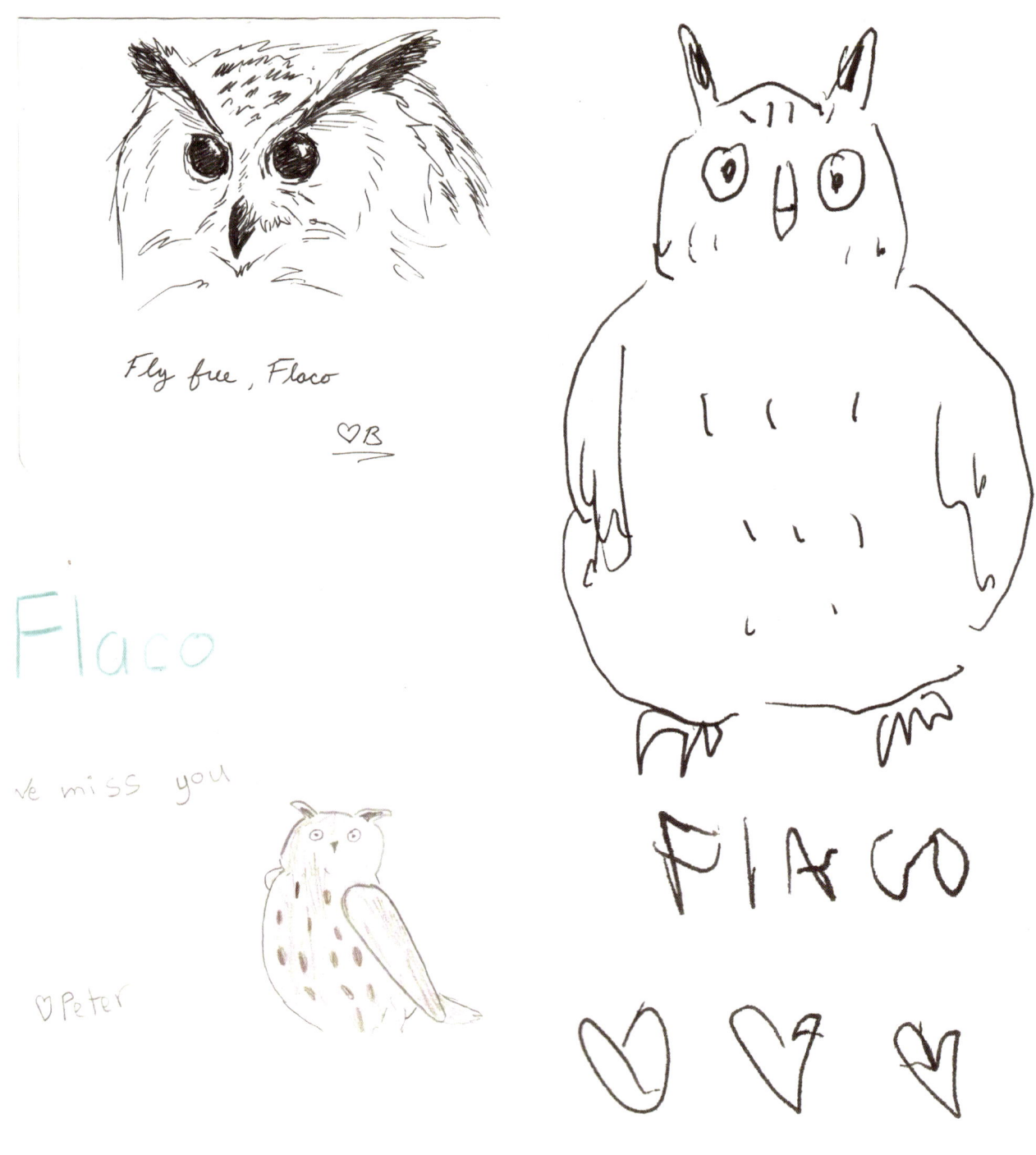

Top B., *Fly free, Flaco,* ink on paper, 5½ x 4½ in., folded.

Bottom Peter, *Flaco, We miss you,* colored pencil on watercolor paper, 7 x 5 in.

Flaco, ink on paper, folded, 5½ x 4½ in. Interior: *Loved Brave Dignified.*

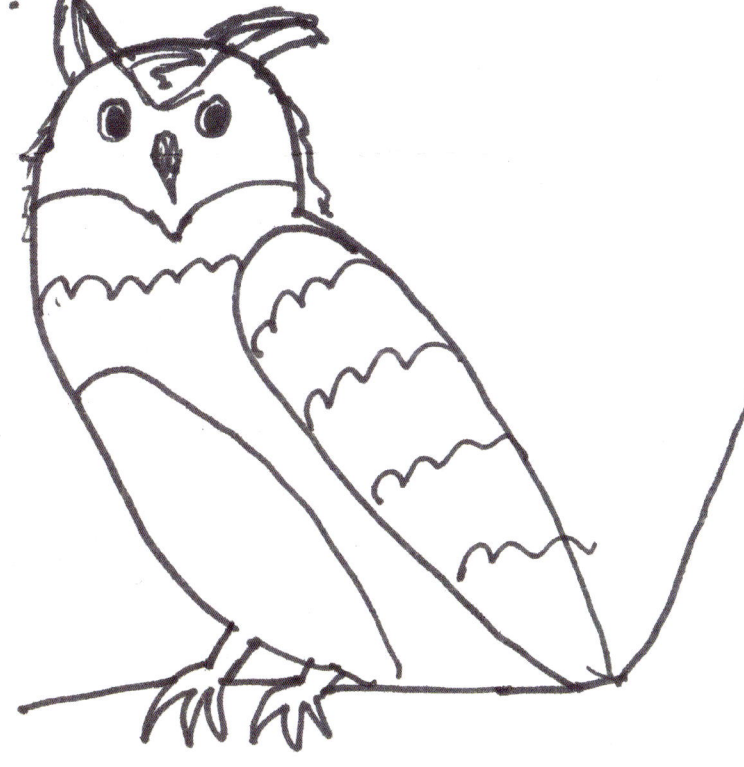

RIP FLACO THE OWL

though I never got to see you in person in all of your beauty you still left a mark on me & many others.
~Fly High

Sincerely, Sarah

Sarah, *RIP Flaco the Owl,* ink on paper, 5 x 5 in.

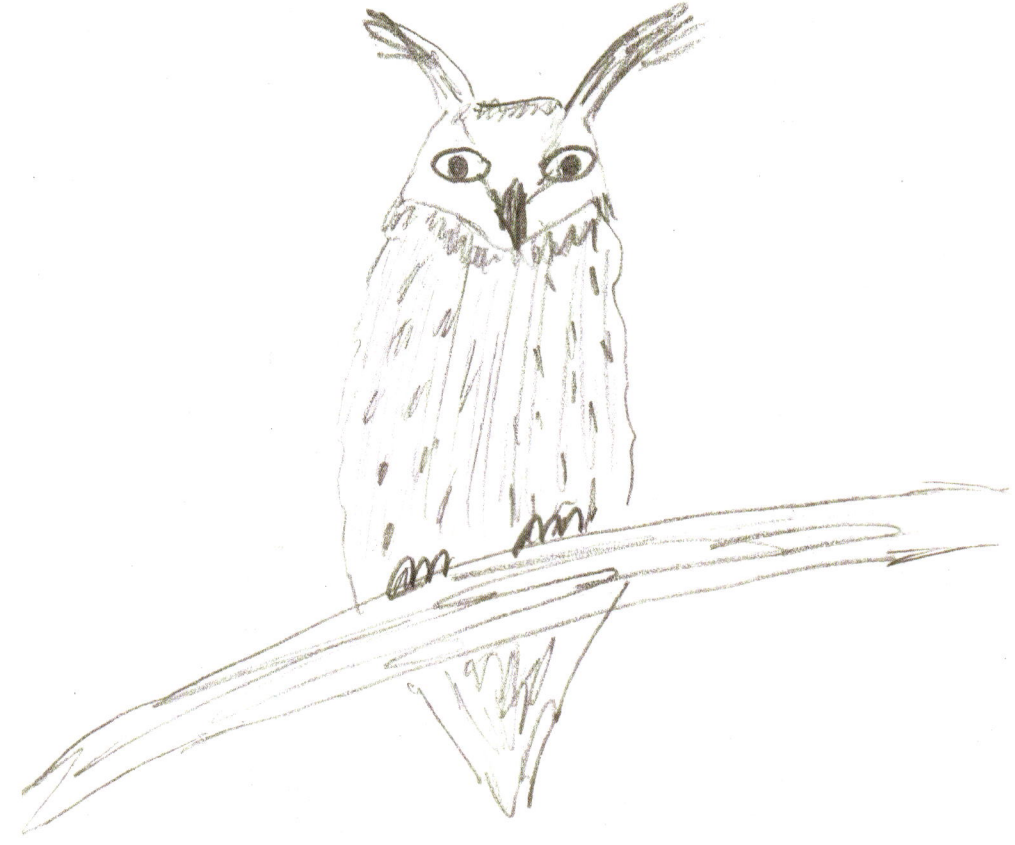

E.H., *Fly High Flaco*, pencil on paper, 4½ x 3½ in.

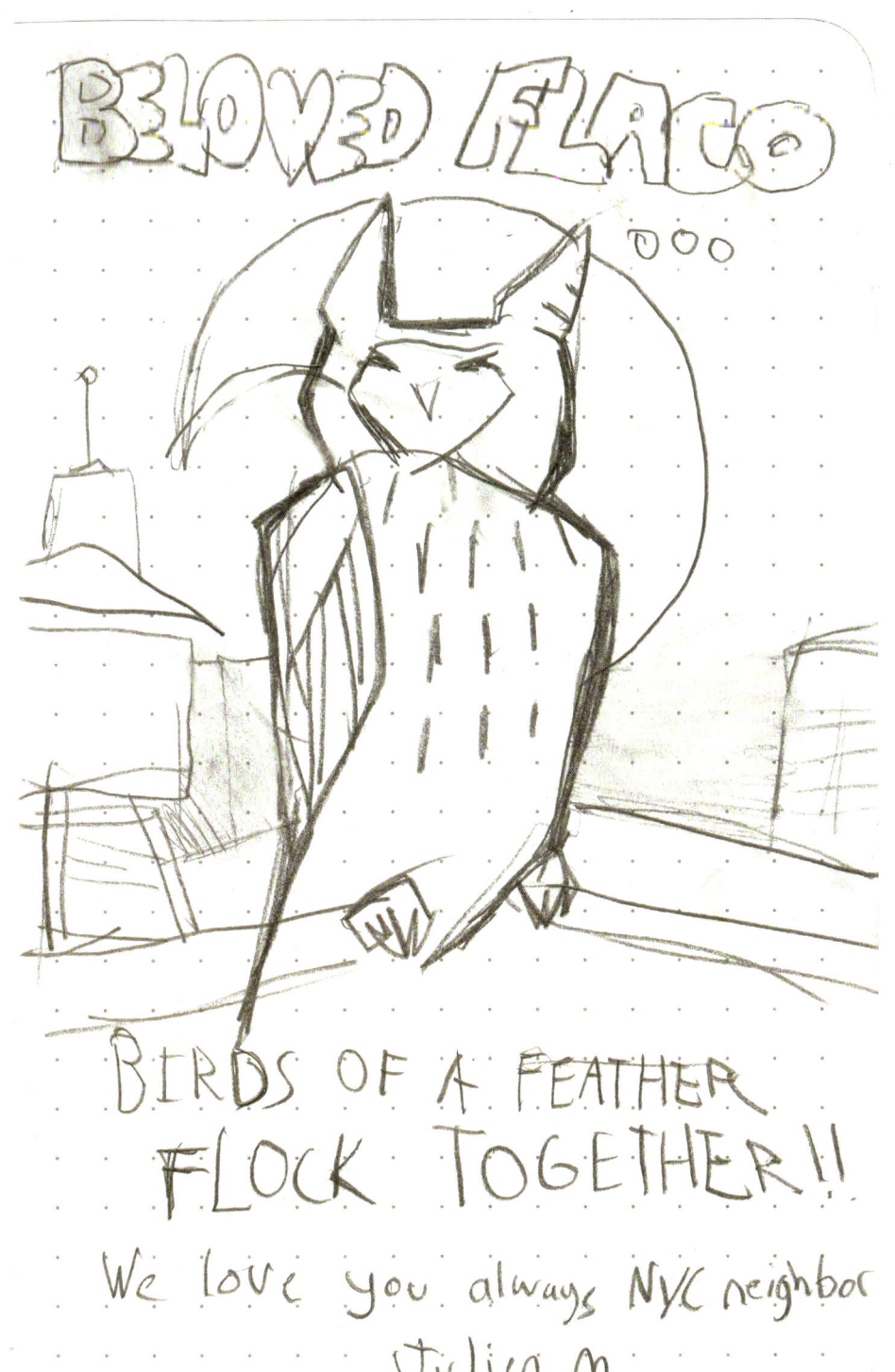

Julien M., *BELOVED FLACO*, pencil on dot grid paper, 5½ x 3¾ in.

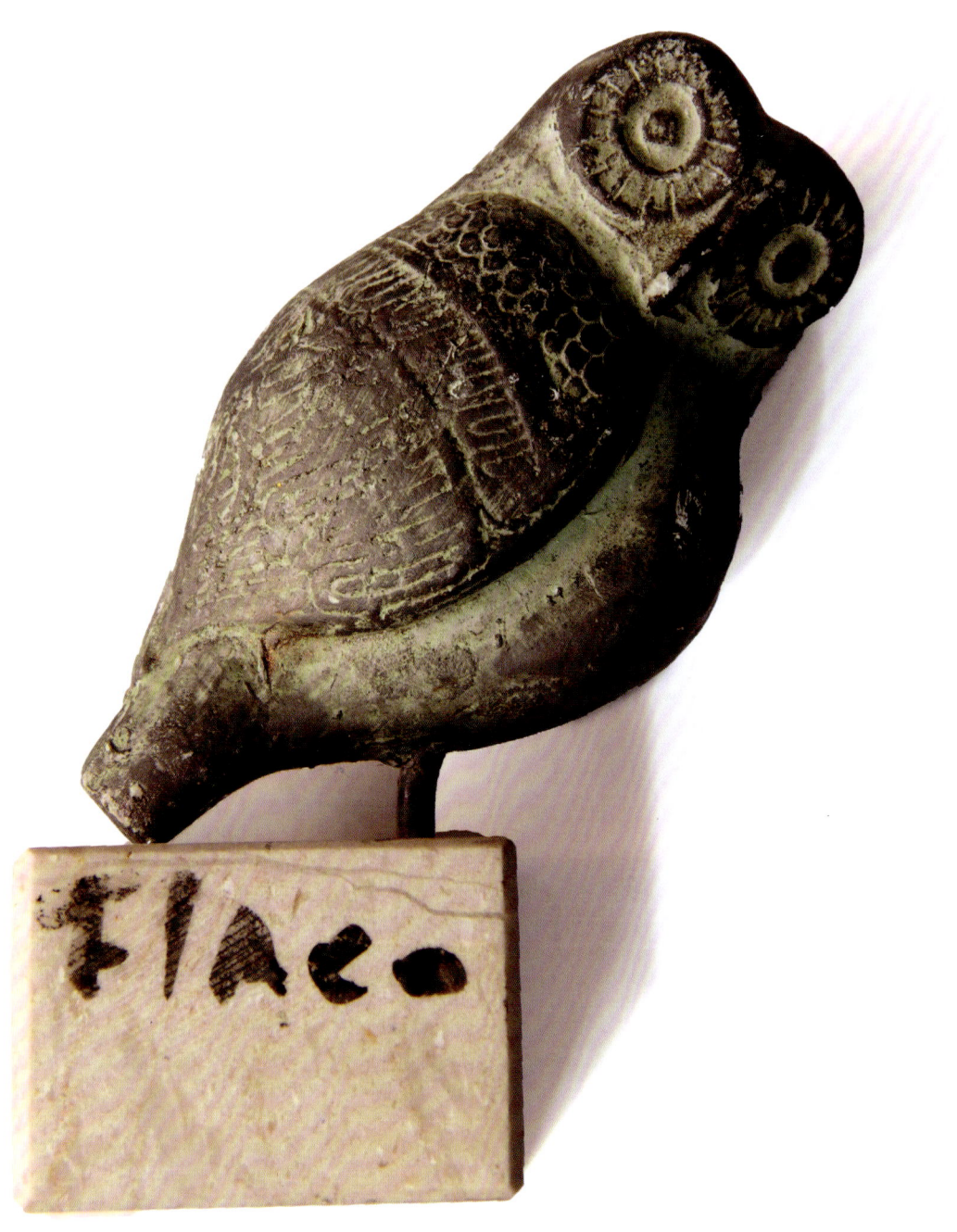

Flaco, bronze owl mounted on stone, "Flaco" written in marker on four sides, Greek letters on reverse, 3½ x 2¾ x 2 in.

Right Series of stenciled images (8), acrylic on multi-colored construction paper, 11 x 8½ in.

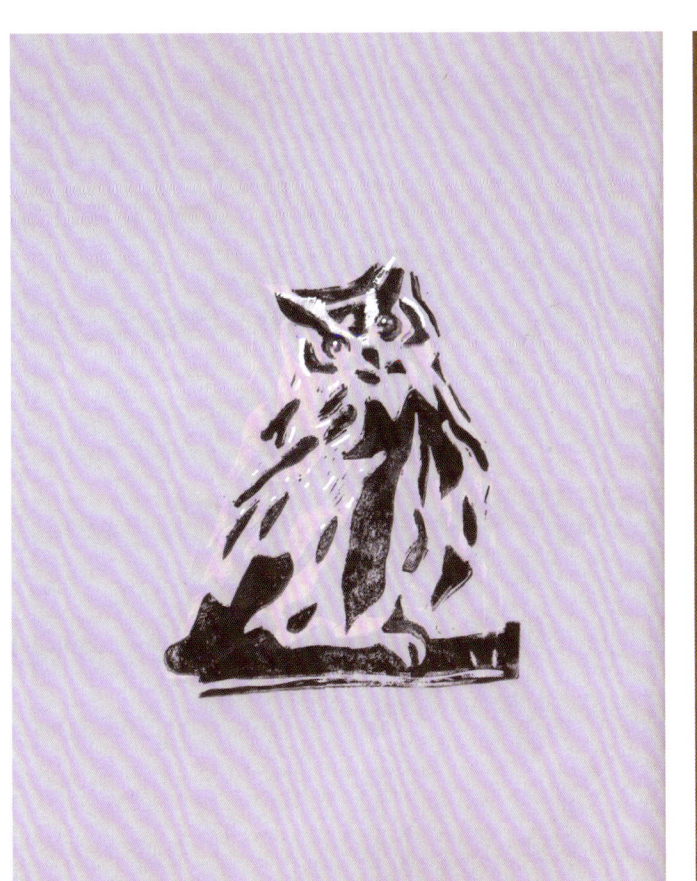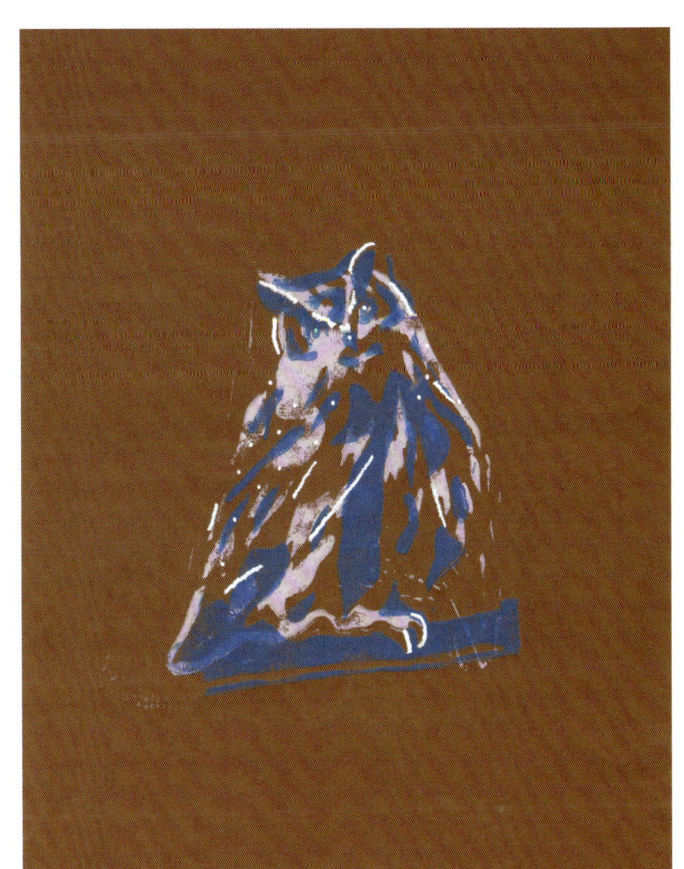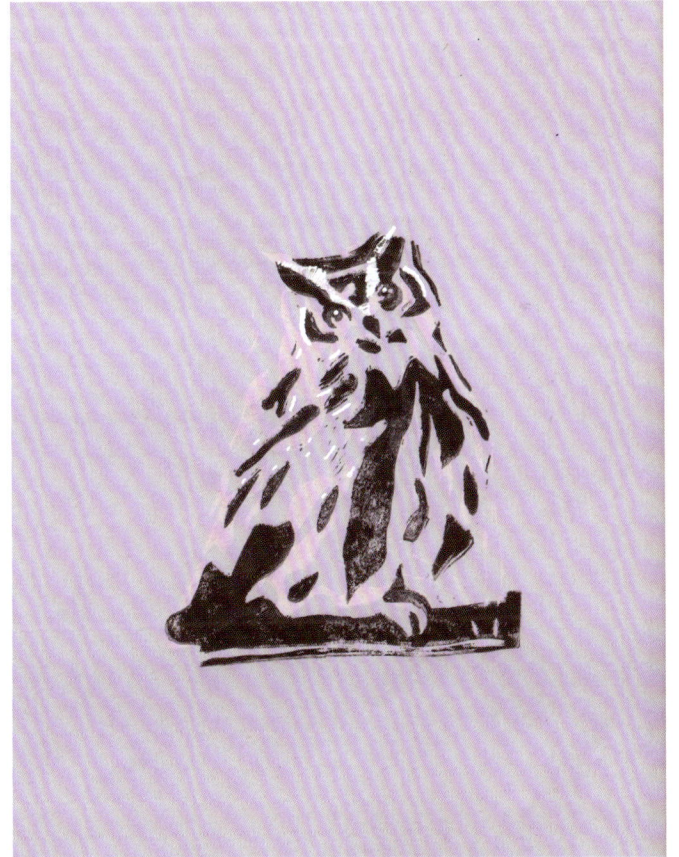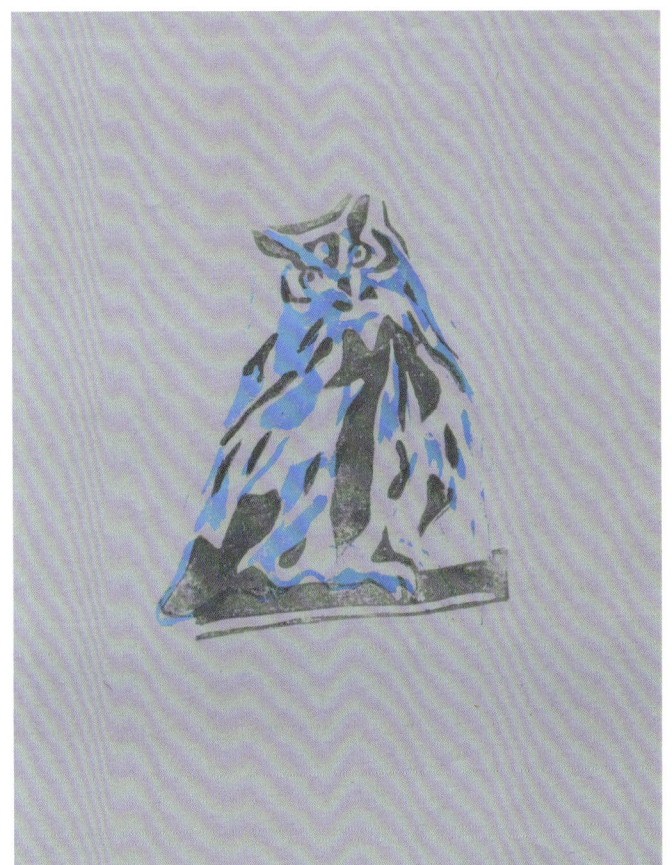

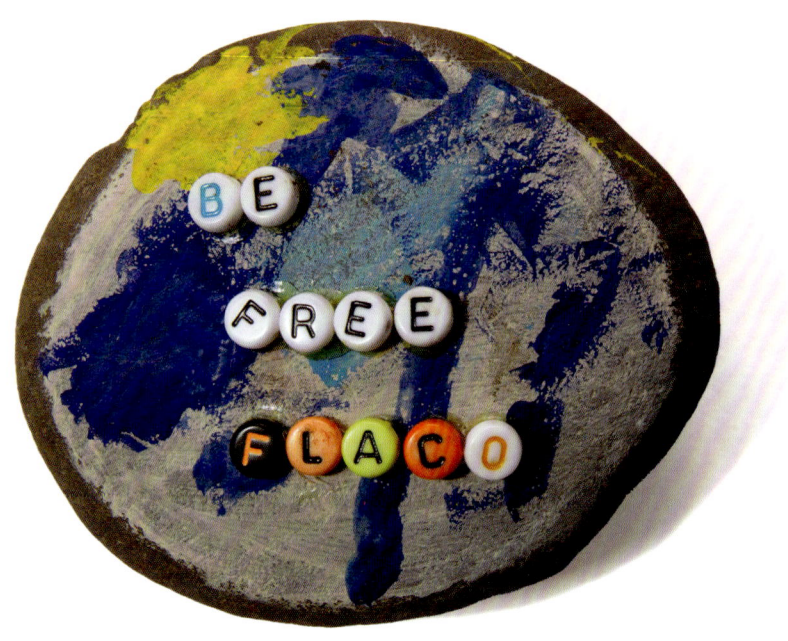

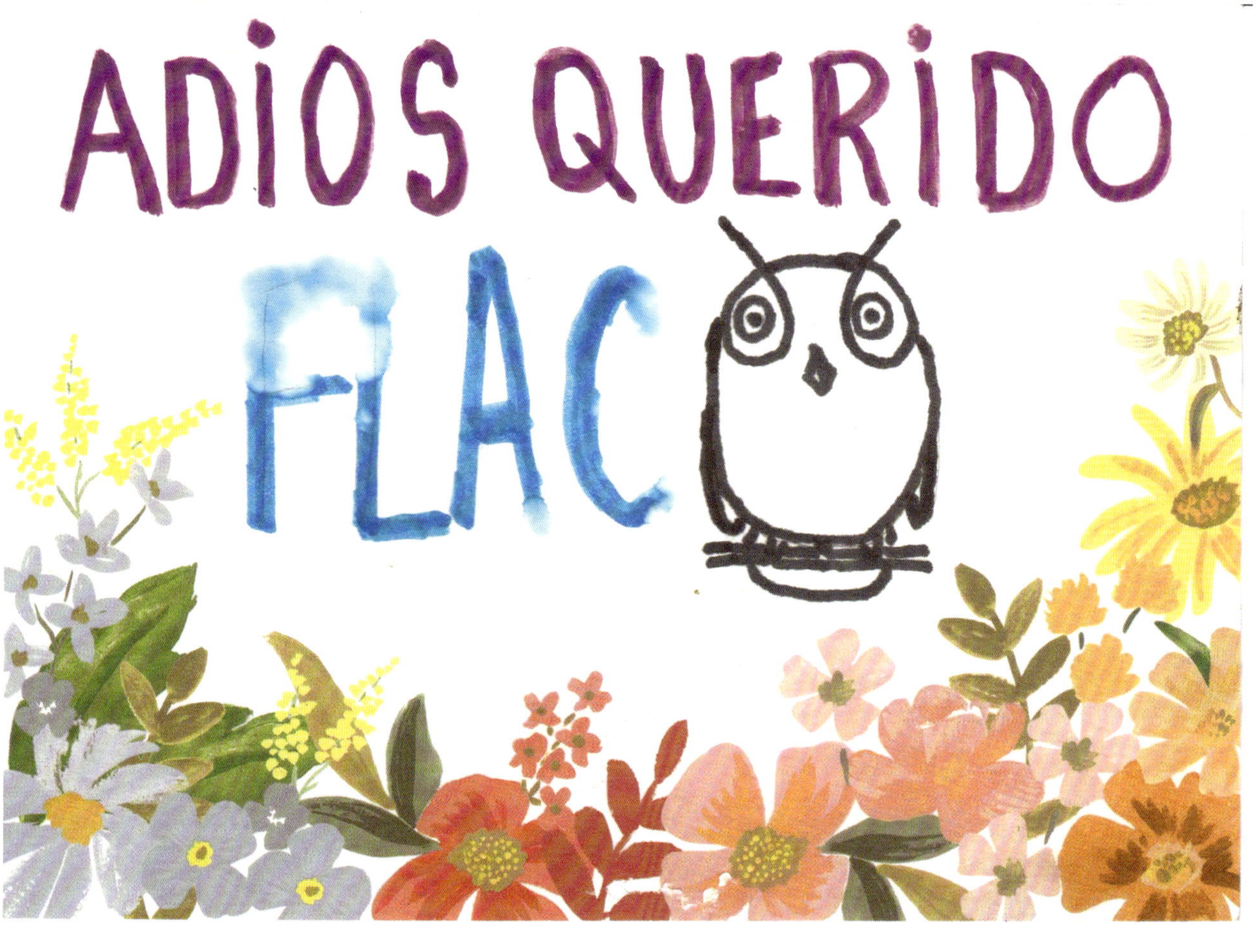

Top *BE FREE FLACO*, acrylic, beads, and glue on stone, 1¼ x 3½ x 3 in.

Bottom *Adios Querido Flaco,* pencil and marker on commercial card stock, 5 x 7 in.

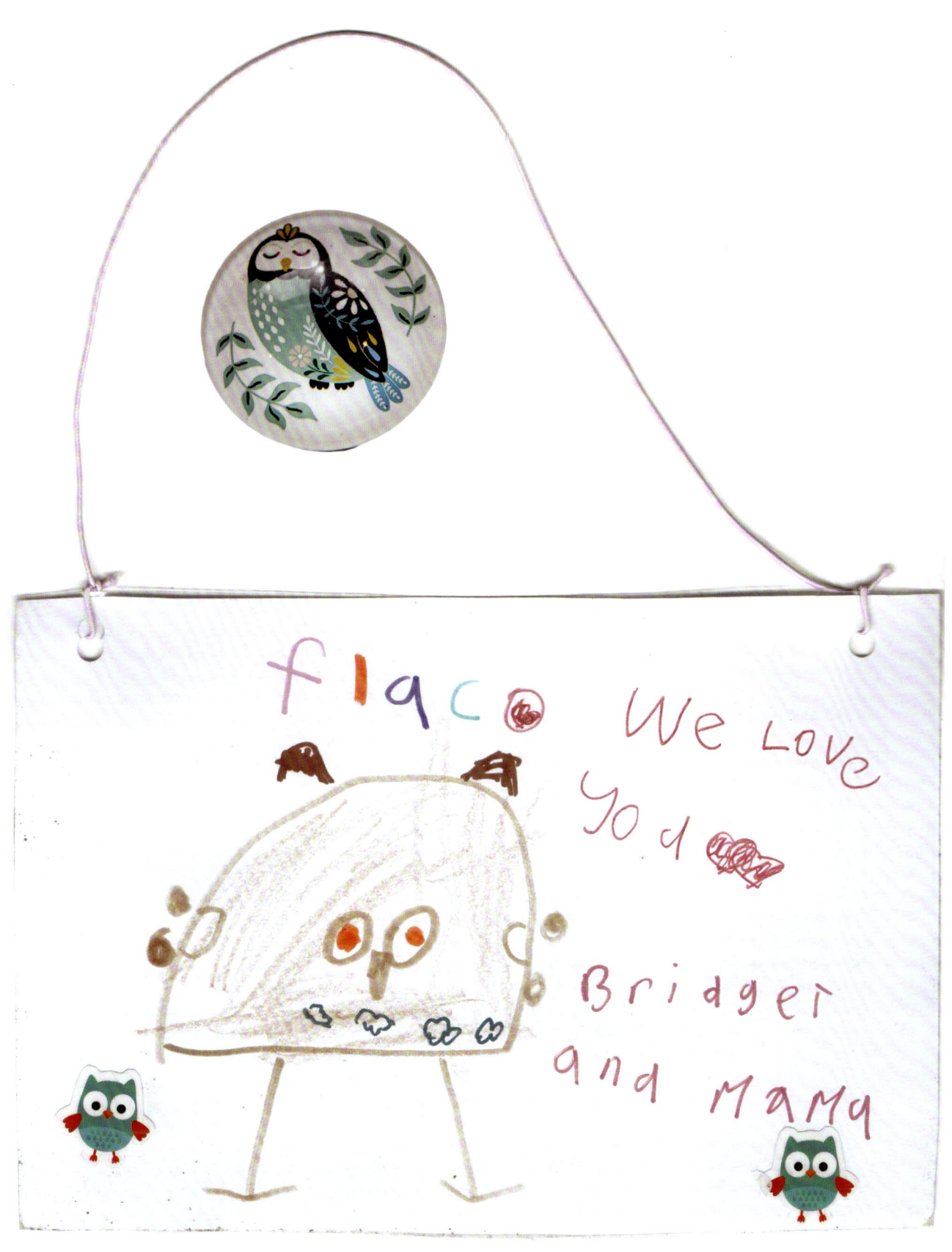

Top Magnet with owl illustration, 2 x 2½ x ½ in.

Bottom Bridget & Mama, *flaco We Love You*, crayon, marker, and stickers on paper, with pink string and mylar, 5½ x 8 in.

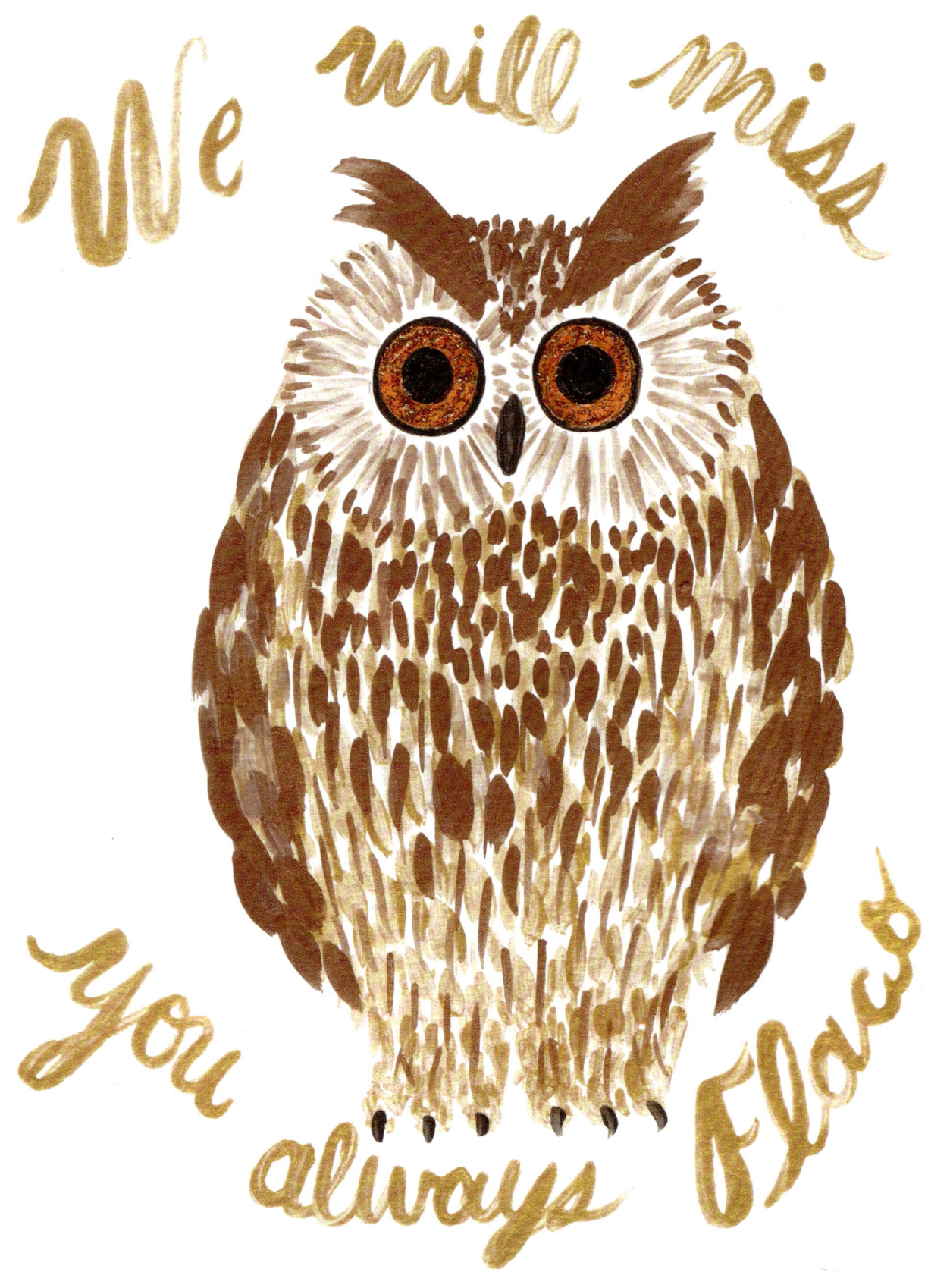

Ashley, *We Will Miss You Always Flaco,* marker, metallic ink, and glitter on card stock, 7½ x 6 in.

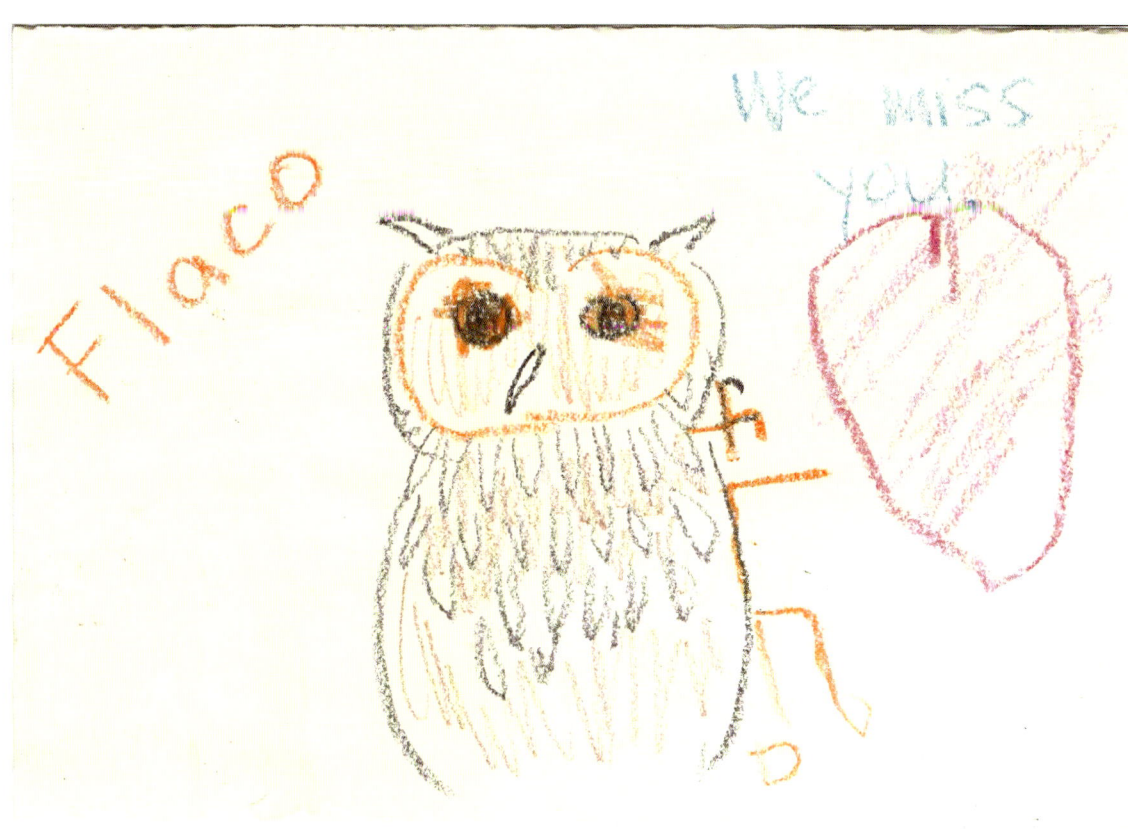

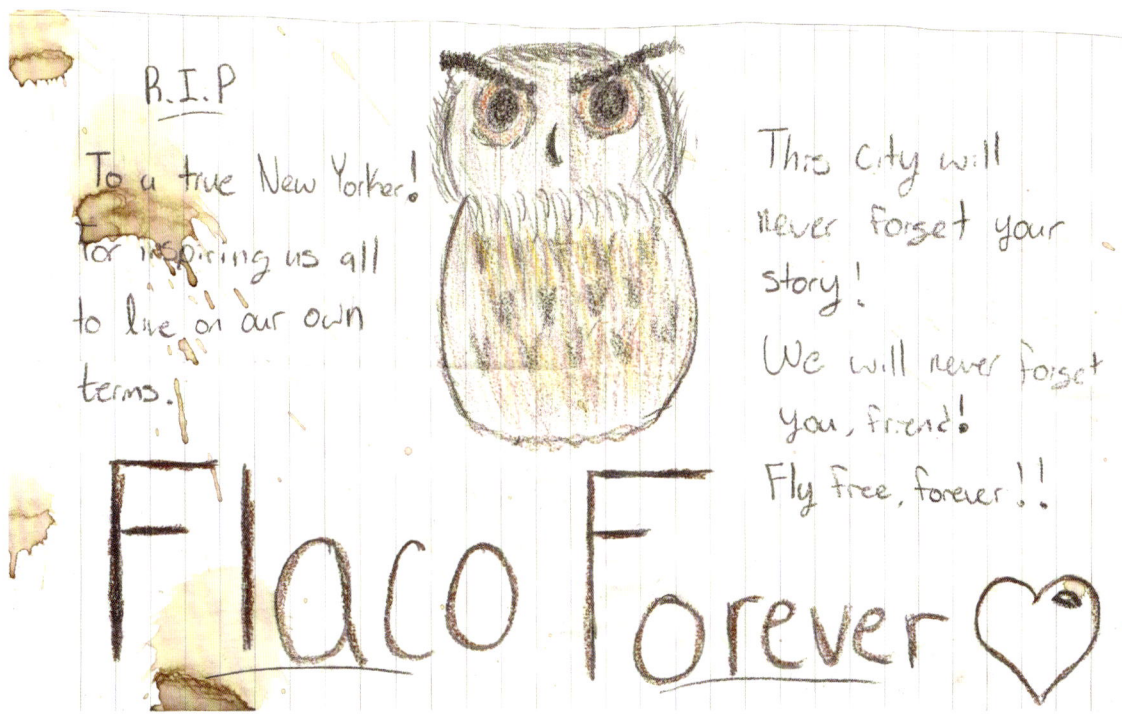

Top *Flaco We Miss You,* crayon on drawing paper, 5¾ x 8½ in., folded.

Bottom *Flaco Forever,* pencil and colored pencil on notebook paper, 5 x 8 in.

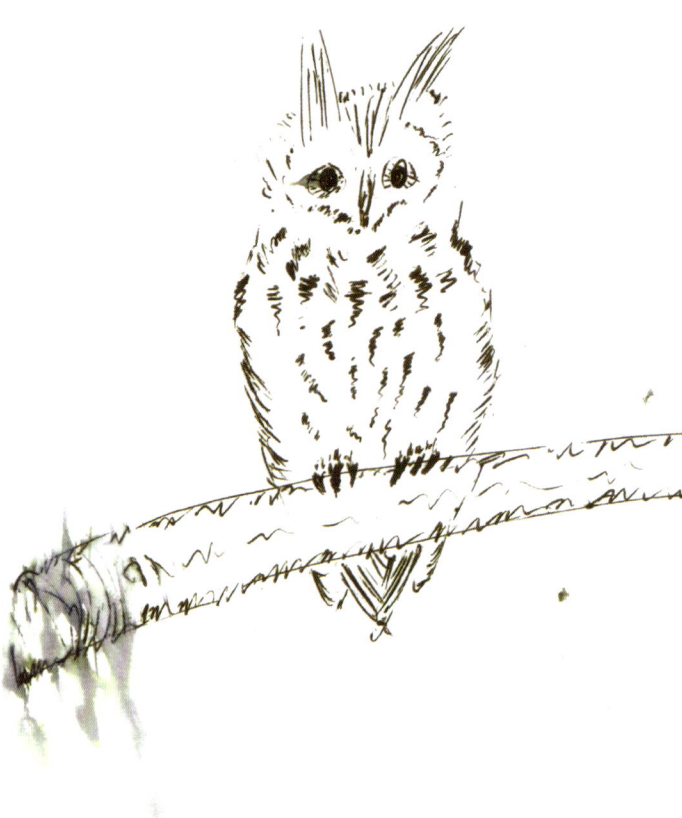

Dear Flaco drawing with handwritten note, ink on card stock, 8½ x 5½ in., folded.

Dear Flaco,

I came to visit you about four times... You were always invisible at first, even when I was looking straight at you... We'd watch you come slowly awake, do your morning routine... You would hop to a different branch, unfolding a mechanical marvel of flight gear and feathers, then folding it up again to sit quietly a while longer...

I wondered what you were thinking about in those moments, what you made of the crowd of people watching you quietly from below–mutual silence. And then when you got the inspiration, you would fly off into the dusk... My heart would break a bit when you called out, because I knew there would be nobody to call back. I wonder if you knew it too? Like an astronaut accidentally left behind on some abandoned space outpost? Maybe hoping someone else got left behind too?

I loved the story of your release — nobody thought you could live, but you thrived in the city — free, with no predators and all the rats an owl could want. I had hoped you would grow old here, living free as a "city bird"... But I suppose that was my dream and not yours. You had an amazing life's journey, and a candle that burned red hot at its fabulous final chapter.

I'm glad that you had a fantastical year as the most famous owl on the planet, a year to live free in Central Park, a year to prove everyone wrong who said you wouldn't survive your first 24 hours. I hope you are in a place where someone special is answering your call. You're a legend and an inspiration, Flaco, and I'll never forget you.

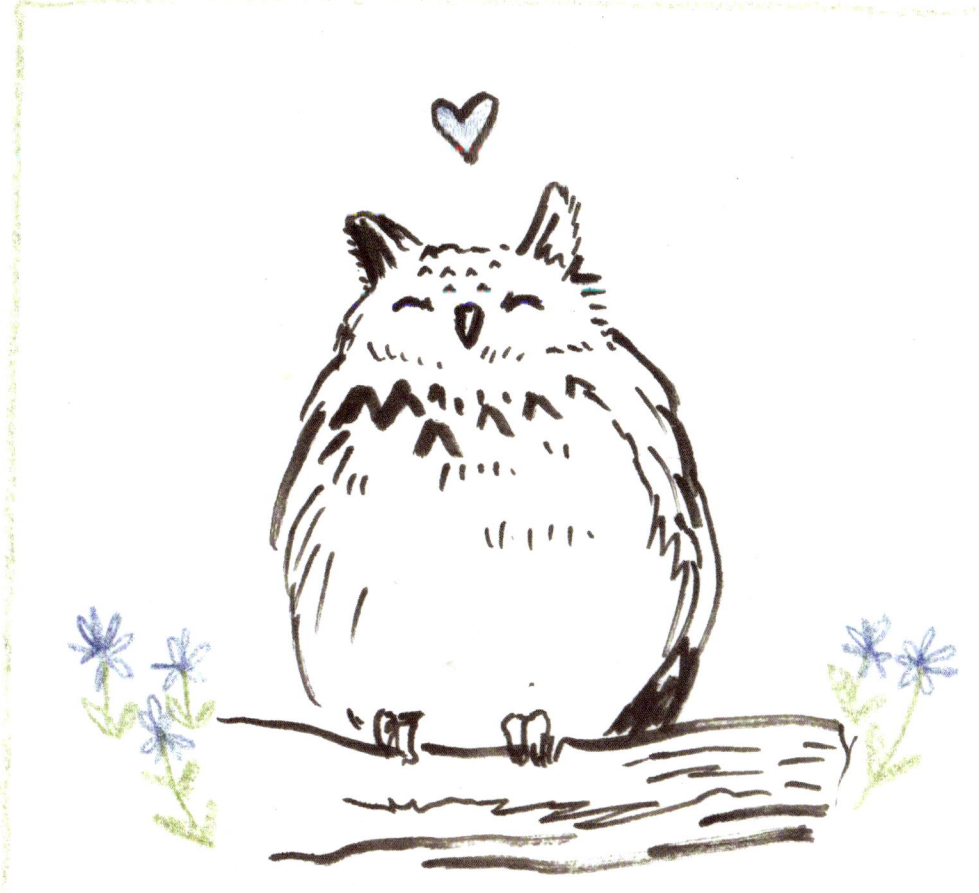

Dear Flaco—

we love you Flaco! thank you for reminding us that anyone can make it in NYC. you brought so many people endless joy all around the world! You've inspired so many to appreciate all the life around them. We will never, ever forget you.

ALL THE LOVE,
SAL   LENA   ANA

Sal, Lena, & Ana, *Dear Flaco,* ink and colored pencil on paper, 6 x 4¼ in.

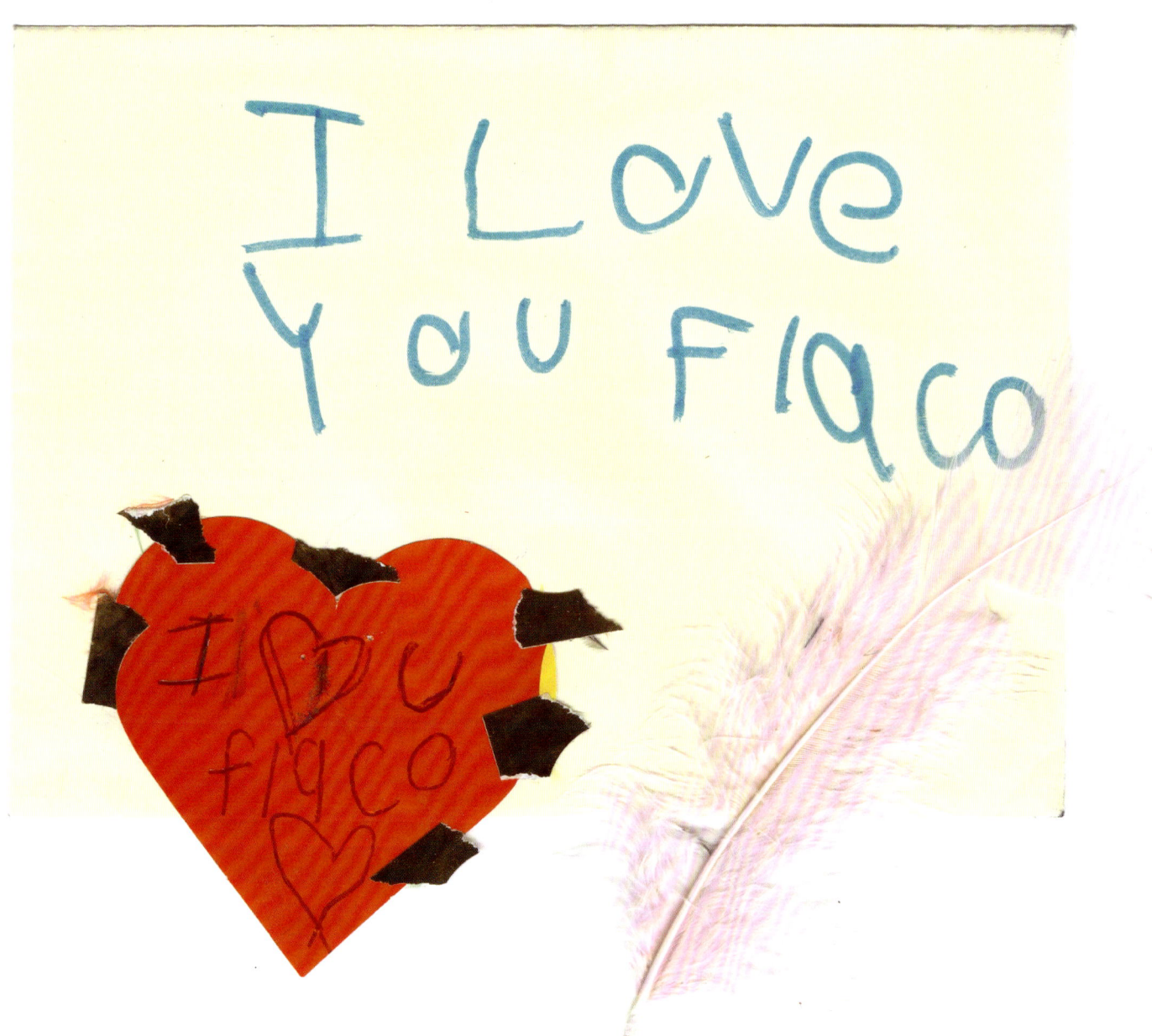

Above, right and following page Charlotte, plastic silver bag (not pictured) with *I Love You Flaco* written on the exterior in green marker.

Envelope with heart and irregular sized adhesive, containing 10 multi-colored feathers and four sheets of paper, 11 x 8½ in., with colored pencil and marker, stapled and folded in quarters.

CHARLOTTE
I miss flaco so much

Flaco the owl was a very cute bird and he was very special to me and I liked his hooting at night and I loved hearing about Flaco like where he was flying around everywhere and I loved seeing him at my house and I miss him so much I was thinking about him every day and how cute he was.

Charlotte

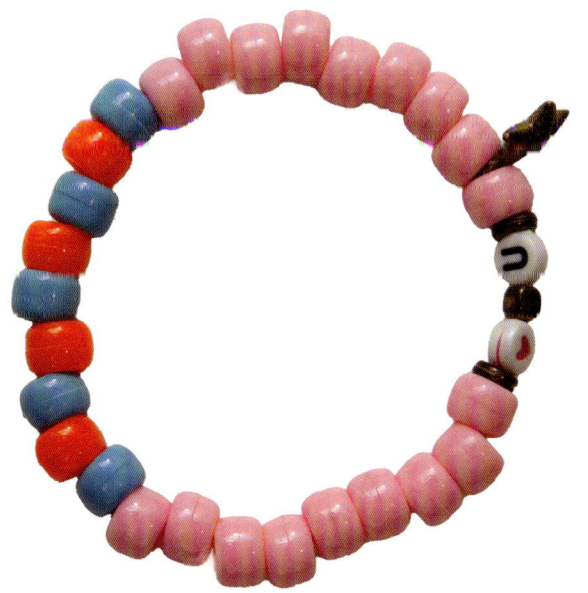
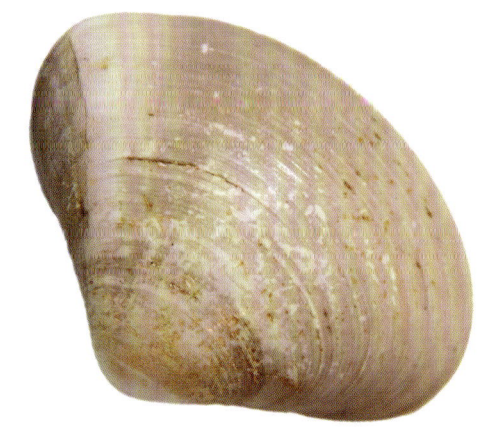
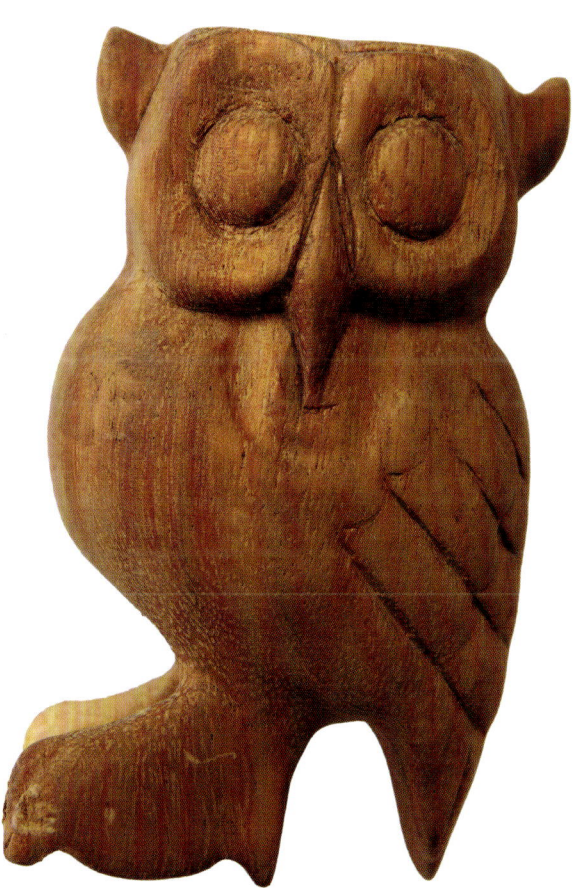
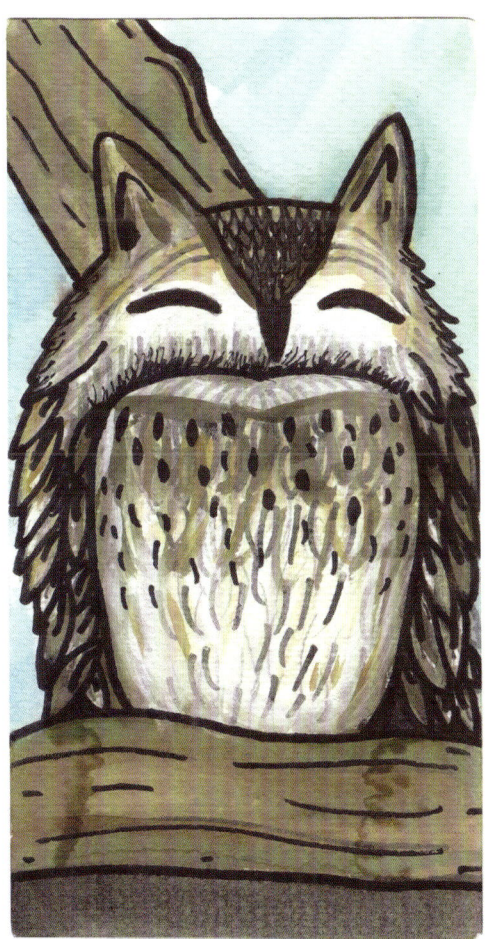

Clockwise Plastic beaded bracelet with bird charm, 3 in. diameter

Shell, 2 x 2½ x ½ in.

Carved owl, wood, 4¼ x 2½ x 2½ in.

Cami & Paul, *Dear Sweet Flaco,* 2/24/24, watercolor on paper, 7 x 3¼ in.

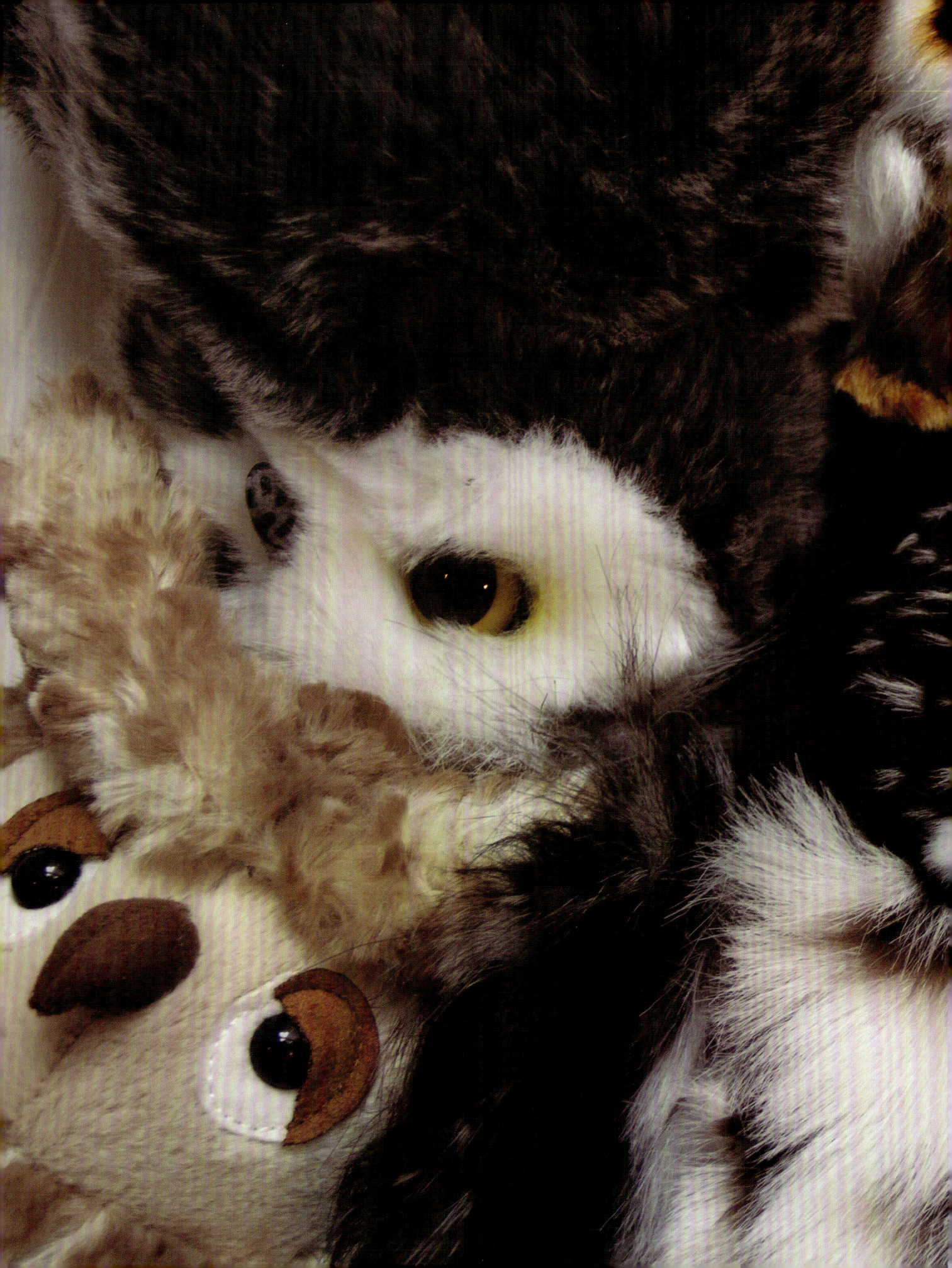

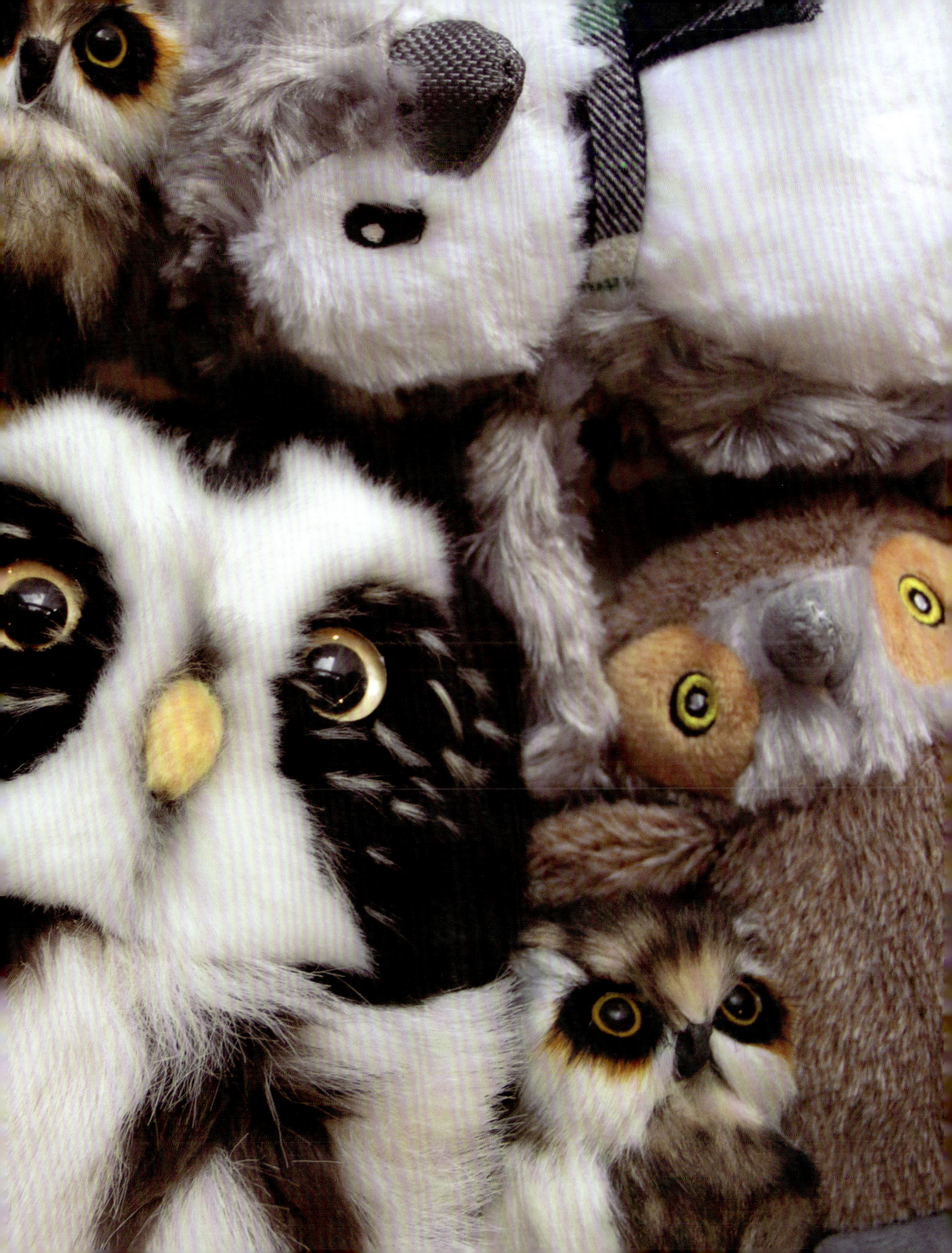

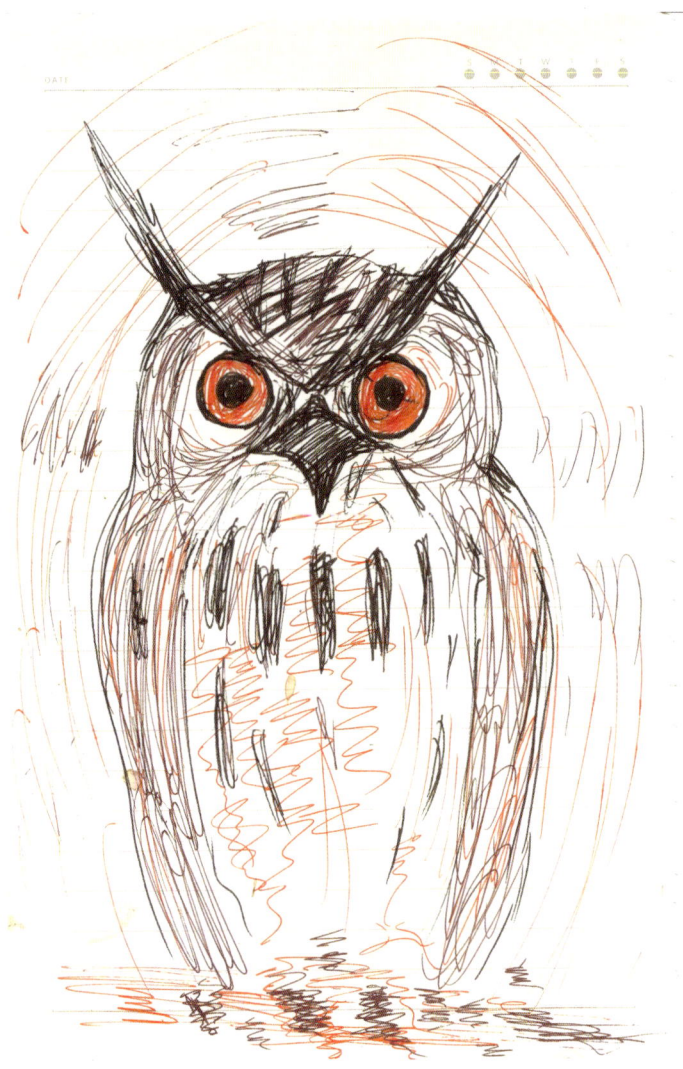

Rest in peace Flaco - You brought joy to the hearts of everyone who got to witness your magical journey.

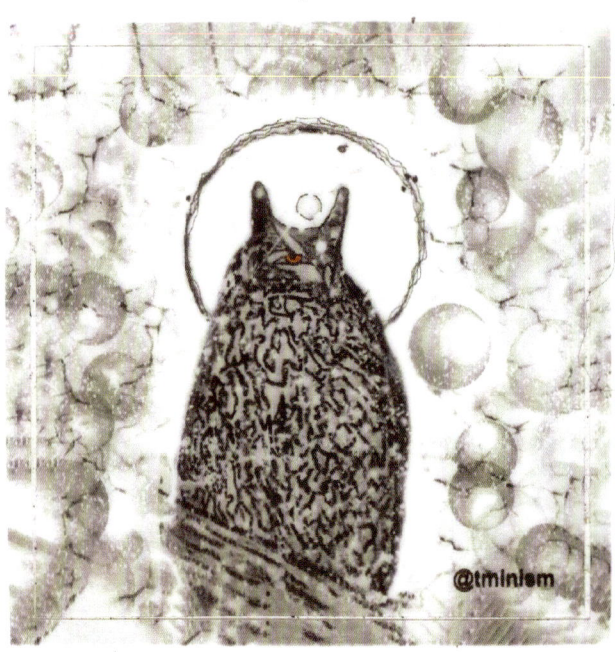

FLACO

WE LOVED FOLLOWING YOU ON SOCIAL MEDIA. IT ALWAYS MADE US SMILE & ADDED A BRIGHT SPOT TO OUR DAY. WE MISS YOU ALREADY. WE THANK YOU FOR BRINGING THE CITY TOGETHER. ♡ THE COLLINS FAMILY

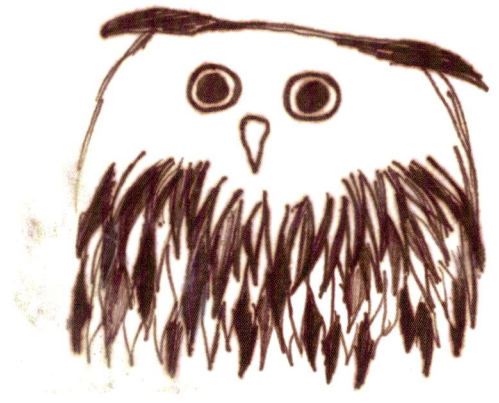

Previous spread Assorted owl stuffed animals, plastic, felt, synthetic plush and fiber, various sizes.

Top left Flaco drawing, ink on paper, 8 x 5½ in.

Above *Rest in Peace Flaco,* ink on paper, 2¼ x 4 in.

Top right @Timinism, Flaco sticker (included with a sheet of 6), 3 x 3 in.

Above Collins Family, *FLACO,* marker on paper, 6 x 4 in.

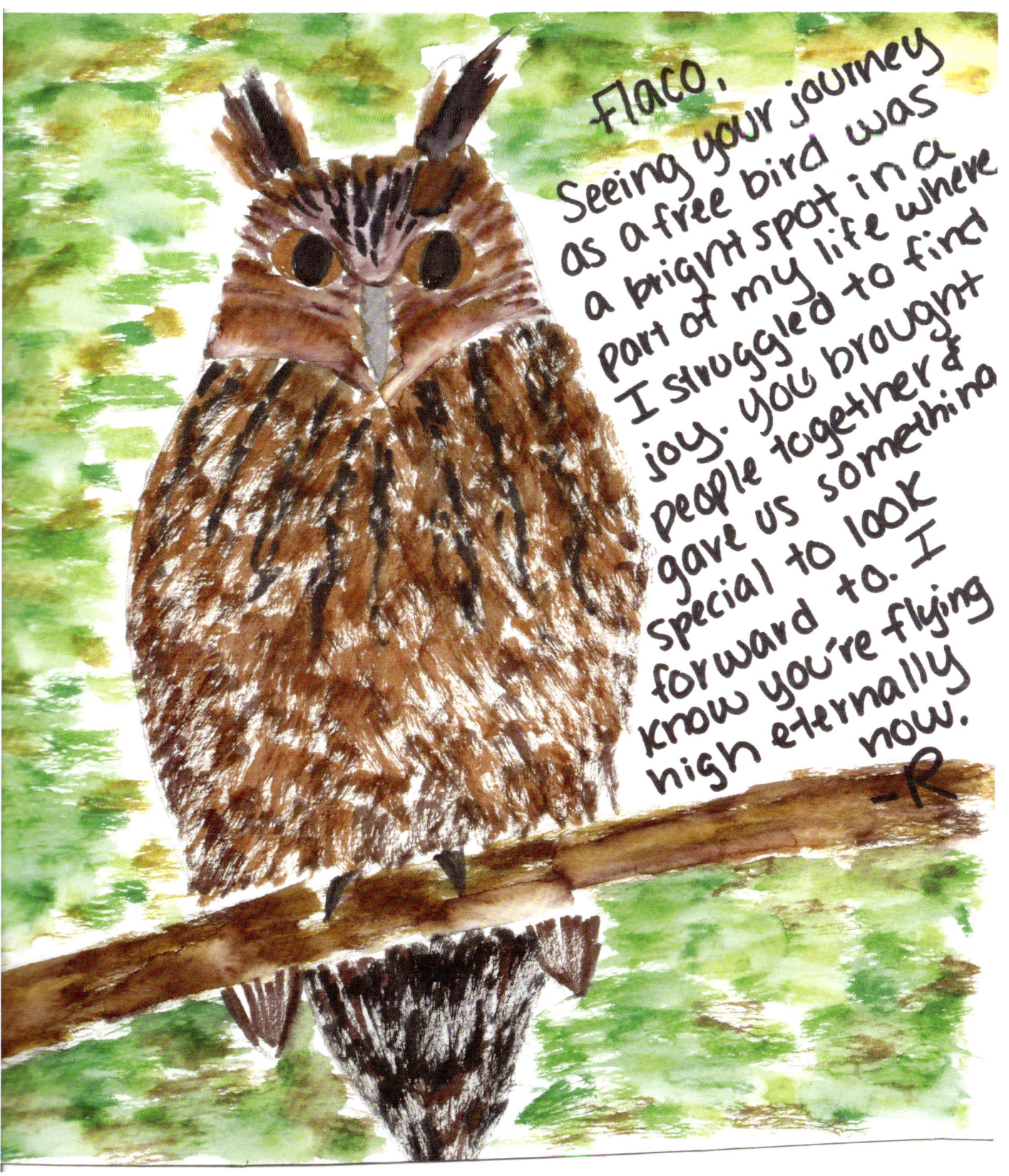

R., *Flaco, Seeing Your Journey*, watercolor and marker on watercolor paper, 9½ x 9 in.

Timeline of Flaco, Eurasian Eagle-Owl

March 15, 2010 — **Hatched in Scotland Neck, North Carolina**

Nov. 10, 2010 — Public debut at the Central Park Zoo; 8 months old

2010-2023 — Spent nearly 13 years in captivity living in cramped conditions; described by some visitors as being grumpy and pudgy.

Feb. 2, 2023 — Vandals (heroes) cut a hole in zoo enclosure, facilitating Flaco's escape. Shortly after, he was seen on the sidewalk near the Sherry-Netherland Hotel on Fifth Avenue before flying south.

Feb. 2-4, 2023 — Spends his first few days of freedom in Central Park; also seen again on Fifth Avenue near Bergdorf's. His flight is wobbly as a result of living in a cramped cage for 12 years.

Feb. 4, 2023 — Owl experts declare that owls aren't smart and predicts that Flaco will be recaptured easily.
Zoo officials attempt to lure Flaco by using a dead rat, a net, dog crates, and a recording of a female mating call.
Flaco rejected all forms of enticement. (Who's stupid now??)

Feb. 5, 2023 — Flaco has taught himself to hunt. Zoo officials end plans for recapture amidst public outcry. Flaco is a bonafide New York celebrity.

Feb. 13, 2023 — **Kim and Ian go to Central Park to meet Flaco.**

March 6, 2023 — Flaco's confidence as a hunter soars; he decides to bring home a squirrel for dinner.

March 10, 2023 — **Kim and Ian use ChatGPT to create the Flaco Soaring Song.**

March 15, 2023 — **Happy 13th Birthday Flaco!** Thousands of devoted fans send their good wishes. He continues to live wild and free in Central Park.

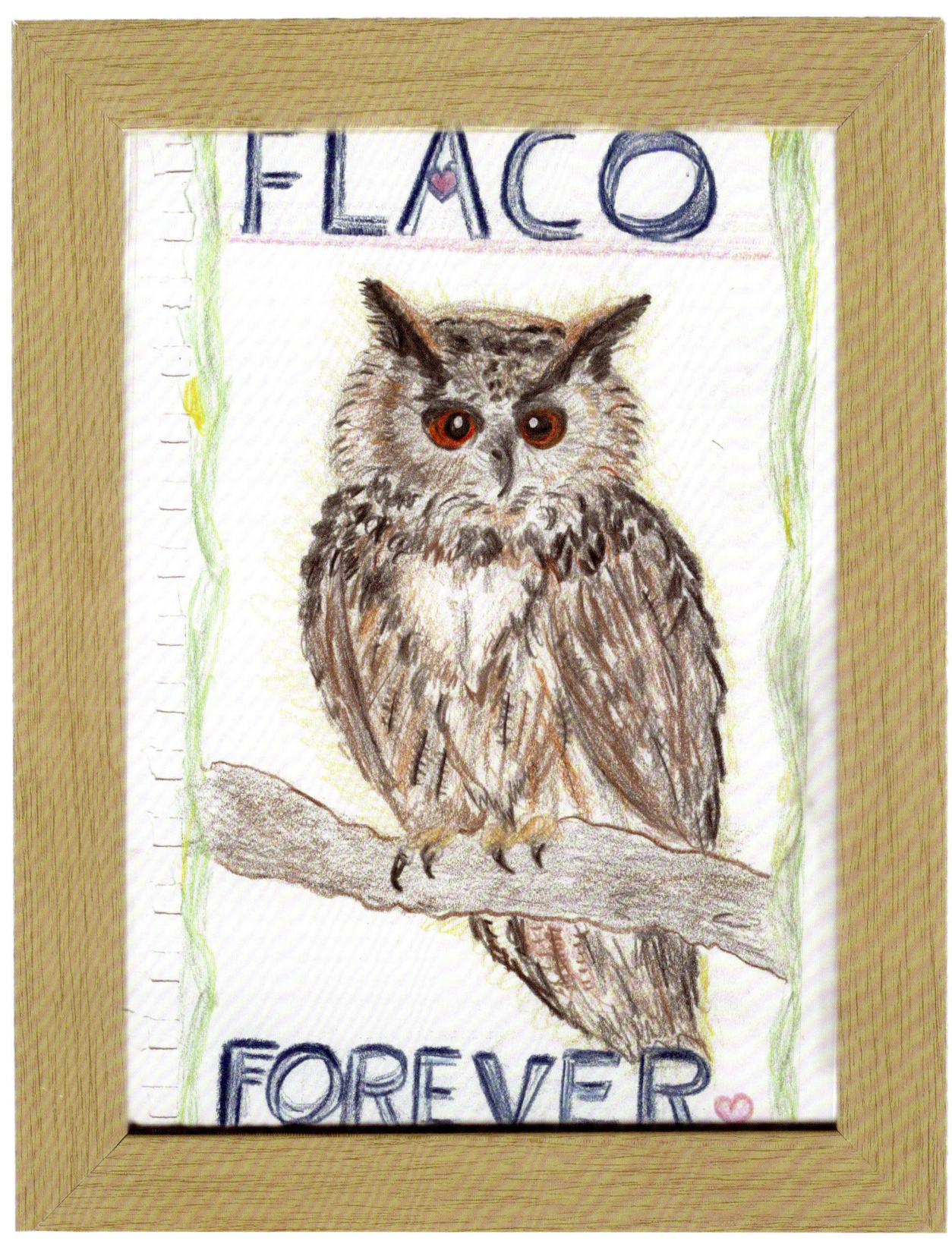

Left Kim & Ian, *Timeline of Flaco, Eurasian Eagle-Owl,* paper, wood, glue and set of four owl rings, 13¼ x 9 x 1 in.

Flaco Forever, colored pencil on paper, framed and inscribed on reverse, artwork: 7½ x 5½ in.

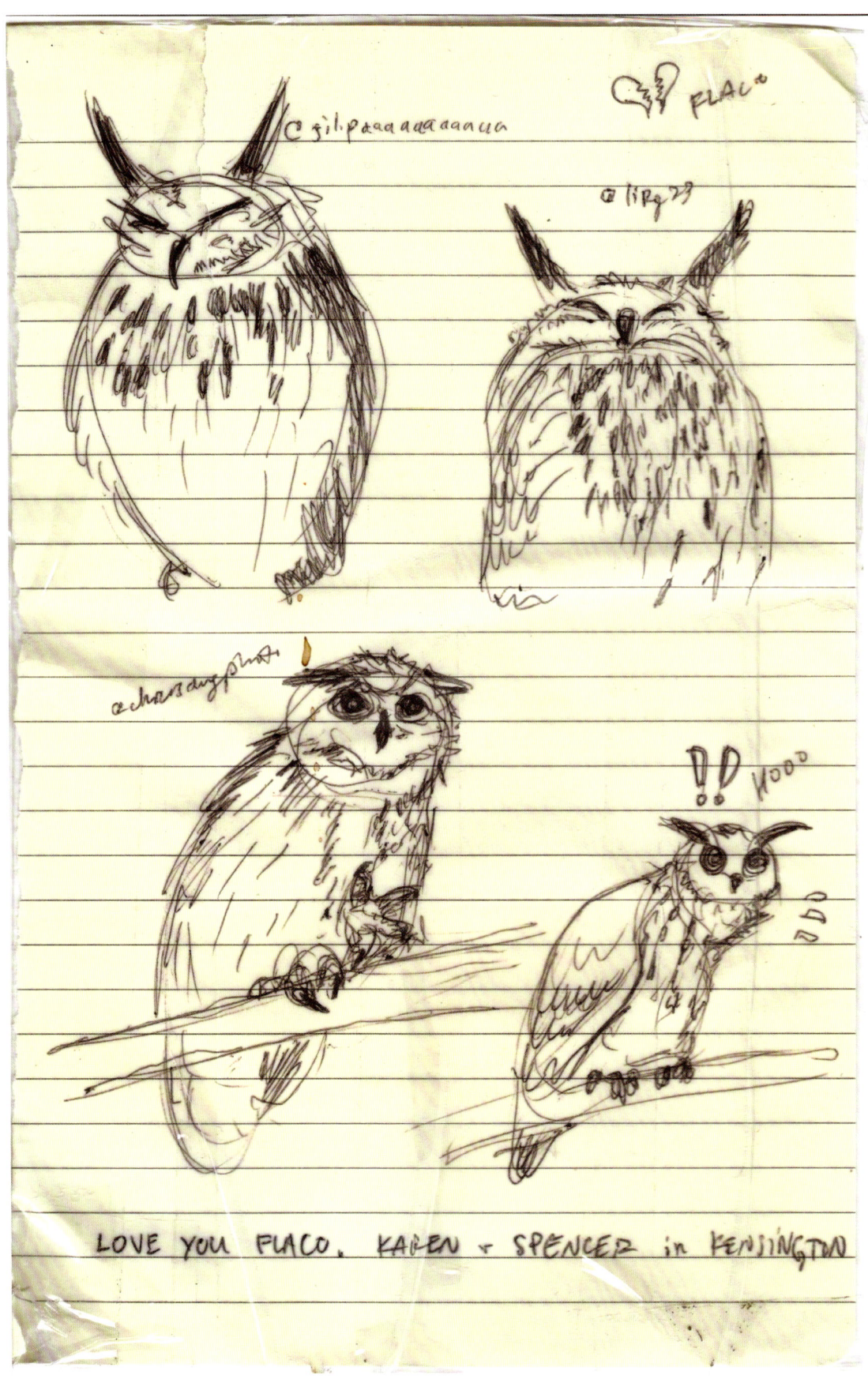

Karen & Spencer, *Love You Flaco,* ink on notebook paper, taped, 8½ x 5½ in.

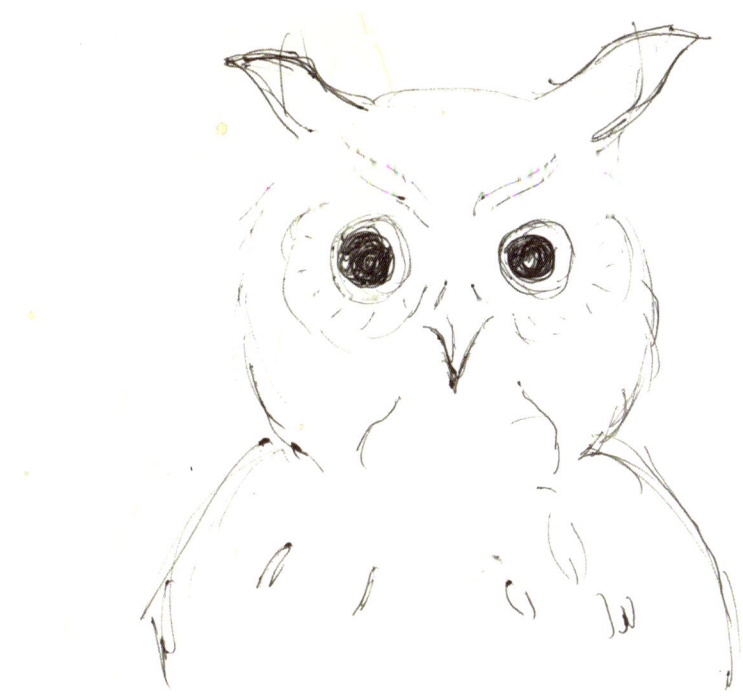

Dear Flaco,
Thank you for your friendship, your patience and your service in teaching us how to better care for your Avian relatives. Fly Free!

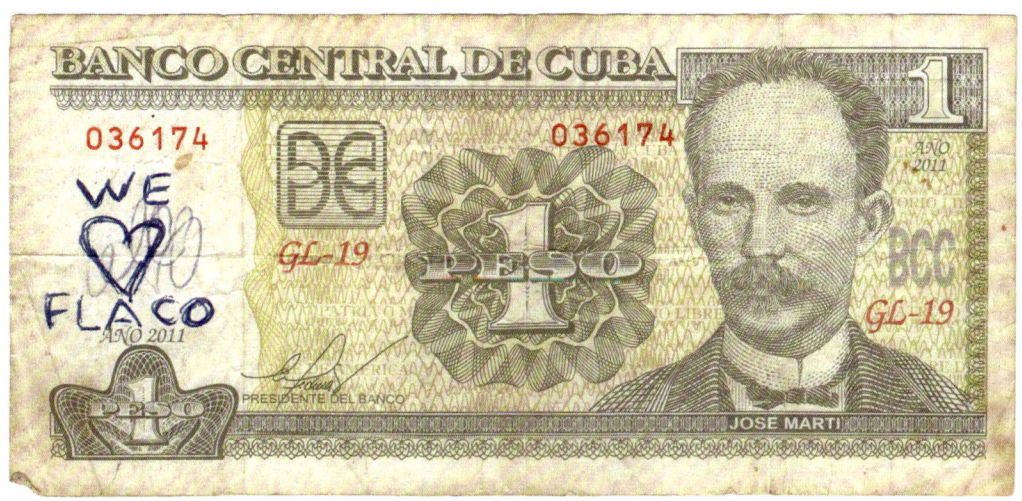

Top *Dear Flaco,* ink on paper (two sheets, taped), 11 x 8½ in.

Bottom *We Love Flaco,* ink on peso, Banco Central de Cuba, 2¾ x 6 in.

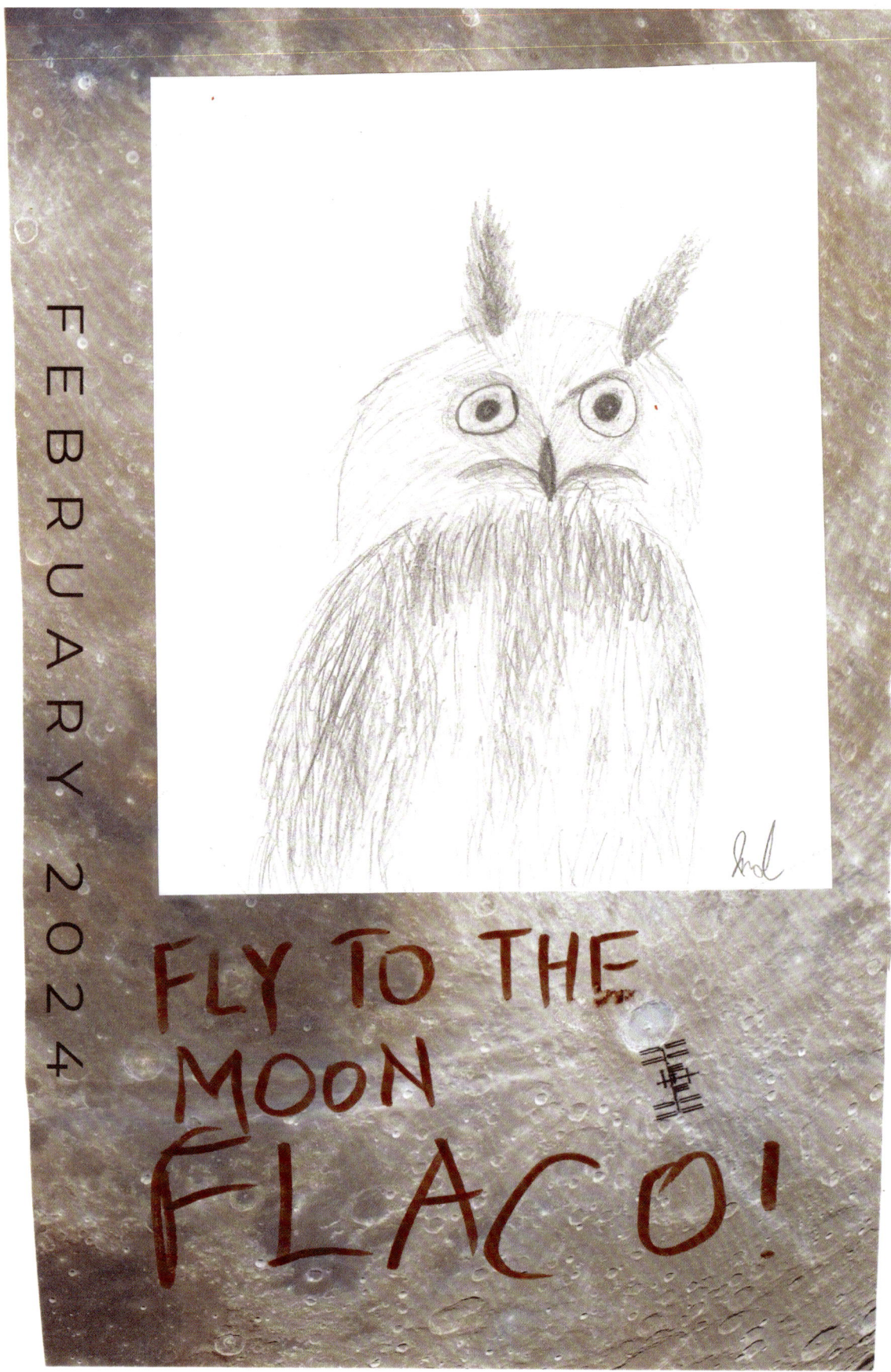

Fly To The Moon Flaco!, pencil on paper, mounted on calendar page, 11 x 7¼ in.

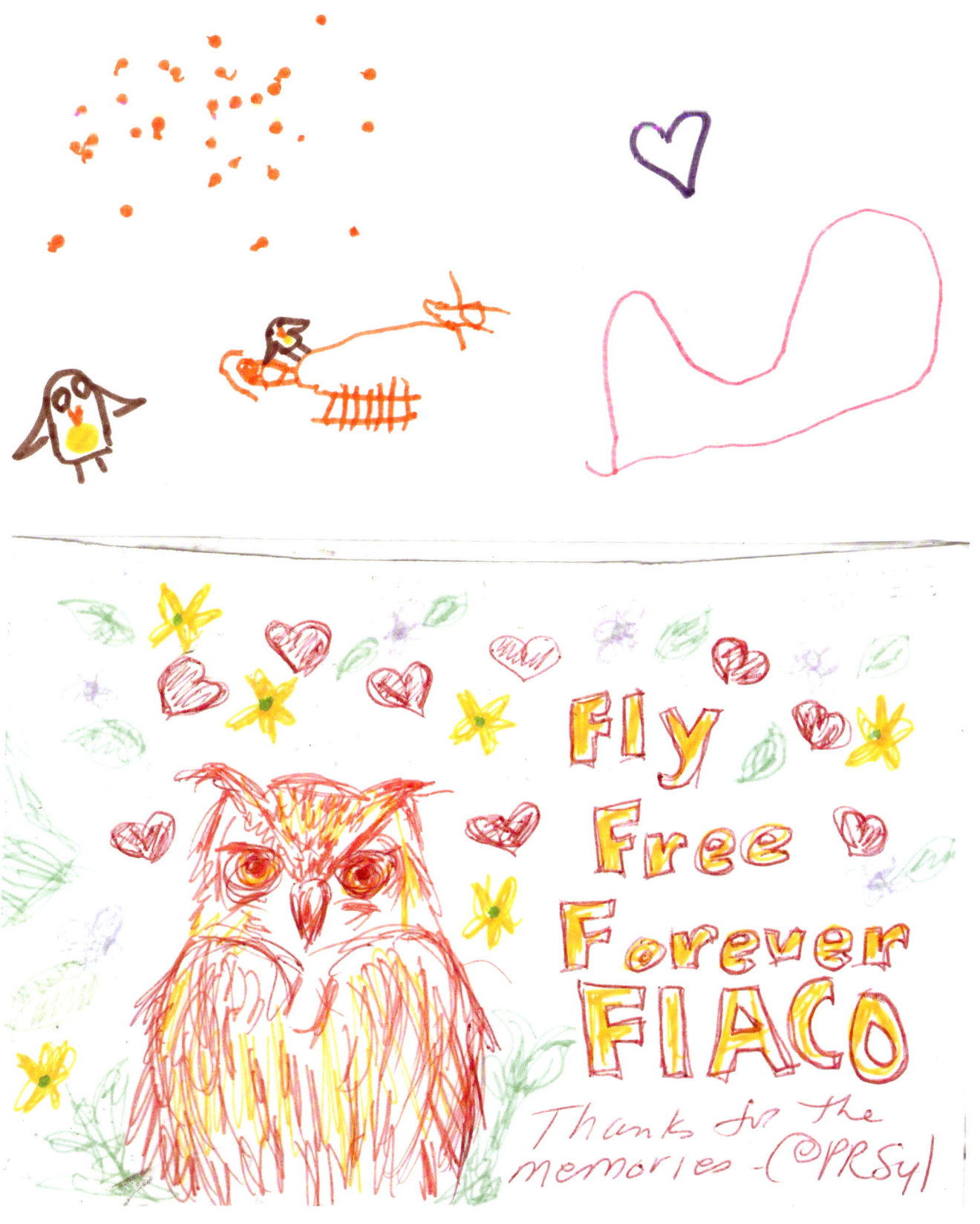

Top Flaco and hearts, marker on paper, 9 × 5½ in., irregular edges.

Bottom @PRSyl, *Fly Free Forever Flaco*, ink and colored pencil on paper in plastic sheeting, 4 × 6 in.

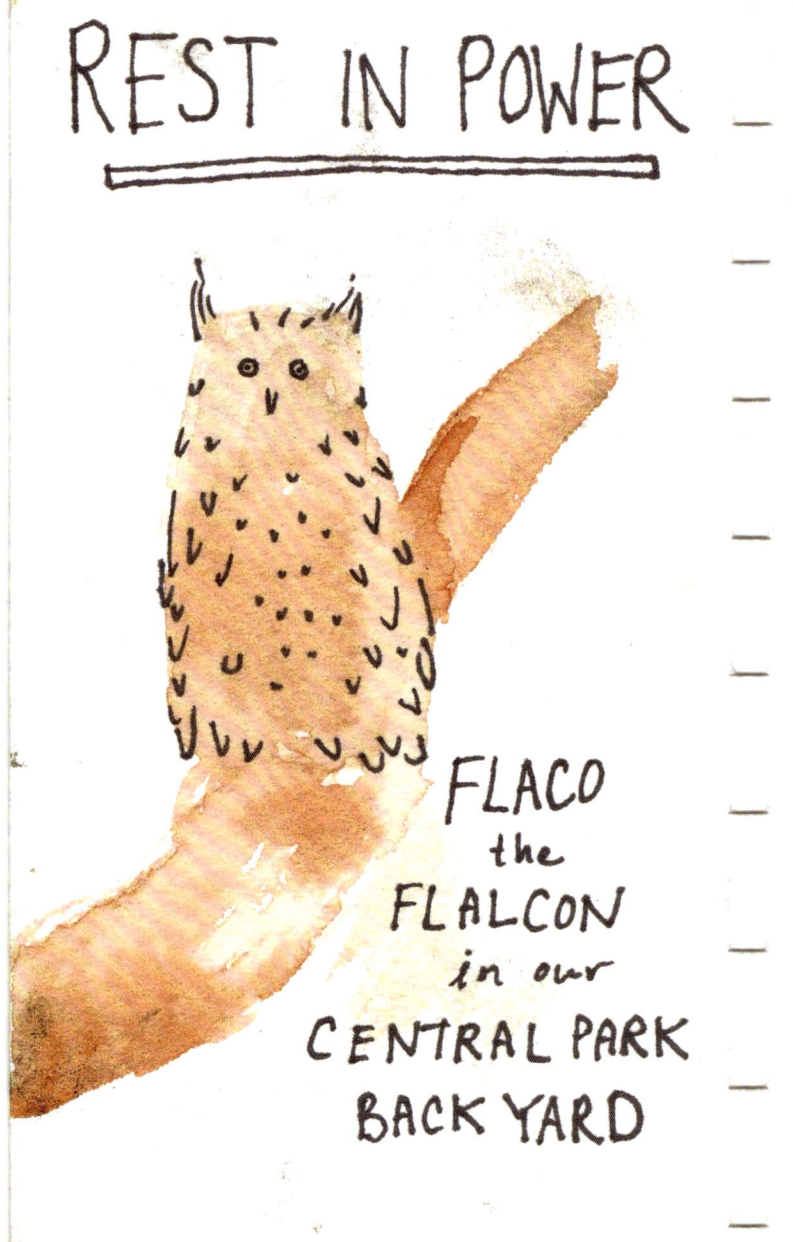

Rest in Power, ink and watercolor on watercolor paper, 5¼ x 3½ in.

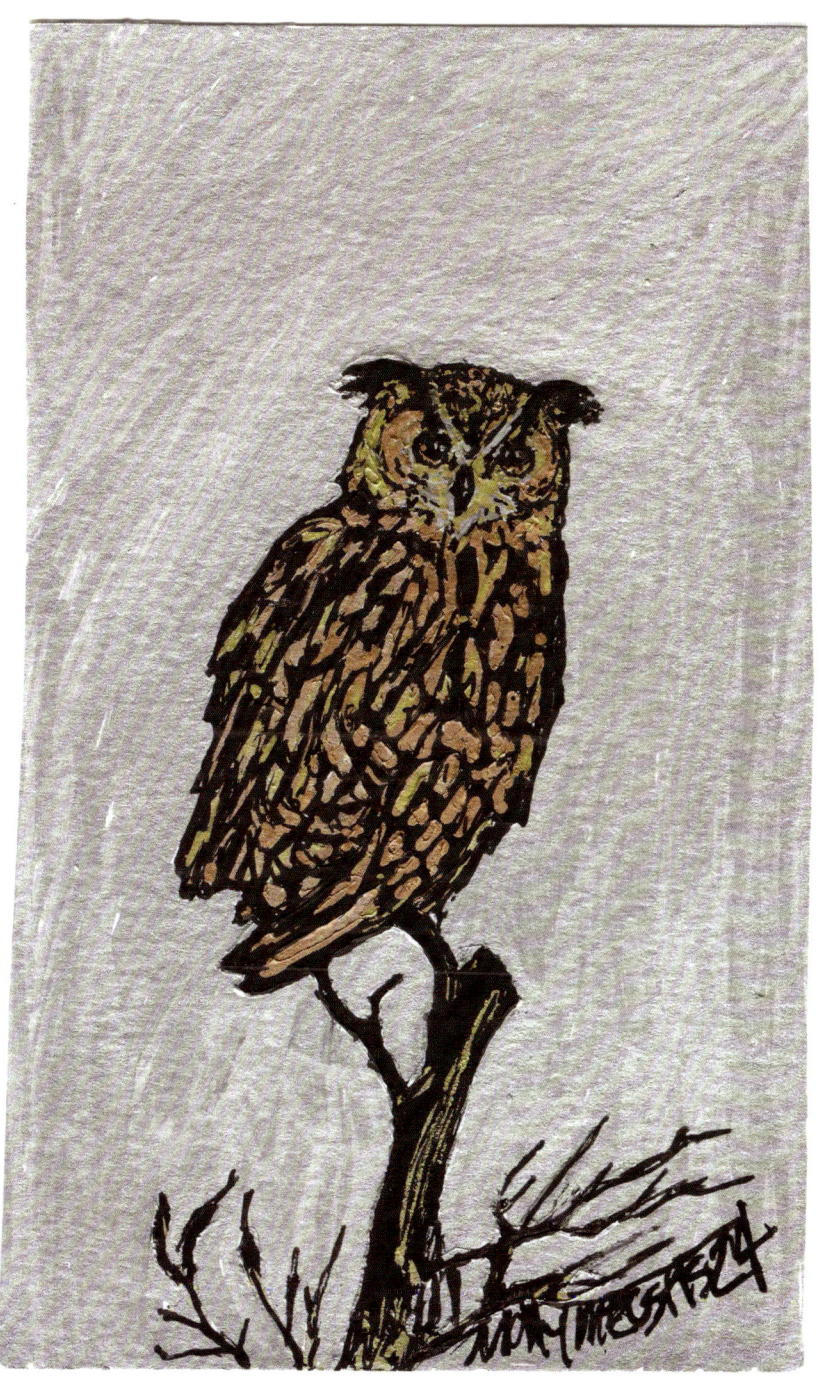

Molly Bangles, Papergoods, *Flaco*, Reverse: *Flaco, Flaco, Wo ist Flaco*, metallic paint and marker on card stock, 7 x 4¼ in.

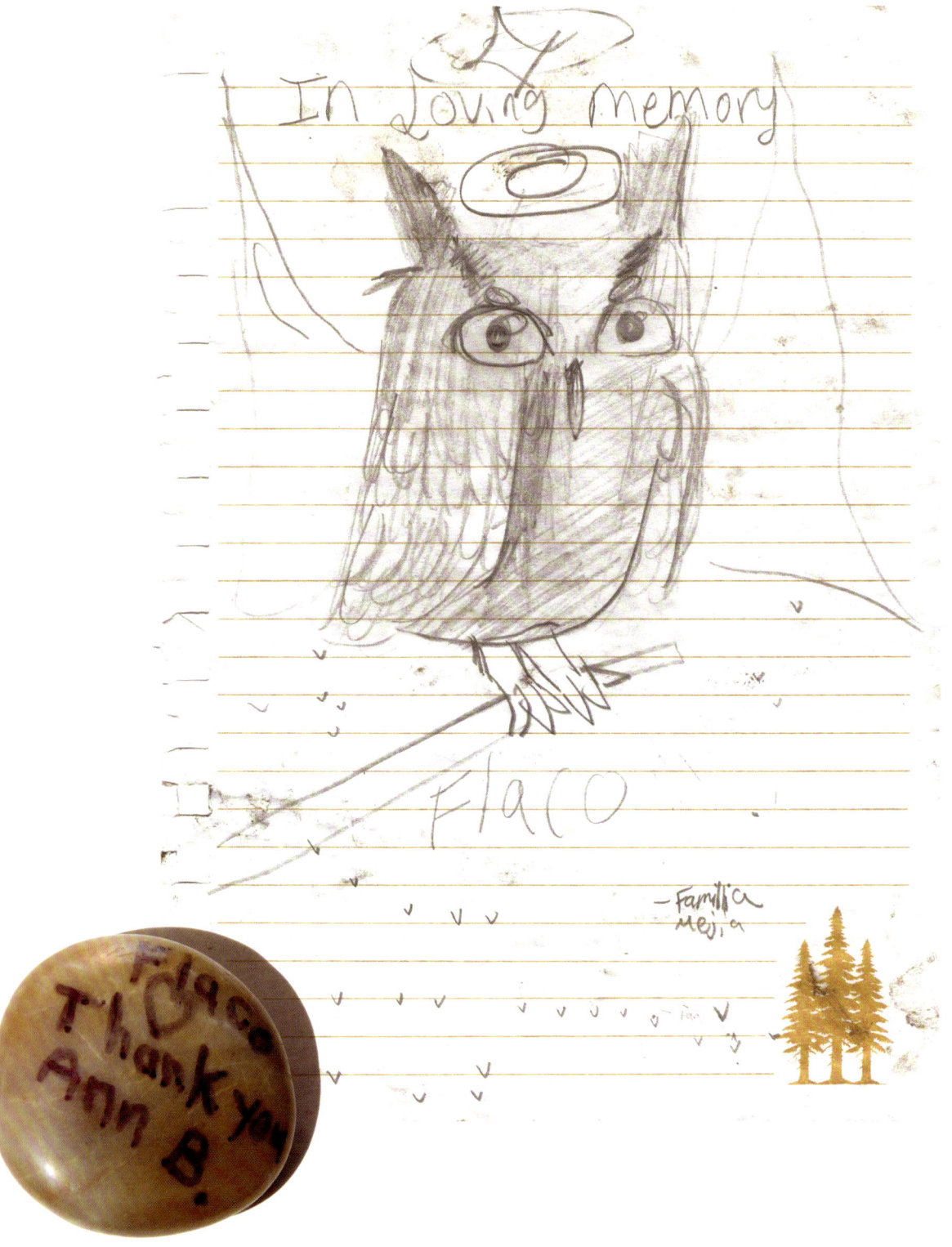

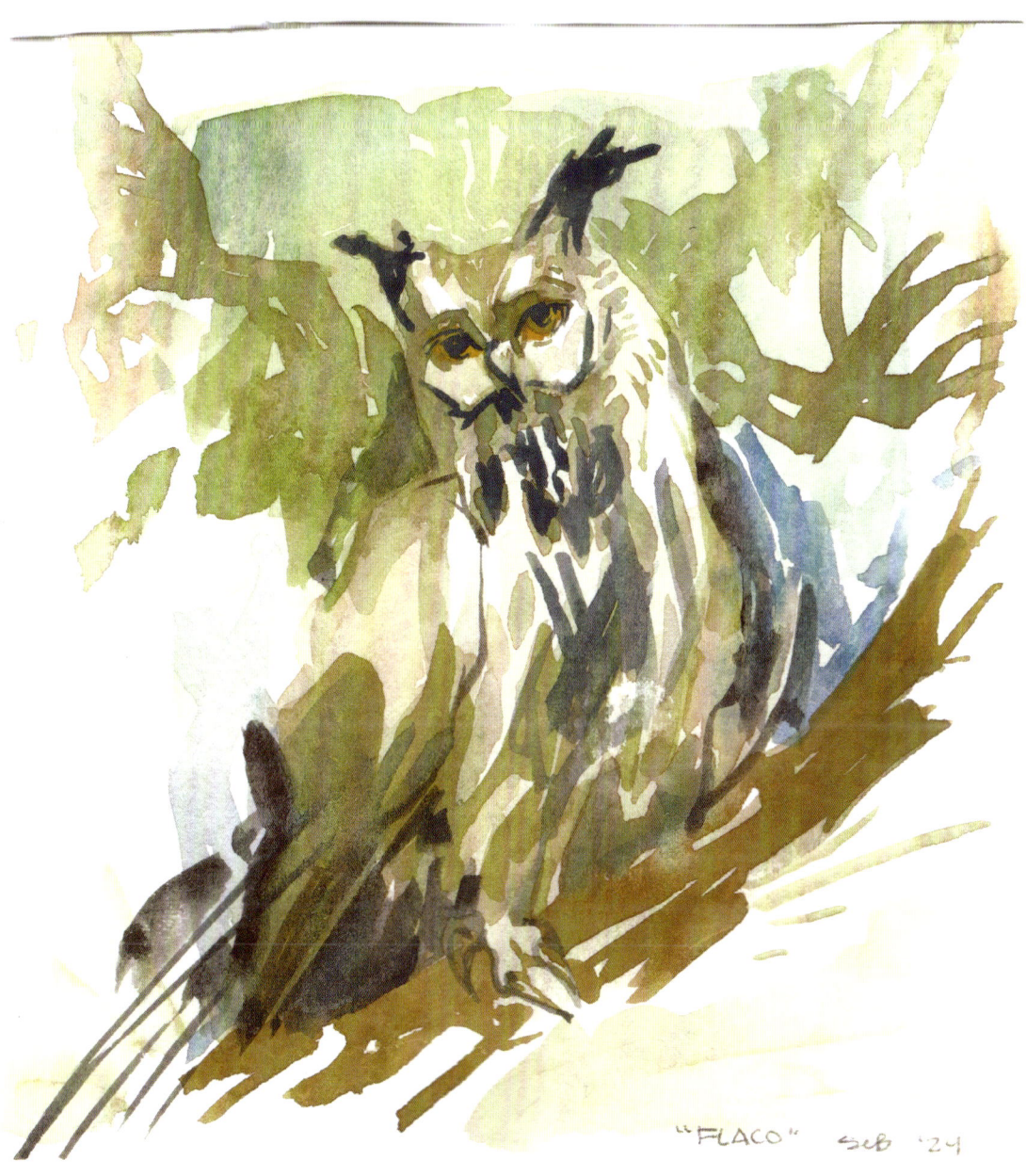

Left top Familia Mejia, *In Loving Memory,* pencil on journal paper, 8 x 6 in.

Left bottom Ann B., *Flaco, Thank You,* marker on polished stone, "Courage" engraved on reverse, ½ x 1½ x 1¾ in.

Above Seb, *Flaco,* 2024, watercolor, 5 x 4¾ in.

We will miss you so much, Flaco! ♥ M. Serra

to behold such beauty and a tenacity
unparalleled

bright orange eyes seemed to reflect
the setting sun

brown and white feathers

pattern

striation

feathery ear tufts heighten his sense
of sound

i wonder if he could hear our awe

MELODY SERRA
Excerpt from "For Flaco"

Melody Serra, *We Will Miss You So Much, Flaco!,* watercolor on watercolor paper, 6 x 6 in., accompanied by an excerpt of Serra's poem, "For Flaco," on identical paper stock.

References

Ackerman, Jennifer. *What an Owl Knows: The New Science of the World's Most Enigmatic Birds*. New York: Penguin Press, 2023.

Calvez, Leigh. *The Hidden Lives of Owls: The Science and Spirit of Nature's Most Elusive Birds*. Seattle: Sasquatch Books, 2016.

DeCandido, Robert, Ph.D., and Allen, Deborah. "Hoo's in the City?: Owls of New York City." New York: *New York State Conservationist,* October 2010.

De Giulio, Bill. "Everything You Wanted to Know About the Eurasian Eagle-Owl." Owlcation.com, December 14, 2023.

Dreier, Frederick. "Flaco the Owl Was Destined to Die Tragically. The Man Who Followed Him for a Year Reveals Why." Santa Fe: *Outside,* February 28, 2024.

Frazier, Ian. "Greetings, Friends!." New York: *The New Yorker*, December 25, 2023.

Garay, Nancy. "On Flaco: The Light That Burns Twice as Bright Burns Half as Long." SuburbanBirds.com, March 5, 2024.

Gessner, David. "Flaco: A Triptych — Part 1: The Escape." Terrain.org, April 9, 2024.

Girardin, Alessia. "Fans Petition Parks Dept. for a Statue Honoring Flaco, But It Could Be a Very Long Wait." New York: *Our Town*, March 8, 2024.

Goldberg, Emma. "Barry the Owl, Beloved by N.Y.C. Birders, Dies in Central Park Collision." New York: *The New York Times*, August 6, 2021.

Honan, Katie. "Barry the Owl Was Poisoned Before Central Park Truck Hit Her." New York: *The City*, September 21, 2021.

Hoylman-Sigal, Brad, Senator. "Legislators, Advocates Rename Statewide Bird Safe Buildings Act the "FLACO" Act." Albany: The New York State Senate, February 26, 2024.

Hoylman-Sigal, Brad, Senator. "Senate Bill S7663." Albany: The New York State Senate, January 5, 2022.

Hutchinson, Bill. "An Outpouring of Tears, Heartbreak as Fans Flock to NYC's Central Park Memorial for Flaco the Owl." ABCNews.com, February 25, 2024.

Jacobs, Julia. "A Mandarin Duck Mysteriously Appears in Central Park, to Birders' Delight." New York: *The New York Times*, October 31, 2018.

Kahfi, Kharishar. "What Should Be Done About Flaco, the Eurasian Eagle-Owl Loose in New York?" New York: *Audubon*, March 3, 2023.

Laing, Olivia. *The Lonely City*. New York: Picador, 2016.

Lane, Charles. "Parts of Flaco the Owl Are Being Housed at the American Museum of Natural History." New York: *Gothamist*, May 28, 2024.

Mistich, David. "Barry, New York City's Captivating and Photogenic Barred Owl, Has Died." *National Public Radio*, August 7, 2021.

Newman, Andy. "Snowy Owl Is Spotted in Central Park, for First Time in 130 Years." New York: *The New York Times,* January 28, 2021.

Oliver, Mary. "Owls" from *Blue Pastures*. New York: HarperCollins Publishers, 1991.

Oliver, Mary. "The Owl Who Comes" from *New and Selected Poems, Volume Two*. Boston: Beacon Press, 1992.

Rivard, Nicole and Smith, Scott. "Wildlife Deaths Expose NYC Rat Poison Problem." FriendsofAnimals.org, September 9, 2024

Safina, Carl. *Alfie & Me: What Owls Know, What Humans Believe*. New York: W.W. Norton & Company, Inc., 2023.

Sain-Baird, Jessica. "From Alaska to Central Park: Balto the Siberian Husky." New York: *Central Park Conservancy Magazine*, January 4, 2018.

Shanahan, Ed. "Flaco, Central Park Zoo Owl, Tastes Freedom and Isn't Rushing to Return." New York: *The New York Times,* February 14, 2023.

Shanahan, Ed. "Flaco the Owl, Zoo Escapee, Leaves Central Park for the East Village." New York: *The New York Times,* November 6, 2023.

Shanahan, Ed. "The Year Flaco the Owl Roamed Free." New York: *The New York Times,* February 2, 2024.

Shanahan, Ed. "New York Mourns Flaco, an Owl Who Inspired as He Made the City His Own." New York: *The New York Times*, February 23, 2024.

Shanahan, Ed. "Flaco, Escaped Central Park Zoo Owl and Defier of Doubts, Is Dead." New York: *The New York Times*, February 24, 2024.

Shanahan, Ed. "Remains of Flaco, the Central Park Owl, to Be Kept at a Museum in His Neighborhood." New York: *The New York Times,* May 28, 2024.

Slaght, Jonathan C. *Owls of the Eastern Ice: A Quest to Find and Save the World's Largest Owl*. New York: Farrar, Straus and Giroux, 2020.

Ungar, Laura and The Associated Press. "Brown Rats Got to America Nearly 300 Years Ago and Wiped Out Black Rats in Just a Few Decades, Says Study That Looks at 32 Piles of Rodent Bones." New York: *Fortune*, April 3, 2024.

Yolton, D. Bruce. "Rest in Peace, Flaco." UrbanHawks.com, February 23, 2024.

Yolton, D. Bruce. "Science Denial Killed Flaco." UrbanHawks.com, February 29, 2024.

Zhou, Naaman. "Evenings in the Park with Flaco." New York: *The New Yorker,* February 22, 2023.

Zhou, Naaman. "Mourning Flaco, The Owl Who Escaped." New York: *The New Yorker*, February 26, 2024.

Zraick, Karen and McCarthy, Lauren. "An Owl Named Flaco Is Loose in Central Park, with Vandals to Blame." New York: *The New York Times,* February 3, 2023.

Wildlife Conservation Society / Newsroom.WCS.org

"Statement from Central Park Zoo on Eurasian Eagle Owl." New York: WCS, February 4, 2023.

"An Update on Eurasian Eagle Owl." New York: WCS, February 12, 2023.

"Update on Eurasian Eagle Owl, Flaco." New York: WCS, February 17, 2023.

"Initial Necropsy Findings for Flaco Are Consistent with Death Due to Acute Traumatic Injury." New York: WCS, February 24, 2024.

"Central Park Zoo Releases Postmortem Results for Flaco, the Eurasian Eagle Owl." New York: WCS, March 25, 2024.

"Central Park Zoo Releases Updates on Remains of Flaco." New York: WCS, May 28, 2024.

Central Park Conservancy / CentralParkNYC.org

Entries: Balto, Delacorte Clock, North Woods, Huddlestone Arch "Still Hunt" and "Eagles and Prey."

Contributors

Chris Ang / @chrisangphoto is an image creator and contributor to several conservation organizations including World Wildlife Fund, Ol Pejeta Conservancy, and World Animal Protection, where he was an ambassador, and he is a collaborator with the Endangered Species Coalition. He is a board director of Wetland Research Center, the parent company of Jaguar Identification Project, Brazil. Following his retirement as a business strategist, he continues to travel extensively as a photographer and conservation advocate for the protection of Earth's biodiversity.

Calicho Arevalo / @calichoart, an internationally recognized architect and artist based in NYC, is celebrated for his vibrant large-scale paintings, murals, sculptures, and digital art. Born in Bogota, Colombia, he integrates three-line stripes, wildlife, doodles, and portals into his creations. Inspired by New York City, his work reflects his Colombian heritage and a deep connection to wildlife. His "Rebirth Darkness" collection masterfully combines these elements, advocating for inclusivity and conveying the value of every human.

David Barrett / @BirdCentralPark (X) earned his undergraduate degree in mathematics from Harvard, and did graduate work in mathematics and computer science at MIT and in finance at the University of Chicago. After a long career as a hedge fund manager, he is now an investor. He is best known for his X account @BirdCentralPark (Manhattan Bird Alert), which features his own nature photography and which has introduced the public to such celebrity birds as Central Park's Mandarin Duck, Snowy Owl, Barred Owl, and Flaco the Eurasian Eagle-Owl, all of which went on to receive worldwide media attention after appearing on his site.

At 10 years old, **Paul Beiboer / @beibsphotography** began birdwatching in the Netherlands and developed his skills of observation and patience. He was given his first camera a few years later and has become a master at catching exquisite moments in time. He has traveled extensively through South America, Australia, Asia, and Africa, always capturing the natural world around him. He lived in New York City from 2016 until 2024 and has recently moved to Europe, where he continues to look for owls and pursue his love of photography.

Growing up in the woods of Upstate New York, **Erika Bleiberg / @ebleiberg** learned to see the world through the eyes of an artist. Self-taught, she has always loved color, texture, and shape. Nature is a consistent theme in Erika's work and she especially loves capturing the personality and spirits of her animal subjects using a range of unconventional acrylic painting techniques. Erika lives in Glen Ridge, NJ with her family and rescue dogs.

Lesley Breen / @lesleybreenillustration is an illustrator of several picture books, including *Bunny Bus* by Ammi-Joan Paquette, *Maximillian Villainous* by Margaret Chiu Greanias, *PEW!* by Cathy Stefanec Ogren, and *You're My Boo* by Kate Dopirak. She is currently working on her debut author-illustrated picture book, *What Rachel Heard* about marine biologist Rachel Carson, to be published by Norton Young Readers.

Sheryl Checkman / @sherylcheckman is an award-winning graphic designer, wildlife and nature photographer, and actor. During the pandemic, she self-published a book, 2020 — *My Photographic Journey Through an Isolating Year,* documenting the year as seen through her camera's lens. Sheryl graduated from Cornell University, studied design at the University of Copenhagen, and attended a Master's program in Communications Design at Pratt Institute. Sheryl is an avid skier, scuba diver, and advanced yoga practitioner. She loves to hike and take long walks, and is rarely without her camera.

Marianne DeMarco / @marianemarco is a professor of screenwriting and film & media production at the CUNY, having received her MFA at Columbia University. An amateur wildlife and underwater photographer, she credits Flaco with introducing her to yet another frustrating new focus: bird photography.

Mark Elliott / @above_96th has been birding on his early morning walks in Central Park since 2019, where he loves the whole experience—the quiet, the greenery, and being in the moment that birding requires. When not birding, he enjoys cooking, playing saxophone, and leading a nonprofit that evaluates promising programs that help low-income people succeed.

Molly Eustis / @molly_bangles (she/her) is a freelance stage manager and artist in Astoria, New York. A New Orleans native, a night owl, and a graduate of both College of Charleston and Columbia University, she spends most of her free time taking pictures of birds and the natural world.

Tony Fitzpatrick / @tonyfitzpatrick9 is a Chicago-based artist best known for his multimedia collages, printmaking, paintings, and drawings. Fitzpatrick's works are inspired by Chicago street culture, cities he has traveled to, children's books, tattoo designs, and folk art. Fitzpatrick has authored or illustrated eight books of art and poetry and, for the last two years, has written a column for the Newcity. Fitzpatrick's art appears in the Museum of Modern Art in New York City, the Museum of Contemporary Art in Chicago, and the National Museum of American Art in Washington, DC.

Anke Frohlich / @anke.frohlich.photography is a New York City-based bird photographer. Her love of birds has been a constant since her childhood in Germany when her father introduced her to birding, but it was the Covid pandemic that led her to purchase a camera and photograph the birds of Central Park on a daily basis. She now travels several times a year to photograph birds in the U.S. and abroad. Her Flaco images have appeared in *The New York Times* and her illustrated Flaco article was published in the January 2025 issue of *Bird Watcher's Digest.*

New York-based German artist **Heide Hatry / @heidihatry,** a former rare book seller, is best known for her work employing animal flesh and organs or other discarded, disdained, or "taboo" materials. Hatry has curated numerous exhibitions and has shown her work at museums and galleries all over the world. She has produced more than 200 artists' books, edited dozens of art catalogues, and four of her larger projects have been documented in monographic books.

Jonathan Hollingsworth / @hollingsworthjd is a New York City-based writer and photographer whose work has been published in *The New York Times, The Independent, The Sunday Times Magazine (London), BBC News Magazine, Die Welt,* and *Photo District News,* among others. He is the author of the monographs *Left Behind: Life and Death Along the U.S. Border* and *What We Think Now: Young People's Response to the War in Iraq.* He has had solo exhibitions at the California Museum of Photography, Santa Fe Art Institute, and Center for Photography at Woodstock. He lives in Brooklyn with a ginger cat and an orange Naugahyde couch.

Bill Hutchinson / @bhutchbroklyn is an award-winning New York City-based journalist and visual artist, who has written and created a series of paintings inspired by encounters he and his wife, Lisa Amand, had with Flaco the Owl in Central Park.

Howard Katz / @katzh76 lives in New York City, where he enjoys observing and photographing the birds of Central Park.

Elizabeth Kennen / @artjazzwine is an artist in the San Francisco Bay Area. A love of nature and art began early, with trips to the ocean and mountains and a sketch pad always handy. She enjoys working in watercolor, as well as colored pencil and oils. Inspiration for compositions comes from her travels and from studying nature and landscapes of Northern California. Her paintings reflect a love of subtle color layering, texture, and detail work. Elizabeth's artwork is exhibited in various Bay Area galleries.

Martha Nishida / @studionishida has sketched and practiced stitchcraft from an early age. She moved to New York City in 1977, where she has lived, for the most part, since that time. Originally from Maryland, where she played in creeks and roamed the woods — and having had the good fortune to travel far and wide— Central Park remains her favorite place on Earth.

Duke Riley / @dukerileystudio, a Boston-born artist based in Brooklyn, NY, and former tattoo artist, lived in a pigeon coop while attending RISD in the early 90s before earning his MFA from Pratt Institute. Over the past two decades, he has produced critically acclaimed works that explore the interface of institutional power and the natural world. His re-imagined narratives comment on a range of issues from the cultural impact of over-development and environmental destruction of waterfront communities to contradictions within political ideologies and the role of the artist in society. Duke Riley has had solo exhibitions at the Brooklyn Museum, Queens Museum of Art, MOCA Cleveland, Havana Biennale, and the Sydney Biennale.

Carl Safina / @csafina is an ecologist, author, and founding President of the Safina Center. He is the first Endowed Professor for Nature and Humanity at Stony Brook University. His work centers on animal psychology and the relationship between humans and nature. His newest book, "Alfie & Me: What Owls Know, What Humans Believe," is a moving account of raising, then freeing, an orphaned screech owl, whose lasting friendship with him illuminates humanity's relationship with the natural world.

Venus N. Sallay / @vee_nab.nyc, a New York City-based nurse practitioner, has discovered a captivating second passion: bird photography. Her journey began as a landscape, cityscape, and wildlife photography enthusiast, but the COVID-19 pandemic ignited a newfound love for capturing the avian world. During the peak of spring migration in 2020, Sallay ventured into Central Park, where she was captivated by the diverse array of migratory birds passing through. Since then, she found herself photographing the fascinating and often rare avian visitors that grace the five boroughs of New York City throughout the year.

Juliet Schreckinger / @julietschreckinger is a Long Island, NY-based artist. Her work is typically created using a stippling technique in pen & ink and graphite, with occasional splashes of color. Juliet's pieces are inspired by the ocean, nature, and all of the creatures within our world. Since the time she was a child, Juliet has been fascinated by black and white photography, colorless television shows, and film noir movies. Being exposed to the lighting effects and sharp contrasts shown in these photographs and films greatly inspired the type of work that she does today. Juliet's work is centered around giving a voice to nature and animals, with the goal of showcasing their importance in this world. Through an illustrative take on fine art, she strives to express a story in each drawing.

Elijah Shiffer / @elijahshiffer is a New York-based musician who has been involved with nearly every facet of the city's jazz scene as a saxophonist, bandleader, composer, arranger, music editor, and critic. He has released four CDs as a leader, each with a regularly performing band. One of these is the first volume of his project, City Of Birds, a collection of compositions inspired by all the birds of New York City. A lifelong birder, Elijah has recently started to lead birding walks; in 2023, he founded Avant Birde, a birding group for musicians (though non-musicians are certainly welcome). Elijah's writings on music can be read on JazzLeadSheets.com and in *New York City Jazz* Record magazine.

Fred Tomaselli / @fredtomaselli has shown his work in museums, biennials, and galleries around the world, including MoMA, LA MoCA, and SF MoMA. Solo shows include the Whitney Museum at Philip Morris, SITE Santa Fe, The Aspen Art Museum, The Brooklyn Museum, The Jocelyn Museum, Laguna Art Museum, and The Orange County Art Museum. His work is represented by James Cohan Gallery in New York and White Cube in London. A native Californian, he has lived in Brooklyn since 1985.

Kamila Zmrzla / @topbunartist is primarily self-taught through a lifetime of creative immersion. Her strongest influences are rooted in her upbringing in the former Czechoslovakia, where folklore, politics, traditional costume, and her grandfather's botanical paintings shaped her imagination from an early age. She favors vivid colors, undulating forms, and repeating patterns. Her lush compositions evoke nature, fertility, and the realm between dreams and reality.

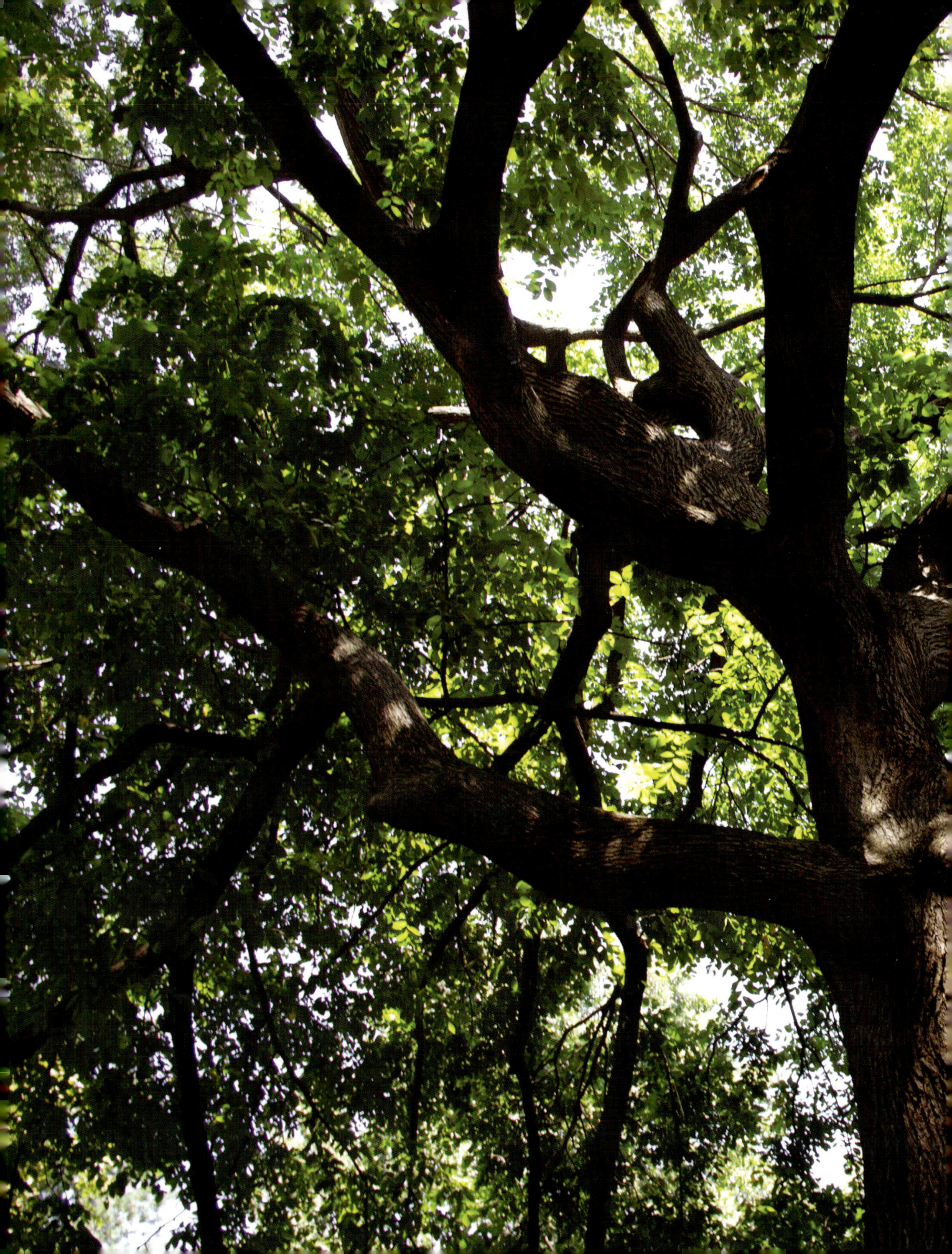

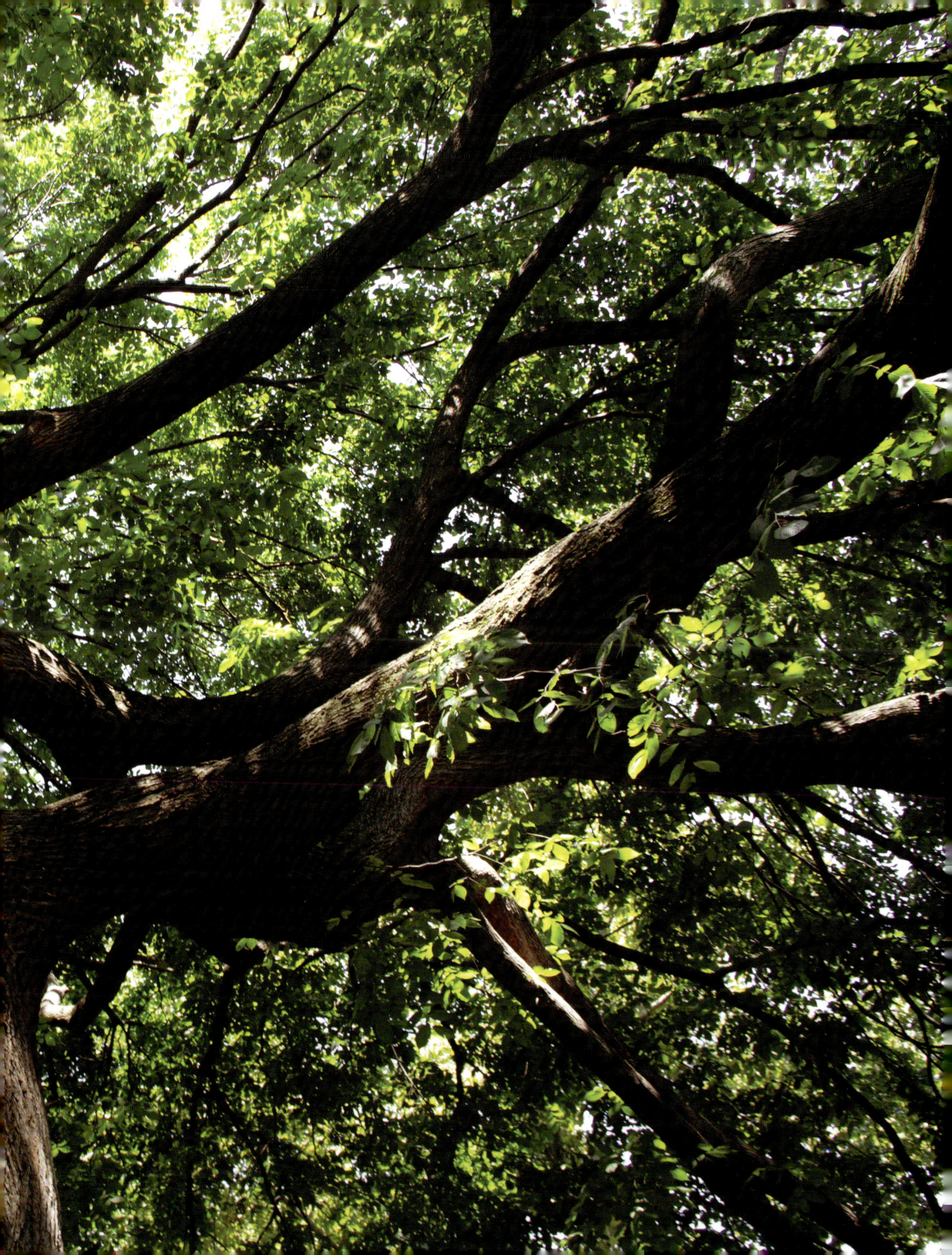

On a clear winter night, Flaco had initially rested on the tower of a nearby water tank, before exploring the tank in this photo, which had a perfect place for him to perch, right at the apex. This is Flaco at his peak, on top of the world.

DAVID BARRETT

Previous spread   Jonathan Hollingsworth, *In Memory of Flaco,* The Elm, 8/10/24, 2:17 p.m.

David Barrett, *Flaco on Water Tower,* 90th Street and Riverside Drive, Upper West Side, 1/8/24, 10:48 p.m.

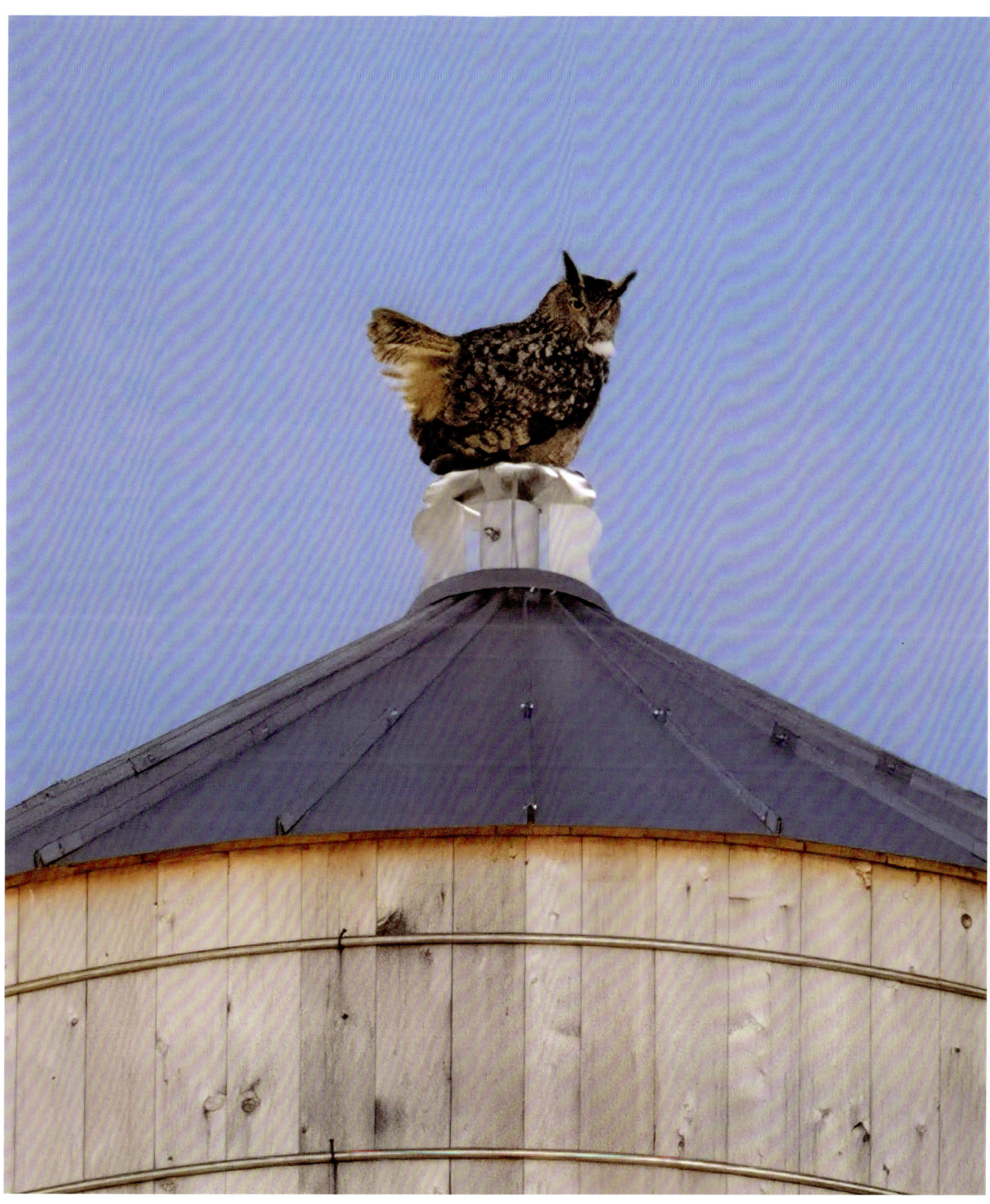

Thank You

The object you're holding in your hands is not just a book but a miracle because there were many, many opportunities for it to never exist at all.

Thank you to Blurring Books and the team (publisher DB Burkeman, Elliott Rogers, and Sean Johnson) for having the vision—and scrappiness!—to publish the book on a breakneck production schedule. The small presses are always the bravest. To designer Jack Lamborn, for their acumen and good humor as we fleshed out these pages. To Arlyn Eve Nathan for the lessons on leading and the happy reunion. To Julie Schumacher for making the connection and lending her keen vision. April Xie carried us across the finish line, overseeing the printing of this book.

Valerie Hartman and Stella Hamilton, fellow stewards of the memorial objects, supported this book and my vision from the beginning. I will always be grateful for their faith and trust.

David Barrett, who in addition to contributing his photographs, was an essential resource and steadfast supporter of this book. The New York City birding community would not be what it is without him.

The work of journalist Ed Shanahan, who meticulously chronicled Flaco's narrative (from beginning to end and beyond) for *The New York Times* was an invaluable resource and point of reference. JenniferAckerman's *What an Owl Knows* (Penguin Random House) provided keen insight on Eurasian eagle-owls and the anatomical mechanics that have allowed owls to evolve over sixty million years.

A huge debt of gratitude to the Estate of Mary Oliver for permitting me to include "The Owl Who Comes" and an excerpt from "Owls". Ian Frazier lent six lines of post-holiday cheer with an excerpt from "Dear Friends!" which first appeared in *The New Yorker*. Leigh Calvez and Sasquatch Books generously permitted inclusion of "Notes from the Field", instructions for living for owls and humans alike, from *The Hidden Lives of Owls*.

Rebecca Klassen, Curator of Material Culture at the New York Historical Society, gave a permanent home to a selection of the memorial objects and contextualized Flaco's story in "The Year of Flaco" exhibition, January 31st — July 6th, 2025.

This book would not be what it is without the generous contributors who shared their words, images, and music: Carl Safina for his insightful foreword, Chris Ang, Calicho Arevalo, Paul Beiboer, Erika Bleiberg, Lesley Breen, Sheryl Checkman, Marianne DeMarco, Mark Elliott, Molly Eustis, Tony Fitzpatrick, Ian Frazier, Kelly Fritz, Anke Frohlich, Emily Gallagher, Heide Hatry, Bill Hutchinson, Howard Katz, Elizabeth Kennen, Megan Mitchell, Kari Nicolaisen, Martha Nishida, Philippe Petit, Duke Riley, Ion Sokhos, Venus N. Sallay, Juliet Schreckinger, Melody Serra, Elijah Shiffer, Fred Tomaselli, Sean Welsh, Kamila Zmrzla, and everyone I interviewed at East River Tattoo.

I'd also like to thank Madeleine Beck, Kelsey Breen, Mary Brower, Hank Cochrane, James D'Elicio, Peter London, Mayra Marino, Liz Nealon, Louis Pagillo, Jesseca Salky, Stefan Shanni, Lottchen Shivers and Scott Weidensaul.

And for always being in my court: my friends, my family, my parents, and Morgan Foxworth.

We owe a huge debt of gratitude to the 259 backers who supported the Kickstarter campaign. This book would not have happened without you.

JH

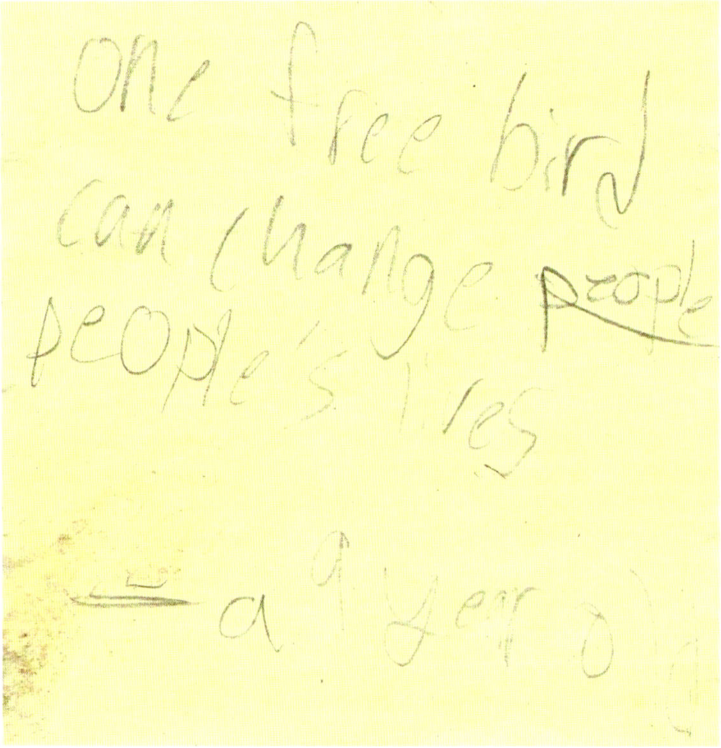

one free bird
can change people
people's lives

— a 9 year o

Colophon

Copyright © 2025 by Jonathan Hollingsworth.

All rights reserved.

Published in the United States by Blurring Books, New York, NY. blurringbooks.com

This first edition of *FLACO* is limited to 2,000 casebound copies. Creative direction by Jonathan Hollingsworth. Book design by Jack Lamborn. Typography by Arlyn Nathan. Project Management by Elliott Rogers and Sean Johnson. Text is set in Minion and Helvetica.

Printed and bound in China.

ISBN 9781963814095

Library of Congress Control Number 2024920750

A portion of the proceeds from *FLACO* will be contributed to the Wild Bird Fund.

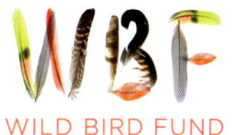

WILD BIRD FUND

Blurring Books

244 5th Avenue, Suite D279
New York, New York, 10001
blurringbooks.com

Left *One Free Bird Can Change People's Lives —A 9 Year Old,* graphite on Post-It note, 3 x 3 in.

Front cover: @chrisangphoto

Half title / Following page / Back cover
Flaco's feathers gathered from the base of the elm, collection of Stella Hamilton.

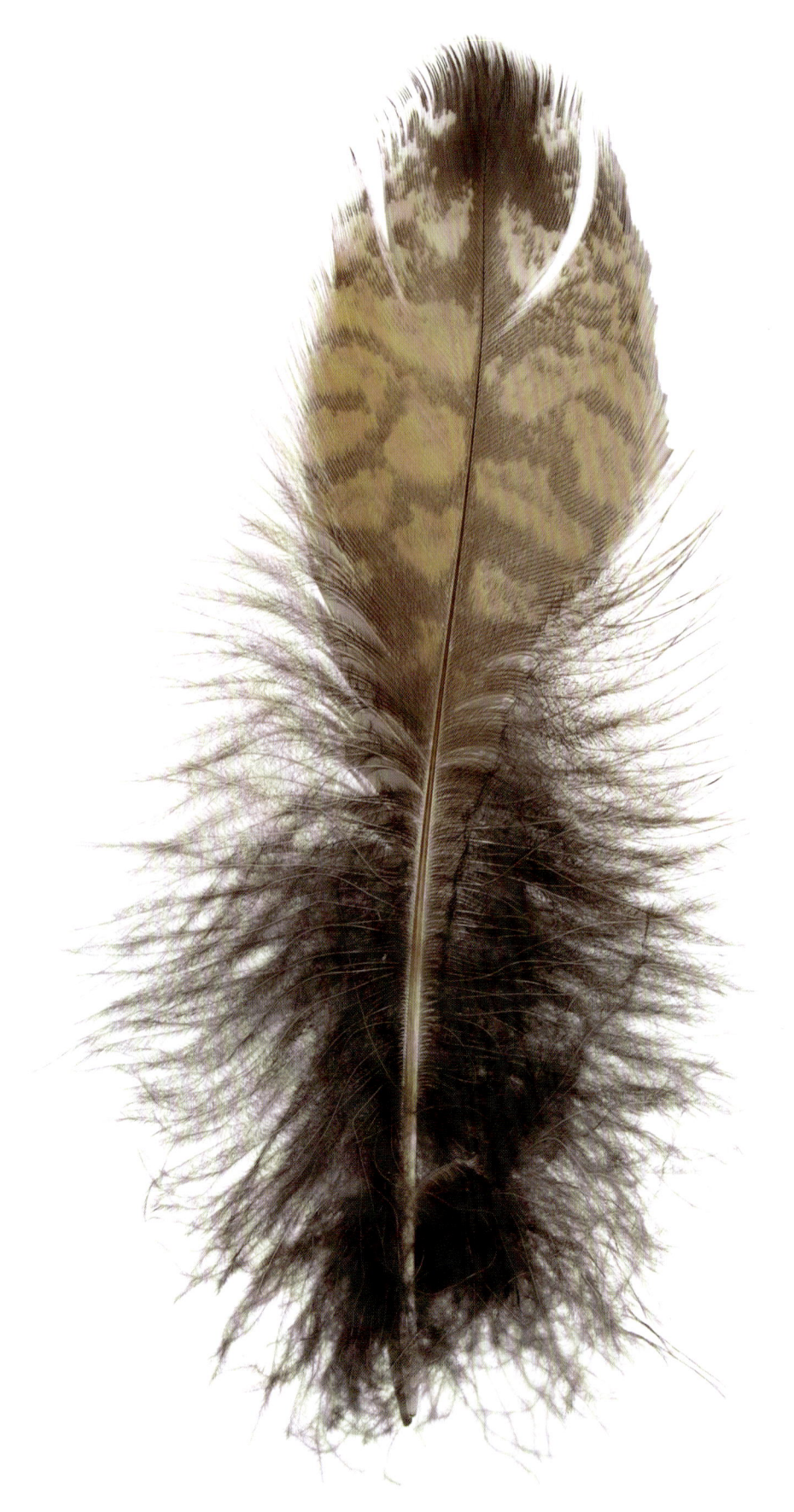